ML

# ADVANCES IN DEVELOPMENTAL AND BEHAVIORAL PEDIATRICS

*Volume* 3 • 1982

# ADVANCES IN DEVELOPMENTAL AND BEHAVIORAL PEDIATRICS

*A Research Annual*

*Editors:* MARK WOLRAICH
*Department of Pediatrics*
*College of Medicine*
*University of Iowa*

DONALD K. ROUTH
*Department of Psychology*
*University of Iowa*

VOLUME 3 • 1982

 JAI PRESS INC.

*Greenwich, Connecticut*          *London, England*

# CONTENTS

# LIST OF CONTRIBUTORS

*David C. Bellinger*

Children's Hospital Medical Center
Boston

*Robert W. Chamberlin*

Department of Pediatrics
University of Rochester Medical Center

*Jesus Fernandez*

Department of Clinical Psychology
University of Florida

*James Hanson*

Department of Pediatrics
University of Iowa Hospitals
and Clinics

*Frances Degen Horowitz*

Department of Human Development and
Family Life, University of Kansas

*Barbara B. Keller*

Department of Pediatrics
University of Rochester Medical Center

*Patricia L. Linn*

Department of Human Development and
Family Life, University of Kansas

*Jan Loney*

Department of Psychiatry
University of Iowa

*Barbara G. Melamed*

Department of Clinical Psychology
University of Florida

*Richard Milich*  
Department of Psychiatry  
University of Iowa

*Herbert L. Needleman*  
Children's Hospital Medical Center  
Boston

*Rochelle L. Robbins*  
Department of Clinical Psychology  
University of Florida

*John J. Spinetta*  
Department of Psychology  
San Diego State University

*Rachel E. Stark*  
John F. Kennedy Institute and  
The Johns Hopkins University School  
of Medicine

*Paula Tallal*  
Department of Psychiatry  
University of California  
at San Diego

J. Kenneth Whitt  
Department of Psychiatry  
School of Medicine  
University of North Carolina

# FOREWORD

In the previous two issues Bonnie Camp has done an excellent job of uniting the behavioral and biological sciences and uniting clinical and research issues. It has been a yeoman's task but one that has been increasing in importance. The Task Force on Pediatric Education (1978)* found that one of the issues which repeatedly emerged at the core of pediatric education was that "Biosocial and developmental problems . . . adversely affect the health of many children and adolescents" (p.ix). Likewise, behavior is very much affected by biological factors.

We have attempted to carry on the exemplary pattern set by Dr. Camp. The authors have each presented subjects which have significance to clinicians in both medicine and behavior. They have attempted to base their reviews on sound scientific data and inform the reader about the present state of the art and current

---

*The Task Force on Pediatric Education: The Future of Pediatric Education, American Academy of Pediatrics. Evanston, Illinois, 1978.

research issues. Some of the chapters, such as that on the effects of low lead exposure, deal with as of yet unanswered questions and attempt to present the issues and relevant data presently available.

In addition to uniting the clinical and research areas in the biological and behavioral sciences, the publication differs from other publications on similar subjects because the articles are able to address subjects in greater depth. It affords the authors, who are extensively involved in research on their topic, the opportunity to present that information in depth. We hope that you will find that the present and future volumes follow the fine example set by Dr. Camp.

Mark L. Wolraich
Donald K. Routh
*Series Editors*

# LOW LEVEL LEAD EXPOSURE AND PSYCHOLOGICAL DEFICIT IN CHILDREN

David C. Bellinger and Herbert L. Needleman

## GENERAL BACKGROUND

*Introduction*

Lead is one of a large number of substances which are useful but can adversely affect health. World production of this metal exceeds 3.5 million tons per year, more than any other heavy metal of equivalent toxicity (U.S. EPA, 1977). Lead is added to gasoline to improve octane rating, used in the manufacture of storage batteries and cable coverings, and is an important component of solder, brass, paint pigments, type metal, PVC plastics, and pipes (Grandjean, 1978).

The toxicity as well as the utility of lead has long been recognized. References to plumbism as an occupational disease can be found as far back as the second

Advances in Developmental and Behavioral Pediatrics, vol. 3, pages 1–49
Copyright © 1982 by JAI Press Inc.
All rights of reproduction in any form reserved.
ISBN: 0-89232-223-3

century B.C. (Gilfillan, 1965). The first public health act passed in the American colonies was a 1724 Massachusetts Bay Colony prohibition against the use of lead-lined apparatus for distilling rum (though the impetus was less a concern for public health than the fear that angry North Carolinians would stop importing Massachusetts rum; McCord, 1953).

Concern over the exposure of the general population to low levels of lead is of relatively recent origin and forms part of the general concern over the health effects of environmental pollutants. There is growing suspicion that chronic exposure to lead, like chronic exposure to alcohol, may take a cumulative toll on one's physical and psychological health, even in the absence of frank intoxication.

Before reviewing the evidence for low level effects on children, we will survey the following issues: historical changes in ambient levels of lead, sources of present-day exposure, the toxicology of lead, and reasons for concern over low level exposure.

## Increases in Ambient Levels of Lead Over Time

The amount of lead available for human uptake has been increasing since man began mining the metal some 4,000 years ago. Sharp increases in the rate of dispersion occurred with the beginning of the Industrial Revolution in the 18th century and the introduction of lead alkyls as gasoline additives in the early decades of this century. The amount of lead used in gasoline increased more than 6-fold between 1935 and 1976 (Lin-Fu, 1979) and, at present, 98% of airborne lead can be attributed to automobile emissions (National Academy of Sciences, 1972). Ambient concentrations of lead have increased proportionately, even in areas well removed from industrial centers. The concentration in the snow strata of Northern Greenland varies inversely with the age of the sample, and has increased 200-fold in the last few centuries (Murozumi, Chow, & Patterson, 1969). Settle and Patterson (1980) reported that, because of a two orders of magnitude increase in the amount of lead in the oceans, fresh albacore muscle contains 10 times the lead it did in prehistoric times. The concentration in albacore packed in unsoldered cans is about 200 times the prehistoric fresh level, and albacore packed in lead-soldered cans is an astonishing 10,000 times greater.

While blood lead level varies with a variety of demographic variables (such as age, sex, and urban versus rural residence), the results of numerous surveys suggest that the mean for members of modern industrialized society is about 20 $\mu$g/dl (U.S. EPA, 1977). Most people in developed countries are in positive lead balance so that the total body burden increases with age (Waldron & Stöfen, 1974), Patterson (1965) calculated from geochemical evidence that before mining and smelting lead began, human blood lead level was 0.2 $\mu$g/dl, approximately 100 times less than today. Recent analyses of the lead in the skeletons of Nubian and Peruvian populations dating from the pre-metallurgical era support this claim (Ericson, Shirahata, & Patterson, 1979; Grandjean, Nielsen, & Shapiro, 1979). Accordingly, some have argued that the terms "average" and "physiologically normal" are not synonymous when applied to the blood lead levels of modern humans (Piomelli, 1980).

## Sources of Exposure

Some exposure to lead is inevitable and occurs via many routes. Airborne lead of small particle size is readily absorbed through the lung. The average air level in certain high-density urban settings may exceed 3 $\mu$g/m$^3$, 10,000 times higher than the "natural" air level calculated by Patterson (1965); concentrations of 70 $\mu$g/m$^3$ have been recorded on Los Angeles freeways during peak traffic hours (National Academy of Sciences, 1972).

Diet is the most significant source of lead for most people. Lead in food can be attributed to the use of pesticides containing lead arsenate, cooking in water with high lead content, or processing and packing procedures. Although canned foods comprise only about 10% of the average diet, they contribute approximately 30% of dietary lead (U.S. EPA, 1977). This may affect young children more than most populations since their diet frequently includes a greater proportion of canned products. Excessive water lead levels may be a particular problem in areas in which the water is acidic and low in mineral content (Moore, 1973) or in which the use of lead pipes and cisterns is widespread (Moore, Meredith, & Goldberg, 1977). Infants who bottle feed may be at particular risk under such circumstances.

There are certain sources of hazardous exposure which pose problems only for specific groups. For adults, sources of high-dose exposure are almost exclusively occupational (e.g., lead smelting, scrap metal handling, storage battery manufacturing and repair, car radiator repair, ship breaking, and welding (Grandjean, 1978; U.S. EPA, 1977).

Other sources or practices which may result in overexposure include swallowing or burning newsprint (Bogden, Joselow, & Singh, 1975; Perkins & Oski, 1976), burning painted wood or discarded battery casings for fuel (Angle & McIntire, 1964), the use of lead-soldered electric kettles (Wigle & Charlebois, 1978), improperly glazed earthenware vessels or glasses with leaded decals (Klein, Namer, Harpur, & Corbin, 1970).

There are several sources of exposure which may endanger children more than adults. House dust, especially in urban areas, may contain enough lead to pose a hazard to children due to their frequent hand-to-mouth activity (Charney, Sayre, & Coulter, 1980; Sayre & Katzel, 1979). This lead may originate with automobile or factory emissions, the flaking or powdering of leaded paint from the interior surfaces of the home, or the clothing of a family member who is occupationally exposed (e.g., Baker, Folland, Taylor, Frank, Peterson, Lovejoy, Cox, Housworth, & Landrigan, 1977).

Lead paint poses the greatest threat to young children and most cases of clinical poisoning can be traced to this source (U.S. HUD, 1978). Although the federal limit on the amount of lead which paint can contain is now 0.06%, there are millions of homes in the United States with paint which is more than 1% lead by dry weight. One gram of such paint contains at least 10 mg of lead, 30 times the daily permissable intake for a 3-year-old child (King, 1971). A child living in a home with leaded paint may accumulate lead even without engaging in pica (the ingestion of nonfood substances; de la Burde & Shapiro, 1975). Exterior as well as interior paint can be hazardous since flaking or powdering may lead to the accumulation of large amounts of lead in play areas near a house (Ter Haar & Aronow, 1974; Bogden & Louria, 1975).

## Toxicology

Unlike many divalent cations such as copper, zinc and manganese which serve as enzyme cofactors, lead has no known biological function. Like other heavy metals, lead binds avidly to sulfhydryl groups on enzyme proteins, altering their molecular conformation and biological activity. The synthesis of hemoglobin, especially the heme component, is the most thoroughly studied of lead's targets. However, lead has also been shown to disrupt many other systems, including the production of collagen, the structural protein of connective tissue (Vistica, Ahrens, & Ellison, 1977), adenyl cyclase, an enzyme important in cellular communication (Nathanson & Bloom, 1975), sodium and potassium ATP'ase, an enzyme important in membrane transport (Hernberg, Vihko, & Hasan, 1967), and 5' pyrimidine nucleotidase, an enzyme important in red blood cell function (Valentine, Paglia, Fink, & Madokoro, 1976). At the organ level, these and other biochemical alterations are expressed in impaired vascular, kidney, liver, thyroid, cardiac, immune, and peripheral and central nervous system function (see reviews by Goyer & Rhyne, 1973; Granick, Sassa, & Kappas, 1978).

The clinical signs of lead toxicity are somewhat different in adults and children. In adults, common symptoms include abdominal colic, motor weakness, palsy, and a variety of other signs of peripheral neuropathy. These effects disappear if exposure is terminated or if the individual is treated with chelating agents, drugs which bind lead and promote its excretion (Chisolm, 1978). The neurotoxic effects of lead in children are most often seen in the central nervous system. The signs are vague and include irritability, vomiting, stupor, ataxia, weakness, abdominal pain, as well as developmental delay and behavior disorder (Center for Disease Control, 1978; Chisolm, 1979). At blood lead levels greater than 80 $\mu$g/dl, children are at risk for lead encephalopathy, a serious condition involving brain edema and hemorrhage (Pentschew, 1965). Children who recover from clinical poisoning are frequently left with permanent residua such as profound retardation, hyperactivity, seizures, optic atrophy, and cerebral palsy (Byers & Lord, 1943; Mellins & Jenkins, 1955; Perlstein & Attala, 1966).

In recent years, clinical lead poisoning has become rare. This can be attributed to efforts to alert both the public and the medical community to the problem, the institution of mass screening programs during the 1960s, the development of more sensitive methods of detecting children at risk, and the discovery of means which permit more effective clinical management.

## The Threshold for Adverse Health Effects

Lin-Fu (1972) observed that lead poisoning has been regarded by many as an "all-or-none" problem. In this view, the lowest blood lead level associated with clinical poisoning is equated with the upper limit of "normal." Lead is assumed to have no adverse effect below this threshold. Because of accumulating biochemical evidence that lead at low dose interferes with a variety of enzymatic systems, the blood lead level at which a child is considered to be "at potential risk" for clinical poisoning has been lowered repeatedly in recent years. In 1970, the surgeon general set the level of "undue lead absorption" at 40 $\mu$g/dl; five years later, the Center for Disease Control lowered it to 30 $\mu$g/dl. Free erythrocyte protoporphyrin (FEP), an index of heme synthesis disruption, begins to accumulate in the red cells at a blood lead level of approximately 15 $\mu$g/dl (Piomelli, Seaman, Zullow, Curran, & Davidow, 1977). The activity of the heme biosynthetic enzyme, delta amino levulinic acid dehydratase (ALA-D) is reduced by 50% at a blood lead level of 15 $\mu$g/dl and by 75% at 30 $\mu$g/dl (Hernberg & Nikkanen, 1970; Millar, Cumming, Battistini, Carswell, & Goldberg, 1970). If there is a threshold for ALA-D inhibition, it is less than 10 $\mu$g/dl (Roels, Buchet, Lauwerys, Hubermont, Bruaux, Claeys-Thoreau, Lafontaine, & van Overschelde, 1976). Millar et al. also found, in rodents, brain levels of ALA-D parallel peripheral blood levels, suggesting that oxidative metabolism in the brain may be affected at low concentrations. Angle and McIntyre (1979a) reported thresholds in the range of 15 to 30 $\mu$g/dl for reductions of red cell pyrimidine 5' nucleotidase and Na/K ATP'ase activity. In rats, Nathanson and Bloom (1975) observed 10 to 20% inhibition of cerebellar adenyl cyclase at brain lead levels of less than 20 $\mu$g/dl and 50% inhibition at about 60 $\mu$g/dl.

The critical issue is whether these are merely biochemical changes without biologic significance or early signs of impaired tissue function. Some argue that the enzymes affected are not rate-limiting or that the inhibitions observed do not exceed "enzyme reserve capacity." Clearly, there is not a single threshold for the many effects of lead. Hernberg (1972) presented a model in which a family of curves represents the responses which a population exposed to lead would be expected to display (Figure 1). Each response is represented by a frequency distribution because of individual differences in the efficiency of lead absorption and physiologic response. Four responses of differing severity are shown in relation to lead dose. Response A represents a low dose response of debatable consequence, for example, inhibition of an enzyme that is not rate-limiting.

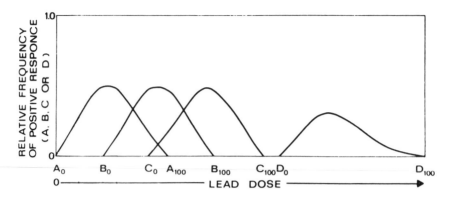

*Figure 1.* A model of the spectrum of responses to lead at increasing dose. Each letter represents a separate biologic response. Each response has a threshold ($A_0$, $B_0$, $C_0$, $D_0$) and a dose at which the entire sample is affected ($A_{100}$, $B_{100}$, $C_{100}$, $D_{100}$). (From Hernberg, "Environmental Health Aspects of Lead" copyright © 1972, reprinted with permission).

Response D represents death. $A_0$, $B_0$, $C_0$, and $D_0$ represent the levels at which no member of a population displays the response, while $A_{100}$, $B_{100}$, $C_{100}$, and $D_{100}$ are the levels at which all members respond. The question addressed by the studies to be reviewed is whether the curve(s) representing psychological deficit most resembles that of response A, B, C, or D.

At present, enzymes in many biosynthetic pathways are being measurably disrupted by lead in many members of modern society. Bryce-Smith (1972) has noted that the average blood lead level of adults in Britain is approximately 40% of that associated with clinical poisoning. An average toxicologic margin of safety of only 60% for an entire population is indeed small. The margin of safety for a syndrome of subclinical poisoning may be considerably smaller. Though it has traditionally been thought that intoxication does not occur in adults at blood levels below 80 $\mu$g/dl, recent studies using sophisticated assessment techniques have found a variety of behavioral and neurophysiological deficits in occupationally exposed workers whose blood lead levels were well below this and who were without clinical symptoms (e.g., Grandjean, Arnvig, & Beckmann, 1978; Seppalainen, Tola, Hernberg, & Kock, 1975; Valciukas, Lilis, Eisinger, Blumberg, Fischbein, & Selikoff, 1978). As a result, the National Institute for Occupational Safety and Health has recommended that the upper limit of safe occupational exposure be lowered to 60 $\mu$g/dl (NIOSH, 1978). While poisoning and encephalopathy may be the end points on a continuum of lead-induced illness, many fear that lesser behavioral and physiological derangements are associated with lower levels of exposure.

## Children: A Particularly Susceptible Population

Some children begin extrauterine life with lead burdens that are already close to what is considered worrisome. Estimates of the correlation between the lead levels of maternal venous blood and newborns' umbilical cord blood range between 0.6 and 0.85 (Barltrop, 1969; Clark, 1977; Gershanik, Brooks, & Little, 1975; Zetterlund, Winberg, Lundgren, & Johansson, 1977). Most studies have reported mean lead levels in cord blood of between 12 and 20 $\mu$g/dl, but individual vlaues ranging as high as 47 $\mu$g/dl. (See Scanlon, 1971; Zetterlund et al., 1977.)

Lead has been shown to be teratogenic in rats (McClain & Becker, 1975) and chicks (Gilani, 1973). While this has not been demonstrated in humans, occupational exposure may cause teratospermia (Lancranjan, Popescu, Găvănescu, Klepsch, & Serbănescu, 1975) or chromosomal changes and mitoses with secondary chromosomal aberrations such as breaks and gaps (e.g., Nordenson, Beckman, Beckman, & Nordstrom, 1978). High rates of sterility, spontaneous abortion, stillbirth, and neonatal mortality have long been noted among occupationally exposed women and wives of occupationally exposed men (see reviews by Rom, 1976; Zielhuis & Wibowo, 1976). The lead levels in the placentae of stillbirths and congenitally malformed births are higher than in those of normal births (Wibberly, Khere, Edwards, & Rushton, 1977).

There has been little investigation of the possibility that lead is a behavioral teratogen, causing damage to the fetal nervous system, which is manifested postnatally as functional disorder.

Young children tend to have higher blood lead levels than their adult relatives, especially in regions near high-dose sources such as smelters (e.g., Landrigan, Gehlbach, Rosenblum, Shoults, Candelaria, Barthel, Liddle, Smrek, Staehling, & Sanders, 1975). There are many differences between children and adults which may be responsible for this.

*Behavioral Differences.* Behavioral differences include children's more frequent outside activities, often involving contact with soil, their more frequent hand-to-mouth activity, and frank pica (Barltrop, 1966). Because of these oral propensities, many lead-containing nonedible items which pose little danger to adults become hazardous to children. Children's lesser height may also increase their exposure relative to adults since there is some evidence that air lead concentration is inversely related to sampling height (Edwards, 1975).

*Physiologic Differences.* The absorption, transport, and distribution of lead differ in the immature and mature organism (Jugo, 1977). Children's gastrointestinal absorption of lead is more efficient than adults'. Adults absorb approximately 10% of the lead ingested, while children absorb approximately 50%

(Ziegler, Edwards, Jensen, Mahaffey, & Fomon, 1978). Furthermore, it has been estimated that dietary intake per kilogram of body weight is two to three times greater for children than adults (U.S. EPA, 1977). Because of children's greater respiratory volume relative to body size, the increase in their blood lead level following an increase in air lead concentration is greater than adults' (U.S. EPA, 1977). In children, a smaller percentage of the total body burden is bound in bone, a relatively inert metabolic site (Chisolm, 1971; Zielhuis, 1972). At the same internal dose (i.e. blood lead level), children suffer greater impairment, as measured by the accumulation of FEP, and the appearance of both anemia and encephalopathy (U.S. EPA, 1977).

Willes, Lok, Truelove, and Sundaram (1977) demonstrated that entry of lead into the brains of monkeys is age-dependent, perhaps due to the greater permeability of the blood-brain barrier in the young. The developing nervous system may be particularly sensitive during periods of active cell proliferation and differentiation. Reduced cortical synaptogenesis in neonatal rats given subhistotoxic doses of lead has been reported (Averill & Needleman, 1980). The greater energy requirements of the immature brain may increase the impact of the inhibitory effects of lead on mitochondrial respiration and oxygen transport (McCauley, Bull, & Lutkenhoff, 1979).

Large numbers of children are at risk. In 1978, 6.48% of the nearly 400,000 children screened nationwide were found to have "undue absorption," though this figure was much higher (up to 20%) in some large cities (Lin-Fu, 1980). This positive find rate is remarkable for a mass screening program (e.g., compared to 0.005% for PKU; California Department of Health Services, 1979), corresponding to an estimated 600,000 children in the United States. Less than 15% of those children identified are treated (Lin-Fu, personal communication). Lin-Fu (1972) has noted that "undue absorption of lead among children living in old neighborhoods is matched by few, if any, other pediatric public health problems" (p. 706).

## REVIEW OF THE EVIDENCE FOR EFFECTS OF LOW LEVEL LEAD EXPOSURE ON CHILD DEVELOPMENT

*Epidemiologic Issues*

A number of population studies of children with differing exposure to lead have been conducted in attempts to measure effects at low dose. As in all epidemiological efforts, the strength and specificity of the causal inferences which can be drawn are limited (Cowan & Leviton, 1980; Lave & Seskin, 1979). The studies to be reviewed fall into two categories. In "cohort" studies, the samples are selected on the basis of degree of exposure to lead. The dependent variable is the incidence of some outcome in children suffering different amounts of exposure. "Case-control" studies compare a group of children who already display a particular outcome, for example, mental retardation, and another group who do not. The critical question is whether the groups differ in their exposure to lead, the suspected risk factor. (See MacMahon & Pugh, 1970, for detailed descriptions and comparisons of these epidemiologic strategies.)

*Methodologic Pitfalls.* Some of the studies report evidence of a link between low level lead exposure and psychological deficit in children; others do not. This discrepancy may stem from one or more of the following issues: (1) the index used to classify level of exposure to lead; (2) the levels on the index accepted as evidence of "exposure" and "nonexposure;" (3) the method of subject ascertainment and sampling; (4) the control of potentially confounding variables; and (5) the indices used to assess psychological outcome.

a.  Index of lead exposure. Most investigators have used as the primary index a direct measurement of the concentration of lead in some body tissue or excreta, most commonly blood, urine, hair, and, more recently, dental tissue. In some studies, other indices, such as radiographic signs of excessive lead intake (e.g., "lead lines" in long bones, radio-opaque intestinal deposits) or assays of the toxic effects of lead on heme synthesis (e.g., urinary coproporphyrin or amino levulinic acid, blood ALA-D, FEP, hemoglobin, hematocrit) have supplemented the direct measurement of lead. A few studies have used distance of residence from a stationary lead source (e.g. a smelter) as the primary index of exposure.

Due to ease of sampling, blood lead is the measure which has been used most frequently. There are several problems in its use. A single blood lead level is a somewhat static "ahistorical" measurement of the interaction of several dynamic forces: the intake, excretion, and sequestration of lead in tissue. The half-life of lead in the blood is approximately 25 to 30 days (Rabinowitz, Wetherill, & Kopple, 1976). About 95% of the total adult burden is bound in bone. As a result, a single blood lead level may accurately reflect current or recent exposure, but not necessarily long-term exposure unless it has remained relatively constant. Blood lead level does not fall immediately after a period of heavy exposure, but the time-course of the decline under conditions of typical human exposure have not yet been worked out in sufficient detail to permit an investigator to reconstruct the parameters of an individual's exposure from a single blood level. Because many of the studies have relied on blood samples taken either after exposure had ended or well before psychological status was assessed, there is usually considerable uncertainty as to the complete exposure history of the children. It is possible that a child with a normal blood lead level may have suffered excessive exposure in the past. This may be discovered only by analyzing shed teeth or measuring lead excretion following provocative chelation (e.g., David, Clark, & Voeller, 1972; Nieburg, Oski, Cornfield, & Oski, 1972).

The amount of lead deposited in bone (for which shed deciduous teeth are the easiest and most universally available assay) may be a better index of an individual's total exposure to lead. Because of the metabolic stability of teeth, once lead enters, it tends to remain. The lead concentration in teeth extracted from baboons at different times (1 to 9 months) following a pulsed dose of lead does not vary, even after chelation (Strehlow, 1972). A study by de la Burde and Shapiro (1975) showed that children who lived in old housing and had a positive history of pica for paint and plaster had higher tooth lead concentrations than a group of control children, despite the fact that the two groups had similar blood lead levels at age eight. Tooth lead concentration was also positively related to the duration of the pica habit.

Unfortunately, there is as yet no practical method of determining from an analysis of tooth lead concentrations the timing or duration of a child's exposure to low levels of lead, though several experimental techniques for determining the spatial distribution of lead in teeth, the first step toward such a goal, are currently under study (e.g., Fremlin & Edmonds, 1980; Sheer, Voet, Watjen, Koenig, Richter, & Steiner, 1977). Because of differences in metabolic stability, there is no fixed relationship between blood lead and tooth lead levels except when the level of exposure is constant or is limited to a single pulsed dose (e.g., see Kaplan, Peresie, & Jeffcoat, 1980). It is difficult to compare the exposure histories of children followed in different studies when blood lead is used as the index of exposure in one study and tooth lead in the other. Serial blood measurements collected every few months from birth, combined with the collection of shed teeth several years later, is probably the best solution to the problem of describing an individual's exposure history and distinguishing chronic from acute effects. However, this would be impractical under most circumstances.

b.  Specification of "exposed" and "nonexposed" levels on the index. In order to maximize the likelihood of detecting an effect for exposure to a putative toxin, the "exposed" and "nonexposed" groups must differ as much as is practically possible in terms of exposure. If the "nonexposed" subjects have actually suffered considerable exposure, their behavior may not appear significantly different from that of the "exposed" subjects, leading to a Type II error. Generally, control subjects are chosen because they have blood lead levels in the "normal" range. As noted, the level which is considered the upper limit of normal has been steadily decreasing with new evidence of possibly adverse biochemical effects at lower and lower concentrations. As a result, in several studies, the mean blood lead level of the controls either exceeded or was just below what is presently considered "undue absorption." As Weiss (1980) and Patterson (1980) note, the average lead burden in our society is so high that a fully adequate control group is probably no longer available. However, some investigators have been more successful than others in obtaining controls with relatively little exposure to lead.

c.   Subject ascertainment and sampling bias. In order to draw conclusions of the widest generality, the investigator must obtain subjects by sampling from the general population. The results of studies which draw their subjects from schools for the retarded or from psychiatric clinics may not apply to other groups. Furthermore, usually not all subjects recruited agree to participate and it is possible that those who are excluded or who exclude themselves differ systematically from those who participate (Cox, Rutter, Yule, & Quinton, 1977), either with respect to the independent variable (lead burden) or the dependent variable (behavior). It is important, therefore, that in population studies, an attempt be made to compare the participants and nonparticipants on these variables in order to evaluate the possibility and extent of ascertainment bias.

d.   Control of confounding variables. Exposure to lead is not distributed randomly throughout the population, occurring most often among the poor. Among the other assaults they experience are poor nutrition, poor prenatal care, exposure to other environmental hazards, increased incidence of infection and trauma, poor schools, and rearing environments that are deficient in the types of stimulation which promote intellectual development. All may seriously compromise a child's development. Unless great effort is made to hold these variables constant for the "exposed" and "nonexposed" groups, the effects of lead may be confounded. Moreover, while exposure to lead may produce developmental deficit, it is also possible that deficit, of whatever origin, increases the likelihood that a child will accumulate a dangerous lead burden (e.g. since pica frequently accompanies deficit; Bicknell, 1975).

e.   Indices used to assess psychological outcome. Frank lead poisoning is difficult to diagnose. The features of a syndrome of subclinical poisoning are likely to be even less dramatic. Care must be taken, then, to choose assessment measures that are sensitive enough to identify subtle deficit. Neither group tests nor clinical screening tests designed to identify children with major developmental disorders are appropriate. Even standardized individual intelligence tests may not be sensitive enough to identify deficits in specific aspects of psychological functioning. Assessment strategies ranging from laboratory procedures designed to dissect cognition into its component processes, to observational procedures for assessing behavior within naturalistic settings may be necessary in order to conduct a comprehensive evaluation of the effects of lead on development.

Table 1 summarizes some of the ways in which various investigators conducting cohort studies have attempted to deal with these methodological issues.
Details of the design of the individual studies will not be discussed unless they
bear on the interpretation of the results.

*Cohort Studies*

*Studies Suggesting a Link Between Low Level Lead Exposure and Psychological
Deficit in Children.*    The only longitudinal study of low level lead exposure was
conducted by de la Burde and Choate (1972, 1975). They found substantial
differences in performance between lead-exposed (LE) and control children at
both 4 and 7 years of age. At 4 years, a significantly greater percentage of LE
children achieved scores on the Stanford-Binet that were indicative of "borderline" or "defective" mental status (24.7 versus 9.8; the mean scores for the LE
and control children were 89 and 94, respectively). The incidence of "suspect"
or "abnormal" behavior on the tests used to assess fine motor development
(Wallin pegboard, copy forms, bead stringing, and Porteus mazes) was twice as
high among the LE children. Overall, their behavior during the testing session
was rated as "suspect" or "abnormal" (along such dimensions as distractibility,
negativity) three times more often than the controls'. The groups did not differ on
gross motor development or on a test of concept formation.

At 7 years of age, twice as many of the LE children presented positive neurological signs (e.g. clumsiness, hyperactivity, difficulties in fine motor performance). The number of children scoring in the "borderline" or "defective"
range on full-scale IQ was again significantly greater in the LE group (23.9
versus 5.7; the mean scores for the LE and control groups were 86.6 and 90.1,
respectively). The groups did not differ with respect to verbal or performance IQ
considered separately. In terms of the frequency of "suspect" or "abnormal"
performance, the LE children did significantly worse than the controls on the
Bender-Gestalt, the auditory-vocal association test, the Goodenough-Harris test,
and the tactile-finger recognition test. Their behavior during the testing session
was rated "suspect" or "abnormal" eight times more frequently; the major
differences (all in favor of the controls) were in self-confidence, fearfulness,
need for attention, attention span, and motivation level. There was no difference
in activity level or on the Wide Range Achievement Test. Parent report and a
review of school records (for a subsample of the children) revealed that the LE
children were experiencing more problems than the controls both at home (e.g.,
stealing, lying, arson) and at school (e.g., poor progress, explosiveness, impulsivity).

In the 1972 study, the authors did not confirm differences between the LE and
control children in tissue lead concentration. Later they obtained shed teeth from
nearly half of the control children and assays of lead content did establish the
children's relative lack of long-term exposure. It was reported by de la Burde and

Shapiro (1975) that the blood lead levels of the LE and control children were not significantly different at the time of the 7 year assessment, suggesting that the recent exposure of the two groups had been similar. The conclusion reached by de la Burde and Choate was that the neurological and psychological deficits which the LE children displayed at this time were not due to an acute pharmacologic effect but to permanent CNS damage produced by early exposure to lead.

Two other aspects of this study warrant comment. First, the control children were chosen because they lived in newer or well-maintained housing where the likelihood of lead exposure was low. The fact that a family lived in such housing may indicate a greater effort to provide a generally more optimal rearing environment for their children. The possibility that groups may have differed in this respect was not assessed by de la Burde and Choate. Second, their statistical treatment of the data was limited to chi square analyses of the percentage of children in each group whose performance was considered, according to criteria left unspecified, "suspect" or "abnormal." A thorough comparison of the distributions would have to include standard parametric tests of the differences between the group means on the dependent variables.

Perino and Ernhart (1974) found that LE children did significantly worse than controls on the General Cognitive (79.8 versus 90.1), Verbal (39.2 versus 43.6) and Perceptual-Performance (37.2 versus 43.6) scales of the McCarthy Scales of Children's Abilities. A multiple regression analysis revealed that lead contributed significantly to the children's scores even after child age, birth weight, and parental intelligence were taken into account. The LE and control children did not differ on the Quantitative, Memory, or Motor scales. The correlation between parent and child intelligence, which is generally about 0.5, was 0.52 for the control group but only 0.10 for the LE group. The authors inferred that some other factor, namely lead, had interfered with the children's cognitive development, disrupting the usual association between parent and child intelligence. Actually, this indicates that the impact of the additional factor(s) varied from child to child. If the effect had been the same on all children, the correlation between parent and child IQ would have remained about 0.5. The uneven impact may have resulted from the fact that the blood lead levels of the children in the LE group ranged from 40 to 70 $\mu$g/dl. It would be interesting to know if the amount by which a child's IQ fell short of that expected on the basis of parent IQ was linearly related to the child's lead burden (i.e., a dose-response effect).

The authors concluded that as a child's burden increases, his cognitive, verbal, and perceptual-performance abilities decrease, noting that this pattern of impairment resembles that of children with minimal brain dysfunction or learning disability. However, they did not explicitly argue that lead is of etiologic significance in these disorders, as others have (e.g., David et al., 1972; Solomon, 1979; see also Pihl & Parkes, 1977).

Perino and Ernhart did not report the way in which they selected the children

**Table 1.** Methodological Features of Cohort Studies on Low Level Lead Exposure

| Study | Subject Ascertainment | Groups | Criteria for Inclusion |
|---|---|---|---|
| de la Burde & Choate (1972) | participants in Collaborative Perinatal Study | (1) lead-exposed (N = 70) | (a) history of paint/plaster ingestion between ages 1–3<br>(b) residence in old house in disrepair<br>(c) elevated urinary coproporphyrin<br>(d) blood lead > .04 mg% or .03 mg% with positive radiographic signs |
| | | (2) control (N = 72) | (a) negative history of paint/plaster ingestion to age 4<br>(b) residence in lead-free environment<br>(c) normal urinary coproporphyrin |
| de la Burde & Choate (1975) | follow-up of same subjects as above | (1) lead-exposed (N = 67)<br>(2) control (N = 70) | same as above<br>same as above |
| Perino & Ernhart (1974) | | (1) lead-exposed (N = 30)<br>(2) control (N = 50) | blood lead .04–.07 mg/dl<br>blood lead .01–.03 mg/dl |
| Landrigan et al. (1975) | children living within 6.6 km of a smelter in El Paso for 12 of 24 months preceding study | (1) lead-exposed (N = 46) | blood lead 40–80 $\mu$g/dl |
| | | (2) control (N = 78) | blood lead < 40 $\mu$g/dl |
| Rummo et al. (1979) | | (1) lead encephalopathy (N = 10) | (a) blood lead > 40 $\mu$g/dl<br>(b) spinal fluid negative for encephalitis or meningitis<br>(c) lethargy, mental confusion, ataxia or convulsions |
| | | (2) long-term lead exposure (N = 20) | (a) blood lead > 40 $\mu$g/dl on two occasions at least 6 months apart or epiphyseal lines on long bones |
| | | (3) short-term lead exposure (N = 15) | (a) blood lead > 40 $\mu$g/dl on two occasions within one month<br>(b) no history of CNS pathology |
| | | (4) control (N = 45) | (a) blood lead < 40 $\mu$g/dl on two occasions<br>(b) no blood lead > 40<br>(c) residence in post-WWII housing<br>(d) no history of CNS pathology |
| Needleman et al. (1979) | all first and second graders in two suburban communities | (1) elevated lead (N = 58) | dentine lead > 20 parts per million |
| | | (2) control (N = 100) | dentine lead < 10 parts per million |
| Hrdina & Winneke (1978) | | (1) lead-exposed (N = 26)<br>(2) control (N = 26) | tooth lead $\geq$ 7 $\mu$g/g; $\bar{X}$ = 9.23 $\mu$g/g<br>tooth lead $\leq$ 3 $\mu$g/g; $\bar{X}$ = 2.41 $\mu$g/g |

| Measure of Lead Exposure | Age at Measure of Lead Exposure | Age at Testing | Confounding Variables Considered | Types of Assessments |
|---|---|---|---|---|
| blood lead: X̄ = .058 mg%; range: .04–.1 mg% | | 3; 11–4; 3 years | age, sex, SES, race, maternal IQ, housing density, number of children under age 6, medical and developmental histories | intelligence, fine motor and gross motor development, concept formation, behavior ratings |
| tooth lead for 29 of the children: X̄ = 202 μg/g   tooth lead for 32 of the children: X̄ = 112 μg/g | | X̄ = 7; 0 years | age, sex, SES, race, maternal IQ, death in family, foster home placement, no father in family, mother working, medical and development histories | intelligence, visuo-motor coordination, language development, neurological status, behavior ratings |
| | 3; 0–5; 11 years | 3; 0–5; 11 years | medical history, age, parental IQ, birth weight, parental education, SES, birth order, number of siblings | intelligence |
| blood lead at: screening: X̄ = 48.3 (range 40–68) testing: X̄ = 40.5 (range 22–58) screening: X̄ = 26.9 (range 1–39) testing: X̄ = 26.5 (range 15–39) | 10 months prior to testing | 8.3 ± 3.4 years   9.3 ± 3.6 years | age, sex, native language, length of residence in smelter area, SES, pica, medical history | medical, neurological status, intelligence, gross motor development, fine motor development, perceptual-motor skills, behavior ratings |
| blood lead: X̄ = 58.8 μg/dl | | 64.0 ± 16.3 months | age, race, sex, SES, complications of pregnancy and birth, neonatal risk factors | neurological status, intelligence, fine motor development, activity |
| blood lead: X̄ = 51.2 μg/dl | | 67.2 ± 13.9 months | | |
| blood lead: X̄ = 45.9 μg/dl | | 65.5 ± 11.5 months | | |
| blood lead: X̄ = 21.4 μg/dl | | 68.1 ± 13.4 months | | |
| | | 87.2 ± 7.7 months   90.7 ± 8.4 months | 39 variables including physical variables at time of testing, medical history, pica, race, sex, a variety of parental variables such as IQ, occupation, age, number of pregnancies, attitudes toward childrearing | intelligence, auditory-linguistic processing, visuo-motor competence, attentional skills, motor coordination, teachers' ratings of behavior, academic achievement, concrete operational intelligence |
| | | 7–10 years | age, sex, paternal occupation, pregnancy, perinatal, and neonatal risk factors | intelligence, visuo-motor coordination, gross motor development, behavior ratings |

(continued)

Table 1. (Continued)

| Study | Subject Ascertainment | Groups | Criteria for Inclusion |
|---|---|---|---|
| Kotok (1972) | | (1) lead-exposed (N = 24) <br> (2) control (N = 25) | |
| Kotok, Kotok, & Heriot (1977) | children enrolled at 3 heath centers and 2 hospital clinics | (1) lead-exposed (N = 31) <br> (2) control (N = 36) | (a) blood lead < 40 μg/dl <br> (b) history of either ingesting on more than one occasion or repetitive chewing of nonfood material |
| Baloh et al. (1975) | chldren at a Hospital lead clinic | (1) lead-exposed (N = 27) <br><br> (2) control (N = 27) | blood lead > 50 μg/dl on two occasions <br><br> blood lead < 30 μg/dl on one occasion |
| Ratcliffe (1977) | children living near a lead works and children of lead workers | (1) high lead (N = 24) <br><br> (2) moderate lead (N = 23) | blood lead > 35 μg/dl <br><br> blood lead < 35 μg/dl |
| McNeil, Ptasnik, & Croft (1975) | children living near a smelter | (1) lead-exposed (N = 138); no fixed groups; children classified into one or more groups on basis of age, blood lead, FEP, length of residence in smelter area, X-ray findings, area of residence <br> (2) matched controls (N = 138) | residence <br><br><br><br><br> residence |
| Hebel et al. (1976) | children living near either a battery factory or electrical equipment factory | (1) lead-exposed (children living near battery factory) (N = 851) <br><br> (2) control (children living near electrical equipment factory) (N = 948) <br> (3) control (children living in residential areas) (N = 694) | residence <br><br><br> residence <br><br> residence |
| Lansdown et al. (1974) | children living near a smelter | no fixed groups; correlational analysis used to examine relationships between: <br> (1) blood lead and distance of home from factory <br> (2) intelligence, distance of home from factory and behavior disturbance <br> (3) intelligence, blood lead, and behavior disturbance | residence |

16

| Measure of Lead Exposure | Age at Measure of Lead Exposure | Age at Testing | Confounding Variables Considered | Types of Assessments |
| --- | --- | --- | --- | --- |
| blood lead: $\bar{X}$ = .081 mg%; range: .058–.137 | | 34 months range: 12–69 | age, sex, race, pica, neonatal condition, quality of environment | gross and fine motor development, language development |
| blood lead: $\bar{X}$ = .038 mg%; range: .02–.055 | | 32 months range: 13–66 | | |
| blood lead: $\bar{X}$ = 79.6 μg/dl; range: 61–200 | | 43.4 months range: 20–65 | age, sex, race, medical history, neonatal condition, SES, pica | social maturity, information-comprehension, spatial relationships, spoken vocabulary, visual attention, auditory memory |
| blood lead: $\bar{X}$ = 28.3 μg/dl; range: 11–40 | | 42.6 months range: 23–67 | | |
| time of testing: $\bar{X}$ = 44.2 μg/dl | up to two years prior to testing | 67 months range: 47–99 | age, sex, race, SES | medical history, physical examination, fine motor development, gross motor development, intelligence |
| time of testing: $\bar{X}$ = 24.6 μg/dl | nine months prior to testing | 68 months range 46–96 | | |
| blood lead: $\bar{X}$ = 44.4 μg/dl; range: 36–64 | two years | 57.6 months range: 50–65 | SES,, length of residence in area, parental education, sex, working mother, primary school attendance, number of siblings, lead worker in family, age, medical history | intelligence, visual-motor integration, fine motor development, behavior ratings |
| blood lead: $\bar{X}$ = 28.2 μg/dl; range: 18–35 | two years | 56.9 months range: 49–67 | | |
| blood lead: $\bar{X}$ = 50.3 μg/dl; range: 14–93 <br><br> blood lead: $\bar{X}$ = 20.2 μg/dl; range: 7–43 | | 1; 9–18 years median: 9 | age, sex, ethnic background, income, pica, medical history, number of children in family, father's age, occupation rating, father's education, length of residence in area, mother's age, education, occupation rating, birth history, birth weight | medical history, neurologic and physical examination, motor function, intelligence, achievement, visual-motor integration, personality adjustment, teacher evaluations, verbal-auditory skills |
| | | 11 years | denisty of occupied dwellings, population density, SES, birthrank, maternal age, sex | intelligence |
| | | 6–16 years | length of residence in area, father's occupation, presence of leadworker in family, SES | intelligence, reading, teachers' behavioral ratings |

17

included in the LE group, leaving open the possibility of ascertainment bias. Also, there was a significant negative correlation between child lead level and parent educational level. Since parental education has been shown to be an important influence on children's cognitive development, it is possible that it was the difference between groups on this variable, not lead, which was responsible for the LE children's deficits. The fact that the relationship between a child's lead level and the child's performance was not disrupted by controlling for parental IQ mitigates somewhat the force of this criticism. Nevertheless, the inferences which can be drawn from these data would have been much stronger if the authors had included parental education in the multiple regression analyses or explored its relationship to child outcome and lead level by means of analysis of variance or partial correlation. Socioeconomic status should also have been included in the regression analyses.

In a study of children living near a lead smelter in El Paso, Landrigan, Baloh, Barthel, Whitworth, Staehling, and Rosenblum (1975) found evidence of non-verbal cognitive and fine motor deficits in those children whose blood lead levels exceeded 40 $\mu$g/dl. Their finger-wrist tapping was significantly slower than that of a group of control children who also lived near the smelter but whose blood lead levels were below 40 $\mu$g/dl. The performance IQ of the LE children or the WISC or WPPSI was also significantly lower (94.9 versus 102.7) than the controls', though verbal (83.8 versus 85.1) and full-scale IQ (88.0 versus 92.9) were not. The groups did not differ in parents' reports of behavioral abnormalities (such as pica, colic, clumsiness, irritability, convulsions, hyperactivity), on quantitative neurological tests (visual or auditory reaction time, two-plate tapping), the Bender-Gestalt test, or on ratings of their behavior during the tests. In a similar study of children living near a smelter in Idaho, Landrigan, Baker, Feldman, Cox, Eden, Orenstein, Mather, Yankel, and von Lindern (1976) found a significant correlation between peroneal nerve conduction velocity and blood lead level ($r = -0.38$).

The index of lead exposure used by Landrigan et al. was blood lead level. However, two blood lead levels, assessed approximately one year apart, were available for each child. The average burden of the children in each group remained relatively constant over this period between screening and psychological assessment (48.3 versus 40.5 $\mu$g/dl for the LE children; 26.9 versus 26.5 $\mu$g/dl for the control children). The correlation between these values is not reported, so it is impossible to ascertain whether the level for an individual child was stable. However, this overall stability suggests that the children in both groups experienced a relatively constant level of exposure, at least over the period of one year.

The LE and control children were not perfectly matched in terms of age or sex. However, all significant group differences persisted when IQ scores and finger-wrist tapping speed were adjusted for age by regression analyses and the groups stratified by sex. There was no attempt, beyond ascertainment of ethnicity, primary language, and Hollingshead Index, to control for quality of rearing environment. The authors noted that the children they studied, unlike those studied in some of the investigations reporting negative results, suffered chronic lead exposure, dating in most cases from the prenatal period. Children whose ingestion of lead occurs mainly through pica for paint may be exposed for shorter periods of time beginning at a later age than the El Paso children. They also raised the possibility that absorption of other metals emitted by the smelter, notably arsenic and cadmium, may have aggravated the effects of lead on the exposed children.

Rummo, Routh, Rummo, and Brown (1979) found consistent, though generally statistically nonsignificant, evidence of a dose-response relationship between level of exposure to lead and deficit in neurological and psychological functioning. With minor exceptions, the only significant differences were between children with a history of lead encephalopathy and controls. The deficits displayed by this group were quite broad, including general intelligence in the borderline range (on the McCarthy Scales), poor motor skills, hyperactivity (as rated by parents), and slow reaction time. On many of the measures, however, the children in the long- and short-term exposure groups achieved scores that were intermediate between those of the encephalopathy and control groups.

Classification of the children into the different groups was based on a variety of criteria, including history of blood lead level, evidence of encephalitis, meningitis, signs or symptoms of CNS pathology, "lead lines," and quality of residence. The exposure groups differed in maternal educational level, with the mothers of the encephalopathy and short-term exposure groups achieving lower levels than the mothers of the other groups of children. There is no indication of how the authors obtained their sample of LE children.

Needleman, Gunnoe, Leviton, Reed, Peresie, Maher, and Barrett (1979) collected shed deciduous teeth from 2,335 of the 3,329 children attending first and second grade in two suburban communities. Teacher ratings of classroom behavior were obtained for 2,146 of the children submitting teeth. The dimensions rated were distractibility, persistence, dependence, organization, hyperactivity, impulsivity, frustration threshold, day dreaming, ability to follow simple directions and sequences of directions, and overall functioning. In addition, the children with the highest (>20 parts per million) and lowest (<10 ppm) dentine lead were given a large battery of neuropsychological tests. The high lead children achieved significantly lower full-scale WISC-R IQs than the low lead children (102.1 versus 106.6). Differences on the verbal subscales were primarily responsible for this overall difference. These children also did significantly worse on three tests of auditory and verbal processing (the Seashore Rhythm Test, the Token Test, and the Sentence Repetition Test), and on an attentional measure (reaction time under various delay conditions). (This later finding replicated the results of a small study reported by Needleman, 1975.) The incidence of negative teacher ratings for the 11 dimensions of classroom behavior increased in a clear dose-related fashion with increasing dentine lead levels, $p = 1.7 \times 10^{-8}$ (unpublished analyses), though it was not possible to control for confounding variables in this analysis. From these data, Cowan and Leviton (1980) calculated that 69% of the low classroom functioning of the children with elevated dentine lead levels and 43% of the low overall classroom functioning in the population as a whole could be attributed to lead exposure (attributable risk).

Thirty-nine non-lead variables were considered possible confounding factors. Those five on which the high and low lead groups differed at the 10% level or less—father's SES, mother's age at child's birth, number of pregnancies, mother's education, and parental IQ—were controlled by analysis of covariance. The two groups also differed significantly in terms of the percentage of children for whom parents reported a history of pica (29% of the high lead group versus 11% of the low), though pica was not included in the analysis of covariance. However, history of pica was not systematically related to the teacher ratings (Needlemen & Bellinger, 1981) and though children with pica tended to achieve IQ scores that were approximately 2 to 3 points below those without, this was true in both the high and low lead groups (unpublished analyses).

The data for only 158 of the 524 children who were eligible for the full neuropsychologic evaluation on the basis of dentine lead are reported, raising the possibility of ascertainment bias. However, these children were very similar to those who did participate, both in terms of lead level and teacher ratings. To our knowledge, this is the only study to establish the equivalence of these two groups on both the independent and dependent variables.

In a study of similar design though much smaller in scale, Hrdina and Winneke (1978) found that a group of children with elevated "dental" lead levels scored lower than control children on all 11 subscales of the Hamburg WISC. (The authors did not clarify whether they measured dentine or whole tooth lead levels). However, none of the group differences reached the 5% level of significance. The mean of the controls exceeded the mean of the LE children by 5 to 7 points on verbal, performance, and full-scale IQ, though only the differences on performance and full-scale IQ reached even the 10% level of significance. The LE children scored lower than the controls on a variety of tests of visuomotor coordination (a diagnostic test for cerebral damage, the Goettingen test for the reproduction of shapes, and the Benton test), though only the difference on the Goettingen test was significant. The groups did not differ on any of the indices of gross motor development (balancing backwards, hopping on one foot, hopping sideways, turning sideways), nor was the children's behavior during the tests rated differently on dimensions such as hyperactivity, affectivity, or distractibility.

Although the group differences did not reach conventional levels of significance, the consistency in their direction led the authors to conclude that "there might be a connection between chronically increased lead absorption in infancy and neurological damage." The authors constructed 26 matched pairs of children on the basis of a pool of 458 children whom they screened. Because of the limited size of the resulting sample, it may have been better to include more children in the study, matching groups rather than individuals on the demographic variables. Also, the authors did not report the source of the screening sample: whether they were selected randomly from the community, were patients in a pediatric or lead clinic, or volunteers for a research project on lead. One possibly confounding factor, which the authors noted, is that there was a higher, though statistically nonsignificant, incidence of perinatal (but not prenatal or neonatal) risk factors in the histories of the LE children. These included disturbances in placental function, prematurity, and low birth weight.

Two additional studies present evidence that children suffer adverse consequences from exposure to low levels of lead (Albert, Shore, Sayers, Strehlow, Kneip, Pasternack, Friedhoff, Covan, & Cimino, 1974; Pueschel, Kopito, & Schwachman, 1972; additional follow-up data reported in Pueschel, 1974). These studies will not be discussed because inadequacies in design and in the reporting of methodology make their results difficult to interpret and impossible to compare to those of other studies.

*Studies Which Report Failure to Find a Link Between Low Level Lead Exposure and Psychological Deficit in Children.* Kotok (1972) reported no significant differences in the performance of LE and control children on the Denver Developmental Screening Test. Both groups performed significantly worse on fine motor, adaptive, and language items, though not on gross motor ability, than the standardization sample. For both groups, however, performance was positively related to the quality of environment, leading Kotok to conclude that the developmental delay of the LE children was due less to lead toxicity than to environmental inadequacies such as poor housing, financial insecurity, drug abuse, and unstable relationships.

As Kotok noted, the Denver was not designed to identify subtle deficits of the type one would expect to follow low level lead exposure. Also, the mean blood lead level of the controls was quite high, 0.038 mg% (approximately 40 $\mu$g/dl), ranging up to 0.055 mg%. Since these levels well exceed that considered evidence of "undue" exposure, such children are not appropriate controls for a study of this sort. Twenty-one of the 24 LE children had received chelation therapy, apparently prior to the developmental assessment, so Kotok's conclusion must be qualified by noting that most of the exposed children had been treated for elevated lead level. Also, the source of the LE children was not identified.

Kotok, Kotok, and Heriot (1977) reported a total failure to find significant differences ($p < .05$) between LE and control children on a variety of assessment measures. However, the scores of the controls averaged 4 points higher on each of the 6 classes of ability assessed (social maturity, spatial relationships, spoken vocabulary, information comprehension, visual attention, and auditory memory). The authors concluded that the "data do not prove that these children have sustained no neurologic damage by lead" and pointed out that longitudinal testing may reveal psychological deficits.

This work is subject to some of the same criticisms as Kotok's earlier study. The blood lead level of many of the control children was quite high: nearly half (15 of 36) over 30 $\mu$g/dl. Also, 14 of the 31 LE children had been chelated.

Baloh, Sturm, Green, and Gleser (1975) also reported the general absence of differences between LE and control children on any of a large battery of psychological and quantitative neurological assessments. A higher frequency of overactive behavior reported by parents of the LE children was the only significant difference, but the instrument used in the collection of these data was unstandardized. In addition, there was a nonsignificant trend toward poorer fine motor control among the LE children.

A child was considered lead-exposed if blood lead levels had been $> 50$ $\mu$g/dl on two prior occasions, though the amounts of time which had elapsed between the two blood samplings or the interval between these samplings and the psychological testing are not reported. At the time of testing, only 11 of the 27 LE children still had blood lead levels $> 50$ $\mu$g/dl; 13 were $\leq 40$ $\mu$g/dl; one only 13 $\mu$g/dl. While all control children had had blood lead levels $< 30$ $\mu$g/dl at screening 9 months prior to psychological testing, 6 had levels of 30 to 40 $\mu$g/dl and one had a level of 63 $\mu$g/dl at the time of testing (though this latter child was not included in the analyses). As a result of these fluctuations in blood lead level between screening and testing, the control child had the higher blood lead level in 2 of the 26 LE-control matches; in another 5 pairs, the levels were within 10 $\mu$gs of one another, and in an additional 5, within 20 $\mu$gs. Given the uncertainty that the exposure histories of the LE and control children were sharply different, it is not surprising that the results of the psychological comparisons were equivocal.

Ratcliffe (1977) reported no significant differences between groups of "high" and "moderate" lead children on any of the subscales of the Griffiths mental development scales, Frostig Perceptual Quotient, a pegboard test of fine motor function, or on ratings of behavior deviance. However, the "high" lead children did score lower on the Frostig and on all 6 subscales of the Griffiths (General Quotient 102.2 versus 107.5), suggesting a consistent, though subtle deficit. A multiple regression analysis indicated that age and primary school attendance were more important than lead in accounting for the variance in the children's performance on the outcome measures.

The numbers of children Ratcliffe included in his study were quite small, only 23 and 24 in the "moderate" and "high" lead groups, respectively. There is also some question as to how different the exposure histories of the two groups really were. The children were classified on the basis of a single blood lead level determined at age 2, three years before the psychological assessments. We cannot be sure that the level of exposure to lead in the intervening period was equivalent for the two groups or that the single blood lead level determined at age

2 accurately reflected the children's total exposure during their early years. Moreover, the difference between groups at 2 years, 28.2 versus 44.4 $\mu$g/dl, was not as large as in most studies.

Hebel, Kinch, and Armstrong (1976) found that children living near a lead-emitting battery factory actually scored higher on all sections of the British 11-plus examination, a group test, than children living in a residential area or near a nonemitting factory. The authors attributed this to the difference across areas in the quality of the children's education. Within the exposed group, the children living closest to the factory did not score significantly lower than those living farther away. Hebel et al. concluded that while "lead pollution . . . did not produce an overall deficiency in school performance, (the data) cannot finally rule out the possibility of such an effect." They noted that given their sample size, the children living closest to the factory would have had to manifest a deficit of 8% on the 11-plus examination for the group difference to be significant (using .05 and .10 as $\alpha$ and $\beta$, respectively). To detect a 5% deficit with the same error parameters, they would have had to nearly triple the size of their sample of children living closest to the factory.

Blood lead levels were not measured in this study, so it is not certain that the groups in the three study areas actually differed in lead burden, especially in light of the fairly low correlation reported by Lansdown, Clayton, Graham, Shepherd, Delves, and Turner (1974) between blood lead level and distance of residence from a smelter ($r = -.18$). There was no attempt to control for pica or other factors which may have led control children to accumulate a significant lead burden.

Like Landrigan et al. (1975), McNeil, Ptasnik, and Croft (1975) studied the children of "Smeltertown," a community very close to a lead smelter in El Paso. Using an extensive battery of neurological and psychological measures, they found few differences between these children and two groups of controls. Only on the California Test of Personality did the groups consistently differ, with the controls demonstrating greater overall adjustment. The authors did not attribute this to lead but to the geographical isolation of the Smeltertown children and to the general disruption of their lives which followed news reports of the public health problems of the Smeltertown area.

A group of 18 Smeltertown children with blood lead levels greater than 40 $\mu$g/dl were involved in litigation against the company owning the smelter and, on the advice of counsel, refused to participate in the McNeil et al. study (U.S. EPA, 1977). The possible impact of this biased ascertainment is a matter of concern since it was the group of subjects who apparently felt most strongly that they had suffered adverse effects for whom data are missing. Another 50 of the 206 children identified as having blood lead levels over 40 $\mu$g/dl did not participate, for reasons unnamed, yielding a total nonparticipation rate of 33% for the high lead group. There are no outcome data to indicate whether their exclusion biased the Smeltertown distribution.

The manner in which the Smeltertown children were assigned blood lead levels for the purpose of classification may have overestimated their actual exposure. Because of their high-risk status, these children had had several lead determinations performed over a period of 18 months. Since these levels apparently varied markedly, the authors averaged the two highest values for a child. Hence, the "exposed" and "nonexposed" groups may actually have had similar blood lead levels at the time of psychological assessment and may not have had different exposure histories since only recent blood levels were available for the controls.

Lansdown et al. (1974), conducting a study of all the children living within 500 meters of a smelter in London, found a significant negative correlation between distance from the smelter and blood lead level, though this relationship accounted for less than 4% of the variance in blood lead level. Blood lead level was not significantly related to reading ability, IQ, or teacher ratings of behavior disorder. Children who had moved into the study area at age 2 or older achieved significantly lower IQ scores and were rated by teachers as more disturbed than those children who were native to the area. This led the authors to conclude that social factors are more important influences than lead on child development. While this is probably true for children in general, it must be regarded as speculation in regard to this specific population, since the authors present no evidence that the late-arriving families differed from the natives in any social characteristics. They concluded that while a blood lead level of 40 $\mu$g/dl suggests excessive exposure, a level of up to 60 $\mu$g/dl does not appear to be a significant cause of behavior disorder or delayed development in children.

Blood lead levels were available for only 78% of the school-age children residing in the area. Why they were not available for the other 22% is not discussed, though the reasons are relevant for deciding whether or not this might have biased the blood lead and IQ distributions. Other potential problems are the restricted range of the blood lead levels of the study population and the fact that only a single blood lead level was available for each child. Finally, the authors did not report any attempt to control for socioeconomic status or rearing milieu. While all families lived in the same neighborhood, there may have been differences across the sample that obscured any effects of elevated blood lead.

There is a series of cohort studies by Sachs and colleagues which warrant mention though they considered the sequelae of clinical lead poisoning rather than low level exposure (Krall, Sachs, Rayson, Lazar, Growe, & O'Connell, 1980; Sachs, Krall, McCaughran, Rozenfeld, Yongsmith, Growe, Lazar, Novar, O'Connell, & Rayson, 1978). They have reported that the psychological functioning of poisoned children (blood lead levels between 40 and 471 $\mu$g/dl) is similar to that of their siblings, as long as they are treated before becoming encephalopathic. In fact, in one study, the poisoned children scored significantly higher than their siblings on visual-motor integration and nonsignificantly higher on 5 of the other 6 outcome measures (Sachs et al., 1978) in addition, several techniques designed to identify brain damage which affects visuospatial functioning from patterns in WISC subtest scores, failed to differentiate groups (Krall et al., 1980). These findings are greatly discrepant from those of other investigations of poisoned children and, if true, would render moot the issue of whether low level lead exposure produces adverse outcomes.

In fact, these studies are seriously flawed in at least three respects. First, only 22% of the children initially considered eligible on the basis of blood lead level were evaluated. The selection process is not adequately explained, nor is the comparability of the included and excluded subjects demonstrated. Sachs et al. provide little information about the exposure histories of the control children. The only criterion for inclusion as a control sibling was a blood lead level less than 40 g/dl ''at screening.'' Apparently, this could have been a single lead level taken from two to eight years earlier, at the time the sibling was diagnosed as lead poisoned. Given the fact that siblings of poisoned children are themselves at high risk for poisoning (Landrigan et al., 1975), an attempt should have been made to document the siblings' lack of exposure during the intervening period. Third, the generally poor performance of the control children, associated with a high incidence of abnormal EEG tracings and mental retardation, raises the question of whether this is a suitable control population. Their performance would be consistent with, though it certainly does not prove the hypothesis that they had suffered an undetected episode of lead poisoning. Kirkconnell and Hicks (1980) noted an additional feature of these studies which weakens Sachs et al.'s interpretation. Since controls were older than their patient siblings in all three studies by periods ranging up to a year, they would be expected to have suffered more of the deterioration in IQ which typically characterizes such disadvantaged populations.

The results of three important cohort studies have been reported since this article was originally written:

a.  Yule, Lansdown, Millar, and Urbanowicz (1981) evaluated the general intelligence (WISC-R) and educational attainment of 166 6-12 year old children with blood lead levels of 7 to 32 $\mu$g/dl. They found significant associations between lead level and intelligence (primarily verbal IQ), reading and spelling achievement scores. These associations were independent of social class, though the authors expressed strong reservations about the adequacy with which this potential confounder was measured.

b.  Relying on whole tooth level as the marker of lead exposure in a sample of 115 West German children, Winneke, Brockhaus, Kramer, Ewers, Kujanek, Lechner, and Janke (1981) replicated many of the findings reported by Hrdina and Winneke (1978) and Needleman et al. (1979). Children with higher levels of tooth lead performed significantly worse than their less exposed peers in terms of verbal IQ (WISC-R), perceptual-motor skill (Bender–Gestalt test), and reaction time. These associations did not appear to be confounded by any of the 19 socioeconomic or medical factors measured.

c.  Ernhart, Landa, and Schell (1981) re-evaluated 63 of the children studied earlier by Perino and Ernhart (1974). They related scores on the McCarthy Scales of Children's Abilities, a reading test, and a variety of other instruments to thre indices of lead exposure: preschool blood lead level, and school-age blood lead and FEP levels. Dentine lead levels were available for approximately half ofthe children. With sex, parent education, and parent IQ controlled, significant associations were observed between school-age lead level and the Verbal and Motor Scales, as well as the General Cognitive Index of the McCarthy Scales, and between school-age FEP and the Verbal Scale. The authors concluded that these were probably not meaningful due to the large number of statistical tests carried out. They generalized their conclusion, attributing the apparent lead effects reported elsewhere in the literature to methodologic difficulties. This interpretation has been challenged (e.g., Needleman, Bellinger, & Leviton, 1981).

*Case-Control Studies*

Much of the interest in lead as a possible etiologic agent in childhood disorder was stimulated by Moncrieff, Koumides, Clayton, Patrick, Renwick, and Roberts (1964), who measured the blood lead levels of four groups of children: normal, mentally retarded or with severe behavior disorder, children with a history of encephalitis, and children with abdominal pain, severe anemia, and a history of pica. The percentage of children in each group with a level greater than 36 $\mu$g/dl, the authors' definition of the upper limit of "normal," was 2.5, 45, 30, and 54, respectively. In a similar study, Cohen, Johnson, and Caparulo (1976) reported significantly higher blood lead levels for autistic children than either nonautistic psychotic or normal children. Because this association is correlational, it is not clear whether the accumulation of lead preceded or followed the manifestation of pathology in these children. Both groups of authors noted that retarded or disturbed children may accumulate lead because of behavioral abnormalities such as pica.

In trying to establish the direction of effect, investigators have generally used one of two strategies: (1) they assess a child's lead burden very early in life, prior to the development of a behavior disorder that might lead to secondary lead accumulation; or (2) they separate those cases for whom no cause for the disorder can be found from those for whom a "probable" cause is known. Both of the outcomes studied in relation to lead (hyperactivity and mental retardation) are final common pathways for a variety of pathological processes. The likelihood of noting a link with lead will increase if cases known to be due to some other factor can be eliminated from the sample or analyzed as a separate group. If lead is not of etiologic significance, this segregation of cases should not affect the strength of the relationship between lead and the disorder.

*Hyperactivity.* David, Clark, and Voeller (1972) compared lead levels in blood and urine after provocatively chelating five groups of children: (1) a "pure" group of hyperactives for whom no cause could be determined, (2) a group for whom a "highly probable" cause could be identified, (3) a group with a "possible" cause, (4) a group with diagnosed lead poisoning, and (5) normal controls. Both the "pure" and "possible" cause hyperactives had significantly higher lead levels than either the controls or the "highly probable" group. The lower levels of the latter group suggest that hyperactivity per se does not predispose a child to develop a high lead burden and supports the interpretation that lead may play a causal role in some cases of hyperactivity. However, there were only 9 children in the "probable" cause group and 11 in the "possible" cause group, too few to provide a firm foundation for such a conclusion. Moreover, the difference between the "pure" hyperactives and the control group in blood lead level was only 4 $\mu$g/dl (26.2 versus 22.2 $\mu$g/dl) (though the difference in urinary lead level was greater: 146 versus 77 $\mu$g/dl). These blood lead levels are comparable to those of the children used as controls in the cohort studies reviewed above. Furthermore, it is not certain that the different groups of hyperactive children were afflicted to the same extent since the teachers' and parents' ratings, the bases for the diagnoses, appear to have been systematically different across groups. Whatever group differences were noted in lead levels may have been related more to the degree of manifest hyperactivity than to the likelihood that a cause for the hyperactivity could be identified.

David, Hoffman, Sverd, and Clark (1977) essentially replicated the earlier study, increasing the numbers of children in the "probable" and "possible" cause groups from 11 and 9 to 12 and 31, respectively. The parents' and teachers' ratings of the severity of hyperactivity were more similar across groups than in the earlier study. As before, the "pure" and the "possible" cause groups did not differ with respect to blood or urinary lead levels, but both had significantly higher levels than the "probable" cause children. The blood lead levels for all groups were again below that usually considered abnormal (24.7 and 26.3 $\mu$g/dl for the "pure" and "possible" cause groups; 20.3 $\mu$g/dl for the "probable" cause group). There were no normal control children in this study.

In both David et al. studies, there may have been a social class bias in the assignment of children to etiologic groups. The information used to classify children apparently came exclusively from mothers rather than medical records. Some of the events considered "possible" or "probable" causes included ABO and Rh blood incompatibility, difficult delivery with low Apgar scores and severe anoxia, eclampsia, and edema serious enough to require diuretics. A mother's ability to report accurately such events, which had occurred a mean of 8 years, 3 months earlier, will probably vary with her social class, particularly her education. David et al. did not indicate whether the etiological groups differed in this regard. Since it has been shown repeatedly that a child's blood lead level varies with social class, it may be that the fact that a child was in the "possible" cause or etiology "unknown" group and had a relatively high blood lead level were not causally related to one another but each separately to the fact that the child's family was of lower socioeconomic class.

David, Hoffman, Sverd, Clark, and Voeller (1976) reported an intriguing approach to the remediation of some cases of hyperactivity. They tested the hypothesis that if an elevated blood lead level is the cause of a child's hyperactivity, lowering that level will reduce the severity of the child's symptoms, but that if the hyperactivity is due to some other factor, this will have no effect. As David et al. predicted, teachers', parents', and physicians' ratings indicated that following 12 weeks of chelation therapy, the etiology "unknown" group displayed a greater reduction than the "probable" cause group in the frequency of behaviors associated with hyperactivity.

These findings should be considered extremely tentative. First, only 13 children received treatment, 6 "probable" and 7 "unknown" cause children. Second, the "unknown" cause children had higher blood lead levels prior to treatment and thus experienced a greater decrease in blood lead level as a result of treatment (since the amount of chelatable lead increases exponentially with arithmetic increases in blood lead level; Chisolm, Mellits, & Barrett, 1976). Behavioral gain might have been related to the magnitude of the decrease, independent of a child's etiologic group. Third, 3 of the 6 children in the "probable" cause group (but only 1 of 7 in the "unknown" cause group) received methylphenidate during chelation. While this drug is generally thought to ameliorate the symptoms of hyperactivity, it is not known how it interacts with chelating agents. In fact, the parent and teacher ratings of the "probable" cause children tended to become somewhat worse following chelation. Fourth, there was no attempt to control for socioeconomic status, so the classification of children into etiologic groups is subject to the same ambiguities as in the other studies in this series. Finally, the protocol did not include a placebo trial, though this is reportedly being carried out (Lansdown, 1979).

Hole, Dahle, and Kløve (1979) failed to find a significant difference between the hair lead levels of a group of 19 hyperactive Norwegian boys and 22 controls.

*Mental Retardation.*    Beattie, Moore, Goldberg, Finlayson, Mackie, Graham, Main, McLaren, Murdock, and Stewart (1975) identified a group of 2–5 year-old mentally retarded children in Glasgow (IQ or DQ < 70) and a matched control group and obtained samples of the drinking water from both the homes in which their mothers lived during pregnancy and their residence during the first year of life. The mean water lead levels at the pre- and postnatal homes of the retarded children were higher than those at the controls' homes. The most striking difference between the two distributions was the number of homes with extremely high levels. For 43 of the 64 matched pairs, the water lead levels fell into the same coarse range (i.e., 0–399, 400–799, and > 800 $\mu g/dl$). For 15 of the 21 discordant pairs, it was the mentally retarded child whose water lead level was higher ($p = .039$). At none of the 64 control homes did the water lead level exceed 800 $\mu g/dl$; but it did so in the homes of 11 of the 64 retarded children, ranging as high as 2,000 $\mu g/dl$. The authors concluded that a child exposed to water with a lead level greater than 800 $\mu g/dl$ is at least 1.7 times more likely to be retarded than a child whose water lead level is unknown. Using Beattie et al.'s data, Leviton and Needleman (1975) determined that "38% of the risk of mental retardation in those exposed to more than 400 $\mu g$ lead per liter of water is estimated to be in excess of the risk among children not so exposed" (p. 983).

Elwood, Morton, and St. Leger (1976) failed to find a similar relationship in an area in which water lead levels are generally lower than in Glasgow. This suggests that a link between water lead level and mental retardation may be evident only at very high levels.

An obvious weakness of the Beattie et al. study is its reliance on an indirect measure of exposure to lead. The dose received by children whose homes had similar water lead levels almost certainly varied with consumption habits and biologic sensitivity to lead. Beattie, Moore, Miller, Devenay, and Goldberg (1972) and Greathouse, Craun, and Worth (1976) have demonstrated a significant positive correlation between water lead and blood lead levels in normal individuals, but the amount of variance in blood lead explained by water lead is extremely small. Studies using indirect measures of exposure should determine whether exposure to lead via other routes is similar for the various outcome groups since any imbalance will confound the results.

Moore, Meredith, and Goldberg (1977) were able to rule out the possibility that an unidentified third factor, such as pre-existing retardation, was responsible for both current blood lead level and poor psychological outcome. For 80 of the 154 children studied by Beattie et al. (1975), they obtained blood samples which had been taken within the first two weeks of life in order to screen the children for phenylketonuria. The children later identified as mentally retarded had significantly higher neonatal blood lead levels than the controls (25.5 versus 20.9 $\mu g/dl$). Furthermore, there was a significant correlation ($r = .54$) between neonatal blood lead level and the water lead level in the home in which a child's mother had lived during pregnancy. Cowan and Leviton (1980) estimated that 35% of mental retardation of "unknown" etiology could be attributed to elevated blood lead levels.

Presumably, the reasons why the PKU cards were unavailable for nearly half of the original sample were clerical in nature rather than related to some characteristic of the children. Therefore, it is unlikely that the failure to follow up more of the children introduced an ascertainment bias.

David, McGann, Hoffman, Sverd, and Clark (1976) found that children with mental retardation of "unknown" etiology had higher blood lead levels than either children with mental retardation of "probable" etiology (most frequently prematurity or eclampsia) or normal children (25.5 versus 18.7 and 18.8 $\mu$g/dl, respectively). Current blood lead level was the only basis for estimating the children's exposure histories and the levels in all groups were moderate. One would not want to conclude that having 25 $\mu$g/dl blood lead was responsible for the low (55–84) IQs of the children in the "unknown" etiology group since many children of normal IQ have blood lead levels on this order. David et al. did not investigate the prevalence of pica among the three groups of children. This is critical in light of Gibson, Lam, McCrae, and Goldberg's (1967) finding, in a study of identical design, that all of the children with a blood lead level over 40 $\mu$g/dl, regardless of diagnostic group, had a history of pica. (Bicknell, Clayton, & Delves, 1968, found that mentally retarded children without pica generally had blood lead levels in the normal range). In Gibson et al.'s study, children with retardation of "unknown" etiology also had higher blood lead levels than children with retardation of known origin (32.4 versus 16.4 $\mu$g/dl). However, the blood lead level of the controls was nearly as high (29.6 $\mu$g/dl). The authors noted that because the retarded children of known etiology (e.g., Down's syndrome, PKU, severe organic disease) were generally less mobile and more closely supervised than the children in either of the other groups, they had less opportunity to ingest lead. The authors concluded that though a high lead burden may aggravate a pre-existing retardation, it is probably more often a concomitant than a cause of this condition.

Youroukos, Lyberatos, Philippidou, Gardikas, and Tsomi (1978) reported similar findings from a study which is subject to many of the same interpretational difficulties.

## EVALUATION OF THE EVIDENCE

In this section, the evidence relating to a variety of outcomes will be summarized and integrated. Then we will discuss several methodological issues which must be addressed more directly in future studies. Finally, we will evaluate the likelihood that the association between low level lead exposure and psychological deficit in children is causal.

*Outcome Variables*

*Intelligence.*   Every cohort study investigating the effects of low level lead exposure has included some measure of intelligence as an outcome variable. A variety of standardized tests have been used. In no study did the children with elevated lead levels achieve a higher full-scale IQ, General Cognitive Index, or General Developmental Index than the control or low lead children. The group differences ranged up to 10 points, with most on the order of 3 to 5 points. In many cases, these differences were not statistically significant, but the consistency in the direction is striking considering the many methodological differences between studies. It is still possible, however, that these studies systematically failed to take account of some third variable which favored the low lead or control groups and which was responsible for the group differences in IQ.

Because few reports are sufficiently detailed, it is difficult to determine whether this trend in full-scale IQ is equally strong in verbal and performance IQ, High lead children have been found to perform worse than controls on primarily verbal tasks (Needleman et al., 1979), performance tasks only (Landrigan et al., 1975), both (Perino & Ernhart, 1974), and neither type of task considered separately (de la Burde & Choate, 1972, 1975). Clearly, more detailed investigation is needed to identify the precise aspects of cognitive functioning which are most vulnerable to low level lead exposure.

Certainly it cannot be said that low level lead exposure produces profound retardation. Some have argued that 3 to 5 IQ points should not be a matter of much concern (e.g., Graham, 1979). However, a 3 to 5 point difference in the mean IQs of two populations does result in rather substantial differences in the numbers of children in the respective populations which fall into the extreme sectors of the scale (cf. Rutter, 1980). Beyond this, however, it is not evident that central tendency is the only property which must be considered in comparing two distributions. The major effect of a toxin on performance may be reflected not only in the average performance, but also in the skewness or kurtosis of the group distribution. Few studies have examined these properties. Certain effects, such as increased within-group variation, would actually lower the likelihood of detecting a significant difference between exposed and nonexposed children, using central tendency as the criterion.

*Hyperactivity.*   Many studies have sought to determine whether low level lead exposure, as well as frank poisoning, produces hyperactivity. Positive evidence of a link between lead and what is historically the most salient characteristic of this syndrome, motor activity, can be found in only two studies. Baloh et al. (1975) reported that nearly three times as many parents of high lead children as parents of controls judged their children to be "overactive" (though the ratings of the children's behavior during testing were not different). David, Hoffman, and Kagey (1978) found that children's blood lead levels correlated 0.15 with teachers' ratings of their hyperactivity, 0.11 with parents' ratings of their impulsivity-hyperactivity, and 0.08 with parents' ratings of their activity. Because of the large sample, these correlations are highly significant, but, obviously, blood lead level accounts for very little of the variance in the ratings. Thus, there is only the slightest of grounds for postulating a link between low level lead exposure and motor overactivity in children.

There is growing evidence, however, that the behavior of lead-exposed children and control children does differ in certain other respects that are central to the definition of hyperactivity. These differences relate mainly to attentional processes. It was reported by de la Burde and Choate (1972, 1975) that while the exposed and nonexposed children did not differ in activity level, many more of the exposed children were distractible, with shorter attention spans. Albert et al. (1974) found that exposed children suffered a higher frequency of "attentional and concentration" problems at school than the controls. Needleman et al. (1979) found that teachers' answers to questions relating to the frequency of difficulties involving distractibility, persistence, impulsivity, and frustration tolerance were reliably different for the high and low lead children, and always in favor of the latter. The inability of the high lead children to sustain attention was further demonstrated by their impaired performance on a task assessing reaction time under varying intervals of delay. In general, these trends are consistent with recent shifts in diagnostic terminology in which "hyperactivity" and "minimal brain dysfunction" syndromes have been replaced by "attentional deficit disorder" in the DSM-III of the American Psychiatric Association (see Shaywitz, Cohen, & Shaywitz, 1979). This shift was motivated by the observation that many children labeled "hyperactive" are, in fact, no more active than their normal peers in terms of feet traversed per unit time. The problem, Cantwell (1979) noted, lies in the quality, not quantity, of their activity. In some cases, this may be manifested as hypoactivity, with few public signs that the child is unable to concentrate. Investigators ought to abandon the expectation that the primary behavioral effect of lead will simply be to increase a child's locomotor activity, in favor of hypotheses that emphasize distortions of cognition whose behavioral manifestations may assume a variety of forms.

*Other Outcomes.*    Strong evidence that fine motor dysfunction is produced by low level lead exposure is generally lacking, though certain findings suggest such a link. In the studies of Landrigan et al. (1975) and Rummo et al. (1979), the finger-wrist tapping of the lead-exposed children was significantly slower than the controls'. (This was true however, only for the dominant hand in the Landrigan et al. study and, in the Rummo et al. study, only the difference between the controls and the lead encephalopathy group was significant.) In neither study were there differences in two-plate tapping, a seemingly related skill. In the de la Burde and Choate (1972) study, significantly more of the exposed children displayed poor fine motor development, as assessed by copy forms, a pegboard, bead stringing, and Proteus mazes. Baloh et al. (1975) reported that the exposed children tended to do worse than the controls on items requiring fine motor ability, but not significantly so.

There are several other tasks on which exposed children sometimes did poorly but, because these involve other abilities besides fine motor ones, it is difficult to identify the reason for the children's failure. In the Rummo et al. (1979) and Perino and Ernhart (1974) studies, exposed children received lower scores on the Perceptual-Performance scale of the McCarthy. This scale includes items requiring fine motor control (e.g., block building, tapping sequence, draw-a-design) but also tests puzzle solving, block classification, right-left orientation, and so on. It was reported by de la Burde and Choate (1975) and Hrdina and Winneke (1978) that the exposed children did significantly worse on the Bender-Gestalt and Goettingen tests, respectively, but these tasks both have a strong perceptual as well as motor component. Also, neither Landrigan et al. (1975) nor McNeil, Ptasnik, and Croft (1975) found significant differences on the Bender-Gestalt. No differences have been found using other perceptual-motor tests such as the Frostig (Needleman et al., 1979; Ratcliffe, 1977; McNeil, Ptasnik, & Croft, 1975) or the Visual Motor Integration Test (Needleman et al., 1979).

It is not at all certain that a child's "intelligence" is the outcome of most importance. Byers and Lord (1943) reported that one of the most striking effects of lead poisoning was that "the usual correlation between the intelligence quotient and the ability to learn in school did not hold up" (p. 479). The children's intelligence did not appear to be grossly impaired when tested in the standardized fashion, but their scholastic achievements were limited due to their impulsivity, short attention span, distractibility, and irritability. In this respect, lead appears similar to malnutrition, which does not affect learning ability and performance per se in a highly structured setting but rather the motivation of an animal to explore and learn about its environment incidentally (Levitsky, 1979).

A more fruitful approach to evaluating the nature of lead-induced deficit may be to assess the manner in which a child tackles a problem rather than simply noting the child's ultimate success in solving it. This would require supplementing conventional standardized tests of intelligence with measures that isolate specific psychological processes; for example, for younger children, the Piagetian-based Ordinal Scales of Infant Development (Uzgiris & Hunt, 1975) or the assessments of perceptual-cognitive responsivity designed by Zelazo and Kearsley (e.g., Zelazo, 1979), or, for older children, the Continuous Performance Test (see Gregory & Mohan, 1977) or the Cincinnati Autonomy Test Battery (Banta, 1970), which includes behavioral measures of curiosity, exploratory behavior, persistence, resistance to distraction, control of impulse, reflectivity, analytical perceptual processes, and innovative behaviors. Yando, Seitz, and Zigler (1979) also report useful behavioral measures of some of these dimensions.

Too much of the research on the relationship between lead and children's behavior has relied on teachers', parents', and testers' ratings of the children. It is not always certain that the different raters, both within and across studies, interpret terms such as "hyperactivity," "impulsivity," and "attentiveness" in precisely the same ways. Moreover, in many of these studies, assessments of the children's behavior was based on the ratings assigned by an individual who had had no contact with a child prior to the relatively brief testing session, and thus a limited basis for drawing global conclusions about the adequacy of that child's functioning. Barocas and Weiss (1974) argued that such impressionistic measures should be replaced by objective methods based on applied behavior analysis and that concepts such as "motivation" and "impulsivity" should be operationalized in terms of specific public behaviors which can be observed and counted. Weiss (1978) also stressed that "behavior" is no more unitary than "health" and underscored the importance of observing behavior in more than one setting.

In a follow-up of some of the children studied initially by Needleman et al. (1979), Bellinger, Needleman, Hargrave, and Nichols (1981) carried out the first observational study of lead-exposed children in a naturalistic setting. They used a method designed by Krupski (1979) to assess distractibility in school-age children. Each child was observed on four separate occasions spread over three days. During each session, which consisted of 36 consecutive 7 second intervals, an observer recorded which of 12 well-defined classroom behaviors a child performed. They found that the children with elevated dentine lead levels engaged significantly more often than controls in a set of "off-task" behaviors which included "interacting with peers," "inappropriate out-of-seat behavior," "glances at the observer," and so on. This observational evidence of more frequent inappropriate classroom behavior was consistent with teachers' ratings of classroom behavior. Furthermore, a significantly disproportionate percentage of the children who were receiving remedial academic aid had elevated lead levels. While one may question the biological significance of the inhibition of an enzyme which is not rate-limiting and the practical significance of a 3 to 5 point reduction in IQ, the importance of impaired school performance is certainly less equivocal.

The measures used to assess the impact of low level lead exposure have generally been limited to the categories of neurological, intellectual, and motor function. Relatively little attention has been paid to children's personality and social development, though the only study to assess this (McNeil, Ptasnik, & Croft, 1975) found the high lead children to be less socially adapted than their peers. Several studies noted, on the basis of school records or teacher reports, that lead-exposed children present more behavior problems than nonexposed children (de la Burde & Choate, 1975; Needleman et al., 1979). However, such records and reports tend to reflect only the public manifestations of intrapsychic conflicts, leaving their dynamics unexplored. While lead may not exert a direct effect on personality development, the motivational and cognitive disturbances it appears to produce may create secondary adjustment problems, leading children to develop a variety of behavior and character disorders (e.g., Cantwell, Baker, & Mattison, 1979, noted that up to 50% of children referred for speech and language problems also have serious psychiatric problems).

*Methodologic Issues*

*Exposure Variables.*    Future studies must take greater care to determine the exposure histories of the children. Exposure variables which are often critical in toxicologic studies include the magnitude of the dose, its duration, the developmental stage of the organism, and route of administration or exposure. Because the human studies of low level lead exposure have been done on populations of children participating unwittingly in natural experiments, they vary unsystematically on these variables, making it virtually impossible to draw conclusions about their relative importance. Furthermore, because of limitations in the indices used as markers of exposure, these parameters of exposure are rarely even known. Unanswered questions include: Is acute exposure to a given dose of lead more debilitating than chronic exposure to the same total dose? Is a small dose suffered early in life worse than a large dose suffered later? Efforts are now underway to measure the contributions of the various sources to blood lead level (e.g., Angle & McIntire, 1979b; Walter, Yankel, & von Lindern, 1980; U.S. EPA, 1977), but, thus far, behavioral effects have not been included as a criterion variable.

Another factor which must be considered more carefully is biologic variability in the absorption, distribution, metabolism, and excretion of lead. It is not the amount of lead in the blood which is responsible for the neurobehavioral deficits observed in heavily burdened children; rather, it is the effect which the lead has on the biologic systems that underlie behavior. Individuals vary in the amount of lead they absorb when exposed to a given source; that is, their "internal" dose will vary despite receiving the same "external" dose. Also, if it were possible to equalize the internal doses, there would be individual differences in the degree to which the biologic systems, such as heme synthesis or the metabolism of certain neurotransmitters, are disrupted. Raghavan, Culver, and Gonick (1980) recently reported that differences in the ability to synthesize a certain as yet uncharacterized lead-binding protein may be responsible for individual differences in biologic response to lead. Furthermore, these variations in response may not be normally distributed but rather log-normal or multimodal with only a subset of subjects responding abnormally (Weiss, 1980). Thus, efforts to relate tissue level of lead to outcome will be hindered by these sources of variability as well as the usual sampling and measurement errors. Measures of biochemical impairment should be substituted for, or should at least supplement, direct measurements of tissue levels of lead as the criteria for classifying children into exposure groups. Another advantage of measures such as FEP over blood lead is that they do not fluctuate as widely in response to periodic exposure to lead or to a variety of pathologic changes in an individual's physiologic state (e.g., acidosis, infection) (CDC, 1978).

*Study Population.*    Another factor to be considered in interpreting these studies is the degree to which the samples of children studied are representative of the general population. This has not been true to any great extent in most studies of low level lead exposure. When enough information is given to determine the composition of the sample, it is apparent that, by and large, the children studied have been black, living in the inner city, usually in families headed by a single parent, generally the mother, and subsisting on welfare. While the lead-exposed and control groups have often been well matched demographically, a comparison of such groups will not indicate the effects that lead exposure would have on middle-class children.

It is interesting to note that in neither of the studies in which the full-scale IQ or General Cognitive Index of the control or low lead children fell below 90 was there a significant difference between their mean and that of the exposed children (Baloh et al., 1975; McNeil, Ptasnik, & Croft, 1975). In most other studies, the mean control IQ was in the 90s. Clearly, the control populations have not usually been representative of the population of all children, limiting the generalizability of the results. It also raises the possibility that some of the studies reporting negative findings may have come up against a floor effect. Lead-exposed and control children alike have generally been drawn from such unfavorable environments that the effects of lead on the exposed children may be difficult to detect amid the broad spectrum of psychological deficits which both groups display, unless the research design includes sophisticated efforts to control other factors known to influence development. Recent work with both young children and animals has shown that adequate amounts of stimulation can largely compensate for the usually deleterious effects of poor nutrition on development (Levitsky, 1979; Cravioto, 1979; Lloyd-Still, Hurwitz, Wolff, & Schwachman, 1974). Similarly, the sequelae of a variety of perinatal complications appear to depend somewhat on the quality of a child's environment (e.g., Sameroff & Chandler, 1975; Werner, Bierman, & French, 1971). The impact of a certain lead level on a child's development may depend on the adequacy of other aspects of the environment, with some combinations of features potentiating the adverse effects and others reducing the child's risk status. Unfortunately, most studies have not gone beyond the Hollingshead Two-Factor Index of social class in characterizing a child's environment. Since parents possessing a wide range of child-rearing attitudes and practices may be assigned to the same social class in this system, it is a poor index of the degree to which the intellectual and emotional climate of a child's environment supports the child's development.

In all fairness, it should be noted that lower-class minority children are the ones at greatest risk for subclinical lead poisoning and, therefore, are the population of the greatest clinical importance. In this sense, these are precisely the children who should be studied, despite the limitations this places on the investigator's ability to draw inferences about the effects of low level lead exposure on children in general. This is the trade-off between clinical and research needs which often complicates applied research.

The effects of low level lead exposure may be different for middle and lower-class children not only because the environments of middle-class children appear to be richer in the types of stimulation which promote intellectual development, but also because of class differences in factors that influence the toxicity of a given dose of lead. Middle-class children generally enjoy better overall nutritional status (Owen & Lippman, 1977). This may be significant because deficiencies in the intake of protein, calories, phosphorus, calcium, copper, magnesium, iron, zinc, selenium, and vitamin E, and excess intake of fats and vitamin D have been shown, in several animal species, to increase the absorption and retention of lead (Levander, 1979; Mahaffey & Michaelson, 1980). In animal studies, Snowden (1977) and Snowden and Sanderson (1974) showed that pica may be related to a deficiency in calcium. Hambridge and Silverman (1973) reported the case of a zinc-deficient girl whose pica for metal disappeared following the initiation of dietary zinc supplementation. In balance studies with infants, Ziegler et al. (1978) found an inverse correlation between the calcium content of the diet and lead absorption. In epidemiologic studies, Mahaffey (1977), Sorrell, Rosen, and Roginsky (1977) and Johnson and Tenuta (1979) have reported that the diets of children with high blood lead levels generally contain insufficient amounts of calcium (though Mooty, Ferrand, & Harris, 1975, found no significant differences in the amounts of protein, calories, and iron).

The racial composition of the study population may affect the generalizability of the findings since there is evidence that the metabolism of lead is affected by genetic diseases which are distributed differently among the races. For example, hemoglobinopathies, such as sickle cell trait and anemia, and thalassemia increase an individual's risk for lead-induced peripheral neuropathies (Chisolm & Barltrop, 1979). Individuals with glucose-6-phosphate dehydrogenase deficiency, the most common genetic metabolic defect, absorb and retain more lead than those without the deficiency (McIntire & Angle, 1972). These genetic disorders are more prevalent in American black than American white populations (Vaughan, McKay, & Behrman, 1979).

*Sample Size.* Besides including children with only a limited range of demographic characteristics, the studies of low level lead exposure have generally employed rather small samples, in some cases less than 30 children per exposed and nonexposed group. Reference to tables which specify sample size requirements for epidemiologic studies (e.g., Schlesselman, 1974) indicates that this may simply be too few children to detect subtle deficit. For instance, in a hypothetical experiment on the relationship between hyperactivity and low lead exposure ($\alpha = .05$, $\beta = .10$, estimated prevalence of hyperactivity among nonexposed children = 5%), using a sample size of under 30 children per group would require that the relative risk (i.e., the ratio of the rate of hyperactivity among lead-exposed children to the rate among nonexposed children) be about 8.0 in order for the difference between groups to be significant. If the relative risk were 4.0, 100 children per group would be required, and 581 if it were 2.0. As these lower risk figures are probably more accurate, given that hyperactivity is the common final pathway for many pathogenic agents, it is clear that every attempt must be made to maximize sample size.

*Is the Lead-Deficit Link Causal?*

Cowan and Leviton (1980), following Hill (1971), cite eight criteria which epidemiologists use in estimating the likelihood that an observed association is causal. Using this framework, we will evaluate the present evidence with respect to the link between low level lead exposure and adverse psychological outcome in children.

a.  *Strength of the association.* "The higher the relative risk or odds ratio the more likely is the suspected etiologic factor to be important in the development of the outcome" (p. 113). In general, outcomes such as slightly lowered IQ, hyperactivity, or even fine motor dysfunction, are sequelae of many different insults, so the number of nonexposed children who develop such disorders will be sufficient to reduce substantially the odds ratio. It might be possible to obtain a better estimate of the strength of the association between lead exposure and deficit if future investigators study less global outcomes in favor of more precisely defined psychological skills and processes. Only when the critical behavioral effects of low level lead exposure have been isolated can progress be made in tracing the complicated path from physiological disruption to behavioral deficit.

b.  *Specificity of the association.* "This criterion requires that the suspected causal factor be associated with only one or a few related outcomes" (p. 113). The evidence linking low level lead exposure to specific outcomes, such as a certain pattern of deficit on IQ tests, is inconsistent. A wide variety of seemingly unrelated adverse outcomes are purportedly associated with lead. However, as Cowan and Leviton note, this does not critically weaken the inference of causality since many clearly harmful factors, such as cigarette smoking, are known to cause a broad range of effects.

c.  *Consistency of the association.* "If a factor and an outcome are repeatedly found to be associated in studies conducted by different investigators, under different circumstances, at varying times and locations and in different population groups, the probability that the factor and the outcome are causally related is increased" (p. 113). A consistent feature of the studies reviewed is that the lead-exposed group scored lower, on the order of 3 to 5 points, in mean IQ than the controls. This difference was sometimes significant at the .05 level and sometimes not. Since sample sizes differed greatly across studies, this inconsistency in significance level is not surprising (Rutter, 1980).

d.  *Temporal sequence.* "The factor should be shown to precede the outcome in time" (p. 113). A persistent problem is the difficulty of distinguishing the child who accumulates lead because the child is impaired and the child who becomes impaired because of an elevated lead burden. Investigators have tried to solve this problem by controlling for pica, though usually only by questioning the mother about the child's ingestion patterns rather than by behavioral observation. A prospective study involving the assessment of children's developmental status prior to the accumulation of elevated lead burdens would overcome this problem but no such study has been carried out. (See Kirkconnell & Hicks, 1980, for a prospective study of lead-poisoned children). Moore et al. (1977) came closest when they demonstrated that children who later become mentally retarded had suffered greater prenatal lead exposure than those who did not.

e.  *Dose-response relationship.* "When the frequency or severity of the outcome is found to increase with increasing levels of exposure, the observed association is more likely to be a direct than an indirect one" (p. 113). Unless dose is known for certain, the search for a dose-response relationship is meaningless. Dose has rarely been well characterized due to ambiguities inherent in relating blood lead level to a developmental evaluation conducted up to several years later. Markers of cumulative exposure, such as dentine lead level, are more desirable. In the only major study using this marker, Needleman et al. (1979) found strong dose-response relationships with respect to teachers' ratings of classroom behavior. This criterion can be tested adequately only in studies which document dose, timing, and duration of children's exposure to lead.

f.  *Biological plausibility.* ". . . biologic plausibility can only be evaluated within the context of current knowledge" and "should not be emphasized as a criterion for causation" (p. 114). At present, our knowledge of the biologic bases of complex behavior such as performance on intelligence tests or even attentional processes is fragmentary, at best. However, it is known that lead affects cholinergic, catecholaminergic, and GABAergic neurotransmitter systems (Silbergeld & Hruska, 1980). Many behavioral and psychological disturbances have been shown to result from disruptions of these systems (Baldessarini, 1972; Schildkraut, 1965). Exposure to lead also results in the accumulation of protoporphyrin. Porphyria, a disorder of porphyrin metabolism, produces a variety of neurological and psychological symptoms. These examples demonstrate the plausibility of the hypothesis that lead may cause psychological deficit.

g.  *Coherence of the evidence.* "The cause-and-effect interpretation of an association should be consistent with the generally known aspects of the natural history and biology of the disease or outcome" (p. 114). An individual with an elevated lead burden manifests essentially the same physiological derangements as an individual who suffers frank poisoning, though on a lesser scale. This similarity appears to extend to the level of behavior, as well. A vast animal literature supports the hypothesis that low level lead exposure produces behavioral disorder (see U.S. EPA, 1977). For example, lead at low dose appears to interfere with nonspatial form discrimination (Rice & Willes, 1979) and reversal learning in monkeys (Bushnell & Bowman, 1979a,b), visual discrimination in lambs (Carson, Van Gelder, Karas, & Buck, 1974), and maze learning in mice (Ogilvie, 1977).

h.  *Experimental or semi-experimental evidence.* "It may be possible to observe the effects of accidental exposure or of elimination or reduction of the exposure" (p. 114). The only study of this sort in the literature is the attempt by David et al. (1976) to alleviate children's hyperactive symptoms by chelation therapy. Although the authors reported success, the methodological problems we noted make it difficult to evaluate the import of these data.

# CONCLUDING REMARKS: DATA, VALUES, AND PUBLIC POLICY

Given the data reviewed in these pages, and the supporting evidence from experimental studies in the rodent and infrahuman primate, certain questions emerge to challenge scientists and regulators. Among them are: (1) Has an adequate case been made for health effects from lead at low dose? (2) If the case against lead is incomplete, what does or should a regulatory agency do?

Causality is a construct that is not accessible to empirical proof (Hume, 1748/1955). The demonstration of an impregnable causal link between lead and behavioral deficit cannot be realized, particularly in real world epidemiological studies. While canons such as those prescribed by Hill (1971) increase the assurance that a causal relationship exists, they do not prove it. The case against lead at low dose derives from many convergent studies. Regulatory decisions necessarily made by government in the face of shrinking, but always present uncertainty are a contentious process in which value judgments become important operators.

While this may seem out of place in a domain labeled as scientific, it is important to recognize that questions of value in fact underlie many of the assertions and actions generally portrayed as objective and rationalistic. The very act of choosing acceptable $\alpha$ and $\beta$ errors for a study is value-laden, even if long consecrated by tradition. If a 5% decrement in a child's intellectual performance is taken as small or negligible because it cannot be recognized without special psychological instruments, that is an assertion of perceived value. Attempts to rationalize or quantitate the value assigned to decrements of this magnitude by maneuvers such as "shadow pricing" are worthwhile, but they diminish comprehension of the phenomenon under study in the same way that a translation of a poem diminishes the original.

This is not to dismiss efforts to quantitate health costs. It is, at the same time, important to examine and understand the structural basis of such a calculus. Costs of reducing or abating a hazard are easy to apply and difficult to verify.

Health benefits, on the other hand, are difficult to price, and such estimates tend to be conservative.

It is into such an arena that regulatory agencies are cast. In 1977, for example, the Environmental Protection Agency, under a suit by the National Resources Defense Council, was ordered by the Circuit Court of Washington, D.C. to write an air lead standard. The process that ensued may well have been one of the most ardous experienced by EPA, and was marked by intense advocacy by industry and public interest groups. The agency defined the most vulnerable group: children. Then it estimated a "no effect" level in that group (30 $\mu$g/dl). Recognizing individual variation in response and absorption, EPA then calculated the mean population blood lead level which would be necessary in order that no more than 0.5% of children would have blood lead levels greater than 30 $\mu$g/dl. The mean level was set at 15 $\mu$g/dl. This allowed EPA to set an air lead standard of 1.5 $\mu$g/m$^3$, averaged over one month.

EPA set what may be considered a pioneering course in the process. It opened itself to scrutiny and advice from many sectors, including industry, public interest organizations, and outside scientists. It moved from a position that initially only recognized frank clinical disease to one that acknowledged the existence of health effects identifiable only by sensitive measures. It set margins of safety which take into account both biological variations and limitations in the state of the science of toxicology. The regulation of lead in the atmosphere is not complete; upon promulgating the standard, EPA was sued by the lead industries.

The regulation of environmental pollutants, of which lead is the most widely recognized, is a difficult and fatiguing enterprise. The stakes, both economic and hygienic, are high. Scientific data, obtained by the most rigorous methods are necessary to guide regulatory action, but they are not sufficient. A clear perception, and perhaps a reshaping of the values inherent in the process must be achieved in order to guide societal choice and to protect those unable to act individually.

## ACKNOWLEDGMENTS

Support during the preparation of this review was provided by Grant HD-08945 from the National Institute of Child Health and Human Development. We would like to thank Dr. Jane S. Lin-Fu for valuable comments on the manuscript.

## REFERENCES

Albert, R., Shore, R., Sayers, A., Strehlow, C., Kneip, T., Pasternack, B., Friedhoff, A., Covan, F., & Cimino, J. Follow-up of children over-exposed to lead. *Environmental Health Perspectives*, 1974, No. 7, 33–39.

Angle, C., & McIntire, M. Lead poisoning during pregnancy. *American Journal of Diseases of Children*, 1964, *108*, 436–439.

Angle, C., & McIntire, M. Low level lead: Concurrence of thresholds for hematologic toxicity. *Toxicology and Applied Pharmacology,* 1979, *48,* A116. (a)

Angle, C., & McIntire, M. Environmental lead and children: The Omaha study. *Journal of Toxicology and Environmental Health,* 1979, *5,* 855–870. (b)

Averill, D., & Needleman, H. Neonatal lead exposure retards cortical synaptogenesis in the rat. In H. Needleman (Ed.), *Low level lead exposure in childhood: The clinical implications of current research.* New York: Raven Press, 1980.

Baker, E., Folland, D., Taylor, T., Frank, M., Peterson, W., Lovejoy, G., Cox, D., Housworth, J., & Landrigan, P. Lead poisoning in children of lead workers: Home contamination with industrial dust. *New England Journal of Medicine,* 1977, *296,* 260–261.

Baldessarini, R. Biogenic amines and behavior. *Annual Review of Medicine,* 1972, *23,* 343–354.

Baloh, R., Sturm, R., Green, B., & Gleser, G. Neuropsychological effects of chronic asymptomatic increased lead absorption: A controlled study. *Archives of Neurology,* 1975, *32,* 326–330.

Banta, T. Tests for the evaluation of early childhood education: The Cincinnati Autonomy Test Battery (CATB). In J. Hellmuth (Ed.) *Cognitive studies.* Vol. 1. New York: Brunner/Mazel, 1970.

Barltrop, D. The prevalence of pica. *American Journal of Diseases of Children,* 1966, *112,* 116–123.

Barltrop, D. Transfer of lead to the human fetus. In D. Barltrop & W. Burland (Eds.), *Mineral metabolism in pediatrics.* Oxford: Blackwell Scientific Publications, 1969.

Barocas, R., & Weiss, B. Assessment of lead intoxication in children. *Environmental Health Perspectives,* 1974, No. 7, 47–52.

Beattie, A., Moore, M., Miller, A., Devenay, W., & Goldberg, A. Environmental pollution in an urban soft-water area. *British Medical Journal,* 1972, *2,* 491–493.

Beattie, A., Moore, M., Goldberg, A., Finlayson, M., Mackie, E., Graham, J., Main, J., McLaren, D., Murdock, R., & Stewart, G. Role of chronic low level lead exposure in the etiology of mental retardation. *Lancet,* 1975, *1,* 589–592.

Bellinger, D., Needleman, H., Hargrave, J., & Nichols, M. Elevated dentine lead level and school success. Presented at the biennial meeting of the Society for Research in Child Development, Boston, April, 1981.

Bicknell, D. *Pica: A childhood symptom.* London: Butterworths, 1975.

Bicknell, D., Clayton, B., & Delves, H. Lead in mentally retarded children. *Journal of Mental Deficiency Research,* 1968, *12,* 282–293.

Bogden, J., Joselow, M., & Singh, N. Extraction of lead from printed matter at physiological values of pH. *Archives of Environmental Health,* 1975, *31,* 442–444.

Bogden, J., & Louria, D. Soil contamination from lead paint chips. *Bulletin of Environmental Contamination and Toxicology,* 1975, *14,* 289–294. Bryce-Smith, D. Behavioral effects of lead and other heavy metal pollutants. *Chemistry in Britain,* 1972, *8,* 240–243.

Bushnell, P., & Bowman, R. Reversal learning deficits in young monkeys exposed to lead. *Pharmacology, Biochemistry & Behavior,* 1979, *10,* 733–742. (a)

Bushnell, P., & Bowman, R. Persistence of impaired reversal learning in young monkeys exposed to low levels of dietary lead. *Journal of Toxicology and Environmental Health,* 1979, *5,* 1015–1023. (b)

Byers, R., & Lord, E. Late effects of lead poisoning on mental development. *American Journal of Diseases of Children,* 1943, *66,* 471–494.

California Department of Health Services. *Progress report on the childhood lead project.* Vol. 1. Sacramento, California: Department of Health and Welfare Agency, 1979.

Cantwell, D. The "hyperactive" child. *Hospital Practice,* 1979, *14,* 65–73.

Cantwell, D., Baker, L., & Mattison, R. The prevalence of psychiatric disorders in children with speech and language disorder. *Journal of the American Academy of Child Psychiatry,* 1979, *18,* 450–461.

Carson, T., Van Gelder, G., Karas, G., & Buck, W. Slowed learning in lambs prenatally exposed to lead. *Archives of Environmental Health,* 1974, *29,* 154–156.

Center for Disease Control. *Preventing lead poisoning in young children.* Washington, D.C.: Department of Health, Education, and Welfare, 1978.

Charney, E., Sayre, J., & Coulter, M. Increased lead absorption in inner city children: Where does the lead come from? *Pediatrics,* 1980, *65,* 226–231.

Chisolm, J. Increased lead absorption: Toxicological considerations. *Pediatrics,* 1971, *48,* 349–352.

Chisolm, J. Treatment of lead poisoning. In *Preventing lead poisoning in young children.* Washington, D.C.: Department of Health, Education, and Welfare, 1978.

Chisolm, J. Increased lead absorption and lead poisoning (plumbism). In V. Vaughn, R. McKay, & R. Behrman (Eds.), *Nelson textbook of pediatrics.* Philadelphia, Pa.: W. B. Saunders, 1979.

Chisolm, J., & Barltrop, D. Recognition and management of children with increased lead absorption. *Archives of Disease in Childhood,* 1979, *54,* 249–262.

Chisolm, J., Mellits, E., & Barrett, M. Interrelationships among blood lead concentration, quantitative daily ALA-d and urinary lead output following calcium EDTA. In G. Nordberg (Ed.), *Effects and dose-response relationships of toxic metals.* New York: Elsevier Scientific Publishing Co., 1976.

Clark, A. Placental transfer of lead and its effects on the newborn. *Postgraduate Medical Journal,* 1977, *53,* 674–678.

Cohen, D., Johnson, W., & Caparulo, B. Pica and elevated blood lead level in autistic and atypical children. *American Journal of Diseases of Children,* 1976, *130,* 47–48.

Cowan, L., & Leviton, A. Epidemiologic considerations in the study of the sequelae of low level lead exposure. In H. Needleman (Ed.), *Low level lead exposure in childhood: The clinical implications of current research.* New York: Raven Press, 1980.

Cox, A., Rutter, M., Yule, B., & Quinton, D. Bias resulting from missing information: Some epidemiological findings. *British Journal of Preventive and Social Medicine,* 1977, *31,* 131–136.

Cravioto, J. Malnutrition, environment and child development. In D. Levitsky (Ed.), *Malnutrition, environment, and behavior: New perspectives.* Ithaca, N.Y.: Cornell University Press, 1979.

David, O., Clark, J., & Voeller, K. Lead and hyperactivity. *Lancet,* 1972, *1,* 900–903.

David, O., Hoffman, S., & Kagey, B. Sub-clinical lead effects. Paper presented at the Conservation Society Symposium on Health Effects of Lead, London, April, 1978.

David, O., McGann, B., Hoffman, S., Sverd, J., & Clark, J. Low lead levels and mental retardation. *Lancet,* 1976, *2,* 1376–1379.

David, O., Hoffman, S., Sverd, J., & Clark, J. Lead and hyperactivity in children. *Journal of Abnormal Child Psychology,* 1977, *5,* 405–416.

David, O., Hoffman, S., Sverd, J., Clark, J., & Voeller, K. Lead and hyperactivity: Behavioral response to chelation: A pilot study. *American Journal of Psychiatry,* 1976, *133,* 1155–1158.

de la Burde, B., & Choate, McL. Does asymptomatic lead exposure in children have latent sequelae? *Journal of Pediatrics,* 1972, *81,* 1088–1091.

de la Burde, B., & Choate, McL. Early asymptomatic lead exposure and development at school age. *Journal of Pediatrics,* 1975, *87,* 638–642.

de la Burde, B., & Shapiro, I. Dental lead, blood lead and pica in urban children. *Archives of Environmental Health,* 1975, *30,* 281–284.

Edwards, H. Environmental contamination by automobile lead. In *Proceedings of the International Symposium on Recent Advances in the Assessment of the Health Effects of Environmental Pollution.* Vol. 3. Luxembourg, Commission of the European Communities, 1975.

Elwood, P., Morton, M., & St. Leger, A. Lead in water and mental retardation. *Lancet,* 1976, *1,* 590–591.

Ericson, J., Shirahata, H., & Patterson, C. Skeletal concentrations of lead in ancient Peruvians. *New England Journal of Medicine,* 1979, *300,* 946–951.

Ernhart, C., Landa, B., & Schell, N. Subclinical levels of lead and developmental deficit—A multivariate follow-up reassessment. *Pediatrics*, 1981, *67*, 911-919.

Fremlin, J., & Edmonds, M. The determination of lead in human teeth. *Nuclear Instruments and Methods*, 1980, *173*, 211-215.

Gershanik, J., Brooks, G., & Little, J. Blood lead values in pregnant women and their offspring. *American Journal of Obstetrics and Gynecology*, 1975, *119*, 408-411.

Gibson, S., Lam, C., McCrae, W., & Goldberg, A. Blood lead levels in normal and mentally deficient children. *Archives of Disease in Childhood*, 1967, *42*, 573-578.

Gilani, S. Congenital anomalies in lead poisoning. *Obstetrics and Gynecology*, 1973, *41*, 265-269.

Gilfillan, S. Lead poisoning and the fall of Rome. *Journal of Occupational Medicine*, 1965, *7*, 53-60.

Goyer, R., & Rhyne, B. Pathological effects of lead. *International Review of Experimental Pathology*, 1973, *12*, 1-77.

Graham, P. (Letter) *Lancet*, 1979, *1*, 1024-1025.

Grandjean, P. Widening perspectives of lead toxicity. *Environmental Research*, 1978, *17*, 303-321.

Grandjean, P., Arnvig, E., & Beckmann, J. Psychological dysfunctions in lead exposed workers: Relation to biological parameters of exposure. *Scandinavian Journal of Work Environment and Health*, 1978, *4*, 295-303.

Grandjean, P., Nielsen, O., & Shapiro, I. Lead retention in ancient Nubian and contemporary populations. *Journal of Environmental Pathology and Toxicology*, 1979, *2*, 781-787.

Granick, J., Sassa, S., & Kappas, A. Some biochemical and clinical aspects of lead intoxication. *Advances in Clinical Chemistry*, 1978, *20*, 287-339.

Greathouse, D., Craun, G., & Worth, D. Epidemiologic study of the relationship between lead in drinking water and blood lead levels. In D. Hemphill (Ed.), *Trace substances in environmental health*. Columbia, Mo.: University of Missouri Press, 1976.

Gregory, R., & Mohan, P. Effect of asymptomatic lead exposure on childhood intelligence: A critical review. *Intelligence*, 1977, *1*, 381-400.

Hambridge, K., & Silverman, A. Pica with rapid improvement after dietary zinc supplementation. *Archives of Disease in Childhood*, 1973, *48*, 567-568.

Hebel, J., Kinch, D., & Armstrong, E. Mental capability of children exposed to lead pollution. *British Journal of Preventive and Social Medicine*, 1976, *30*, 170-174.

Hernberg, S. Biologic effects of low lead doses. In *Proceedings of the International Symposium on Environmental Health Aspects of Lead*. Luxembourg: Commission of the European Communities, 1972.

Hernberg, S., & Nikkanen, G. Enzyme inhibition by lead under normal urban conditions. *Lancet*, 1970, *1*, 63-66.

Hernberg, S., Vihko, V., & Hasan, J. Red cell membrane ATPases in workers exposed to inorganic lead. *Archives of Environmental Health*, 1967, *14*, 319-324.

Hill, A. *Principles of medical statistics*. New York: Oxford University Press, 1971.

Hole, K., Dahle, H., & Kløve, H. Lead intoxication as an etiologic factor in hyperkinetic behavior in children: A negative report. *Acta Pediatrica Scandinavica*, 1979, *68*, 759-760.

Hrdina, K., & Winneke, G. Neuro-psychological investigations on children with increased lead content in the teeth. Paper presented to the German Society for Hygiene and Microbiology, Mainz, Germany: October, 1978.

Hume, D. *An inquiry concerning human understanding*. Indianapolis: Bobbs-Merrill, 1955. (Originally published, 1748)

Johnson, N., & Tenuta, K. Diets and lead blood levels of children who practice pica. *Environmental Research*, 1979, *18*, 369-376.

Jugo, S. Metabolism of toxic heavy metals in growing organisms: A review. *Environmental Research*, 1977, *13*, 36-46.

Kaplan, M., Peresie, H., & Jeffcoat, M. The lead content of blood and deciduous teeth in lead-exposed beagle pups. In H. Needleman (Ed.), *Low level lead exposure in childhood: The clinical implications of current research.* New York: Raven Press, 1980.

King, B. Maximum daily intake of lead without excessive body lead burden in children. *American Journal of Diseases of Children,* 1971, *122,* 337-340.

Kirkconnell, S., & Hicks, L. Residual effects of lead poisoning on Denver Developmental Screening Test scores. *Journal of Abnormal Child Psychology,* 1980, *8,* 257-267.

Klein, M., Namer, R., Harpur, E., & Corbin, R. Earthenware containers as a source of fatal lead poisoning. *New England Journal of Medicine,* 1970, *283,* 669-672.

Kotok, D. Development of children with elevated blood lead levels: A controlled study. *Journal of Pediatrics,* 1972, *80,* 57-61.

Kotok, D., Kotok, R., & Heriot, J. Cognitive evaluation of children with elevated blood lead levels. *American Journal of Diseases of Children,* 1977, *131,* 791-793.

Krall, V., Sachs, H., Rayson, B., Lazar, B., Growe, G., & O'Connell, L. Effects of lead poisoning on cognitive test performance. *Perceptual and Motor Skills,* 1980, *50,* 483-486.

Krupski, A. Are retarded children more distractible? Observational analysis of retarded and non-retarded children's classroom behavior. *American Journal of Mental Deficiency,* 1979, *84,* 1-10.

Lancranjan, I., Popescu, H. I., Găvănescu, O., Klepsch, I., & Serbănescu, M. Reproductive ability of workmen occupationally exposed to lead. *Archives of Environmental Health,* 1975, *30,* 396-401.

Landrigan, P., Baker, E., Feldman, R., Cox, D., Eden, K., Orenstein, W., Mather, J., Yankel, A., & von Lindern, I. Increased lead absorption with anemia and slowed nerve conduction in children near a lead smelter. *Journal of Pediatrics,* 1976, *89,* 904-910.

Landrigan, P., Baloh, R., Barthel, R., Whitworth, R., STaehling, N., & Rosenblum, B. Neuro-psychological dysfunction in children with chronic low level lead absorption. *Lancet,* 1975, *1,* 708-712.

Landrigan, P., Gehlbach, S., Rosenblum, B., Shoults, J., Candelaria, R., Barthel, W., Liddle, J., Smrek, L., Staehling, N., & Sanders, J. Epidemic lead absorption near an ore smelter: The role of particulate lead. *New England Journal of Medicine,* 1975, *292,* 123-129.

Lansdown, R. Moderately raised blood lead levels in children. *Proceedings of the Royal Society of London,* 1979, *205,* 145-151.

Lansdown, R., Clayton, B., Graham, P., Shepherd, J., Delves, H., & Turner, W. Blood lead levels, behavior, and intelligence: A population study. *Lancet,* 1974, *1,* 538-541.

Lave, L., & Seskin, E. Epidemiology, causality and public policy. *American Scientist,* 1979, *67,* 178-186.

Levander, O. Lead toxicity and nutritional deficiencies. *Environmental Health Perspectives,* 1979, *29,* 115-125.

Leviton, A., & Needleman, H. (Letter). *Lancet,* 1975, *1,* 983.

Levitsky, D. Malnutrition and the hunger to learn. In D. Levitsky (Ed.) *Malnutrition, environment and behavior: New perspectives.* Ithaca, New York: Cornell University Press, 1979.

Lin-Fu, J. Undue absorption of lead among children. *New England Journal of Medicine,* 1972, *286,* 702-710.

Lin-Fu, J. Lead exposure among children: A reassessment. *New England Journal of Medicine,* 1979, *300,* 731-732.

Lin-Fu, J. Lead poisoning and undue lead exposure in children: History and current status. In H. Needleman (Ed.), *Low level lead exposure in childhood: The clinical implications of current research.* New York: Raven Press, 1980.

Lloyd-Still, J., Hurwitz, I., Wolff, P., & Schwachman, H. Intellectual development after severe malnutrition in infancy. *Pediatrics,* 1974, *54,* 306-311.

MacMahon, B., & Pugh, T. *Epidemiology: Principles and methods.* Boston, Mass.: Little, Brown, 1970.

Mahaffey, K. Relation between quantities of lead ingested and health effects of lead in humans. *Pediatrics*, 1977, *59*, 448-456.

Mahaffey, K., & Michaelson, I. The interaction between lead and nutrition. In H. Needleman (Ed.), *Low level lead exposure in children: The clinical implications of current research*. New York: Raven Press, 1980.

McCauley, P., Bull, R., & Lutkenhoff, S. Association of alterations in energy metabolism with lead-induced delays in rat cerebral cortical development. *Neuropharmacology*, 1979, *18*, 93-101.

McClain, R., & Becker, B. Teratogenicity, fetal toxicity, and placental transfer of lead nitrate in rats. *Toxicology and Applied Pharmacology*, 1975, *31*, 72-82.

McCord, C. Lead and lead poisoning in early America: Benjamin Franklin and lead poisoning. *Industrial Medicine and Surgery*, 1953, *22*, 393-399.

McIntire, M., & Angle, C. Air lead: Relation to lead in blood of Black school children deficient in glucose-6-phosphate dehydrogenase. *Science*, 1972, *177*, 520-522.

McNeil, J., Ptasnik, J., & Croft, D. Evaluation of longterm effects of elevated blood lead concentrations in asymptomatic children. *Archives of Industrial Hygiene and Toxicology*, 1975, *14*, 97-118.

Mellins, R., & Jenkins, C. Epidemiological and psychological study of lead poisoning in children. *Journal of the American Medical Association*, 1955, *158*, 15-20.

Millar, J., Cumming, R., Battistini, V., Carswell, F., & Goldberg, A. Lead and delta aminolevulinic acid dehydratase activity in mentally retarded children and in lead-poisoned suckling rats. *Lancet*, 1970, *2*, 695-698.

Moncrieff, A., Koumides, O., Clayton, B., Patrick, A., Renwick, A., & Roberts, G. Lead poisoning in children. *Archives of Disease in Childhood*, 1964, *39*, 1-13.

Moore, M. Plumbosolvency of waters. *Nature*, 1973, *243*, 222-223.

Moore, M., Meredith, P., & Goldberg, A. A retrospective analysis of blood-lead in mentally-retarded children. *Lancet*, 1977, *1*, 717-719.

Mooty, J., Ferrand, C., & Harris, P. Relationship of diet to lead poisoning in children. *Pediatrics*, 1975, *55*, 636-639.

Murozumi, M., Chow, T., & Patterson, C. Chemical concentrations of pollutant lead aerosols, terrestrial dusts and sea salts in Greenland and Antarctic snow strata. *Geochimie, Cosmochimie Acta*, 1969, *33*, 1247-1294.

Nathanson, J., & Bloom, F. Lead-induced inhibition of brain adenyl cyclase. *Nature*, 1975, *255*, 419-420.

National Academy of Sciences. *Airborne lead in perspective*. Washington, D.C.: NAS, 1972.

National Institute for Occupational Safety and Health. *Criteria for a recommended standard. Occupational exposure to inorganic lead. Revised criteria*. Washington, D.C.: NIOSH, 1978. (Publication No. 78-158).

Needleman, H. Incidence and effects of low level lead exposure. *Proceedings of the International Conference on Heavy Metals in the Environment*. Toronto, 1975.

Needleman, H., & Bellinger, D. The epidemiology of low level lead exposure in childhood. *Journal of the American Academy of Child Psychiatry*, in press.

Needleman, H., Bellinger, D., & Leviton, A. Does lead at low dose affect intelligence in children? A reply to Ernhart et al. *Pediatrics*, 1981, *68*, 894-896.

Needleman, H., Gunnoe, C., Leviton, A., Reed, R., Peresie, H., Maher, C., & Barrett, P. Deficits in psychologic and classroom performance of children with elevated dentine lead levels. *New of the American Academy of Child Psychiatry*, 1981, *20*, 496-512.

Nieburg, P., Oski, B., Cornfield, D., & Oski, F. Red cell ALA-D activity as an index of body heat burden. *Pediatric Research*, 1972, *6*, 366.

Nordenson, I., Beckman, G., Beckman, L., & Nordstrom, S. Occupational and environmental risks in and around a smelter in northern Sweden. IV. Chromosomal aberrations in workers exposed to lead. *Hereditas,* 1978, *88,* 263-267.

Ogilvie, D. Sublethal effects of lead acetate on the Y-maze performance of albino mice (*Mus musculus* L.). *Canadian Journal of Zoology,* 1977, *55,* 771-775.

Owen G., & Lippman, G. Nutritional status of infants and young children. *Pediatric Clinics of North America,* 1977, *24,* 211-227.

Patterson, C. Contaminated and natural lead environments of man. *Archives of Environmental Health,* 1965, *11,* 344-360.

Patterson, C. An alternative perspective: Lead pollution in the human environment: Origin, extent, and significance. In National Academy of Sciences. *Lead in the human environment.* Washington, D.C.: NAS, 1980.

Pentschew, A. Morphology and morphogenesis of lead encephalopathy. *Acta Neuropathologica,* 1965, *5,* 133-160.

Perino, J., & Ernhart, C. The relation of subclinical lead level to cognitive and sensorimotor impairment in black preschoolers. *Journal of Learning Disabilities,* 1974, *7,* 26-30.

Perkins, K., & Oski, F. Elevated blood lead in a 6 month old breast-fed infant: The role of newsprint logs. *Pediatrics,* 1976, *57,* 426-427.

Perlstein, M., & Attala, R. Neurologic sequelae of plumbism in children. *Clinical Pediatrics,* 1966, *5,* 292-298.

Pihl, R., & Parkes, M. Hair element content in learning disabled children. *Science,* 1977, *198,* 204-206.

Piomelli, S. The effects of low level lead exposure on heme metabolism. In H. Needleman (Ed.), *Low level lead exposure in childhood: The clinical implications of current research.* New York: Raven Press, 1980.

Piomelli, S., Seaman, C., Zullow, D., Curran, A., & Davidow, B. Metabolic evidence of lead toxicity in "normal" urban children. *Clinical Research,* 1977, *25,* 459A.

Pueschel, S. Neurological and psychomotor functions in children with an increased lead burden. *Environmental Health Perspectives,* 1974, No. 7, 13-16.

Pueschel, S., Kopito, L., & Schwachman, H. A screening and follow-up study of children with an increased lead burden. *Journal of the American Medical Association,* 1972, *222,* 462-466.

Rabinowitz, M., Wetherill, G., & Kopple, J. Kinetic analysis of lead metabolism in healthy humans. *Journal of Clinical Investigation,* 1976, *58,* 260-270.

Raghavan, S., Culver, B., & Gonick, H. Erythrocyte lead-binding protein after occupational exposure. I. Relationship to lead toxicity. *Environmental Research,* 1980, *22,* 264-270.

Ratcliffe, J. Developmental and behavioral functions in young children with elevated blood lead levels. *British Journal of Preventive and Social Medicine,* 1977, *31,* 258-264.

Rice, D., & Willes, R. Neonatal low-level lead exposure in monkeys (*Macaca Fascicularis*): Effect on two-choice non-spatial form discrimination. *Journal of Environmental Pathology and Toxicology,* 1979, *2,* 1195-1203.

Roels, H., Buchet, J-P., Lauwerys, R., Hubermont, G., Bruaux, P., Claeys-Thoreau, F., Lafontaine, A., & Van Overschelde, J. Impact of air pollution from lead on the heme biosynthetic pathway in school-age children. *Archives of Environmental Health,* 1976, *31,* 310-316.

Rom, W. Effects of lead on the female and reproduction: A review. *The Mount Sinai Journal of Medicine,* 1976, *43,* 542-552.

Rummo, J., Routh, D., Rummo, N., & Brown, J. Behavioral and neurological effects of symptomatic and asymptomatic lead exposure in children. *Archives of Environmental Health,* 1979, *34,* 120-124.

Rutter, M. Raised lead levels and impaired cognitive/behavioral functioning: A review of the evidence. *Developmental Medicine and Child Neurology,* Suppl. No. 42, 1980, *22,* 1-26.

Sachs, H., Krall, V., McCaughran, D., Rozenfeld, I., Yongsmith, N., Growe, G., Lazar, B.,

Novar, L., O'Connell, L., & Rayson, B. IQ following treatment of lead poisoning: A patient-sibling comparison. *Journal of Pediatrics, 1978, 93,* 428–431.

Sachs, H., McCaughran, D., Krall, V., Rozenfeld, I., & Yongsmith, N. Lead poisoning without encephalopathy: Effect of early diagnosis on neurologic and psychologic salvage. *American Journal of Diseases of Children, 1979, 133,* 786–690.

Sameroff, A., & Chandler, M. Reproductive risk and the continuum of caretaking casualty. In F. Horowitz, M. Hetherington, S. Scarr-Salapatek, & A. Siegel (Eds.), *Review of Child Development Research.* Vol. 4. Chicago, IL.: University of Chicago Press, 1975.

Sayre, J., & Katzel, M. Household surface lead dust: Accumulation in vacant homes. *Environmental Health Perspectives, 1979, 29,* 179–182.

Scanlon, J. Umbilical cord blood lead concentration. *American Journal of Diseases of Children, 1971, 121,* 325–326.

Schildkraut, J. The catecholamine hypothesis of affective disorders: A review of supporting evidence. *American Journal of Psychiatry, 1965, 122,* 509–522.

Schlesselman, J. Sample size requirements in cohort and case-control studies of disease. *American Journal of Epidemiology, 1974, 99,* 381–384.

Seppalainen, A., Tola, S., Hernberg, S., & Kock, B. Subclinical neuropathy at "safe" levels of lead exposure. *Archives of Environmental Health, 1975, 30,* 180–183.

Settle, D., & Patterson, C. Lead in albacore: Guide to lead pollution in Americans. *Science, 1980, 207,* 1167–1176.

Shaywitz, B., Cohen, D., & Shaywitz, S. New diagnostic terminology for minimal brain dysfunction. *Journal of Pediatrics, 1979, 95,* 734–736.

Sheer, J., Voet, L., Watjen, U., Koenig, W., Richter, F., & Steiner, U. Comparison of sensitivities in trace element analysis obtained by X-ray excited X-ray fluorescence and photon induced X-ray emission. *Nuclear Instruments and Methods, 1977, 142,* 333–338.

Silbergeld, E., & Hruska, R. Neurochemical investigations of low level lead exposure. In H. Needleman (Ed.), *Low level lead exposure in childhood: The clinical implications of current research.* New York: Raven Press, 1980.

Snowden, C. A nutritional basis for lead pica. *Physiology and Behavior, 1977, 18,* 885–893.

Snowden, C., & Sanderson, B. Lead pica produced in rats. *Science, 1974, 183,* 92–94.

Solomon, B. Dyslexia: A lead toxicity symptom? *Maryland State Medical Journal, 1979, 28,* 43–45.

Sorrell, M., Rosen, J., & Roginsky, M. Interactions of lead, calcium, vitamin D, and nutrition in lead-burdened children. *Archives of Environmental Health, 1977, 32,* 160–164.

Strehlow, C. The use of deciduous teeth as indicators of lead exposure. Unpublished Ph.D. thesis, New York University, 1972.

Ter Haar, G. & Aronow, R. New information on lead in dirt and dust as related to the childhood lead problem. *Environmental Health Perspectives, 1974, No. 7,* 83–89.

United States Department of Housing and Urban Development. *Lead paint poisoning research: Review and evaluation, 1971–1977.* Washington, D.C.: Office of Policy Development and Research, 1978.

United States Environmental Protection Agency. *Air quality criteria for lead.* Washington, D.C.: Office of Research and Development, 1977.

Uzgiris, I., & Hunt, J. *Assessment in infancy: Ordinal scales of psychological development.* Urbana, Illinois: University of Illinois Press, 1975.

Valciukas, J., Lilis, R., Eisinger, J., Blumberg, W., Fischbein, A., & Selikoff, I. Behavioral indicators of lead neurotoxicity: Results of a clinical field survey. *International Archives of Occupational and Environmental Health, 1978, 41,* 217–236.

Valentine, W., Paglia, D., Fink, K., & Madokoro, G. Lead poisoning: Association with hemolytic anemia, basophilic stippling, erythrocyte pyrimidine 5'-nucleotidase deficiency and intra-erythrocytic accumulation of pyrimidines. *Journal of Clinical Investigation, 1976, 58,* 926–932.

Vaughan, V., McKay, R., & Behrman, R. *Nelson textbook of pediatrics.* Philadelphia, Pa.: W. B. Saunders, 1979.

Vistica, D., Ahrens, F., & Ellison, W. The effects of lead on collagen synthesis and proline hydroxylation in the Swiss Mouse 3T6 fibroblast. *Archives of Biochemistry and Biophysics,* 1977, *179,* 15-23.

Waldron, H., & Stöfen, D. *Subclinical lead poisoning.* New York: Academic Press, 1974.

Walter, S., Yankel, A., & von Lindern, I. Age-specific risk factors for lead absorption in children. *Archives of Environmental Health,* 1980, *35,* 53-58.

Weiss, B. The behavioral toxicity of metals: Biological and pharmacological effects of metal contaminants. *Federation Proceedings,* 1978, *37,* 22-27.

Weiss, B. Conceptual issues in the assessment of lead toxicity. In H. Needleman (Ed.), *Low level lead exposure in childhood: The clinical implications of current research.* New York: Raven Press, 1980.

Werner, E., Bierman, J., & French, F. *The children of Kauai: A longitudinal study from the prenatal period to age ten.* Honolulu: University of Hawaii Press, 1971.

Wibberly, D., Khere, A., Edwards, J., & Rushton, D. Lead levels in human placentae from normal and malformed births. *Journal of Medical Genetics,* 1977, *14,* 339-345.

Wigle, D., & Charlebois, E. Electric kettles as a source of human lead exposure. *Archives of Environmental Health,* 1978, *33,* 72-78.

Willes, R., Lok, E., Truelove, J., & Sundaram, A. Retention and tissue distribution of $^{210}Pb(NO_3)_2$ administered orally to infant and adult monkeys. *Journal of Toxicology and Environmental Health,* 1977, *3,* 395-406.

Winneke, G., Brockhaus, A., Kramer, U., Ewers, U., Kujanek, G., Lechner, H., & Janke, W. Neuropsychological comparison of children with different tooth-lead levels. Preliminary report. Presented at the International Conference Heavy Metals in the Environment, Amsterdam, September, 1981.

Yando, R., Seitz, V., & Zigler, E. *Intellectual and personality characteristics of children: Social-class and ethnic-group differences.* Hillsdale, New Jersey: Erlbaum, 1979.

Youroukos, S., Lyberatos, C., Philippidou, A., Gardikas, C., & Tsomi, A. Increased blood lead levels in mentally retarded children in Greece. *Archives of Environmental Health,* 1978, *33,* 297-300.

Yule, W., Lansdown, R., Millar, I., & Urbanowicz, M. The relationship between blood lead concentrations, intelligence and attainment in a school population: A pilot study. *Developmental Medicine and Child Neurology,* 1981, *23,* 567-576.

Zelazo, P. Reactivity to perceptual-cognitive events: Application for infant assessment. In R. Kearsley & I. Sigel (Eds), *Infants at risk: The assessment of cognitive functioning.* Hillsdale, New Jersey: Erlbaum, 1979.

Zetterlund, B., Winberg, J., Lundgren, G., & Johansson, G. Lead in umbilical cord blood correlated with the blood lead of the mother in areas with low, medium or high atmospheric pollution. *Acta Pediatrica Scandinavica,* 1977, *66,* 169-175.

Ziegler, E., Edwards, B., Jensen, R., Mahaffey, K., & Fomon, S. Absorption and retention of lead by infants. *Pediatric Research,* 1978, *12,* 29-34.

Zielhuis, R. Lead absorption and public health: An appraisal of hazards. In *Proceedings of the International Symposium on Environmental Health Aspects of Lead.* Luxembourg: Commission of the European Communities, 1972.

Zielhuis, R., & Wibowo, A. Susceptibility of adult females to lead: Effects on reproductive function in females and males. Paper presented at the Second International Workshop on Permissible Limits for Occupational Exposure to Lead, 1976.

# PSYCHOSOCIAL ISSUES IN CHILDHOOD CANCER:

## HOW THE PROFESSIONAL CAN HELP

John J. Spinetta

## INTRODUCTION

Some chronic diseases of childhood, while debilitating, follow a known course. Because the course is predictable, parents and patients alike can learn to cope well, given sufficient time, energy, and assistance. The uncertain and the unpredictable diseases make it more difficult to cope well. The varieties of childhood cancer fall into the category of the uncertain.

Less than 20 years ago, childhood cancer was invariably considered fatal. The general course of each type of cancer was fairly predictable, and parents were counseled in ways of preparing for the death of the child. The time lag between diagnosis and death was brief. Today, the outlook for the survival of the child with cancer has improved dramatically. Many children live five years and more beyond the point of diagnosis. Many are considered cured. This increased chance

Advances in Developmental and Behavioral Pediatrics, vol. 3, pages 51–72
Copyright © 1982 by JAI Press Inc.
All rights of reproduction in any form reserved.
ISBN: 0-89232-223-3

for survival of the child with cancer has changed the psychosocial needs of caregivers and families. While medical advances have bettered the survival rates, the psychosocial problems faced by the children and their families have multiplied. Even when the child achieves a five-year or longer survival, uncertainty remains (Koocher & O'Malley, 1980). The cancer can recur.

How do parents live with this uncertainty? How do the children adapt to living with a life-threatening illness? What happens to the siblings? Are there ways that professionals can help facilitate the coping and adaptation of patient and family? Can we be satisfied with merely helping the patient and family adapt, or can we help the child continue to grow and develop, despite the illness?

The literature on the psychosocial repercussions of childhood cancer ranges from the pessimistic tones of a decade ago, when it was believed that the majority of children suffered psychological damage, to the more optimistic tones of recent years. Much has been written about the child, the child's family, and those who treat the child. This chapter will deal with these, as well as with the child's attempts to return to a normal school life. It is the theme of helping the child *live* with the cancer that will be the primary focus of the present chapter.

## HISTORY

There is no doubt that the lengthening of the course of the disease has had a profound impact on the interests and the approach of mental health professionals and researchers working in pediatric oncology over the last two decades. A masterful literature review by Slavin (1980) highlights the trends over the past 20 years, with careful attention given to the way that the cancer experience has changed as a result of the evolving medical outlook for these patients, and to the new issues that have emerged as childhood cancer is increasingly viewed as a chronic disease. A comparison of newer volumes (such as those by Adams, 1980; Kellerman, 1980; Koocher & O'Malley, 1980; Schulman & Kupst, 1980; and Spinetta & Deasy-Spinetta, 1981) with the classic volumes and papers of a decade ago (Binger, Albin, Feuerstein, Kushner, Zoger, & Mikkelson, 1969; Bozeman, Orbach, & Sutherland, 1955; Easson, 1970; Friedman, Chodoff, Mason, & Hamburg, 1963) points to the change in emphasis from one of preparing for death to one of preparing for life.

When the early work on psychosocial aspects of childhood cancer was undertaken, children invariably died. Psychosocial concern focused on helping the parents prepare the child for death, and themselves for what would inevitably and shortly become life without the child. A major question was whether or not to tell the child about the impending death, and at what age. In our early work (Spinettta, 1974; Spinetta & Maloney, 1975; Spinetta, Rigler, & Karon, 1973, 1974), we demonstrated that children as young as five years of age became aware that theirs was no ordinary illness, even when no one had told them. At a level often preceding their ability to conceptualize their awareness in adult terms, the children were very aware that they had a very serious illness. Eventually they came to know that they too might die from the illness. Our advice to the adults dealing in the children's lives was to allow the children to speak openly about their concerns so that they could receive support in their struggles.

As the medical prognosis becomes more optimistic, it is easier to discuss the illness and its prognosis, because the future can be discussed with a great deal more optimism than was the case previously. In addition, it has become clear over recent years that children's coping skills are much more adequate and mature than had been previously thought (Spinetta, 1977). In addition, there is growing evidence that talking about one's fears and fantasies relative to the cancer can be supportive and reassuring, and can lessen levels of anxiety (Slavin, 1980).

Concern has shifted from the issue of telling or not telling, to one of communication as an effective support mechanism. Research has centered on how to maintain, effectively, open levels of communication within a family, allowing the parents to remain in their role as support network for the child. It was shown that as a child who knows little about his or her illness nears death, he or she tends to separate from those around, and exhibits increased feelings of isolation and loneliness (Spinetta, Rigler, & Karon, 1974). In contrast, children whose families maintained an open level of communication throughout the course of the illness not only demonstrated a higher level of self-regard, but were closer to family members than children whose families did not maintain an open level of communication (Spinetta & Maloney, 1978; Spinetta, Swarner, & Sheposh, 1981).

Even now, with all of the medical advances, some children do die of cancer, and they must be prepared for that death, as must the parents and caregivers. However, children typically live longer before their death than in years past. Even those children who will die can live fully until the moment of their death (Martinson, 1976). Allowing them to attend school and encouraging a positive outlook toward their future can be as helpful to those who will eventually die as to those who will become long-term survivors (Clapp, 1976; Deasy-Spinetta & Spinetta, 1980; Lansky, Lowman, Vats, & Gyulay, 1975; van Eys, 1977). Kagen-Goodheart (1977) wrote of helping children with cancer continue in their forward growth and commitment to life by helping them to re-enter their normal world as soon as possible after initial cancer treatment. This "re-entry" often involves having the child go to school despite outward signs of sickness such as hair loss or excessive weight, or despite negative effects of medication on ordinary bodily functioning. Regular school attendance is considered vital, not only to normal development, but to maintenance of normal social behavior (Deasy-Spinetta 1981, Greene, 1975; Kagen-Goodheart, 1977; Kaplan, Smith, Grobstein, & Fishman, 1973; Katz, Kellerman, Rigler, Williams, & Siegel, 1977). A positive school experience can provide the child with a sense of accomplishment and social acceptance, strengthen his or her faltering self-esteem, and

lessen maladaptive emotional responses to the illness (Slavin, 1980). The theme
of the child's re-entry into a normal world will be addressed in detail throughout
this chapter.

## COPING WITH DIAGNOSIS AND TREATMENT

The childhood cancers are a group of diseases. Each disease has its own natural
history, a relatively predictable course from the time that it first becomes apparent, through a period of spreading, to death. The goal of treatment is to interrupt
or alter the natural history of the disease. The psychological impact of the cancer
is complex.

The time of diagnosis and initial treatment is the first of a series of events with
which the child and family must cope. In fact, many families have pointed to the
event of diagnosis as the most serious of the entire disease course. When a child
is diagnosed with cancer, each family member is affected. Parents and siblings
must develop methods of dealing with the child's cancer. They must also adjust
to the practical limitations placed on their lives by the child's illness. Basically
sound families are confronting an inordinate amount of stress, and need help to
begin to master at least some of the day-to-day elements of the task. Families
must live with the uncertainty of the illness. They hope for a sustained remission,
while at the same time preparing for the possible loss of their child. About half of
the children will make it; the other half will not.

Therapeutic programs in the past were aimed at keeping the child comfortable.
Today, treatment is undertaken with the hope of cure. Such therapy is often
aggressive to the point that the effects of the treatment are often as painful as the
effects of the disease (Koocher & Sallan, 1978). Parents and children must
accept and incorporate this aggressive treatment in the hope of a greater good, the
child's ultimate cure. Not only are the chemotherapies tolerated differently by
each child; wide variations occur within the same individual at various times.

As issues relative to diagnosis become less immediate, the issues that come to
the fore for the children center about coping with the cancer treatments. Recently, we set forth a series of tasks, originally described by Lazarus (1976), as
helpful in evaluating the adaptational efforts of children with cancer (Spinetta,
1977). These coping tasks are: (1) tolerating or relieving distress associated with
the illness; (2) maintaining a sense of personal worth; (3) maintaining positive
personal relationships with parents, peers, and caregivers; and (4) meeting the
specific requirements of particularly stressful situations, utilizing the resources
available. Researchers are now addressing each of these issues (Adams, 1980;
Kellerman, 1980; Schulman & Kupst, 1980; Spinetta & Deasy-Spinetta, 1981).
The increased use of self-relaxation or hypnosis techniques for relieving distress
associated with the treatments has resulted in less pain for the children (Dash,
1980; Hartman, 1981; Zletzer, 1980). The area of preparation for untoward
events has received much emphasis in recent literature (Slavin, 1980).

The treatments can result in a variety of side effects. Hair loss can be an emotionally trying experience for all children, the very young as well as teens. Although family and friends become accustomed to the children's appearance and the hair does grow back eventually, the hair loss can be very embarassing. Other problems include dramatic weight gain or loss, mouth ulcers, muscle spasms, skin rashes, skin discolorations, scars, organ losses, and amputations (Koocher & Sallan, 1978). Preparation for these can be helpful, but the problems are not resolved at a single intervention. Problems in adaptation continue throughout the disease course. As old problems are resolved, new ones appear. Chronic vomiting is a virtually inescapable part of chemotherapy. Some children may even become so conditioned to expect the side effect of vomiting that they begin to vomit hours before the medication is given, in anticipation of receiving it.

Depression of a child's immune responses presents a constant concern because of the child's increased susceptibility to all manner of infection (Koocher & Sallan, 1978). When a child with cancer develops infections during the course of treatment, the infections are considerably more dangerous than in the normal child. The frequency of these interruptions in daily living adds considerably to the family's level of stress. Commonly voiced concerns of the children themselves include forced dependence on others and loss of bodily control, both coming at a time when they have begun to mature. The painful muscle spasms, nausea, and disorientation that are side effects of chemotherapy cause the child concern.

The age and level of development of the child make a difference in how the child responds to the illness and treatments. A brief review of a child's age-related responses and concerns will follow.

## THE CHILD'S AGE, EXPERIENCE, AND LEVEL OF DEVELOPMENT

A prerequisite to meaningful communication with a child about his or her illness and treatment is a basic understanding of developmental levels in the growth of the child's thought processes, notably those surrounding the concepts of life and death. There are many books and articles which speak to this issue (Easson, 1970; Grollman, 1967; Hostler, 1978; Jackson, 1965; Koocher, 1973; Spinetta, Spinetta, Kung, & Schwartz, 1976; Spinetta, Deasy-Spinetta, Koenig, Lightsey, Schwartz, Hartman, & Kung, 1979). Although it is difficult to do justice to so complex a topic in a brief space, the issue will be addressed at this point in an overview fashion, so that it can be placed in proper perspective. The topic will be considered in two phases: (1) the child's concept of death, and (2) the seriously ill child's concept (or understanding) of death.

### The Child's Concept of Death

Concepts of death are age-related in children and differ with intellectual ability and development (Anthony, 1940; Hostler, 1978; Koocher, 1973; Nagy, 1948;

White, Elsom, & Prawat, 1978). It is generally believed that during the first two years of life, there is no understanding of death as such, but fear of separation from protecting, comforting persons is present in its most terrifying intensity. While death is not yet a fact of life for the child going on three, anxiety about separation remains all-pervasive. Some time between the ages of three and five, most children first comprehend the fact of death as something that happens to others. At this time, the concept of death is still vague. It is associated with sleep and the absence of light or movement and is not yet thought of as permanent. In contrast to toddlers, most children of this age are able to withstand and understand short separations. They often respond more spontaneously and with less anxiety to questions about death than do older children. They are also curious about dead animals and flowers. However, children between three and five typically deny death as a final reality. They believe death is accidental and they themselves will not die.

Attitudes and concepts of children do not change abruptly at any given age, but evolve gradually and with wide individual variation. This is true whether one is talking about the concept of time, the concept of space, or the concept of death. From approximately the age of six onward, the child seems gradually to be accommodating himself or herself to the proposition that death is final, inevitable, universal, and personal. Many six and seven year olds suspect that their parents will die some day, and that they too may die, but only in the very distant future. Children in these early school years show a strong tendency to personify death. Many children at their initial awareness and discovery of death are horrified, confused, and angered. Although some authors feel that because of exposure a child in the present day and age is coming to grips with the concept of death at a young age (Hansen, 1973), most still agree that the child under 10 has not yet attained a well-developed understanding of death (White, et al., 1978). As children approach adolescence, they are equipped with the intellectual tools necessary to understand time, space, life, and death in a logical manner. At about the age of 10 or 11 the fact of the universality and the permanence of death becomes understandable.

What we have discussed to this point is the normal development of the ability to conceptualize death in children. A speeding-up of the process occurs when the child is faced with death at an early age, often at a level preceding the child's usual ability to conceptualize it (Bluebond-Langner, 1974, 1977; Spinetta, 1974; Waechter, 1971).

### The Seriously Ill Child's Concept of Death

It is important when speaking to children with a life-threatening illness about the concept of death to understand differences in ability to conceptualize because of the child's age and level of development. At the same time, it must be remembered that a child who is experiencing the day-to-day effects of a life-threatening illness and often the drastic changes in the emotional climate that accompany this disease, may become aware of his or her impending demise at a much younger age than do the child's healthy peers (Spinetta, 1974). As shown above, recent studies of 6- to 10-year-old children with life-threatening illnesses reveal that, despite efforts by parents and medical personnel to keep the child from becoming aware of the prognosis, he or she somehow picks up a sense that the illness is no ordinary one. The fear of abandonment and separation, characteristic of the younger child, has added to it a fear of bodily harm and injury and possible awareness at a level preceding his ability to conceptualize it, that something very serious is happening. The awareness of his or her own impending death becomes stronger as the child nears death (Bluebond-Langner, 1977; Spinetta, Rigler, & Karon, 1973, 1974).

Adolescence brings with it additional problems and concerns. There are changes and conflicts that accompany ordinary adolescence; the addition to these of the diagnosis of cancer makes it traumatic (Adams, 1980; Clapp, 1976; Drotar, 1977; Easson, 1970; Katz et al., 1977; Plumb & Holland, 1974). There are basic developmental tasks the adolescent must accomplish, whether he or she has cancer or not: achieving a sense of personal identity, establishing independence from parents, adjusting to sexuality, forming mature relationships with peers of both sexes, and planning for a future in terms of job and marriage. Adolescents have a need to assert their independence at the same time that their illness forces dependence on physician, hospital staff, and parents. Anything that can be done to allow them a sense of independence, some participation in decision making while under treatment is most helpful. Building up trust and rapport will help to diminish the rebelliousness that is common among teenagers. Communicating directly with them will help them maintain a level of maturity and independence that will help them sustain self-esteem.

Adolescents normally look forward to what their lives will be like in the future. Most begin thinking about careers and marriage. The adolescent with cancer may be concerned about whether the disease will limit the possibilities open to him or her (National Cancer Institute, 1979). Sterility may be a possible side effect of some treatments. They may see their friends getting married and having children, and wonder if they will be able to do so as well. Yet in spite of the uncertainty about their future, adolescent cancer patients must be encouraged to make realistic plans. Parents and caregivers must provide the emotional support for them to do so. Psychological support for adolescent cancer patients must take into account their developmental needs. Peer support groups are good ways to help them talk about the illness with someone who will understand. Often adolescents have a difficult time talking to adults. Forming a group of adolescents with cancer allows them to talk openly with peers about common disease-related and other problems. An ongoing adolescent support group has been an integral part of our own intervention program (Deasy-Spinetta, 1980).

How do health care professionals begin to help a child and family deal with the cancer diagnosis, aggressive treatment regime, and life-threatening prognosis? It is essential that they understand the family's role as support system for the child, and make an effort to help establish open communication from the beginning.

## COMMUNICATION WITH FAMILY MEMBERS

While the health care professional must attempt to understand the particular family structure and environment under which an individual child must live and grow, and while each family's adaptive capabilities and coping styles may differ, there are common patterns of communication among family members that are peculiar to the families of children with a life-threatening illness. It is these common elements that this section will address.

If it is true that children as young as four or five are aware of the serious nature of their illness, what do they do with this knowledge and awareness? Do they talk openly with their families about the prognosis, or do they live in silence with the knowledge? What roles do the families play in the children's wish to talk or not to talk about the illnesses? Studies of family communication patterns about the issue of serious illness in children show that the level of family communication about the illness, as expressed in the mother's judgment of communication, relates to coping strategies in the child (Spinetta & Maloney, 1978). Families in which levels of communication about the illness are high are those families in which the children: (1) exhibit a nondefensive personal posture, (2) express a consistently close relationship with the parents, and (3) express a basic satisfaction with self. The parental level of willingness to discuss the illness is most important in the child's decision about what to do with the knowledge. Children who have the personal desire and parental permission to discuss their illness openly within the family structure are in the best position to receive the type of support they need (Spinetta, 1978).

Circumstances of pain, reactions to medication and treatment, and the death of other children from the illness all play a role in children's increasing awareness of the severity of their illnesses. Some professionals encourage denial in order for the children to maintain mental as well as physical comfort, and to a point, some brief denial may appear helpful (Alby & Alby, 1973; Howarth, 1974; Lazarus, 1980). However, children, siblings, and parents are best served in the long run by being encouraged to bring into the open their anxieties about the illness and its possible consequences (Alby & Alby, 1973; Futterman & Hoffman, 1973; Spinetta & Deasy-Spinetta, 1981; Spinetta, Spinetta, Kung, & Schwartz, 1976).

In a series of interviews conducted with families whose children had died from a life-threatening illness after the age of six, the most frequently discussed issue was the extent to which the family had communicated with the child about the possible terminal effects of the illness (Spinetta, Swarner, & Sheposh, 1981). About one-half of the families interviewed felt they had talked freely and openly with their children about their impending deaths. None of the parents who had spoken openly with their child felt that too much had been said; on the contrary, these parents felt that a higher level of closeness was achieved with the child than might have occurred otherwise. The memory of the open discussions and exchange of family values before the child's death had sustained the families during the mourning process. The siblings in the open group reported having had time to say goodbye to their dying brother or sister, to resolve old quarrels, and to help their dying sibling in his or her own efforts to say goodbye as well.

The families whose children had died without open discussion of the illness or of the imminent death usually wished they had spoken more openly with their child. These parents reported feelings of incompleteness and nonresolution. Those siblings who reported unresolved feelings regretted not having been forewarned or not having had time to say goodbye and settle differences before the child's death.

Further studies are needed as to what to say and when, taking into consideration the severity of the illness, parental and sibling readiness, and age levels of the children. Nevertheless, studies to date point to the fact that children understand that their illnesses are serious, and encouraging children to talk about the illness usually has beneficial short- and long-term effects on all family members, including the life-threatened child.

Though desirable, open communication in all families in all circumstances is not always possible. Although open communication is generally of supportive value to the sick child, a forced openness too soon can be destructive for some specific families. Some parents are initially unable to communicate openly under the stress of a seriously ill child and exhibit maladaptive behavior, becoming inaccessible, withdrawn, and remote (Spinetta, 1978). The goal in working with these parents should be to help them become aware of the false sense of equilibrium that comes from excessive denial of the problem, and the harm such denial can cause the sick child. Temporary use of denial of a serious illness can allow the family time to pull adaptive resources together. However, in dealing with such a family, care should be taken to prevent the ''temporary'' state of denial from becoming self-perpetuating.

We have found that the life-threatened child chooses whether or not to talk about the illness depending on his or her experiences within the family regarding openness of communication about illness. A child may choose silence becuase he or she senses that the family forbids discussion of the illness, or the child may communicate openly because the family reinforces openness. Either choice represents a different style of coping. The choice of silence can lead to excessive denial and avoidance, and a feeling of rejection and isolation; the child may feel that he or she has been left alone to work out his or her problems. In contrast, open discussion, stemming from the sincere attempts of family members to communicate concern and support, encourages expression of feelings. Open expressions of the child's fears relative to the illness can lead to mutual support among family members, helping the child to achieve a balanced adaptive equilibrium.

## The Family as a Support System

When open communication begins in a family, complex sets of feelings emerge. Openness increases expressed levels of anxiety within the family and commits family members, as well as others who must deal with the family members, to a confrontation with the severity of the illness. The open family may be torn apart by the confrontation, or it may come through the adaptive struggle with members having grown closer together, having gained an ability to struggle valiantly in future life conflicts, and having achieved a level of confidence, strength, and re-evaluation of basic life commitments that will make for a more effective and fulfilled life.

People deal with crises, well or poorly, using various coping mechanisms (Lazarus, 1981). Even escape through suicide or mental illness represents a mechanism for coping. In families coping with a life-threatening illness, it is important to place the coping patterns of each member within the context of the family's primary role as support environment for its members. If a family loses its common objectives, reduces cooperation among members, if members do not reciprocate services (most notably in the sexual roles of the spouses) or fail to coordinate functions or lack consensus of emotional attitudes, then, no matter how well an individual member adapts to a life-threatening diagnosis, the family itself has failed in its primary function of social support of its members. The result is family disorganization and possible disintegration if the situation continues for long. While individual family members may cope effectively and well without family support, effective coping is the exception in families in which communication is minimal and disorganization is high.

In the family of a child with a life-threatening illness, parents are often so overwhelmed by the illness that they do not prepare for ordinary events; for example, a child diagnosed with a life-threatening illness at two years of age can at five begin to have problems in school simply because the mother did not engage in the ordinary preparatory steps for school. An event such as the child's beginning school is such a minor one to the mother in comparison to the illness itself, that she does not prepare the child to enter school. If the child had not developed a life-threatening illness some time earlier, the mother would have placed into perspective the child's needs for preparation for school, with the accompanying social demands from the child's school-aged peers. What happens is a basic failure in family communication: the mother's attempts at coping with her child's illness, though successful regarding the illness, leave the mother with little energy to deal with the child's new problem, entry into school. The mother, while coping with the illness, is not giving her child the type of support the child needs to cope with a task that is not related to the disease. Similarly, other ordinary life transitions of children, such as entry into junior high school, pubescence, or transfer to a new city, can become crises because the family, overwhelmed by a life-threatening diagnosis in the child, has frozen efforts at growth. It is as if the family unit were saying to itself: "If only we can hold it all together and keep from falling apart, we'll make it." Such a mode of coping with the illness precludes the type of openness to growth and change that is necessary as the children move through various developmental crises on their way to adulthood. Such a family fails to devote the necessary energy to help the child in his or her times of greatest need.

## Siblings

What has been stated about the child with a life-threatening illness also holds for the siblings. The siblings of a child with a life-threatening illness are often neglected by the parents, not because sibling needs are not important, but because their needs take on a lesser importance relative to the diagnosis of a life-threatening illness. Siblings in the families of children with a life-threatening illness often face alone the developmental tasks necessary to achieve adulthood. Attempts by the siblings to seek help from parents often meet with a plea to be mature and generous, and to respect the needs of the ill child. Even the mentally strong and healthy sibling cannot be expected to go through life's transitional stages without support from parents who have "burned out" from strategies used in coping with their ill child's diagnosis (Cairns, Clark, Smith, & Lansky, 1979; Johnson, Rudolph, & Hartman, 1979; Kagen-Goodheart, 1977; Kaplan, Grobstein, & Smith, 1976; Lavigne & Ryan, 1979; Slavin, 1980; Sourkes, 1977, 1980; Spinetta, 1981).

## Spouses

What has been said about the child with a life-threatening illness and his or her siblings also holds for the parents. The parents, occasionally in unison but more often in their own separate ways, expend their energies dealing with the illness. Often, remaining life tasks, such as career, finances, and sexual life, take on a lowered significance (Stehbens & Lascari, 1974). When a parent's needs are not met within the family unit, the parent may turn outside the family to fulfill the needs. Often, separation and divorce can result from this activity (Johnson, Rudolph, & Hartman, 1979; Spinetta & Deasy-Spinetta, 1981). However, with proper and continued counseling support, spouses can be drawn closer together because of their shared experiences. Divorce is not inevitable (Lansky, Cairns, Hassanein, Wehr, & Lowman, 1978; Spinetta, Swarner, & Sheposh, 1981).

In summary, a family spends a large amount of energy in attempting to keep itself from becoming disorganized and disintegrated under the overwhelming threat to the life of one of its members. In the process of dealing with a life-threatening illness, the family finds itself with little energy left to fulfill its primary function as a support system to each of its members. Individual members may find their own special needs unmet. What must occur is that family members communicate their needs at a level that can be effectively understood by others in the family. Unless this communication occurs and individual family members are able to continue to receive support for their own needs from the family system, those individuals will be forced to look elsewhere for the support the family no longer gives.

As parents prepare to meet the new demands imposed upon them by their child's illness, it is wise for them to take an inventory of what individuals or systems of belief they can rely on as a source of support in this time of stress (Spinetta et al., 1976). It might be good to look back and analyze who or what helped during previous stressful times.

A group of parents who had lost their child to cancer was asked to list the sources of support they depended upon during the long haul of their child's illness (Spinetta, Swarner, & Sheposh, 1981). Not all indicated the same sources, but the list included: spouse, friends, relatives, hospital staff, religious beliefs, clergy, professional counselors, the sick child, and other parents of sick children.

The spouse was a supportive factor in many but not all of the marriages. Some people turned to friends because they accepted the fact that they could not communicate with their partner. The hospital staff was of assistance to many families. Parents as a whole had great respect for the medical competence of their physician and appreciated the doctor's and nurses' understanding and sensitive care of their child. Religion was a powerful factor in the lives of many parents who had a strong religious belief prior to the diagnosis. By far the strongest source of support was the presence of an understanding spouse or close friend to whom the parent could turn as problems arose. It was not unusual for parents to derive strength from their own child. Finally, parents have found other parents of children with cancer a source of support. Other parents with a child with cancer have an understanding that cuts across social, economic, and racial barriers because both share a common problem so fundamental in nature.

In many hospitals, parents have organized parents' groups that meet on a regular weekly or monthly basis to share common problems and concerns (Adams, 1980; Heffron, Bommelaere, & Masters, 1973; Knapp & Hansen, 1973). These parental groups serve a healthy function in helping parents attain a feeling of mastery in coping with some of the more difficult aspects of the illness and diagnosis.

The goal of working with the families of children with a life-threatening illness is to help them strengthen their own adaptive capacities and coping styles. The health care professional treating the child must take into account the family structure and environment (van Eys, 1977). To help family members use the support systems they will need during the remaining months or years of their child's life and after the child's death, is the goal for which the professional dedicated to the care of the total child must strive.

# RETURNING TO SCHOOL

A major part of normal growth and development for all children involves school. For a child with a life-threatening illness, a return to school represents a continuation of life, hope for the future, and an attempt to re-establish equilibrium—an equilibrium that does not deny the fact of the illness, but encompasses the new reality base of a potential threat to life (Greene, 1975; Kagen-Goodheart, 1977; Kaplan et al., 1973; Katz et al., 1977; Kirten & Liverman, 1977; Lansky et al., 1975; Zwartjes & Zwartjes, 1980). School personnel play a crucial role in determining whether or not the child with a potentially life-threatening illness can live a normal life, since so much of the child's day is centered around school. Teachers, counselors, school nurses, and administrators must be prepared to deal with this added responsibility (Deasy-Spinetta & Spinetta, 1980). The physician, either directly or through a school-trained educational liaison who is an integral member of the health care team can best help the child by opening, and keeping open, lines of communication with the school.

A return to school for a child with a life-threatening illness involves personal interaction, typically with one teacher at the elementary school level, five or more at the secondary level, plus school nurses, counselors, administrators, and peers. Each of these individuals brings to the child his or her own philosophy of life, attitudes toward death, and understanding of the illness. Furthermore, each school often has an identifiable attitude toward working in the regular classroom with any child with a medical problem. It is, therefore, imperative to prepare significant school personnel for the re-entry of the patient-student. The school needs first, accurate medical information specific to the particular child; second, an understanding of the psychosocial implications of the illness as it relates to the child and the family; and finally a referral resource, someone who is part of the health care team, who can answer questions as they arise. When this is done, the school, the environment in which the child spends many hours each day, will promote rather than interfere with the child's efforts to cope with school life within the context of the child's illness. If the school is not adequately prepared, the environment in which the child spends many hours each day may interfere with the child's efforts to cope with school life within the context of the child's illness.

## Preparing the Teacher

Health care professionals associated with the medical management of potentially life-threatening illnesses in children realize that the children are living longer than in the past. However, professionals outside the medical environment, such as school teachers, frequently equate life-threatening illnesses with death. Since such illnesses no longer always result in death, this attitude must be addressed if teachers are to be adequately prepared to handle children with life-threatening illnesses in the classroom. Just as each member of the medical staff has his or her own philosophical position on death, so too does each member of the school staff. A specific teacher's philosophy of death may differ from that of colleagues, and from that of the parents of the child. The presence of a possibly life-threatened child in the classroom causes reflection and concern among the school staff. For some teachers this may be a personally unsettling experience. It is necessary to assist teachers in understanding their own attitudes and emotional responses toward the concept of death. The teacher must also gain an appreciation of the child's understanding of death, and realize that each family has its own manner of dealing with such a crisis. It is important to help teachers realize that all children are very sensitive to nonverbal cues in their environment. If the teacher is uneasy about having a child with a potentially life-threatening illness in the classroom, the child will sense this at a nonverbal level, and there may be negative consequences in his or her academic and social performance. The child will also sense a warm, caring, supportive attitude on the part of the teacher. Teachers must realize that they are working not only with a child, but also with a family in crisis.

It is also important to help teachers understand that a child with a serious illness can continue to achieve and develop, and may have years of valuable life ahead. Hope is essential in dealing with these students. Hope, unlike denial, does not interfere with healthy adjustment and is entirely compatible with an acceptance of reality (Lazarus, 1981). When caregivers lose the hope for cure, development can be hampered. Some caregivers may expect a child to die and, therefore, not do what is needed to help the child develop. This attitude, termed "psychological euthanasia" (Van Eys, 1977), may serve to protect caregivers, but is devastating to the child in the classroom. It is imperative, then, that teachers be helped to understand that a child with a life-threatening illness is a living, growing, developing child valiantly trying to learn in spite of a difficult situation.

*Specific Issues Relative to School*

Many children with a potentially life-threatening illness have difficulties in school for a variety of reasons. Hair loss, weight loss or gain, and reduced stamina are the most obvious and most often discussed. Yet, many children who have an understanding of the reasons for these obvious physical changes and have been well prepared by both the medical staff and their parents, can explain to their classmates the reasons for the physical changes, and thereby gain the understanding and support of their peers. The more directly school-related problems can be more devastating than the disease-related problems, simply because the former are more subtle and easily overlooked. For example, a child with a serious illness may either have or develop a reading problem. Teachers who view the child as living despite the illness see the need for referring the child for appropriate diagnostic evaluation and remediation. Teachers who view the child as dying do not refer, and the child goes from grade to grade carrying the burden, not only of the illness, but also of a worsening reading difficulty.

Attendance at school may be a problem because of frequent clinic visits and occasional hospitalizations. Many teachers are very cooperative and flexible, and allow the child to make up work. Others, especially at the secondary level, do not. The adolescent's need for privacy, coupled with a teacher's need for an excuse for absence, can often conflict. This especially becomes a problem when the child's teachers do not accept the fact of the illness, or the adolescent refuses to tell the teacher what he or she really has. Bridging this communication gap is critical, and can best be done by a professional trained both in the school and in the hospital environments.

A well-prepared teacher is a valuable link in the total care of the child. A teacher who is prepared to deal with the family in crisis, as well as with the child, is in a position to communicate with parents in a way health care professionals might not be. Many children, for example, are found to have the illness before entering school. Beginning school is a significant step for all children and their parents. If the child is successful in entering school, the parents feel rewarded in their efforts to promote normal growth and development. If a child has problems in school, parents may link the problems to some other cause. If the child has an illness, they may blame the illness for unrelated difficulties. A well-prepared teacher will point out to these parents that many other children have difficulties at the beginning of school as well, and that the difficulties are not those only of children with a serious illness. This support of the parents at a critical transition time by a competent teacher helps the child.

The transition from elementary to junior high school is stressful for all students, not merely for the student with a life-threatening illness. School-related activities are particularly significant for the adolescent patient. Diseases and their treatment may prevent or impede successful development of autonomy, acquisition of consistent body image and sex roles, establishment of peer relations, and the adoption of future-oriented social and intellectual preparation. It is important to allow an adolescent to maximize his or her sense of control, and the school is one area where the adolescent patient can do this. It is essential that school personnel understand the particular illness and its related consequences as they apply to the adolescent.

Since children with life-threatening illnesses are living longer and seeking a normal life by attending school, communication with the school becomes, not a luxury, but a vital and essential element in the total care of the child. Everyone involved benefits from expanded communication with the child's school. The child is happier in school; teachers are more comfortable in their roles; parents are content that the child is safe, productive, and functioning like other children the same age; and the physician obtains a more complete picture of the child. Teachers and other school personnel play a significant role in the life of the child. Given adequate preparation, information, and support, they are an essential and valuable link in the total care of the child.

# CONCLUSION

The major dilemma facing parents of a child with cancer is balancing the amount of time and mental effort to be devoted to concern for the cancer and its treatment, and the amount of time to be devoted to the continuation of a normal living pattern, both for the child with cancer and for the remaining family members. Work, the home, the siblings, the schools, the normal life of the patient—all of these must continue. The critical factor is at what level these will continue. Does coping merely mean getting on with the task of life, or can it include a healthy growth that includes the joy of living? Parents need help to keep their lives moving forward. Our research has demonstrated that the parental self-image does not change because of the illness (Spinetta, Swarner, & Sheposh, 1981). What does change is the parent's ability to handle day-to-day kinds of problems (Kalnins, Churchill, & Terry, 1980). These are problems that come to the fore during the course of remission. During ordinary clinic visits for treatments, it is the day-to-day issues that become important; issues that may have been readily resolvable prior to the illness now take on a different challenge. Many parents feel unable to make the needed decisions alone without the help, understanding, support, and input of an understanding team member. What the parents need is not therapy, but a listener who is willing to tell them that what they are experiencing—indecision, lack of zest for life, and the excessive burdens of day-to-day living tasks—are the normal responses of parents who are struggling with the continual task of maintaining normalcy while their child has cancer and is undergoing treatment. It is during times of relapse/recurrence that the strain becomes greatest, that parents feel expecially overwhelmed by the tasks, when life in effect does stop, because the child becomes the central and sole focus for a while. What is needed from the team is an attitude of understanding that expresses itself in concern for the family's needs, most especially the nonmedical needs. The attitude must begin with the physician and extend to the team. It is most helpful to have a professional assigned to the team whose primary task is dealing with the psychosocial concerns of the family (Koocher & Sallan, 1978). This will give the family members a pivotal person on whom they can depend, even though they may also turn to the nurse or physician for counsel.

The availability of psychological consultation services in pediatric oncology cannot be considered a luxury. The ever-increasing complexity and variables in the treatment programs demand a relatively sophisticated consultant who can function smoothly as a member of an oncology treatment team (Koocher &

Sallan, 1978). Issues about side effects of treatment, troublesome symptoms, relations with staff members, and a hundred other potential concerns cannot be met effectively by a therapist at the local mental health center, a school counselor, or a private practitioner away from the clinic. The other members of the oncology treatment team must have consultants they know, whose judgment they trust, and with whom they can relate on a regular basis.

It is therapy in the broadest sense which is being addressed here. Often parents are reluctant to talk to an assigned therapist directly about a problem, for fear of being labeled abnormal or pathological. What is critical is that the parent, sibling, and child realize that talking about day-to-day concerns is not only appropriate and acceptable, but that the need to do so is normal. While parental concerns from the outset may be existential and very much related to the potentially life-threatening nature of the illness, what will emerge after a time will be the day-to-day concerns, first the medical and treatment-related concerns, and then the nonmedical family concerns. When the initial shock has worn off, the family members need to know that there is someone on the team to whom they can turn to have their questions resolved, both medical and nonmedical. This rapport must be established from the outset; the parents will fare best when they are able to return to the business of living as soon as possible after diagnosis and initiation of treatment.

Lazarus (1981) talks about the aspects of denial. One must maintain hope at all costs, hope that this particular child will be the one to make it. Use of the best medical treatment will be one step toward that goal. A second and equally important step is the psychological commitment toward life on the part of the parents, siblings, and patient. A child who is going to live will need to continue to develop and grow, and to continue to pursue schooling with the objective of full adult participation in life. If the child does make it as a survivor of the cancer experience, the patient should not have fallen so far behind that catching up to normal living becomes an additional burden.

If the child relapses, hope can still be kept alive, though it becomes more difficult to do so. It is not uncommon for family members to be committed to growth and development, and, at the point of relapse or recurrence, to give up hope. When a child does not achieve a remission again, the family members then bear the additional burden of having to regroup forces and continue moving forward, with diminished hope. The parents need help to pull them through these phases of relapse/remission to keep their commitment to life fully functional.

If the child does eventually become terminal, as a large number of children still do, then a point comes when the parents must face the fact of the child's death. Even at this point, a family must continue its commitment to the value of life for each of its members. The patient will have been well served by having tried as much as possible to live a fulfilled life, despite the cancer. At the point of death, such a child will die with the memory of having lived fully at least for a while. Such a child may continue to fight the death, but at least when death comes will have felt that life was set aside because of the cancer. A continued commitment of the family to schooling and family activities during the course of the child's disease will be a memory the child can cherish at the end. It is very important for children and adolescents to achieve as much as possible during the time they have left. Keeping up physical appearance, keeping up with school-work, most especially during the final phases of the illness, are critical to the self-esteem of the patient. For adolescents, love, security, and freedom from pain are equally as important as for younger children. The more their parents can be with them and communicate with them with openness and honesty, the more adolescents can be helped to resolve their feelings at the time of death (Adams, 1980).

Parents who have given this commitment to continued life and living, who have allowed the siblings to live their lives as well, and who have continued their own spouse relationships will find the strength to accept the death of the child when it comes. While the sadness and grieving will not be diminished after the death of the child, the ability to return to a full and functioning life after the death will be greatly enhanced for those who were able to go on with the business of living during the life of the child (Spinetta, Swarner, & Sheposh, 1981).

There are effects on caregivers as well. It is difficult to see so many children die without being depressed when the deaths occur. The emotional costs are high, but the rewards are even higher. There is the opportunity to work with highly motivated family members and to see significant beneficial progress in short periods of time. There is the continuous reward of playing an important role, helping at a crucial time in the life of a family. Some patients die. The caretaker who has depressed feelings, and can reasonably accept them, will remain in the field and be productive (Koocher, 1980; Koocher & Sallan, 1978).

While a family's responses at the point of diagnosis may be so exceptional as to single out the family as one with low risk, most families are in need of care throughout. Some families ebb and flow in their abilities to handle issues; some do well at the beginning but grow progressively more in need of help. There is no single pattern.

There is also no single prescription for dealing with childhood cancer. There are many variables involved: the type of cancer, the severity of the illness, the prognosis, the age of the child, the family history of coping, the present family support system, as well as economic and other factors which may impinge in an ongoing manner on the course of treatment and response to the treatment.

One group of pioneers in this work have expressed the problem exceptionally well:

Each parent and sibling reacts to a fatal illness individually, in a manner consistent with his own personality structure, past experience, current crises, and the particular meaning or special circumstances associated with the loss threatening him. To help them, one must know each one and his relations to his or her friends, how they react to the initial diagnosis, how their grief process begins and how they cope. One should know, too, something of their beliefs about life, death, and religion, their response to previous crises, and their current burdens and sources of support (Binger et al., p. 418).

This is a large task, but then, the life of a child is not a small responsibility. Will we meet the task of helping the child with cancer live a full and happy life, even if that life will be foreshortened?

## ACKNOWLEDGMENTS

During the preparation of this chapter, the author was supported in part by Grant Number CA 21254, awarded by the National Cancer Institute, Department of Health and Human Services. The author wishes to thank Faith Kung, M.D., of the University of California, San Diego, School of Medicine, Donald Schwartz, M.D., and Gary Hartmen, M.D., of Children's Hospital and Health Center, San Diego, and their staffs for their continued support and encouragement. Reprinted by permission of the publisher from *Coping with Medical Issues: Living and Dying with Cancer* by P. Ahmed, (Ed.) copyright © 1981 by Elsevier North Holland, Inc.

## REFERENCES

Adams, D. W. *Childhood malignancy: The psychosocial care of the child and his family.* Springfield: Thomas, 1980.

Alby, N., & Alby, J. M. The doctor and the dying child. In E. J. Anthony & C. Koupernik (Eds.), *The child and his family.* Vol. 2. *The impact of disease and death.* New York: Wiley, 1973.

Anthony, S. *The child's discovery of death.* New York: Harcourt Brace, 1940.

Binger, C. M., Ablin, A. R., Feuerstein, R. C., Kushner, J. H., Zoger, S., & Mikkelsen, C. Childhood leukemia: Emotional impact on patient and family. *New England Journal of Medicine,* 1969, *280,* 414-418.

Bluebond-Langner, M. I know, do you? Awareness and communication in terminally ill children. In B. Schoenberg, A. Carr, D. Peretz, & A. Kutscher (Eds.), *Anticipatory grief.* New York: Columbia, 1974.

Bluebond-Langner, M. Meanings of death to children. In H. Feifel (Ed.), *New meanings of death.* New York: McGraw-Hill, 1977.

Bozeman, M. F., Orbach, C. E., & Sutherland, A. M. Psychological impact of cancer and its treatment: The adaptation of mothers to the threatened loss of their children through leukemia. *Cancer,* 1955, *8,* 1-33.

Cairns, N. U., Clark, G. M., Smith, S. D., & Lansky, S. B. Adaptation of siblings to childhood malignancy. *Journal of Pediatrics-* 1979, *95,* 484-487.

Clapp, M. J. Psychosocial reactions of children with cancer. *Nursing Clinics of North America,* 1976, *11,* 73-82.

Dash, J. Hypnosis with pediatric cancer patients. In J. Kellerman (Ed.), *Psychological aspects of childhood cancer.* Springfield, Ill.: Thomas, 1980.

Deasy-Spinetta, P. The adolescent with cancer: A view from the inside. In J. J. Spinetta & P. Deasy-Spinetta (Eds.), *Living with childhood cancer.* St. Louis: Mosby, 1981. (a)

Deasy-Spinetta, P., The school and the child with cancer. In J. J. Spinetta & P. Deasy-Spinetta (Eds.), *Living with childhood cancer.* St. Louis: Mosby, 1981. (b)

Deasy-Spinetta, P., & Spinetta, J. J. The child with cancer in school: Teachers' appraisal. *American Journal of Pediatric Hematology/Oncology,* 1980, *2,* 89-94. (a)

Drotar, D. Family oriented intervention with the dying adolescent. *Journal of Pediatric Psychology*, 1977, *2*, 68–71.

Easson, W. M. *The dying child*. Springfield, Ill.: Thomas, 1970.

Friedman, S., Chodoff, P., Mason, J., & Hamburg, D. Behavioral observations of parents anticipating the death of a child. *Pediatrics*, 1963, *32*, 610–625.

Futterman, E., & Hoffman, I. Crisis and adaptation in the families of fatally ill children. In E. J. Anthony & C. Koupernik (Eds.), *The child and his family: Impact of disease and death*. New York: Wiley, 1973.

Greene, P. The child with leukemia in the classroom. *American Journal of Nursing*, 1975, *75*, 86–87.

Grollman, E. A. (Ed.) *Explaining death to children*. Boston: Beacon Press, 1967.

Hansen, Y. *Development of the concept of death: Cognitive aspects*. Doctoral dissertation, California School of Professional Psychology. Ann Arbor, Michigan: University Microfilms, 1973. (73-19, 640)

Hartman, G. Hypnosis as an adjuvant in the treatment of childhood cancer. In J. J. Spinetta & P. Deasy-Spinetta (Eds.), *Living with childhood cancer*. St. Louis: Mosby, 1980.

Heffron, W. A., Bommelaere, K., & Masters, R. Group discussions with the parents of leukemic children. *Pediatrics*, 1973, *52*, 831–840.

Hostler, S. I. The development of the child's concept of death. In O. J. Z. Sahler (Ed.), *The child and death. St. Louis: Mosby, 1978*.

Howarth, R. The psychiatric care of children with life-threatening illnesses. In L. Burton (Ed.), *Care of the child facing death*. Boston, Mass.: Routledge and Kegan Paul, 1974.

Jackson, E. N. *Telling a child about death*. New York: Hawthorn Books, 1965.

Johnson, F. L., Rudolph, L., & Hartman, J. Helping the family cope with childhood cancer. *Psychosomatics*, 1979, *20*, 241, 251.

Kagen-Goodheart, L. Re-entry: Living with childhood cancer. *American Journal of Orthopsychiatry*, 1977, *47*, 651–658.

Kalnins, I. V., Churchill, M. P., & Terry, G. E. Concurrent stresses in families with a leukemic child. *Journal of Pediatric Psychology*, 1980, *5*, 81–92.

Kaplan, D., Grobstein, R., & Smith, A. Predicting the impact of severe illness in families. *Health and Social Work*, 1976, *1*, 72–81.

Kaplan, D. M., Smith, A., Grobstein, R., & Fishman, S. Family mediation of stress. *Social Work*, 1973, *18*, 60–69.

Katz, E. R., Kellerman, J., Rigler, D., Williams, K. O., & Siegle, S. E. School intervention with pediatric cancer patients. *Journal of Pediatric Psychology*, 1977, *2*, 72–76.

Kellerman, J. (Ed.) *Psychological aspects of cancer in children*. Springfield, Ill.: Thomas, 1980.

Kirten, C., & Liverman, M. Special educational needs of the child with cancer. *Journal of School Health*, 1977, *48*, 170–173.

Knapp, V., & Hansen, H. Helping the parents of children with leukemia. *Social Work*, 1973, *18*, 70–75.

Koocher, G. P. Childhood, death, and cognitive development. *Developmental Psychology*, 1973, *9*, 369–375.

Koocher, G. P. Pediatric cancer: Psychological problems and the high costs of helping. *Journal of Clinical Child Psychology*, 1980, *9*, 2–5.

Koocher, G. P., & O'Malley, J. E. (Eds.) *The Damocles syndrome: Psychosocial consequences of surviving childhood cancer*. New York: McGraw-Hill, 1980.

Koocher, G. P., & Sallan, S. E. Pediatric oncology. In P. R. Magrab (Ed.), *Psychological management of pediatric problems*. Vol. 1. *Early life conditions and chronic diseases*. Baltimore: University Park Press, 1978.

Lansky, S. B., Cairns, N. U., Hassanein, R., Wehr, J., & Lowman, J. T. Childhood cancer: Parental discord and divorce. *Pediatrics*, 1978, *62*, 184–188.

Lansky, S., Lowman, J. T., Vats, T., & Gyulay, J. School phobia in children with malignant neoplasms. *American Journal of Diseases in Children,* 1975, *129,* 42–46.

Lavigne, J. V., & Ryan, M. Psychological adjustment of siblings of children with chronic illness. *Pediatrics,* 1979, *63,* 616–627.

Lazarus, R. S. *Patterns of adjustment.* New York: McGraw-Hill, 1976.

Lazarus, R. S. The costs and benefits of denial. In J. J. Spinetta & P. Deasy-Spinetta (Eds.), *Living with childhood cancer.* St. Louis: Mosby, 1981.

Martinson, I. M. (Ed.) *Home care for the dying child: Professional and family perspectives.* New York: Appleton-Century-Crofts, 1976.

Nagy, M. The child's theories concerning death. *Journal of Genetic Psychology,* 1948, *73,* 3–27.

National Cancer Institute. *Coping with childhood cancer: A resource for the health professional.* Bethesda, Maryland: U.S. Department of Health and Human Services, 1979.

Plumb, M. M., & Holland, J. Cancer in adolescents: The symptom is the thing. In B. Schoenberg, A. C. Carr, A. H. Kutscher, D. Peretz, & J. Goldberg (Eds.), *Anticipatory grief.* New York: Columbia University Press, 1974.

Schulman, J. L., & Kupst, M. J. *The child with cancer: Clinical approaches to psychosocial care—Research in psychological aspects.* Springfield, Ill.: Thomas, 1980.

Slavin, L. S. Evolving psychosocial issues in the treatment of childhood cancer: A review. In G. P. Koocher & J. E. O'Malley (Eds.), *The Damocles syndrome: Psychosocial consequences of surviving childhood cancer.* New York: McGraw-Hill, 1980.

Sourkes, B. Facilitating family coping with childhood cancer. *Journal of Pediatric Psychology,* 1977, *2,* 65–67.

Sourkes, B. Siblings of the pediatric cancer patient. In J. Kellerman (Ed.), *Psychological aspects of childhood cancer.* Springfield, Ill.: Thomas, 1980.

Spinetta, J. J. The dying child's awareness of death: A review. *Psychological Bulletin,* 1974, *81,* 256–260.

Spinetta, J. J. Adjustment in children with cancer. *Journal of Pediatric Psychology,* 1977, *2,* 49–51.

Spinetta, J. J. Communication patterns in families dealing with life-threatening illness. In O. J. Z. Sahler (Ed.), *The child and death.* St. Louis: Mosby, 1978.

Spinetta, J. J. The sibling of the child with cancer: In J. J. Spinetta & P. Deasy-Spinetta (Eds.), *Living with childhood cancer.* St. Louis, Mosby, 1981.

Spinetta, J. J., & Deasy-Spinetta, P. Coping with childhood cancer: Professional and family communication patterns. In M. G. Eisenberg J. Falconer, & L. C. Sutkin (Eds.), *Communications in a health care setting.* Springfield, Ill.: Thomas, 1980. (a)

Spinetta, J. J., & Deasy-Spinetta, P. *Living with childhood cancer.* St. Louis: Mosby, 1981.

Spinetta, J. J., Deasy-Spinetta, P., Koenig, H. M., Lightsey, A. L., Schwartz, D. B., Hartman, G. A., & Kung, F. H. *Talking with children with a life-threatening illness: A handbook for health care professionals.* San Diego: Childhood Adaptation Project, San Diego State University, 1979.

Spinetta, J. J., & Maloney, L. J. Death anxiety in the out-patient leukemic child. *Pediatrics,* 1975, *65,* 1034–1037.

Spinetta, J. J., & Maloney, L. J. The child with cancer: Patterns of communication and denial. *Journal of Consulting and Clinical Psychology,* 1978, *48,* 1540–1541.

Spinetta, J. J., Rigler, D., & Karon, M. Anxiety in the dying child. *Pediatrics,* 1973, *52,* 841–845.

Spinetta, J. J., Rigler, D., & Karon, M. Personal space as a measure of the dying child's sense of isolation. *Journal of Consulting and Clinical Psychology,* 1974, *42,* 751–756.

Spinetta, J. J., Spinetta, P. D., Kung, F., & Schwartz, D. B. *Emotional aspects of childhood cancer and leukemia: A handbook for parents.* San Diego: Leukemia Society of America, 1976.

Spinetta, J. J., Swarner, J. A., & Sheposh, J. P. Effective parental coping following the death of a child from cancer. *Journal of Pediatric Psychology,* 1981, *6,* 251–263.

Stehbens, J. A., & Lascari, A. D. Psychological follow-up of families with childhood leukemia. *Journal of Clinical Psychology,* 1974, *30,* 394–397.

van Eys, J. (Ed.) *The truly cured child: The new challenge in pediatric cancer care.* Baltimore: University Park Press, 1977.

Waechter, E. H. Children's awareness of fatal illness. *American Journal of Nursing,* 1971, *7,* 1168–1172.

White, E., Elsom, B., & Prawat, R. Children's conceptions of death. *Child Development,* 1978, *49,* 307–310.

Zeltzer, L. The adolescent with cancer. In J. Kellerman (Ed.), *Psychological aspects of childhood cancer.* Springfield, Ill.: Thomas, 1980.

Zwartjes, W. J., & Zwartjes, G. School problems of children with cancer. In J. L. Schulman & M. J. Kupst (Eds.), *The child with cancer: Clinical approaches to psychosocial care—Research in psychological aspects.* Springfield, Ill,: Thomas, 1980.

# FACTORS TO BE CONSIDERED IN PSYCHOLOGICAL PREPARATION FOR SURGERY

Barbara G. Melamed, Rochelle L. Robbins and
Jesus Fernandez

## PSYCHOLOGICAL INFLUENCES IN HOSPITAL RECOVERY

The stress of hospitalization for a child includes fears of separation from the parents, the distress of unfamiliar surroundings, anxiety about painful procedures, the actual physical discomfort of surgery or recovery from illness, and loneliness precipitated by isolation from peers and the daily school routine. The estimates of behavioral disturbances resulting from the hospital experience range from 10 to 92% of all children hospitalized (Cassell, 1965; Chapman, Loeb, & Gibbons, 1956; Gellert, 1958; Goffman, Buckman, & Schade, 1957). Although some children suffer severe transient and long-term disturbances such as regress-

Advances in Developmental and Behavioral Pediatrics, vol. 3, pages 73–112
Copyright © 1982 by JAI Press Inc.
All rights of reproduction in any form reserved.
ISBN: 0-89232-223-3

ive behaviors, increased dependency, loss of toilet training, excessive fears, and sleep or eating disturbances, *not all* children are equally vulnerable to the negative effects of the hospital experience. It is necessary at this time to evaluate which factors enhance the emotional stress that can accompany hospitalization and to identify which children are at high risk for developing behavioral disturbances without psychological preparation for hospitalization.

In the past decade, there has been increased research demonstrating that psychological factors influence the course of illness and bodily response to stress (George, Scott, Turner, & Gregg, 1980; Melamed & Siegel, 1980). It is not surprising that this recognition has led to an increase in the use of psychological preparation in hospitals. A recent survey (Peterson & Ridley-Johnson, 1980) reported that over 70% of the hospitals providing pediatric care for nonchronic conditions use psychological preparation routinely with patients undergoing diagnostic or surgical procedures.

It is often assumed that *all* children can benefit to some extent by receiving support and information about what to expect. However, children's prehospital adjustment and personality characteristics may make them more or less prone to psychological consequences, due to the hospital experience. Some children may even benefit from the mastery of their fears and anxieties following a successful experience (Sipowicz & Vernon, 1965). Conversely, some youngsters may become more frightened or even overwhelmed by the presentation of hospital-relevant information if they are too young to understand it, if it is presented too far in advance, or if it is incompatible with their way of coping with stress (Melamed, Robbins, & Graves, 1981). Even adults have been shown to suffer negative consequences if the materials being presented are inconsistent with their coping styles or if they perceive themselves as inadequate in handling the threatening aspects of the medical procedure (Kendall, in press).

The goal of this review is to identify what preparation is appropriate for an individual child given the requirements for his or her behavior, parental support, the hospital environment and policies, and the child's own coping resources.

## EVALUATION OF TREATMENT EFFECTIVENESS

Many of the procedures being employed, such as puppet therapy, bibliotherapy, and film modeling have developed out of the practical experience of nursing and pediatric patient education specialists. Their aim is to inform the child about what will happen during the hospitalization. Decisions about how much information to give and at which time prior to surgery seem to be based upon the clinical experience of the staff with children of different ages. Hospital regimens also determine the availability of personnel and time for the implementation of such programs. There are few studies in the research literature derived from specific theoretical positions, instead, different treatment packages are compared with one another. This does not encourage sequential research and replications which would allow us to converge upon a network of findings that can guide selection of presurgery preparation.

There seems to be a general assumption that the goal of surgery preparation is to reduce anxiety. The thought of denying a child some form of preparation is often rejected as unethical. Yet, the theoretical and research literature makes several predictions regarding the adaptive function of anxiety in helping the patient to cope with the stressful event. Lazarus (1966) postulated that in the face of threat an individual experiences arousal and that the person's appraisal of the situation can motivate adaptive coping behaviors. Janis (1958) predicted that a moderate level of anxiety prior to surgery facilitated a more satisfactory postsurgical adjustment. The process by which this occurs is described as the ''work of worrying'' in which thoughts and fantasies about the outcome of surgery are elicited and dealt with. Johnson and Leventhal (1974) examined the influence of accurate expectations regarding sensory and procedural information on patients' cooperation with and recovery from surgery. Melamed and Siegel (1975) applied Bandura's (1969) social learning theory, which predicted that if individuals are exposed to a model of someone dealing with the fearful event in the absence of adverse consequences, their fear would be vicariously extinguished.

One of the difficulties in evaluating these theories is the poorly defined use of such terms as ''moderate arousal,'' ''vicarious extinction,'' ''coping mechanism,'' and ''anxiety.'' Thus, one goal of this chapter is to elaborate on the effective mechanism of change that may contribute to a particular child's successful experience with the hospitalization or medical experience. An organized schema will be presented based upon what we know about individual factors such as age, conceptual level of understanding, coping style preference, and previous experience, within the context of the type of preparatory procedures employed, the support of the nursing/medical staff, and the degree of parents' involvement. ''Success'' of the preparation will be defined by broad-based measurement of the child's subjective experience, autonomic arousal, cooperation with procedures, and physical recovery.

The practical questions which are asked by psychologists and other health care professionals about to prepare a child for stressful medical events include: (1) What does the child need to know in order to cooperate with the physician? How do we know if the child can understand and make use of the information being presented? (2) Given the child's previous experience, age, and/or level of anxiety, which of the preparatory treatment approaches would be the most useful? (3) Should preparation be given in advance of the hospitalization or at the time of the stressful procedure? (4) Should parents be included in the preparation of their child?

Most of the research literature has been organized into types of programs such as puppet therapy, modeling, cognitive control, systematic desensitization, familiarization, and stress-point nursing. Often, there are compound packages, making it difficult to parcel out the effective components of a given procedure.

The question of treatment efficacy must be readdressed in terms of the type of patient that we need to prepare rather than searching for a universal panacea. The psychologist can provide a useful service in helping to evaluate these questions. Ultimately, profiles of each patient's competencies and anxieties need to be developed so that treatment can be individualized. At this point, we have found it useful to reorganize the treatment literature, by evaluating the factors often controlled to minimize extratherapeutic effects. Thus, age, conceptual development, timing of preparation, and parental involvement become the focus of our schema. The importance of carefully assessing each child's psychological and physiological reactions to the stress of hospitalization becomes a significant aspect of deciding what preparation, if any, to administer and under what conditions. It is hoped that this approach will generate new hypotheses based on specific predictions regarding the interaction of these individual and contextual factors in order to optimize the efficiency and benefit of the preparatory procedures.

# AGE OF THE CHILD

## Cognitive Development

A general belief held by health professionals involved in the psychological preparation of hospitalized children is that younger children are more vulnerable to the hospital experience and in turn may need different types of preparation than older children. Few studies, however, have empirically investigated this notion. Most studies in the area have routinely ignored the effect of cognitive development when preparing children or when formulating preparatory packages for use in hospitals.

Because of earlier research in which we found that younger children were sensitized by receiving information in advance (Melamed, Meyer, Gee, & Soule, 1976), we have turned our attention to the issue of cognitive development and its role in preparatory packages. The study of Melamed, Robbins, Small, Fernandez, and Graves (1980) investigated children who were hospitalized at the Shands Teaching Hospital of the University of Florida. All children were seen the night before their scheduled surgery and shown a slide-tape presentation made specifically for children at Shands. By this time, many of the preoperative procedures, including blood tests and X-rays, had been completed. A wide range of physiological, cognitive, and behavioral measures were collected. A significant relationship was found between the age of the child and the amount of information retained from the film. Children age seven or younger averaged 64% correct responses to the information test, while children between the ages of 7 and 15 averaged 87% correct items.

Examination of developmental studies of normal children yields considerable support for our findings. Flavell (1977) has noted that, of course, children differ in cognitive abilities as a function of their age. Similarly, developmental studies of memory, a key consideration for any preparatory package, indicate that older children recall more items correctly than younger children (Belmont & Butterfield, 1969; Hagen, Jongeward, & Kail, 1975; Jablonski, 1974; Perlmutter & Myers, 1976). Researchers have noted that older individuals store, retain, and retrieve a larger number of memory inputs better and differently than do younger ones, simply because developmental advances in the content and structure of their semantic or conceptual systems render these inputs more familiar, meaningful, and otherwise more memorable for them (Flavell & Wellman, 1976).

Finally, there have been recent efforts to understand the development of children's concept of illness (Campbell, 1975; Peters, 1978; Simeonsson, Buckley, & Monson, 1979). It is widely known that children's awareness and knowledge of health, illness, and hospitalization increase as a child gets older (Neuhauser, Amsterdam, Hines, & Steward, 1978; Steward & Regalbuto, 1975). For example, there is extensive evidence that children of different ages have different conceptions of illness causality. Nagy (1951) asked 350 healthy children, ranging from 3 to 12 years of age, "What makes us ill?" The responses she obtained could be separated into four age-related stages of causal belief. Children under six based their cause-and-effect connections on the time contiguity between events. Thus, if a child becomes sick after drinking milk, the child concludes that milk makes him or her sick. Six and seven-year-olds made reference to an unspecified infection. Eight to 10-year-olds believed all illnesses were caused by micro-organisms, but did not differentiate between types. A full understanding of the fact that different organisms lead to different illnesses characterizes the responses of 11 and 12-year-olds. It has been clearly demonstrated in a number of studies that the conceptual ability of children regarding their understanding of what a doctor does increases with age (Blos, 1956; Steward & Regalbuto, 1975).

The application of Piaget's theory of stage development has clarified the relationship between age and conceptions of illness (Neuhauser, Amsterdam, Hines, & Steward, 1978; Simeonsson et al., 1979). The hypothesis that the concrete operational children would be able to give more accurate causal statements about healing inside the body was demonstrated by dividing the groups of children into their stage of cognitive development by a conservation task, and interviewing them about their concepts of illness.

Simeonsson, Buckley, and Monson (1979) used hospitalized children of three age groups (5, 7, and 9). A significant age progression was found to exist across several cognitive tasks with responses becoming more abstract. Children's conceptions of illness were also significantly related to performance in conservation, egocentrism, and physical causality measures. The children in this study were heterogeneous regarding illness, and the generalizability of these findings to nonchronically ill or healthy children must be explored since other research suggested that children with chronic illness have a lower level of cognitive development on Piagetian tasks than age-matched healthy controls, but an illness causality notion equal to that of peers (Myers-Vando, Steward, Folkins, & Hines, 1979).

The importance of these findings is highlighted by the belief that a person's acquired knowledge, or memory in the "wider sense," powerfully influences what that person stores and retrieves from storage, or memory in the "strict sense" (Piaget & Inhelder, 1973). In other words, if a child of seven is given preparatory material which indicates that illnesses are caused by viruses, this will be of little use, as the child's knowledge is limited to the belief that illness is the result of the contiguity of two events. However, if a child of 12 is given the same information, it is likely that he or she will be able to process the information and abstract the preparatory material embedded in it.

Taken collectively, these studies suggest that there is some theoretical and empirical support for the notion that younger children retain less of the preparatory information afforded them in many packages. Thus, there appears to be some support for the notion that younger children be prepared differently than older children. However, more empirical research is needed in this area in order to identify what types of preparatory information young children can process and how best to present information to the younger child.

## TIMING OF PREPARATION

The beneficial effect of psychological preparation has been clearly demonstrated in the research literature (Melamed, 1977; Melamed, Meyer, Gee, & Soule, 1976; Melamed & Siegel, 1975). However, there is some disagreement surrounding the selection of an optimal time of preparation. For example, data exist suggesting that some patients can be sensitized by advanced preparation (Melamed, Meyer, Gee, & Soule, 1976; Shipley, Butt, Horwitz, Farbry, 1978; Shipley, Butt, & Horwitz, 1979). Melamed, Meyer, Gee, and Soule (1976) found that a film which utilized a child narrating his feelings and fears about the hospital experience sensitized younger children (under 7 years) when they were prepared a week in advance of the hospitalization. These children had higher levels of palmar sweating upon admission and at preoperative and postoperative assessments than younger children who were shown the videotape at the time of admission. Ferguson (1979), with a different videotape, demonstrated a similar age effect. Children prepared at home by a visiting nurse were compared with those receiving film preparation during hospital admission. With a wide range of measures, it was found that the younger child (age 3 to 5) benefited from the videotape modeling exposure at the time of admission, whereas older children (age 6 to 7) did as well with simple verbal home preparation, given one week in advance.

These findings support earlier theoretical positions taken by investigators. For example, Mellish (1969) suggested that younger children, particularly very anxious ones, need only a few days of preparation since longer intervals could increase anticipatory anxiety. Newswanger (1974) used a two-day preparatory period to prepare mothers and their preschool children for hospitalization for tonsillectomy and adenoidectomy. Home visits were made to children and either various hospital procedures were demonstrated (experimental) or an unrelated story was read (control sample). Observational data were obtained in the hospital during critical medical procedures. Children who had received relevant preparation showed significantly more positive mastery behaviors and fewer behaviors classified as negative or passive than those children in the control group. However, there were no longer any group differences found at the two-week posthospital interview, during which a questionnaire was filled out by the parents to indicate if any behavioral problems had occurred. This study failed to assess the children's degree of understanding of the materials presented at the home visit, and it is difficult to interpret their in-hospital findings. Perhaps parental anxiety was reduced, leading to more appropriate preparation by the mother.

Wolfer and Visintainer (1975) conducted a similar study in which children were presented materials developed in their earlier hospital studies, 3 to 4 days prior to admission. One hundred and sixty-three children between 2 and 12 years of age were assigned to one of five groups: advanced preparatory materials; stress-point preparation in the hospital (no home preparation); home preparatory materials plus stress-point preparation; home preparation plus supportive care from a single nurse; and a routine care control condition.

The results from using the preparatory materials at home alone were as effective as preparation plus supportive care or stress-point preparation. The children receiving this preparation were rated as less upset and more cooperative during the blood test, venipuncture, and transport to the operating room. Parental ratings of satisfactory care and anxiety reduction were improved only for mothers in those conditions where home preparation was combined with stress-point preparation or consistent supporting nursing care in the hospital. In fact, data indicated that 20% of the parents did not use the home preparatory materials, either because they felt they already knew what to expect, or their children did not seem to need preparation. It was surprising that there were no differences due to an interaction of age with type of preparation, although younger children were rated as more upset than older children during the blood test, preoperative medication, and the time of first voiding. The authors reported a lack of differences between the groups as to the effects of previous experience in the hospital influencing the treatment results. Perhaps the statistical methods required for main treatment evaluation masked the results due to age.

In a second study, Visintainer and Wolfer (1975) hypothesized "that stress-point preparation would be the most effective stress-reducing condition followed by the single-session preparation, then the consistent supportive care condition, and finally, the control condition" (p. 190). Children in the stress-point preparation and single-session preparation conditions tended to have lower upset and higher cooperation and ease of fluid intake ratings than those in the supportive care and control groups. Children in stress-point preparation showed this improvement only on the preoperative medication upset and ease of fluid intake ratings. It would appear that the information given in both the stress-point preparation and single-session preparation was an important condition to the child's behavioral adjustment. In terms of posthospital adjustment, however, the single-session preparation was not significantly different from the supportive care condition, which in turn was not significantly different from the control condition. Parents in the stress-point preparation condition were less anxious, more adequately informed, and more satisfied with the care they received than parents in the other three conditions. Thus, the benefit of combining information with the opportunity of a supporting relationship with a nurse at particularly stressful points during the hospital experience was demonstrated.

Finally, in a recent study, Melamed, Robbins, Small, Fernandez, and Graves (1980) reported data which suggest that an individual's pattern of autonomic responding affected the individual's readiness to acquire information. In other words, a person's physiological state may determine the optimal time of preparation. The results are encouraging, as they support the theoretical position posited by Lacey and his associates. Lacey (1967) has proposed that patterns of autonomic responding in a given situation reflect the individual's readiness to receive information from the environment. Lacey and his colleagues (Libby, Lacey, & Lacey, 1973) have demonstrated that when the primary task of the situation is to attend to information, deceleration in heart rate, accompanied by other sympathetic activation such as palmar skin conductance increases are likely to occur. Similarly, when the primary task of the situation is to reject information, acceleration in heart rate will occur. The data from the study clearly support the theory. The higher the prefilm level of sweat gland activity, and the lower the heart rate, the greater the amount of information that was retained on a postpreparation questionnaire concerning the content of the slide-tape.

The above suggests that Lacey's (1967) theory of fractionation as it related to information processing can lead to testable predictions about who is likely to learn from preparatory information. Perhaps a patient can be calibrated on the degree of receptiveness he or she is likely to display when faced with noxious information by measuring the pattern of autonomic responsivity when the patient is confronted by a loud noxious tone, or anticipation of aversive stimulation. Then we can present the information in a manner, and at a time when it is most likely to be attended to. The need to assess what information is actually obtained is clear. Unfortunately, there are very few studies that have obtained such a measure. Interpretations of treatment effectiveness therefore rely on the inference that if the children exposed to preparatory information improved in behavior, and anxiety was reduced, it was something they learned from the treatment package.

# INDIVIDUAL COPING PREDISPOSITIONS

When faced with a threat, individuals may exhibit vigilance, denial, and a host of other coping behaviors. There are certain response styles which may influence whether or not a particular patient will be receptive to information given during psychological preparation. Research on hospital preparation with adults has suggested that different therapeutic effects are possible depending on the patient's coping style, given that the method of preparation is standardized across subjects (Kendall, in press).

The literature on coping or defensiveness in children is very sparse. Coping styles may be in early stages of development and thus unstable. Compounding this is the general unavailability of inventories by which to classify predisposing coping tendencies. Burstein and Meichenbaum (1979) did find less hospital toy/doll play in children rated as high in defensiveness. However, the relationship between this characteristic and postsurgery recovery is not significant. The defensiveness measure was a self-report questionnaire (Wallach & Kogan, 1965). This 27-item self-report measure gives a score of the degree of a child's denial of concern.

Knight, Atkins, Eagle, Evans, Finkelstein, Fukushima, Katz, and Weiner (1979) classified children as to their degree of defense effectiveness based on interview data and the Rorschach test. Types of defenses included: intellectualization, denial, intellectualization and isolation, denial and isolation, mixed, displacement, and projection. The degree of defense reserve was measured by the patient's capacity to mobilize defenses further in the face of increasingly threatening situations. All children were prepared by being told what procedures they would encounter during their hospital stay. During the discussion of needles, surgery, and other frightening procedures, the clinician would challenge their defenses to judge their defense reserve. It was found that a significant relationship existed between Rorschach anxiety rating and cortisol production rates. There was a relationship between defenses used and rated effectiveness of defenses. Two weeks prior to hospitalization for surgery, there was no relationship between cortisol production and effectiveness of defense. However, during the hospitalization, the cortisol production rates obtained the day before surgery were inversely related to defense effectiveness. Children who used certain types of defenses, such as intellectualization with or without isolation, mixed, and flexible defenses, seemed to cope more successfully than children who used denial, with or without isolation, displacement, or projection in a rigid defense structure. These findings have implications with regard to the way doctors and parents prepare children for their hospital experience. The authors suggest that "careful attention must be paid to the way a child copes with stimuli in his environment before he is prepared and hospitalized for surgery" (p. 48). While children who intellectualized wanted to hear every detail of the upcoming experience, the children who denied often covered their ears, trying to block out all the information. These latter children would probably do best with little information, whereas those who seek out information might do better with specific information.

Kendall and Williams (1981) found that using interview and self-report inventories in identifying adult patients as repressors or sensitizers, or as having an internal or external locus of control, helped determine prior coping preferences. They cite studies (Andrew, 1970; Cohen & Lazarus, 1973) in which identification of these patterns led to clear differences in the usefulness of preparatory information. Recent research on the effects of videotape preparation of adults for endoscopy found that when the data were re-analyzed according to the distinction between repression and sensitization, the patients viewing material were either sensitized or helped to cope. Repressors who saw one videotape model experiencing discomfort during the insertion of the endoscope became more anxious when this information interfered with their denial defense. However, on repeated showing of the videotape in patients who had already experienced this procedure, the information promoted more cooperation with the procedure and lower heart rate during insertion of an endoscope. On the other hand, patients who preferred to know what to expect showed a positive linear relationship between the number of exposures and cooperation with the procedure. The issue of whether or not the patient could really exercise any control over the procedure was also raised. Perhaps it may not be useful to provide sensory or procedural information in a situation where the patient cannot control, only endure a stressful procedure.

Coping styles in children are not well understood. In children, we are often unable to pinpoint whether they have obtained the information being presented. It is only recently that investigators (Melamed et al., 1980; Roberts, Wurtele, Boone, Ginther, & Elkins, 1981) have reported the necessity of obtaining a measure of the acquisition of the information.

In the modeling studies used to prepare children for surgery or dental treatment, physiological levels of arousal during and preceding the exposure have been related to whether the child benefited from the material presented. We found that one major advantage of a peer model over a demonstration of what would occur in the dental operatory, was that the children seemed to orient to the material more efficiently when a peer model was used. In the measure of information acquired, it was found that those children who had been shown the modeling film retained more information than those who viewed the same information without a model present. The examination of heart rate revealed acceleration accompanying exposure to familiarization (no model) condition, whereas there was deceleration of cardiac rate ("taking in") accompanying the modeling film.

In our current studies we are directly measuring this orienting component of heart rate prior to presenting hospital-relevant information. We have found that those children who acquire the most information from a slide-tape presentation were those who were "set" to attend. In other words, they showed heart rate activity at a low level, while simultaneously experiencing sympathetic activation of the palmar sweat glands. The self-reports of anxiety were inversely related to the acquisition of information. Those children who were most anxious obtained the least information from the preparation. A pilot study is now underway to evaluate children's self-reported defensiveness as it affects the processing of relevant hospital information versus irrelevant information. Thus, an individual's self-report of denial of concerns is predicted to relate to his or her set to attend to information regarding the impending event. It is plausible to hypothesize that the individual's prior experience in the situation influences the level of anticipatory anxiety that the patient brings to the present situation, which may directly affect his or her defensive style.

## PREVIOUS EXPERIENCE

If the main ingredient of psychological preparation is providing the patient with information about what to expect and how to behave in the stressful situation, then what the patient brings with him or her because of previous experience needs to be assessed. The nature of the previous experience affects the patient's expectations regarding his or her ability to cope, and information about the controllability or lack of controllability of the situation. Thus, just knowing that the patient has had prior experience does not clearly tell us what new preparation may be required. In fact, Wolfer and Visintainer (1975) have stressed the importance of accurate expectations about what the experience will be like. Others have found that sensory information is often more important than procedural information (Johnson, Kirchoff, & Endress, 1975). If the prior experience left the patient feeling competent about his or her ability to get through the experience, then one would predict that little new preparation would be required. Rather than needing a model, the patient has his or her own experience upon which to rely in facing the stress. Thus, in a situation which is not intensely frightening or prolonged, such as dental treatment, we might expect prior experience to decrease the patient's stress response. In fact, studies have shown (Melamed & Siegel, 1975; Siegel & Peterson, 1980; Venham, Bengston, & Cipes, 1975) that with subsequent treatment patients tend to confine their anxiety responses to the imminent injection and can deal with the restorative process. Melamed, Yurcheson, Fleece, Hutcheson, and Hawes (1978) investigated the effects of previous experience on the patient's tendency to benefit from videotape preparation. It was found that children with no previous experience were sensitized by exposure to the injection segment, unless they were shown a child coping with this procedure. On the other hand, older children who had already been through dental restorative treatment benefited equally well when presented only with a short demonstration of what would occur during the injection segment (no model) or a peer model coping with the entire restoration. Thus, they already had coped and had a prototype of how to get through the experience without further prompts. Siegel and Peterson (1980) showed that sensory and procedural information were equally effective in preparing preschool children for their first dental treatment. Subsequent sessions were handled without further preparation.

However, in a situation where patients have little actual control over the course of events (i.e., as in surgery or chemotherapy, or bone marrow aspirations), and if their previous experience has made them aware of the discomfort that they would experience, then preparation might be contraindicated. Re-exposure to the stimuli which were present at the time of the previous experience might sensitize them and reinvoke conditioned emotional responses that are aversive. This could lead to avoidance behavior and greater disruption than would be expected without preparation. Melamed and Siegel (1980) presented data pertinent to this sensitization effect. Children who had already had elective surgery and were about to undergo a second operation did not benefit from film modeling in comparison with an unrelated film. In fact, the physiological data would suggest that their sympathetic activation (palmar sweating) at the time of the preparation would lead to a rejection rather than a taking in of more information.

It is necessary prior to deciding whether to prepare a youngster who had already experienced a similar noxious event, to evaluate carefully whether he or she had been successful in the previous situation. In obtaining this information, the psychologist needs to know what coping strategies were effective and how the prior experience may have differed from what the patient now needs to undergo. In the situation where unsuccessful coping occurred, the learning situation must incorporate discrimination and reduction of interfering responses that the patient may have acquired. In addition, new coping skills need to be learned and rehearsed to the point that the patient feels he or she can get through this experience.

Longitudinal research would be a far more appropriate way to investigate the effects of repeated experience with stress than trying to piece together retrospectively what the previous experience involved. Thus, future investigations of stress management techniques need to be carried out on populations where chronic conditions (orthopedic, cancer treatments, etc.) require repeated medical stress.

## PARENT INVOLVEMENT

Hospital admission is not only stressful to the child but may also be quite anxiety-producing and disruptive to the life of the parent. The parent must often cope with his or her uncertainty about outcome, try to mitigate the child's fears, pains, and discomforts, juggle his or her own expectations, past experiences, and needs, as well as maintain his or her continuing familial, occupational, marital, and personal roles.

There are a variety of factors likely to influence the nature of the parental involvement. These include: parents' psychological state concerning illness and hospitalization (Mahaffy, 1965; Roskies, Bedard, Gauvreau-Guilbault, & Lafortune, 1975; Roskies, Mongeon, & Gagnon-Lefebvre, 1978; Skipper, Leonard, & Rhymes, 1968); their relationship with the child (Robertson, 1958, 1976); parents' coping strategies under stress; support available to the parent both from within the family and from the larger community (Skipper & Leonard, 1968; Visintainer & Wolfer, 1975); competing demands on the parent's time; and amount of supportive information available to the parent concerning the role that he or she may play concerning his or her child's hospitalization (Eckhardt & Prugh, 1978; Prugh, Staub, Sands, Kirschbaum, & Lenihan, 1953; Roskies, Mongeon, & Gagnon-Lefebvre, 1978).

It is a question of great concern to doctors and medical staff whether or not it is important to encourage parent participation or whether parental presence is more of a burden on the staff, and not likely to contribute to the welfare of the child. The degree of parental involvement may depend on a variety of factors, not the least of which is the policy, both implicit and explicit, of the hospital or clinic toward the involvement of the parent. Theoretically, one could posit a range of possible points on a continuum that express the degree of parental involvement in the child's hospitalization. The parent may be the agent who delivers and retrieves the child from the hospital. The parent may be the noninvolved visitor who arrives periodically and remains uninvolved with the ongoing treatment or care of the child. The parent may dutifully visit during the prescribed hours, entertain the child, but still remain separate from the care of the child. Or the parent may become an intricately involved member of the child-care team, becoming involved in and responsible for the nonmedical care of his or her own child.

There is a good deal of clinical literature that has focused on the child's relationship with his or her mother during the time of hospitalization. It appears that if a parent is uncomfortable and anxious about the child's welfare, the child will experience the parent's anxiety in his or her interaction with the parent. This will in turn increase the child's level of stress and anxiety. Escalona (1953) discussed how such feeling states may be communicated between mother and child on a nonverbal as well as verbal level. This may occur with children of all ages and may not be under the voluntary control of the mother. Escalona called this nonverbal communication ''contagion.''

Recent literature concerned with the examination of parental involvement in preparation of children for surgery and medical procedures is sparse indeed. As early as the mid-1950s, professionals had acknowledged that the parent-child relationship was a critical one to be maintained during the child's hospitalization. Subsequent literature has focused on the parental involvement in terms of the parent's ability to affect the child's response to hospitalization.

Vernon, Foley, Sipowicz, and Schulman (1965) presented a comprehensive review of articles and books concerning the psychological responses of children to hospitalization and illness. Of the over 200 references cited, Visintainer and Wolfer (1975) point out that "only six of the studies reviewed were some form of clinical experiment where preparation was given to children or their parents along with an attempt to determine if the preparatory communication had a positive outcome" (p. 188). A review of these pre-1965 studies provides six noncomparable investigations which yield tentative neutral-to-positive findings for the varied attempts to provide psychological preparation for children and their families.

The present reviewers have chosen seven generally well-controlled studies to examine the best and most recent research concerning parental involvement in preparation for children's hospitalization. Prugh et al. (1953) focused on the use of an experimental program of ward management with 100 two- to twelve-year-old children. They compared the effects of traditional ward practices (weekly two-hour parent visits, and limited encouragement of parental ward care of the child) with an experimental program that included daily visiting periods, a play program, early ambulation of patients, psychological preparation for, and support during, potentially emotionally traumatic diagnostic or treatment procedures, attempt at clearer definition and integration of parent's role in the care of the child, weekly ward conferences for staff that focused on the adjustment of each child. They reported that children who

> showed the most successful adjustment on the ward were those who seemed to have the most satisfying relationship with their parents, especially the mother, and whose parents accomplished the most balanced adaptation themselves to the experience of illness and hospitalization on the part of their child (pp. 81-82).

They tentatively concluded that the most diffusely supportive aspects of the experimental program were most prophylactic in effect. The Prugh et al. study contrasted the most limited form of parental involvement and staff support with a varied, nonspecific array of techniques designed to decrease child stress and parental distance from the child. This study set the stage for studies to identify more specifically techniques that might be employed to decrease the potentially traumatic effects from a pediatric hospitalization.

In a related series of well-controlled studies by Mahaffy (1965), Skipper, Leonard, and Rhymes (1968), Wolfer and Visintainer (1975) and Visintainer and Wolfer (1975) the effect of preparing the mothers of children having minor surgery was evaluated. This work bears on the emotional contagion hypothesis (Campbell, 1957; VanderVeer, 1949) which holds that a parent's emotional state may be transmitted to a young child, and the clinical observation that emotionally upset or uninformed parents often are unable to assist their children to cope with stress.

Mahaffy (1965) investigated the possibility of improving the hospital care of children by involving their parents. The author supported parental involvement by referring to the mother's unique understanding of her own child. He emphasized the importance of the mother herself feeling comfortable so that she can more adequately meet her own child's needs. He felt that most hospitals made the parents feel uncomfortable, because the parent's role in the child's care during hospitalization was not well specified. Peterson and Shigetomi (1981) compare a variety of preparation techniques for parents and children to test their hypothesis "that the use of a cognitive coping procedure would further improve previously used techniques" (p. 4). Parents were taught how to help their children. Sixty-six children, aged 2½ to 10½ (mean age 5½) and their parents were treated in small groups using minimal information preparation and one of the following procedures: control (minimal preparation only), self-coping, filmed modeling, or self-coping plus film modeling.

The results indicated that children receiving coping plus modeling techniques were more calm and cooperative during the blood test and presurgical injection than children receiving coping or modeling alone. Other measures indicated that the coping procedures were more effective than modeling-only procedures for both parents and children.

The authors matched groups for previous hospitalization, although none of the children had been hospitalized within the last year. The client population was white and middle class. It is not clear that the youngest children could perform the self-coping procedures. It was not specified what effect group viewing (by parents and children) of the Melamed film would have in relation to its previous effectiveness. Also, all groups received a hospital tour and party, making it difficult to interpret which ingredient was responsible for change.

Peterson and Shigetomi felt that consistency of their results suggested that "coping skills" may be a useful addition to a presurgical preparation program. With younger children especially, they felt that the parents could be actively involved in helping the child to employ the coping techniques.

Unfortunately, the follow-up of parents of children in this study at the end of one year (Peterson & Shigetomi, in press) revealed that few parents reported using any of this coping training once their child left the hospital. It was reported, however, by 60% of the original participants, that their children recalled more of the positive aspects of their hospital experience than negative aspects, such as the pain or preoperative injections. The results do not clearly support the contention that coping skills were a useful presurgical preparation in that only 30% of the mothers reported that they made use of this training.

Recent research data exist (Brown, 1979) that have demonstrated that a child's response to hospitalization varies with the child's relationship to the family at home, the mother-child interactions, and mother's anxiety. Through the use of personality tests, structured interviews, and direct observation of children 3 to 6 years old and their mothers during a short stay in the hospital, it was revealed that those children who have close proximity to their families were most likely to withdraw and show stress during their hospital experience. Mothers who are themselves anxious and highly accepting of hospital authorities tend to have children who are distressed and withdrawn.

The age of the child may influence his or her susceptibility to parents' communication of anxiety. Vardaro (1978) examined the anxiety of the parent prior to the hospitalization of the preschool child. She found that anxiety in the parent was correlated with anxiety in the child. She concluded that one method of decreasing the preschool child's anxiety prior to hospitalization is by assisting his or her mother in coping with anxiety. One method of preadmission teaching would be through the parent because of the ability of the mother to affect the child's emotional response. Vardaro's study was methodologically quite weak but did point out an important focus for intervention, namely the mother and her relationship to the child.

In summary, the care and preparation of each child needs to be individualized. What is proposed is the obtaining of a profile of an individual child so that the treatment approach selected is directed at creating a balanced approach, where an individual is provided with information appropriate to the child's age, predisposing coping style, and family support system. This means also that the child should be evaluated for psychological stress, behavioral disruptiveness, and self-reported apprehension. A review of the available preoperative preparation literature will emphasize the system (self-report, physiological, or behavioral) which is most often found to reflect the treatment effectiveness.

# BEHAVIORAL TREATMENT APPROACHES

*Systematic Desensitization*

Children and adults have been treated successfully by exposing them either in imagination or in real life to medical events and concerns. Fear of injections (Taylor, Ferguson, & Wermuth, 1979), dental treatment (Gale & Ayer, 1969), intervenous procedures, and hemodialysis phobias (Katz, 1974; Nimmer & Kapp, 1974) have been treated by desensitization. The basic procedure is to train the individual in a reponse antagonistic to anxiety, such as relaxation, and then gradually expose the patient to a fear hierarchy that reflects his or her degree of increasingly fearful situations. This requires a number concept so that ordering can be individualized, although hierarchies can often be standardized. The child must be cooperative in order to learn to relax effectively. Children under 7 years have not done as well with this technique and often emotive imagery (Lazarus & Abramovitz, 1962) can be substituted by having the child emit prideful or pleasant scenes to substitute for fear.

The use of systematic desensitization would be a primary choice where the child does show a visceral component of anxiety such as increased heart rate or sweating. In addition, for children who are so afraid as to exhibit avoidance responses (hiding, refusal to cooperate) which are likely to interfere with direct exposure, then imaginal graduated hierarchy approach is most likely to enable the patient to prepare for the stressful procedure. The adult literature showed greater long-term reduction of dental fears and more attitude changes in patients receiving systematic desensitization as compared with modeling (Shaw & Thoreson, 1974) or general coping and stress management training (Krop, Jackson, & Mealiea, 1976). Children have also been shown to benefit from being introduced to the dental setting via systematic desensitization. The specific component that promotes change is not clear. When Machen and Johnson (1974) compared film modeling and desensitization, both were found equally effective and better than a control group. Sawtell, Simon, and Simeonsson (1974) demonstrated that the dental assistant's having a friendly chat with the child outside of the dental operatory also reduced fear behaviors. Again, the results suggest that supportive treatment within the context of the relevant situation may be sufficient to reduce anxiety. Kleinknecht and Bernstein (1980) reported unexpected positive results with a placebo condition of merely providing the patient with a supportive dentist with no pretreatment. It is likely that the children who have little or no previous experience and do not show disruption would most likely benefit from support along with clear instructions at the time of a given procedure (Melamed et al., 1980).

## Modeling

The presence of a cooperative peer or older sibling has led to less disruption in younger children (Ghose, Giddon, Shiere, & Fogels, 1969) and has encouraged the adaptation of this technique within a modeling context. Modeling provides the observer with an exposure to aspects of the feared situation through the eyes of another child. The question of what modeling conveys beyond observation has been subjected to careful studies using children receiving injections during dental restorative work or preoperative procedures. When 4- to 8-year-old children (White & Davis, 1974) were exposed to the dental situation with no model, they were more cooperative during treatment. However, in terms of "hiding" and "refusal to receive treatment," patients were less likely to avoid the treatment after exposure to a model. Therefore, disruptive children probably benefit from having a prototype of cooperative behavior.

In a more explicit attempt to evaluate the effective component of modeling, Melamed, Yurcheson, Fleece, Hutcheson, and Hawes (1978) found that overall a peer modeling was superior to a demonstration (no model) preparatory videotape in reducing the disruptive behavior of children undergoing dental restorative procedures including novocain injection. They attempted to examine the reason for this. Follow-up work has related this to the autonomic reactivity of the children to the fearful segment during the videotape observation (Melamed, in press). The children viewing the peer model showed increased sympathetic activation, accompanied by cardiac deceleration which facilitated the intake of information from the videotape. Children watching the demonstration tape, on the other hand, showed sympathetic activation (palmar sweating) accompanied by cardiac acceleration. These children "rejected" the information being presented. In fact, they scored much lower on the test of information recalled than those children who had viewed a peer model. Thus, it does appear that an active ingredient in the modeling situation is learning how to behave by watching another child cope with stress. The opportunity for viewing the ingredients while simultaneously remaining in an appropriate psychological attitude for obtaining information is best achieved by watching a peer model. However, children who had previous experience benefited as much by being exposed to a short demonstration (no model) of the anesthetic injection as they did from a long version of a peer modeling film. They already knew what to expect and how to behave. On the other hand, children with no prior experience were sensitized by a short demonstration (no model) and showed a greater degree of disruptiveness than those given an unrelated control videotape.

The modeling approach has been found to facilitate cooperation with general anesthesia induction. Early work by Vernon (1973) suggested that film modeling did facilitate the cooperation of children during the anesthetic induction procedures. Unfortunately, the measure of anxiety was strictly a global rating of fear and an adequate control condition was lacking.

Peterson, Schultheis, Ridley-Johnson, Miller, & Tracy (in press) compared the effectiveness of a puppet model, a local film-modeling videotape accurate for procedures in the particular setting, *Ethan Has An Operation* (Melamed & Siegel, 1975), and a control group receiving minimal preparation from the nursing staff. The surgery procedure involved excisions of nonmalignant tumors in the gums or impacted teeth, and required general anesthetic and a hospital stay of less than 24 hours. The children were 2 to 11 years of age, with a mean age of 4.77. Ratings consisted of behavior checklists compiled by parents, nurses, and observers both before and after surgery. Results demonstrated a lack of difference among the three experimental groups, though each facilitated reduction of anxiety more than the informal preparations. Thus, there is little support for the hypothesis that the preparation must be providing information specific to the hospital experience; rather, exposure to medical situations seems to suffice. However, the research did not provide information about age differences.

In our laboratory, age and prior experience were found to influence the modeling effect. It was demonstrated that for children with no prior hospital experience, film modeling was more effective than routine in-hospital preparation (Melamed & Siegel, 1976). However, a further investigation (Melamed et al., 1976) revealed that age played an important role in determining the optimal time for preparation. Older children (7 years and above) benefited when preparation was presented a week in advance of hospitalization. They came in to admissions with lower physiological arousal, reported less anxiety, and had fewer behavior problems after discharge. On the other hand, the results on younger children (less than 7 years old) suggested that no advanced preparation should be undertaken and the film should be presented at the time of hospital admission. The effect of the film on younger children (under 7 years) viewing the model 6 to 9 days in advance of hospitalization appeared to be sensitization. They had higher levels of palmar sweating upon admission and at preoperative and postoperative assessments than younger children who were shown the videotape only at the time of admission.

Ferguson (1979) with a different videotape, demonstrated a similar age effect. Children prepared at home 5 to 7 days in advance by a visiting nurse were compared with those receiving film preparation during hospital admission. With a wide range of measures, it was found that the younger child (age 3 to 5) benefited from the videotape modeling exposure at the time of admission whereas older children (age 6 to 7 years) did as well with simple verbal home preparation. The need to consider the age of the child then relates to both the amount of arousal such exposure might generate, and the length of time over which they can deal with knowing what will happen.

The need to evaluate the effect of a child's prior hospital experience on the preparation via modeling was suggested by the fact that the children who had experience with hospitals already knew what to expect. Melamed and Siegel (1980) demonstrated that the hospital videotape during an admission for a second operation produced no additional benefit over the viewing of an unrelated film. The level of autonomic arousal, as measured by palmar sweat activity, was significantly higher prior to film exposure for the experienced than inexperienced children. This may reflect their having been sensitized by the exposure to staff and equipment on the prior hospitalization in a way that conditioned them to painful stimulation. Thus, at a second hospital admission, the autonomic component of orienting was not optimal for obtaining the information being presented.

In a recent study discussed briefly earlier in this chapter, which focused more on examining the children's readiness to process the information presented (Melamed et al., 1980), this was examined. We recorded the child's pulse rate and sweat activity (Palmar Sweat Index) prior to exposing them to a slide-tape preparation made specifically for children at Shands Teaching Hospital. Table 1 summarizes the patient characteristics. Each child was individually prepared the night before his or her scheduled surgery. By this time, many of the preoperative procedures, including blood tests and X-rays, had been completed.

The child was read the Hospital Fears Rating Scale so that his or her prefilm level of medical concerns could be obtained. An independent rater observed the frequency of verbal and nonverbal anxiety behavior during the assessment. Following the slide-tape, pulse rate measurement and palmar sweating were reassessed. An information acquistion test was completed.

The results are encouraging, as they support the theoretical position (Lacey, 1967) regarding the pattern of autonomic responding and the individual's readiness to acquire information. The correlations presented in Table 2 reveal the fractionation of the heart rate and sweat gland response that was previously found in children who observed the peer modeling version of the dental injection videotape. The higher the prefilm level of sweat gland activity, and the lower the heart rate, the greater the amount of information that was retained on a postpreparation questionnaire concerning the content of the slide-tape. It was revealing to examine the child's age and prefilm level of subjective anxiety as they influence information processing. In general, the younger the child, the less information was retained. In addition, those children who reported a high degree of medical concern had lower levels of sweat gland activity and remembered less information, whereas children with low medical concerns had higher sympathetic activity and retained more information. This discordance between self-report and level of sympathetic activation (palmar sweat activity) had been found to underlie the denial disposition in adult patients watching a distressful film (Opton & Lazarus, 1976). Perhaps the issue of coping style can be readdressed in terms of the individual's autonomic response characteristics that set him or her to receive information from the environment. Support for this notion comes from the results of Knight et al. (1979) in which children who used denial (held their ears) to block out information about their surgery showed higher cholesterol rates and coped more poorly with the experience than children who used intellectualization to master this situation. The stress reaction, as measured by its physiological counterparts, may mediate the child's information-processing capacities. Thus, for children emotionally and physiologically aroused, systematic desensitization,

*Table 1.*   Major Characteristics of Patient Population

| Age | Previous Experience | Type of Surgery | Sex | Race |
|---|---|---|---|---|
| 6 | No | Hydroureter | M | W |
| 7 | No | Cabitus Varus of left elbow | M | W |
| 7 | No | Aortic Stenosis | F | NW |
| 7 | Yes | Umbilical Hernia | F | NW |
| 7 | Yes | Hernia | M | NW |
| 9 | No | Femoral Anteversion | F | W |
| 10 | Yes | Tonsillectomy | M | W |
| 10 | Yes | Catheterization of aorta | M | W |
| 10 | No | Rectal Mass | M | NW |
| 10 | No | Urinary Tract | M | W |
| 10 | Yes | Hernia | M | W |
| 10 | Yes | Heart Valve Closure | M | NW |
| 11 | Yes | Renal Staghorn calculus | M | W |
| 15 | Yes | Congenital Scoliosis | F | W |
| 15 | Yes | Urinary Retention | M | W |

*Source:* Melamed et al., 1980.

*Table 2.* Intercorrelations between Measures of Autonomic Arousal, Self-Report of Hospital Fears, Age, and Percent of Information

| Measure | Correlation with Percent Information | Correlation with Hospital Fears |
|---|---|---|
| Prefilm Heart Rate | −.23 | .002 |
| Postfilm Heart Rate | −.31 | .09 |
| Prefilm Palmar Sweat Index | .52* | −.52* |
| Postfilm Palmar Sweat Index | .10 | −.26 |
| Age | .76** | −.32 |
| Hospital Fears Rating Scale | −.51* | −.32 |

*Notes:*
*$p < .07$.
**$p < .001$.
*Source:* Melamed et al., 1980.

or relaxation, or premedication must accompany or precede the dissemination of information.

## Behavioral Rehearsal

Behavioral rehearsal is a procedure which includes many aspects of modeling, but encourages the participant actually to try out new behaviors or coping techniques, either in imagination, through role-playing, or in real life. Thus, young children or those having no actual experience in a given situation could most likely benefit from this approach. Ayer (1973) used emotive imagery to improve three 10-year-old children's cooperation in "mouth opening" prior to injection of local anesthetic. Chertok and Bornstein (1979) used covert rehearsal to reduce dental fears in children 5 to 13 years of age. It was found that imagining someone else coping with or mastering their fears was equally effective as merely imagining the relevant stimuli associated with the dental operatory. However, the data were not analyzed in terms of previous experience, and it is possible that a differential effect could have been obtained with exposure to relevant stimuli sensitizing the inexperienced patient. In addition, age effects could be masking treatment differences. Anecdotal reports indicated that younger children were not able to follow the instruction as well as one might have expected. Therefore, it is likely that there was no real difference in what these children actually imagined and not surprising that the different cognitive instructions were equally effective.

Although cognitive instructions have been reported to help children reduce fears of the dark (Kanfer, Karoly, & Newman, 1975) and improve task performance (Kendall, 1977), there is as yet little evidence that it has helped children cope with hospitalization and surgery. Kendall, Williams, Pechacek, Graham,

Shisslak, and Herzoff (1979) demonstrated improved behavior of adult patients undergoing cardiac catherterization if they had received cognitive-behavioral coping training in addition to procedural information. Peterson and Shigetomi (1981) demonstrated a similar beneficial effect for hospitalized children who received self-instruction and guided practice (parent assisted) in relaxation, distraction, and comforting self-talk.

Kendall (in press) reminds the clinician to consider the compatibility between the parents' own coping preferences and the style of behavioral coping strategies selected. Thus, patients who tend to deny or repress their concerns may do better with little information and with procedures which force distraction or reinterpretation of pain, whereas those patients who have sought out information and are vigilant regarding what to expect might do better when provided with sensory information and cognitive coping strategies focused on controlling stress.

*Operant Reinforcement*

The studies reviewed suggest that parent support and the health professional's style of interacting influence the child's cooperation with medical procedures. Unfortunately, few studies have investigated the specific manner in which feedback in terms of positive or negative rewards or instructions influence the effectiveness of these procedures. In a study designed to parcel out the specific contribution of a supportive relationship, the role of information alone, or the combination of information and a supportive relationship was examined (Visintainer & Wolfer, 1975). Information given in either a single session or at various stress points was more important in reducing upset scores and improving cooperation in children ages 3 to 12 who were hospitalized for tonsillectomies than was consistent supportive care given by nurses.

Currently, we have investigated the effect of dentist-reinforcement style on the cooperativeness of children undergoing dental restorative treatments (Melamed, Bennett, Hill, & Ronk, 1980). Different styles of reinforcement are compared with neutral instructions (show-tell-do). Interestingly, it appeared that directive guidance was generally more effective than praise for cooperative behavior or punishment for inappropriate or disruptive behaviors. This was also found by Weinstein (1980). However, a closer examination of the data looking at the children's fear level and previous experience revealed differential effectiveness of reinforcement. Those youngsters who were least fearful and new to the dental operatory benefited most from direction or praise alone. On the other hand, children who have had previous experience or high fear self-reports behaved more cooperatively when they received information by having both the appropriate behavior rewarded and the inappropriate behavior punished. The child with previous experience who has learned to be disruptive needs discrimination training to learn what is acceptable and to unlearn the interfering responses. However, if a child who is low in fear and disruptiveness receives punishment in the form of criticism, he or she becomes more apprehensive and shows a greater likelihood of being disruptive in the future.

A self-report questionnaire of parental discipline techniques for helping their child cope with many fear-evoking situations predicted children's behavior during hospitalization. Zabin and Melamed (1980) found that mothers who reported that they predominantly used positive reinforcement, reassurance, and modeling to handle their children's fearful behaviors tended to have children who coped well with the hospital experience. Those who used punishment or force, or allowed their child to avoid a fearful situation, had children who reported more stress and coped less well with the hospital experience.

## DECISION MAKING

Practical recommendations regarding preparatory procedures follow from the literature reviewed. Although these are based on less than ideally obtained empirical findings, future studies to validate these recommendations will, it is hoped, promote a clearer understanding of the determinants and their interactions with different treatments.

A tabular presentation will allow the health care professional to make a more educated decision regarding preparation of a given child for medically stressful events. Table 3 provides this. To determine the effectiveness of the method selected, the clinician needs to provide some objective measures of adaptive functioning that tap the child's subjective anxiety, physiological stress, cooperative behavior, and recovery from the medical procedure.

Self-report measures of anxiety have been reviewed (Johnson & Melamed, 1979) and provide scales for trait and state anxiety. A new assessment device (Dearborn & Melamed, in press; Silverman & Melamed, in press) provided accurate and reliable information that related fear ratings to dimensions of arousal, dominance, and pleasure.

Rating scales have been specifically adapted for hospital stress (Ferguson, 1979; Melamed & Siegel, 1975) for use by staff. Peterson, Schultheis, Ridley-Johnson, Miller, and Tracy (in press) have used behavior checklists and parent and nurses' ratings to measure adjustment during the hospital stay. Cataldo, Bessman, Parker, Pearson, and Rogers (1979) have developed behavioral categories such as attention, engagement, and positive affect to measure pediatric patients' responses to intensive care units.

Physiological indices of stress can be measured by nonintrusive observations of flushing, sweating, heart rate, or nurse's records of blood pressure and body temperature. In addition, polygraph recordings during preparation are providing concurrent physiological measures as the child orients to materials being presented.

Although posthospital adjustment scales (Vernon et al., 1965) have been widely used, it is also important to assess more immediate aspects of recovery

Table 3. An Aid to Decision Making regarding Preparation of a Child for Medically Stressful Events

| Author(s) | Patient Characteristics | Types of Procedure | Types of Presentation | Measures | Results |
|---|---|---|---|---|---|
| 1) Burstein & Meichenbaum (1979) | $N = 20$ Age Range = 4.8–8.6 Sex = 10 males, 10 females previous exp. w/ hosp.* | Tonsillectomy Adenoidectomy Myringotomy | None | 1 wk. prior to surgery: Defensiveness questionnaire 1 wk, prior, day of, wk after surgery. 2-minute play observation periods 1 wk prior to surgery anxiety scale | Two classes of children can be identified, those who distinguish themselves in terms of their disposition to engage in the work of worrying, and those who were highly defensive. |
| 2) Ferguson (1979) | $N = 82$ Age Range = 3 and 7 Sex = 43 males, 39 females previous experience | Elective tonsillectomy alone or in combination with adenoidectomy (5–7 days in advance) | 1. Nonhospital-related film 2. Hospital-related peer modeling film 3. Preadmission visit by nurse at home and nonhospital-related film 4. Preadmission visit from nurse at home | Hospital fears rating scale Mood adjective checklist Electromyographic recording Observer rating scale of anxiety Posthospital behavior rating scale | A preadmission visit contributed to the lessening maternal anxiety during and after the child's hospitalization. A preadmission visit reduced negative posthospital behaviors in 6- and 7-year olds. Viewing a peer modeling film reduced children's hospital specific physiologic anxiety response at the preoperative measure particularly in 3–6 year olds. Viewing the film also reduced posthospital negative behavior. |
| 3) Johnson, Kirchoff & Endress (1975) | $N = 84$ Ages = 6–11 years $M = 8.4$ years 52 males, 32 females No prior cast removal within 3 months | Orthopedic cast removal (outpatient) | 1. Sensory information 2. Procedural information 3. Control group | Radical pulse rate Self-report of fear Observed distress score | Sensation message group showed less distress during cast removal than the no information control group and had no increase in pulse rate during the removal of the cast, whereas control and procedural information subjects had increased pulse rates. |

| | | | | | |
|---|---|---|---|---|---|
| 4) Knight, et al. (1979) | $N = 25$<br>Age Range = 7–11<br>Sex = 19 males, 6 females<br>Previous exp. w/ hospitalization = 18 | Hernia Repair = (10)<br>Cyst Removal = (4)<br>Removal of foreign body = (1)<br>Undescended testes = (2)<br>Cardiac catheterization = (4)<br>Circumcision = (2)<br>Pharyngeal flap repair = (2). | None | 2 wks. prior to hospitalization:<br>—extensive interview<br>—Rorschach<br>—urine sample<br>Day of admission:<br>—interview<br>—Rorschach<br>—urine sample<br>1 day postsurgery:<br>—interview<br>—ward behavior questionnaire | No relationship between defense effectiveness (as measured by Rorschach) and cortisol production rates in the out-patient department and an inverse relationship between cortisol production and defense effectiveness under the stress of hospitalization. Defense style was found to correlate with coping under stress. Four different types of reactions to hospitalization emerged. |
| 5) Mahaffy (1965) | $N = 43$<br>Age = 2–10<br>Sex = *<br>No previous hospital exp. | Tonsillectomy Adenoidectomy | 1. Routine nursing care<br>2. Supportive nursing care | Temperature measures<br>Blood pressure<br>Pulse rate<br>Incidence of vomiting<br>Incidence of crying<br>Ability to take fluids<br>Ability to void | Supportive nursing care made the hospitalization less anxiety provoking and reduced negative behaviors in both children and their mothers. |
| 6) Melamed, Meyer, Gee and Soule (1976) | $N = 48$<br>Age Range = 4–12<br>Sex = 25 males, 23 females<br>No previous hospital experience | Tonsillectomies<br>Hernia<br>Genital-Urinary Tract | Ethan has an Operation hospital film | Children's Manifest Anxiety Scale<br>Palmar sweat index<br>Hospital fears rating scale<br>Observer rating scale of anxiety<br>Parents questionnaire<br>The anxiety scale of the personality inventory for children | No main effect for time of preparation. Film modeling was found to reduce anxiety in children. Older children benefited from seeing the film one week in advance of the actual hospitalization. Younger children needed more immediate preparation. The effectiveness of the film in reducing anxiety was enhanced when the child observer was similar in age, sex and race to the child narrator in the film. |

(continued)

*Table 3. (Continued)*

| Author(s) | Patient Characteristics | Types of Procedure | Types of Presentation | Measures | Results |
|---|---|---|---|---|---|
| 7) Melamed and Siegel (1975) | N = 60<br>Age Range = 4–12<br>Sex = 37 males, 23 females<br>No previous hospital exp. | Hernia<br>Tonsillectomy<br>Urinary Genital Tract | Hospital film *Ethan has an Operation* viewed at admission. In-hospital preparation by staff. | Children's Manifest Anxiety Scale.<br>Human Figure Drawing.<br>Palmar Sweat Index.<br>Obs. Rat. Sc. of Anx.<br>Hospital fears rating scale.<br>Anxiety scale of the Personality Inventory for children. | State measures of anxiety revealed a significant reduction of preoperative and postoperative fear arousal in the experimental group as compared to an unrelated film to the control group. Parents reported a higher number of posthospital behavior problems in the children who had not seen the modeling film. |
| 8) Newswanger (1974) | Age = preschool | Tonsillectomy<br>Adenoidectomy | 2-day preadmission home visit<br>1. Hospital procedures demonstration<br>2. Unrelated story read. | Observations in hospital. | More mastery behavior and fewer negative or passive behaviors in children prepared with relevant information. No differences at 2-week posthospital interview. |
| 9) Peterson, Schultheis, & Ridley-Johnson (in press) | N = 44<br>Age Range = 2–11<br>Sex = *<br>previous exp.* | Removal of impacted teeth<br>Oral tumors | All children received informal preparation from a nurse in addition the following conditions existed:<br>1. a puppet model<br>2. a local videotape that presented information accurate to setting and | Child disposition measure<br>Parent self-report<br>Child rating scales<br>Behavior checklist<br>Child self-report | All experimental modeling conditions were more effective in reducing anxiety and distress than the informal preparation received by the control group. There were no consistent differences among the three modeling procedures. No sex differences were found. |

| | | | | | |
|---|---|---|---|---|---|
| | | | 3. a commercial film with a live child patient that presented information that was often inaccurate to setting and order. | | |
| 10) Peterson and Shigetomi (1981) | $N = 66$<br>Age Range = 2.5–10.5<br>Sex = 31 males, 35 females<br>No previous exp. with surgery<br>No hospitalization in previous year. | Elective tonsillectomy | —Information about hosp. delivered at a party<br>—*Ethan Has an Operation* plus inform.<br>—Coping procedures plus information plus *Ethan.*<br>—Coping procedures plus information. | Child disposition measure<br>Pulse rate; temperature<br>Fluid, food consumption latency to void.<br>Child observational rating scale.<br>Behavior checklist.<br>The Faces Scale Hospital Fear Survey | Children receiving coping plus modeling techniques were more calm and cooperative during the blood test than children receiving coping or modeling alone. Parents receiving coping procedures rated themselves as less anxious and more competent than those receiving other treatments. |
| 11) Prugh, Staub, Sands, Kirschbaum & Lenihan (1953) | $N = 100$<br>Age = 2–12<br>Sex = 48 males, 52 females<br>Previous hosp. experience = 41<br>None within 6 months | Infection, renal disease, cardiac disease, C.N.S. or emotional | Parent involvement 1-week visiting<br>Daily visits and parent participation in care | (In hosp., 3 weeks, 3 mos., 1 yr. follow-up)<br>Parent interview<br>Play therapy<br>Behavioral observations<br>Intellectual and developmental data | Children of parent-involved group were better adjusted. Preschool children most disturbed. Children who had good relationship with parents did better. Children with good adaptive functioning prehospital had fewer severe disturbances. |

*(continued)*

*Table 3.* (*Continued*)

| Author(s) | Patient Characteristics | Types of Procedure | Types of Presentation | Measures | Results |
|---|---|---|---|---|---|
| 12) Roberts, Wurtele, Boone, Ginther, & Elkins (in press) | N = 18<br>Age Range = 7-12 yrs.<br>Sex = 18 males, 18 females<br>Previous hospital experience* | Not applicable | A hospital slide and tape package<br>A nonhospital-related slide and tape package | Children's Manifest Anxiety Scale<br>Medical Fears Subscale-Fear Survey Schedule for Children<br>Hospital Fears Questionnaire<br>Information Test | In comparison to a group of control subjects who viewed a travelogue slide package, the subjects who viewed the Hospital Package reported significantly reduced fears on measures of anxiety related to medical situations. Further reductions were obtained two weeks after the package presentation. |
| 13) Vernon (1974) | N = 38<br>Age Range = 4-9 yrs.<br>(M=6)<br>Sex = 19 males, 19 females<br>Previous hospital experience* | Herniorraphy<br>Tonsillectomies<br>Other forms of elective minor surgery | Peer modeling film dealing with anesthesia induction. | Global Mood Scale<br>Projective Testing<br>Posthospital behavior questionnaire | Subjects exposed to the experimental film behaved as if they were less afraid of anesthesia induction than did controls. |
| 14) Visintainer and Wolfer (1975) | N = 84<br>Age range = 3-12<br>Sex = *<br>Previous hospital experience* | Elective tonsillectomies alone or in combination with adenoidectomies, myringotomies or PE tubes. | 1. Combination of systematic preparation, rehearsal, and supportive in-hospital care conducted prior to each stressful procedure. | Manifest Upset scale<br>Cooperation Scale<br>Recovery room medication requirement.<br>Ease of fluid intake.<br>Time to first voiding.<br>Posthospital Behavior Questionnaire.<br>Information Questionnaire.<br>Anxiety Questionnaire. | Children who received condition 1 showed significantly less upset and more cooperation. Their parents reported significantly greater satisfaction and less anxiety than did children or parents in the other groups. Younger children were significantly more upset and less cooperative than older children. |

| | | | | |
|---|---|---|---|---|
| 15) Wolfer and Visintainer (1979) | $N = 163$<br>Age Range = 3–12<br>Sex = *<br>Previous hospital experience*<br>No hospitalization within last year | Elective tonsillectomies and adenoidectomies | 2. Single-session preparation conducted after admission.<br>3. Consistent supportive care given prior to each stressful procedure.<br>5 groups (1 wk. in advance):<br>1. Home preparation; routine care in hospital.<br>2. Stress-point preparation in hospital.<br>3. Home preparation; stress-point preparation in, hospital.<br>4. Home preparation; supportive nursing care.<br>5. Routine nursing care. | Satisfaction Questionnaire.<br>Manifest Anxiety Scale.<br>Cooperation Scale.<br>Time of first voiding.<br>Posthospital Behavior Questionnaire.<br>Satisfaction with Information Questionnaire.<br>Anxiety Questionnaire.<br>Satisfaction Questionnaire. | Children who used home-preparatory materials alone or in combination with in hospital preparation showed better adjustment than children in the control group. In-hospital preparation was effective either alone or in combination. Parents reported more satisfaction with hospital care and less anxiety when prepared in the hospital as opposed to home preparation alone. |

Note:
*No information provided.

from surgery such as time to first solid foods, amount of nausea or vomiting, and sleeping behavior. Even the rate of recovery from swelling and blood loss have been found to be affected by psychological and individual factors with physical trauma partialed out (George et al., 1980).

The critical review of the literature summarized in Table 3 includes those studies which employed at least two different systems of measurement in evaluating their results. Each of these studies included a control condition to provide a comparison with standard hospital practices in effect or the presentation of nonrelevant material.

Table 4 must be used with knowledge from the studies from which it was

*Table 4.*  Guide to Use of Different Types of Preparation

| Method of Preparation | When Used | Probable Effective Component |
|---|---|---|
| Systematic Desensitization | To reduce physiological arousal: children over 7 years; when avoidance behaviors likely | Pairing of anxiety antagonistic response (relaxation or imagery) with graduated hierarchy of fearful situations |
| Modeling | No previous experience at time of hospital admission. Children 3–6 years. | Provides vicarious exposure; shows cooperative peer |
| Information Alone | Previous experience controllable situation. Children over 7 years | Reinstate coping mechanisms already available |
| Behavior Rehearsal (including cognitive self-talk, distraction, guided relaxation) | Previous experience, especially when inappropriate responses; no previous experience | Practice in positive coping. Provides increased self-competence |
| Operant Reinforcement | No previous experience | Shaping cooperation in neutral context or praise of appropriate behavior. |
|  | Previous experience | Contingent feedback; praise for cooperation; punishment for disruptiveness; discrimination training |
| Parental Involvement | Children under 7 years; low parental anxiety; daily visit; participation in hospital care to teach coping skills | Supportive relationships; model for low anxiety; Prototype of coping behavior |
| No Preparation | In advance for young children (3–6 years) High anxious or defensive children; noxious stress which allows no control or escape; previously experiences youngsters with good coping mechanisms, particularly over 7 years of age | Avoid sensitization

Information already available |

devised. In most cases the variables defined interact with treatment, either singly or jointly. Thus, it is necessary at this point to elaborate on the decisions by recommending specific predictions that need to be validated in future research. Numbers in parenthesis indicate which studies (Table 3) are related to the prediction.

*Age*

a. Younger children (under 7 years of age) show greater adjustment to hospitalization when they are prepared at the time of admission rather than a few days in advance, regardless of type of preparation (2, 6, 11).

b. Younger children should benefit more from coping and modeling than through information presented in demonstration, particularly if they have no experience in the stressful procedure (2, 6, 8, 10, 12, 13; Melamed et al., 1978).

c. The more congruent the children's level of illness conception with the model presented, the greater the information obtained (Nagy et al., 1951).

d. The older the child, the more information obtained due to the older child's greater ability to abstract, synthesize, and recall material presented (2, 6; Melamed et al., 1980).

e. Preschool children, 3 to 6 years of age, are most likely to show the adverse reactions to parental separation. Thus, children at this age with good relationships with their mothers will be most withdrawn and distressed during the hospital experience. Parental anxiety affects the anxiety of their children, with younger children particularly prone to this distress. Parental involvement during hospitalization should be encouraged (2, 5, 8, 10, 11, 14, 15).

f. Children most susceptible to adverse effects of hospitalization are below the age of four, have good relationships with their parents, have poor adaptive defense mechanisms prior to hospitalization, tend to show regressive behaviors, and use denial excessively (4, 11; Brown, 1979).

*Previous Experience*

a. If the stressful situation is controllable to some extent, then those children without prior experience benefit from psychological preparation (modeling) at the time of the impending event (2, 6, 7, 8, 9, 10, 14).

b. If the situation cannot really be controlled, then children without prior experience should be taught to use distraction techniques and avoid focusing on sensory information related to pain. Reinterpretation of pain as a signal that the procedure is almost over, or in terms of pleasant consequences after surgery may be helpful, particularly if the child's prehospital adaptive mechanisms are good (1, 4, 10).

c.  Children without prior experience benefit from seeing a peer coping with a similar experience, more than from simply receiving information regarding what will occur (2, 9, 10; Melamed, Yurcheson, Hutcheson, Fleece, & Hawes, 1978).
d.  Children with prior experience do not benefit as much from modeling or procedural information as they do from behavioral rehearsal or coping instructions and practice.
e.  Children with prior experience in a situation that was handled adequately benefit from mere information about the impending event, which may activate previous coping strategies (Melamed et al., 1978).
f.  Children with prior experience in a situation where the stress is not easily controlled should not be prepared prior to the impending event. They may be too highly aroused autonomically to obtain information from the preparation, and may be sensitized through reinvoking the aversive emotional reaction (Siegel, 1980; Melamed et al., 1980).

## Anxiety Level and Prehospital Coping Style

It is difficult to generalize about anxiety since the level of self-reported fear may not correlate, or may correlate inversely with the physiological arousal or tendency to show avoidance behaviors. Therefore predictions from various theories need to be tested by multidimensional approaches where interrelationships can be examined.

a.  Moderate levels of arousal facilitate the process of information acquisition (1, 2, 4, 6, 7; Melamed, in press).
b.  Levels of increased sweat activity simultaneous with lowered heart rate suggest enhanced attention to information that results in the taking in of material presented (Melamed, 1980).
c.  Low reported anxiety will be accompanied by a lack of use of coping skills. High cortisol production will be present where defensiveness is inadequate (2,4).
d.  High defensiveness (high anxiety) will lead to avoidance of hospital-relevant play. Information presented to children who report high anxiety or high levels of heart rate will not be easily retained. Thus, no information, or information in advance of hospitalization would be recommended (1, 4; Melamed, 1980).
e.  Children preferring avoidant (denial) styles of coping would do best with little or no psychological preparation, whereas those who use intellectualization or seeking of information should be presented with coping strategies prior to hospital experience (untested).
f.  Presentation of peer models will promote identification and increase attention over a demonstration (no model) (2, 7, 9, 10; Melamed et al., 1978).

## Time of Preparation

a.   In general, studies have failed to manipulate this as a primary independent variable. Melamed et al. (1976) found no overall advantage of modeling preparation 6 to 9 days in advance for children over 7 years of age, although they were less anxious and more cooperative at the admission procedure. However, children below the age of 7 become sensitized by preparation a week in advance and showed elevated levels of arousal (sweat activity) throughout the hospital experience. Children over 7 years of age benefited from home preparation (5 to 7 days prior to admission) as much as from a videotape model in the hospital (2).

b.   Stress-point preparation by nursing staff was more beneficial than either single session preparation or supportive therapy (14; Visintainer & Wolfer, 1975).

c.   Physiological set to receive information may be more important than any arbitrary time selected to prepare children (Melamed et al., 1980).

## Parent Involvement

a.   Preparation which focuses on reducing parents' anxiety concerning their child's hospitalization will reduce the child's anxiety (2, 5, 8, 10, 11, 14, 15).

b.   Parents who are given coping instructions to guide their child's hospital experience are less anxious and report feeling more competent than parents who are uninvolved. Their children were rated as less anxious during the blood test (10).

c.   Parents who were encouraged to visit their child daily and taught to be actively involved in the hospital care had children with fewer behavior problems during and following hospitalization (10, 11).

d.   Highly anxious mothers had children who were more withdrawn and less mobile during their hospital experience, especially those under four years of age (11; Brown, 1979).

e.   Parents who tend to use modeling and reassurance rather than punishment or force or reinforcement of dependency have children who cope better with the hospital experience (10; Zabin & Melamed, 1980).

# SUMMARY AND CONCLUSIONS

This chapter has critically reviewed the literature on hospital preparation for children in order to identify which factors need to be considered before deciding what preparation would be most useful. The notion that every child could benefit from psychological preparation was rejected given the evidence that many children get through the experience with few adverse side effects and that occasionally a child can be sensitized by the presentation of information. Behavioral treatment approaches were recommended after the basic considerations of age, conceptual development, previous experience, and coping styles were discussed in formulating what different types of preparation might be required. Decision making regarding optimal time and type of preparation, given the degree of parental involvement and the hospital setting in which the intervention would occur, was approached on the basis of the current literature review. Important predictions regarding the interaction between patient variables and treatment ingredients were presented for future research consideration.

The review of the literature provided much support for the fact that psychological preparation influences children's ability to cooperate with medical procedures. The rate of recovery from surgery as reflected by medical indices such as time of first voiding, eating of solids, nausea, vomiting, sleep disturbances, and actual physical recovery, are influenced by patients' expectancies, ability to cope, and parental support during the hospital experience. Children's adverse psychological reactions, including disruptive behavior, regression, or increased anxiety, may be reduced by providing the child with information in advance of the actual experience.

The major shortcoming of the research literature is its failure to provide specific guidance for selection of a particular preparation which takes into account the individual's current level of functioning. This has resulted from the fact that most studies compare compound treatment packages against one another without looking at the effects of psychological preparation as it varies with the nature of the specific situation as well as the personality of the patient. Instead, standardized approaches with unselected children are employed.

The identification of children at high risk for emotional disturbances would allow attention to be focused on those in most need of psychological preparation. The studies reviewed indicate that children under the age of seven, who have no previous experience in the medical procedures, and who have highly anxious but involved parents, are most susceptible to the adverse effects of the hospital experience. Preparation too far in advance of hospitalization, particularly for those who tend to be highly anxious and use denial to cope with stress, may be contraindicated. Instead, preparation needs to be geared to the child's level of functioning, both psychological and intellectual.

Measures are available which provide the clinician with information regarding the anxiety level of the child. Given the individual differences in the expression of anxiety, a multidimensional approach is recommended. The self-reported apprehensiveness of the child can be assessed in interviews, through response to questions regarding their medical concerns, or through fantasy play with hospital-relevant toys. The behavioral observations that are most critical include the child's ability to cooperate with the medical procedures. Therefore, the child's reaction to various presurgery routines, such as the blood test, X-rays, or urine testing can be used to evaluate the efficacy of the preparation. In addition, the physiological arousal of the patient, particularly at the time the information is being presented, can be used to predict if the information will be acquired.

Parental anxiety has been shown to affect the child's adjustment during hospitalization. Therefore, questionnaires regarding the parents' concern about the forthcoming operation would be most useful in identifying the families who would benefit the most from psychological preparation.

The treatment recommendations made are tentative in that the predictions that they are based on need to have a better empirical base. Instead of comparing one treatment package with another to demonstrate that something works better than nothing, we need to identify what we feel are the active therapeutic ingredients. There is much overlap between systematic desensitization, modeling, and behavior rehearsal, in that they all provide information to the patient about what will occur. It is not surprising then that many outcome studies report that they are equally effective in reducing anxiety. One must parcel out the common ingredients, such as supportive relationships, and information, and examine their separate and then combined results. In modeling, for example, are we teaching a coping strategy or merely presenting information? If relaxation is included, how would this differ from systematic desensitization? Is exposure alone sufficient from some children in order to elicit their use of mastery coping mechanisms?

The selection of appropriate control groups is very important. Are surgeries comparable in terms of amount of stress, days in the hospital, chronicity, or recovery period? Age interactions with types of treatments might lead to better predictions than trying to control by matching samples on this variable. Previous experience as it affects the amount of information obtained or the type of coping strategies already available should likewise be studied as an independent variable.

The selection of treatment should be based on the individual child's needs. Psychological preparation must be geared to the child's intellectual level of understanding and be consistent with the child's coping styles, understanding of illness, and previous knowledge of medical procedures. There are developmental influences on the child's ability to cope with hospitalization. The age of the child is a highly predictive variable regarding when and how he or she should be prepared. There is a definite need for longitudinal studies which would allow us to understand the changes in children over time. The effects of hospitalization are often delayed; thus longer follow-up periods are required.

The need for further psychological outcome studies designed to answer questions such as does conjoint preparation with the family improve adjustment, and how does mothers' anxiety affect children's behavior, is paramount before hospital policies such as rooming-in or open visiting can be promoted.

We have made much progress in the past decade. Statistics reveal that over 70% of nonchronic care pediatric hospitals provide some type of preparation. Thus, the research arena is set. The data derived from studying behavioral methods of reducing fear in this setting will provide information that is relevant to many other situations in which an individual must cope with life stress. It is an excellent place for developmental psychologists to apply their theories about the ability of children to cope as they change over time and develop greater cognitive control. It is an ideal problem area in which to bridge the gap between medicine and psychology. The mutual contributions of professionals from the different specialties promote the most holistic, and probably most beneficial approach. The next decade will provide us with specific answers to the questions about how to individualize treatment in an efficient manner so that the appropriate people get the most advantageous preparation.

# REFERENCES

Andrew, J. M. Recovery from surgery, with and without preparatory instruction, for three coping styles. *Journal of Personality and Social Psychology*, 1970, *15*, 223-226.

Ayer, W. A. Use of visual imagery in needle phobic children. *Journal of Dentistry for Children*, 1973, *40*, 125-127.

Bandura, A. *Principles of behavior modification*. New York: Holt, Rinehart and Winston, 1969.

Belmont, J. M., & Butterfield, E. C. The relation of short-term memory to development and intelligence. In L. P. Lipsitt & H. W. Reese (Eds.), *Advances in child development and behavior*. Vol. 4. New York: Academic Press, 1969.

Blos, P. *An investigation of the healthy child's understanding of the cause of illness*. Unpublished Ph.D. thesis, Yale University, School of Medicine, 1956.

Brown, B. Beyond separation. In D. Hall & M. Stacey (Eds.), *Beyond separation*. London: Roubedge and Kegan Paul, 1979.

Burstein, S., & Meichenbaum, D. The work of worrying in children undergoing surgery. *Journal of Abnormal Child Psychology*, 1979, *7*, 121-132.

Campbell, E. *The effects of mothers' anxiety on infants' behavior*. Unpublished doctoral dissertation, Yale University, 1957.

Campbell, J. D. Illness is a point of view: The development of children's concepts of illness. *Child Development*, 1975, *46*, 92-100.

Cassell, S. Effect of brief puppet therapy upon the emotional responses of children undergoing cardiac catheterization. *Journal of Consulting Psychology*, 1965, *29*, 1-8.

Cataldo, M. F., Bessman, C. A., Parker, L. H., Pearson, J. E. R., & Rogers, M. C. Behavioral assessment for pediatric intensive care units. *Journal of Applied Behavior Analysis*, 1979, *12*, 83-97.

Chapman, A. H., Loeb, D. G., & Gibbons, M. J. Psychiatric aspects of hospitalizing of children. *Archives of Pediatrics*, 1956, *73*, 77-88.

Chertok, S. L., & Bronstein, P. H. Covert modeling treatment of children's dental fears. *Child Behavior Therapy*, 1979, *1*, 249-255.

Cohen, F., & Lazarus, R. S. Active coping processes, coping dispositions, and recovery from surgery. *Psychosomatic Medicine*, 1973, *35*, 375-389.

Dearborn, J. M., & Melamed, B. G. *Lang's self-assessment mannequin as a measure of emotion*. Unpublished manuscript, University of Florida, 1981.

Eckhardt, L. O., & Prugh, D. G. Preparing children psychologically for painful medical and surgical procedures. In E. Gelbert (Ed.), *Psychosocial aspects of pediatric care*. New York: Grune & Stratton, 1978.

Escalona, S. Emotional development in the first year of life. In M. J. Senn (Ed.), *Problems of infancy and childhood*. New Jersey: Foundation Press, 1953.

Ferguson, B. F. Preparing young children for hospitalization: A comparison of two methods. *Pediatrics*, 1979, *64*, 656-664.

Flavell, J. H., & Wellman, H. M. Metamemory. In R. V. Karil & J. W. Hagen (Eds.), *Memory in cognitive development*. Hillsdale, N.J.: Lawrence Erlbaum, 1976.

Flavell, J. H. *Cognitive development*. Englewood Cliffs, N.J.: Prentice-Hall, 1977.

Gale, E. N., & Ayer, W. A. Treatment of dental phobias. *Journal of the American Dental Association*, 1969, *78*, 1304-1307.

George, J. M., Scott, D. S., Turner, S. P., & Gregg, J. M. The effects of psychological factors and physical trauma on recovery from oral surgery. *Journal of Behavioral Medicine*, 1980, *3*, 291-310.

Gellert, E. Reducing the emotional stress of hospitalization for children. *American Journal of Occupational Therapy*, 1958, *12*, 125-129.

Ghose, L. J., Giddon, D. G., Shiere, F. R., & Fogels, H. R. Evaluation of sibling support. *Journal of Dentistry for Children*, 1969, *36*, 35-49.

Goffman, H., Buckman, N., & Schade, G. The child's emotional response to hospitalization. *American Journal of Diseases of Children*, 1957, *93*, 157-164.

Hagen, J. W., Jongeward, R. H., Jr., & Kail, R. V., Jr. Cognitive perspectives on the development of memory. In H. Reese (Ed.), *Advances in child development and behavior*. Vol. 10. New York: Academic Press, 1975.

Jablonski, E. M. Free recall in children. *Psychological Bulletin*, 1974, *81*, 522-539.

Janis, I. L. *Psychological stress*. New York: Wiley, 1958.

Johnson, J. E., Kirchoff, K. T., & Endress, M. P. Altering children's distress behavior during orthopedic cast removal. *Nursing Research*, 1975, *24*, 404-410.

Johnson, J. E., & Leventhal, H. Effects of accurate expectations and behavioral instructions on reactions during a noxious medical examination. *Journal of Personality and Social Psychology*, 1974, *29*, 710-718.

Johnson, S. B., & Melamed, B. G. The assessment and treatment of children's fears. In B. Lacey & A. Kazdin (Eds.), *Advances in clinical child psychology*. Vol. 2. New York: Plenum, 1979.

Katz, R. C. Single session recovery from a hemodialysis phobia: A case study. *Journal of Behavior Therapy and Experimental Psychiatry*, 1974, *2*, 205-206.

Kanfer, F. H., Karoly, P., & Newman, A. Reduction of children's fear of the dark by competence-related and situational threat-related verbal cues. *Journal of Consulting and Clinical Psychology*, 1975, *43*, 251-258.

Kendall, P. C. On the efficacious use of verbal self-instructional procedures of children. *Cognitive Therapy and Research*, 1977, *1*, 331-341.

Kendall, P. C. Stressful medical procedures: Cognitive-behavioral strategies for stress management and prevention. In D. Meichenbaum & M. Jaremko (Eds.), *Stress management and prevention: A cognitive-behavioral approach*. New York: Plenum, in press.

Kendall, P. C., & Williams, C. L. Preparing patients for stressful medical procedures. In T. J. Coates (Ed.), *Behavioral medicine: A practical handbook*. Champaign-Urbana, Illinois: Research Press, 1981.

Kendall, P. C., Williams, L., Pechacek, T. F., Graham, L. E., Shisslak, C., & Herzoff, N. Cognitive-behavioral and patient education interventions in cardiac catheterization procedures: The Palo Alto medical psychology project. *Journal of Consulting and Clinical Psychology*, 1979, *47*, 49-58.

Kleinknecht, R., & Bernstein, D. Short-term treatment of dental avoidance. *Journal of Behavior Therapy and Experimental Psychiatry*, in press.

Knight, R. B., Atkins, A., Eagle, C. J., Evans, N., Finkelstein, J. W., Fukushima, D., Katz, J., & Weiner, H. Psychological stress, ego defenses, and cortisol production in children hospitalized for elective surgery. *Psychosomatic Medicine*, 1979, *41*, 40-49.

Krop, H., Jackson, E., & Mealiea, W. *Effects of systematic desensitization and stress management training in reducing dental phobia*. Paper presented at the American Psychological Association, Montreal, 1980.

Lacey, J. I. Somatic response patterning and stress: Some revisions of activation theory. In M. H. Appley & R. Trumball (Eds.), *Psychological stress: Issues in research*. New York: Appleton-Century-Crofts, 1967.

Lazarus, A., & Abramovitz, A. The use of "emotive imagery" in the treatment of children's phobias. *Journal of Mental Science*, 1962, *108*, 191–195.

Lazarus, R. S. Some principles of psychological stress and their relation to dentistry. *Journal of Dental Research*, 1966, *45*, 1620–1626.

Libby, W. L., Lacey, B. C., & Lacey, J. I. Pupillary and cardiac activity during visual attention. *Psychophysiology*, 1973, *10*, 270–294.

Machen, J. B., & Johnson, R. Desensitization, model learning, and the dental behavior of children. *Journal of Dental Research*, 1974, *53*, 83–87.

Mahaffy, P. R., Jr. The effects of hospitalization on children admitted for tonsillectomy and adenoidectomy. *Nursing Research*, 1965, *14*, 12–19.

Melamed, B. G. Psychological preparation for hospitalization. In S. Rachman (Ed.), *Contributions to medical psychology*. London: Pergamon Press, 1977.

Melamed, B. G. Reduction of medical fears: An information processing analysis. In J. Boulougouris (Ed.), *Learning theories in psychiatry*. New York: Wiley, in press.

Melamed, B. G., Bennett, C., Hill, C., & Ronk, S. Strategies for patient management in pediatric dentistry. In B. Ingersoll & W. McKutcheon (Eds.), *Proceedings of the Second National Conference on Behavioral Dentistry. Clinical Research in Behavioral Dentistry*. Morgantown, West Virginia: University of West Virginia Press, 1980.

Melamed, B. G., Meyer, R., Gee, C., & Soule, L. The influence of time and type of preparation on children's adjustment to hospitalization. *Journal of Pediatric Psychology*, 1976, *1*, 31–37.

Melamed, B. G., Robbins, R., & Graves, S. Psychological preparation for surgical and medical procedures. In D. Russo & J. Varni (Eds.), *Behavioral pediatrics: Research and practice*. New York: Plenum, in press.

Melamed, B. G., Robbins, R., Small, N., Fernandez, J., & Graves, S. *Coping strategies in children undergoing surgery: The need to evaluate individuals' predisposition to process preparatory information*. Paper presented at the American Psychological Association, Montreal, 1980.

Melamed, B. G., & Siegel, L. J. *Behavioral medicine: Practical applications in health care*. New York: Springer, 1980.

Melamed, B. G., & Siegel, L. J. Reduction of anxiety in children facing hospitalization and surgery by use of filmed modeling. *Journal of Consulting and Clinical Psychology*, 1975, *43*, 511–521.

Melamed, B. G., Yurcheson, R., Fleece, E. L., Hutcheson, S., & Hawes, R. Effects of film modeling on the reduction of anxiety-related behaviors in individuals varying in level of previous experience in the stress situation. *Journal of Consulting and Clinical Psychology*, 1978, *46*, 1357–1367.

Mellish, R. W. P. Preparation of a child for hospitalization and surgery. *Pediatric Clinics of North America*, 1969, *16*, 543–553.

Myers-Vando, R., Steward, M. S., Folkins, C., & Hines, P. The effects of congenital heart disease on cognitive development, illness causality concepts, and vulnerability. *American Journal of Orthopsychiatry*, 1979, *49*, 617–625.

Nagy, M. Children's ideas of the origin of illness. *Health Education Journal*, 1951, *9*, 6–12.

Neuhauser, C., Amsterdam, B., Hines, P., & Steward, M. Children's concepts of healing: Cognitive development and locus of control factors. *American Journal of Orthopsychiatry*, 1978, *48*, 335–341.

Newswanger, A. *Hospital preparation of preschool children as related to their behavior during and immediately following hospitalization for tonsillectomy and adenoidectomy.* Unpublished M.S. thesis, University of Delaware, 1974.

Nimmer, W. H., & Kapp, R. A. A multiple impact program for the treatment of an injection phobia. *Journal of Behavior Therapy and Experimental Psychiatry,* 1974, *5,* 257-258.

Opton, E. M., Jr., & Lazarus, R. S. Personality determinants of psychological response to stress: A theoretical analysis and an experiment. *Journal of Personality and Social Psychology,* 1967, *6,* 291-303.

Perlmutter, M., & Myers, N. A. A developmental study of semantic effects on recognition memory. *Journal of Experimental Child Psychology,* 1976, *22,* 438-453.

Peters, B. M. School-aged children's beliefs about causality of illness: A review of the literature. *Maternal Child Nursing Journal,* 1978, *7,* 143-154.

Peterson, L., & Ridley-Johnson, R. Pediatric hospital response to survey on prehospital preparation for children. *Journal of Pediatric Psychology,* 1980, *5,* 1-7.

Peterson, L., & Shigetomi, C. The use of coping techniques to minimize anxiety in hospitalized children. *Behavior Therapy,* 1981, *12,* 1-14.

Peterson, L., & Shigetomi, C. One year follow-up of elective surgery child patients recovering pre-operative preparation. *Journal of Pediatric Psychology,* in press.

Peterson, L., Schultheis, K., Ridley-Johnson, R., Miller, D. J., & Tracy, K. Comparison of three modeling procedures in the presurgical preparation of children. *Behavior Therapy,* in press.

Piaget, J., & Inhelder, B. *Memory and intelligence.* (trans. A. J. Pomerans) New York: Basic Books, 1973. (Originally published, 1968)

Prugh, D. G., Staub, E. M., Sands, H. H., Kirschbaum, R. M., & Lenihan, E. A. A study of the emotional reactions of children and families to hospitalization and illness. *American Journal of Orthopsychiatry,* 1953, *23,* 70-106.

Roberts, M. C., Wurtele, S. R., Boone, R. R., Ginther, L. J., & Elkins, P. D. Reduction of medical fears by use of modeling: A preventive application in a general population of children. *Journal of Pediatric Psychology,* in press.

Robertson, J. *Young children in hospitals.* New York: Basic Books, 1958.

Robertson, J. The child in hospital. *South African Medical Journal,* 1976, *50,* 749-752.

Roskies, E., Bedard, P., Gauvreau-Guilbault, M., & Lafortune, P. Emergency hospitalization of young children: Some neglected psychological considerations. *Medical Care,* 1975, *13,* 570-581.

Roskies, E., Mongeon, M., & Gagnon-Lefebvre, B. Increasing maternal participation in the hospitalization of young children. *Medical Care,* 1978, *16,* 765-777.

Sawtell, R. O., Simon, J. F., Jr., & Simeonsson, R. J. The effects of five preparatory methods upon child behavior during the first dental visit. *Journal of Dentistry for Children,* 1974, *41,* 37-45.

Shaw, D. W., & Thoresen, C. E. Effects of modeling and desensitization in reducing dentist phobia. *Journal of Counseling Psychology,* 1974, *21,* 415-420.

Shipley, R. M., Butt, J. H., & Horwitz, E. A. Preparation to reexperience a stressful medical examination: Effect of repetitive videotape exposure and coping style. *Journal of Consulting and Clinical Psychology,* 1979, *47,* 485-492.

Shipley, R. M., Butt, J. H., Horwitz, E., & Farbry, J. E. Preparation for a stressful medical procedure: Effect of amount of prestimulus exposure and coping style. *Journal of Consulting and Clinical Psychology,* 1978, *46,* 499-507.

Siegel, L. J., & Peterson, L. Stress reduction in young dental patients through coping skills and sensory information. *Journal of Consulting and Clinical Psychology,* 1980, *48,* 785-787.

Silverman, W., & Melamed, B. G. Measurement of emotion in children. *Behavioral Assessment,* in press.

Simeonsson, R. J., Buckley, L., & Monson, L. Conceptions of illness causality in hospitalized children. *Journal of Pediatric Psychology,* 1979, *4,* 77-84.

Sipowicz, R. R., & Vernon, D. T. Children's stress and hospitalization. *Journal of Health and Social Behavior*, 1965, *9*, 275-287.

Skipper, J. K., & Leonard, R. C. Child hospitalization and social interaction: An experimental study of mothers' feelings of stress, adaptation, and satisfaction. *Medical Care*, 1968, *6*, 496-506.

Steward, M., & Regalbuto, G. Do doctors know what children know? *American Journal of Orthopsychiatry*, 1975, *45*, 146-149.

Taylor, C. B., Ferguson, J. M., & Wermuth, B. M. Simple techniques to treat medical phobias. *Postgraduate Medical Journal*, 1977, *53*, 28-32.

Vardaro, J. A. R. Preadmission anxiety and mother-child relationships. *Journal of the Association for the Care of Children in Hospitals*, 1978, *7*, 8-15.

Vanderveer, A. H. The psychopathology of physical illness and hospital residence. *Quarterly Journal of Child Behavior*, 1949, *1*, 55-71.

Venham, L., Bengston, D., & Cipes, M. Children's response to sequential dentist visits. *Journal of Dental Research*, 1977, *56*, 454-459.

Vernon, D. T. Use of modeling to modify children's responses to a natural, potentially stressful situation. *Journal of Applied Psychology*, 1973, *58*, 351-356.

Vernon, D. T., Foley, J. M., Sipowicz, R. R., & Schulman, J. L. *The psychological responses of children to hospitalization and illness*. Springfield, Illinois: Thomas, 1965.

Visintainer, M. A., & Wolfer, J. Psychological preparation for surgical pediatric patients: The effects on children's and parents' stress responses and adjustment. *Pediatrics*, 1975, *56*, 187-202.

Wallach, M. A., & Kogan, N. *Modes of thinking in young children*. New York: Holt, Rinehart & Winston, 1965.

Weinstein, P. Identifying patterns of behavior during treatment of children. In B. Ingersoll & W. McKutcheon (Eds.), *Proceedings of the Second National Conference on Behavioral Dentistry: Clinical Research in Behavioral Dentistry*. Morgantown, West Virginia: West Virginia University Press, 1980.

White, W. C., Jr., & Davis, M. T. Vicarious extinction of phobic behavior in early childhood. *Journal of Abnormal Child Psychology*, 1975, *2*, 25-32.

Wolfer, J., & Visintainer, M. A. Pediatric surgical patients' and parents' stress responses and adjustment as a function of psychological preparation and stress point nursing care. *Nursing Research*, 1975, *24*, 244-255.

Zabin, M. A., & Melamed, B. G. Relationship between parental discipline and children's ability to cope with stress. *Journal of Behavioral Assessment*, 1980, *2*, 17-38.

# HYPERACTIVITY, INATTENTION, AND AGGRESSION IN CLINICAL PRACTICE

Jan Loney and Richard Milich

## BACKGROUND

*Current Definitions: Vague and Various*

Every researcher who must decide whether or not to admit a child to a study of childhood hyperactivity and each clinician who must diagnose a child as having or not having the hyperkinetic syndrome must answer an identical question: What is childhood hyperactivity? Either explicitly or implicitly, both investigators and practitioners use a definition of childhood hyperactivity in an attempt to produce a homogeneous group of children, and the absence of an accepted and valid operational definition of childhood hyperactivity has negative effects on both research and clinical practice. Vague definitions that produce large heterogeneous groups defeat everyone's purpose. So do idiosyncratic definitions which,

**Advances in Developmental and Behavioral Pediatrics, vol. 3, pages 113–147**
**Copyright © 1982 by JAI Press Inc.**
**All rights of reproduction in any form reserved.**
**ISBN: 0-89232-223-3**

however precise, are used only by a few. Most definitions of childhood hyperactivity fall into one or both of those categories. There are many sketchy and subjective definitions, rather than a single specific one.

## Central Dimensions: Candidates and Controversies

Although existing definitions are vague and various, there has been general agreement about which symptoms or behavioral traits are important to the concept of childhood hyperkinesis or minimal brain dysfunction. Perhaps the three most commonly nominated symptoms are: hyperactivity, attention deficits, and aggression. However, even this short list is subject to some debate, and if we attempt to move beyond it we will encounter repeated examples of the confusion and controversy for which this childhood behavior disorder is well known. In particular, there are continuing controversies about the relative importance of the three symptoms and about their relationships to one another.

Some authorities have considered aggression and hyperactivity to be inseparable expressions of a childhood conduct disorder. From their vantage point, children with hyperactive and/or aggressive symptoms may be called externalizing, noncompliant, or disruptive, but their central problem is seen as a conduct disorder. Such views have been common among psychologists (Barkley, 1981; Quay, 1979) and among British child psychiatrists (Sandberg, Rutter, & Taylor, 1978). American child psychiatrists, on the other hand, have typically considered hyperactivity and aggression to reflect two separate disorders. In their view, there are children who have an unsocialized aggressive reaction (DSM-II, American Psychiatric Association, 1968) or an aggressive conduct disorder (DSM-III, American Psychiatric Association, 1980), and there are children who have the hyperkinetic reaction of childhood (DSM-II) or its contemporary equivalent, the attention deficit disorder (DSM-III). Although it is accepted that hyperkinetic children can display or develop aggressive problems, such children are considered in both DSM-II and III to have two distinct disorders.

The change in diagnostic nomenclature between the DSM-II and DSM-III shifted the emphasis from hyperactivity to inattention. In DSM-III hyperactivity and inattention were considered to be inseparable expressions of the hyperkinetic syndrome; in DSM-III there are two forms of the newly named attention deficit disorder: one with and one without hyperactivity. Thus, inattention is now considered to be the central diagnostic concept.

The present authors and their colleagues (Loney, Langhorne, & Paternite, 1978; Milich & Loney, 1979) believe that hyperactivity and aggression are relatively independent and associated with different etiological antecedents and different prognostic consequences. In our studies, an aggression factor derived from ratings of children's psychiatric charts was associated at referral with low socioeconomic status, parental rejection, absence of neurological signs, and self-esteem deficits. A similarly derived hyperactivity-inattention factor was associated with poor performance on the Bender Visual-Motor Gestalt Test and with better initial response to stimulant drug treatment. Further, the aggression factor was more stable across situations, informants, and time than was the hyperactivity factor. Our findings are summarized in a predictive theory (Loney, Kramer, & Milich, 1981) that links aggression with early environment and with later symptom behavior and delinquency, while hyperactivity is linked with both childhood and adolescent cognitive and academic functioning. These accumulated studies led us to suggest the formulation of four diagnostic groups (Langhorne & Loney, 1979), based on scores on the hyperactive and aggressive dimensions: *exclusive hyperactives* (low scores on aggression and high scores on hyperactivity), *exclusive aggressives* (high on aggression and low on hyperactivity), *aggressive hyperactives* (high on both aggression and hyperactivity), and *normals* or *psychiatric controls* (low on both aggression and hyperactivity). With respect to childhood hyperactivity, this model suggests that aggressive hyperactive children differ from exclusive hyperactive children in ways that have implications for both research and clinical practice.

An important step toward validating the differential importance of hyperactivity and aggression was taken by Roberts (1979). Roberts based her assignment to diagnostic groups on material from the children's psychiatric charts, teachers' ratings of hyperactivity, and parents' ratings of aggression. Using an elaboration of the playroom methods of Routh and Schroeder (1976), Roberts found that differences in on-task behavior in a restricted academic situation were sufficient to allow 86% of referred boys with externalizing disorders to be correctly assigned to one of the three diagnostic categories: exclusive hyperactive, exclusive aggressive, and aggressive hyperactive. She demonstrated that boys from the three diagnostic groups suggested by the four-group model could in fact be differentiated in terms of their observable behavior in both free play and schoollike situations. Up to that point, differences had been shown for dependent variables that were less direct and/or less naturalistic: parent and teacher ratings, ratings of chart information about presenting symptoms and response to medication, demographic factors, and children's performance on visual-motor and self-esteem tests. Roberts' data suggest that aggressive hyperactive children are more overactive and inattentive in playroom situations than are their exclusive hyperactive counterparts. Exclusive hyperactives are in turn more overactive and inattentive than are exclusive aggressives; and, in the playroom, exclusive aggressives are in most ways indistinguishable from normal controls.

## Constructing Diagnoses: The Need for "SCOPE"

One of us has said elsewhere (Loney, 1980) that a truly satisfactory diagnostic approach to childhood hyperactivity would need to have "SCOPE," an acronym denoting a diagnostic method that is *S*ystematic, *C*omplete, *O*perational, *P*ractical, and *E*mpirical. No one who has read the literature on childhood hyperactivity can fail to notice the limited SCOPE of existing definitions.

There are numerous scales of childhood externalizing behavior based on factor analyses of parent or teacher questionnaires or interview schedules. Some of these scales are considered to measure a broad-band conduct disorder dimension, while others are believed to measure a narrow-band hyperactivity factor (Achenbach & Edelbrock, 1978). But, as Quay (1979) has pointed out, so-called hyperactivity factors have tended to be highly correlated with factors labeled conduct disorder. Those who consider such correlations evidence that the two dimensions are synonyms naturally do not tend to offer a diagnostic definition of childhood hyperactivity per se.

Even for those who believe that there is an independent hyperkinetic syndrome, there are many difficulties in deciding how to proceed from an individual score on one of these factors to assignment to a diagnostic category. Werry, Sprague, and Cohen (1975) suggested that we consider as potentially hyperactive those children who fall at or above a screening score of 15 on the 10-item Conners Abbreviated Teacher's Rating Scale (approximately 2 standard deviations above the mean in a sample of normal children). This suggestion has gained wide acceptance, and while the technique is not *complete* and is of questionable discriminant validity, it is *systematic* and *practical*. Most important, it is apparently the only *operational* diagnostic method in the child hyperactivity literature.

The DSM-II (American Psychiatric Association, 1968) method for diagnosing the Hyperkinetic Reaction of Childhood involved matching one's impressions of a given child to a general word-portrait of the prototypical hyperactive child. In application, this method could be approached in a *systematic* (orderly) and *practical* (rapid and inexpensive) fashion. It was relatively *complete* in its inclusion of relevant symptoms and in its implication that symptoms should persist across informants, time, and situations. However, although it was derived to some extent from *empirical* studies, it had serious shortcomings in its reliability and validity.

The revised DSM-III (American Psychiatric Association, 1980) method for diagnosing Attention Deficit Disorder is even more *systematic, complete,* and *practical*. It offers general advice about how to deal with situational variability and developmental changes. Despite the fact that it is based on an additional decade of empirical investigation, however, it appears to be no more reliable than was DSM-II (see Cantwell, Russell, Mattison, & Will, 1979; Mattison, Cantwell, Russell, & Will, 1979), and its validity is presently unknown.

The fourfold method advocated by the present investigators is relatively systematic and complete, but because it has depended upon ratings of material from children's psychiatric charts, it has not been *practical* (O'Leary & Steen, 1980). Its *empirical* reliability and validity have been promising, but largely confined to a group of medicated hyperkinetic boys referred to a single clinic.

The fact that none of these approaches to diagnosing childhood hyperactivity has SCOPE should probably be considered an inevitable reflection of both the complications of diagnostic systems in general and the confusions of the hyperactive syndrome in particular. However, the fact that so few of these approaches to diagnosing childhood hyperactivity are completely *operational* should concern us. A genuine operational definition would provide detailed information on: (1) which symptoms are to be measured, (2) what specific instruments are to be used, (3) where to draw the line separating symptomatic behavior or scores from asymptomatic behavior or scores, and (4) how to combine the symptom information into a diagnostic decision. In constructing their partially operational definition (steps 1 and 4 were taken) of the attention deficit disorder, the architects of DSM-III correctly noted that operational definitions tend to increase reliability, and that reliability is a necessary prerequisite for satisfactory clinical diagnosis. And if we cannot agree on exactly what childhood hyperactivity is, there is little probability that research proceeding from our divergent definitions will converge upon the truth.

But, however essential operational diagnostic methods may be to clinical practice and scientific progress, childhood hyperactivity is not a condition upon which one rushes to impose an invariant definition. The absence of a standard diagnostic method is not a mere oversight. It is a product of the variation that is the hallmark of what is called childhood hyperactivity. These are children who vary from situation to situation, and from time to time within situations. Their parents' views of their problems often differ from those of their teachers; perhaps their mother's views differ from their father's. "Experts" about childhood hyperactivity disagree among themselves, and they change their minds over time.

We therefore set about developing operational definitions of childhood hyperactivity and aggression with considerable reluctance. Although we believe that operational definitions are needed, and that one pays for the flexibility of "clinical" decision making with decreased accuracy (Meehl, 1954), we are aware of the fact that only operational definitions can be rapidly and resoundingly disconfirmed. Our central goals were: (1) to develop a more practical and prospective method than chart rating for measuring the central dimensions of our fourfold model, (2) to provide a more explicit technique than mean or median splits for assigning children to diagnostic groups, (3) to begin empirical studies of these new methods, and (4) to use these preliminary studies to estimate the distance between our methods and our goals.

## OPERATIONALIZING THE FOURFOLD MODEL

The fourfold model (Loney, Langhorne, & Paternite, 1978; Langhorne & Loney, 1979) calls for clinic referrals to be separated into diagnostic groups based on their hyperactive and aggressive symptom behaviors. It may be useful to start with some examples of Hyperactivity and Aggression as we now understand them.

*What are Hyperactivity and Aggression?*

In our studies, the Hyperactivity dimension involves three major kinds of behavioral descriptors: hyperactivity, inattention, and judgment deficits. Those that refer to hyperactivity[1] tend to describe inappropriate large and small motor behaviors: always on the go, restless, wiggly and squirmy, wound up, and so on. These are frenetic and peripatetic behaviors, and they are considered symptomatic clinically to the degree that they are not commensurate with the child's age and to the extent that they interfere seriously with the learning or relationships of the child or of others in the given situation. Another group of descriptors that characterize the Hyperactivity dimension in our studies are those that refer to inattention.[2] Some descriptors considered to typify inattention are: distractible, can't concentrate, forgetful, and short attention span. The final set of symptoms that are associated with the Hyperactivity dimension are those that describe judgment deficits or impulsivity. As we use the term, impulsivity refers to deficits in social judgment and "common sense." Thus, the relevant descriptors tend to be: doesn't plan ahead, immature, talks too much, and so on. Failure to control aggressive impulses is specifically excluded.

Behavior characteristic of the Aggression dimension can also be considered to fall into three major categories: negative affect, peer aggression, and adult aggression. Negative affect descriptors often refer to disagreeable aspects of disposition or temperament that do not necessarily involve overtly aggressive interpersonal behavior. The operation of negative affect is suggested by descriptors such as: irritable, sullen, sulky, explosive, and grouchy. A second type of behavior that falls on the Aggression dimension is peer aggression,[3] both verbal and physical. Descriptors here include: cruel, teases, bullies, and picks fights. The third kind of aggressive behavior is resistive and contentious hostility displayed with adult authority figures such as parents and teachers. Again, this hostility may be expressed either verbally or physically, but generally peer aggression is more apt to be physical while adult aggression is more apt to be verbal. Adult aggression includes such descriptors as: acts smart, defiant, sassy, rebellious, belligerent, swears, and so forth.

We believe that a child high on the Hyperactivity dimension, like an inattentive puppy, has a problem of *aptitude*; when it comes to adult expectations, the child is essentially willing but unable, and as a result he or she wants to comply, but usually *cannot*. In contrast, a child high on the Aggression dimension, like an irritable bear, has a problem of *attitude;* confronted with adult demands, this child is basically able but unwilling,[4] and consequently he or she could comply, but often will not. A child high on both the Hyperactivity and the Aggression dimensions is unwilling *and* unable; as a result, this child usually cannot comply, and often would not if he or she could. Such a combination of hyperactive and aggressive symptoms makes for the most deviant behavior across both situations and time (Langhorne & Loney, 1979; Roberts, 1979).

It is obvious that arriving at a placement on the Hyperactivity and Aggression dimensions may require drawing indirect inferences and making subtle distinctions. Both hyperactive and aggressive children can be described as "disobedient" and "noncompliant," and parents' and teachers' attitudes can determine whether they speak of a child who "can't concentrate" or one who "won't listen." Adult attributions can likewise play a role in whether a child is said to "refuse to mind" or is merely called "forgetful." Children who cannot perform may defend themselves by saying they did not want to in the first place, and children who do not want to comply may say that they cannot. The necessary judgments may to some degree require an extended personal familiarity that is beyond a clinician, an objectivity that eludes a parent, and a psychological-mindedness that may be unavailable to a teacher. Thus, no single source of information (clinic examination, psychiatric interview, parent report, or teacher rating scale) will be totally satisfactory in every case, and there is little reason to believe that several sources of information will be much better. Even direct observations of the child at home and in school are subject to several sources of error and bias. For these reasons, all information about a given child will contain errors, and no hyperactivity or aggression score will be completely accurate.

## Derivation of the Prospective Scales

Our goal was to provide an explicit method of estimating our Hyperactivity and Aggression dimensions for research and screening purposes. We started by attempting to replicate our original factor analysis in a second sample (Milich, Loney, & Landau, 1980). This new sample was a group of 50 consecutive diagnostic referrals to the University of Iowa child psychiatry outpatient clinic. All were male, between 6 and 12 years of age, and enrolled in first to sixth grade in public or private school settings. No boy had a full-scale IQ below 70, and none had peripheral sensory loss, frank organic damage, or outright psychosis. Otherwise, all diagnostic problems were represented (unlike our previous samples, which consisted only of diagnosed hyperkinetic/minimal brain dysfunction boys who had been recommended for a trial of CNS stimulant medication). The current sample of 50 included two boys who were being maintained on medication (but who were not on medication on the day of the outpatient evaluation) and eight boys who had had a previous trial of stimulant medication. The remaining 40 boys had no history of treatment with a stimulant drug.

Two trained judges independently reviewed a set of materials from each boy's psychiatric chart. These materials included written accounts of the child's problems at home and at school taken from intake forms filled out by both teacher and parent, as well as lengthy typed summaries of the psychiatric evaluation. For each boy, the judges rated the frequency and/or severity of nine symptoms: attention problems, fidgetiness, hyperactivity, impulsivity, negative affect, aggressive interpersonal behavior, self-esteem deficits, anxiety, and depression.

Effective rater reliabilities (Rosenthal, 1973) for these two judges ranged from .77 to .86. A factor analysis of the correlations among the nine symptoms replicated our previous work by producing a Hyperactivity factor (consisting of attention problems, fidgetiness, hyperactivity, and impulsivity) and an Aggression factor (consisting of negative affect and aggressive interpersonal behavior). For the analyses that we will describe, each of the 50 boys was given two factor scores. For a given factor, a child's score was the sum of both judges' ratings of him on all of the symptoms that loaded on that factor.

As part of an ongoing study of cross-situational variation in childhood behavior problems, each of the 50 boys and their parents and teachers had provided responses to a number of questionnaires and rating scales. We chose to use the Conners rating scales (Conners, 1973) as the basis for our operational measures of the Hyperactivity and Aggression dimensions. Scores on the Conners Teacher's Rating Scale have been shown to separate hyperactive from normal children, to differentiate between medicated and nonmedicated hyperactive children, and to correlate with classroom behavior. It was felt that the ubiquitousness of these scales in both clinic settings and research studies would facilitate independent testing of the reliability and validity of any subscales that we might develop. Furthermore, there are numerous practical advantages because the Conners scales can be administered with a minimal expenditure of time and money and repeated by phone or mail for treatment monitoring.

Numerous investigators have factor analyzed the Conners parent and teacher rating scales. Separate aggression (conduct problem), inattention, and hyperactivity factors have typically resulted. Our initial hope was that scores on these existing Conners factors might prove to be satisfactorily discriminating measures of the criterion scores on the Hyperactivity and Aggression dimensions that we had derived from the chart ratings. This would have been true for hyperactivity if, for example, the Conners Hyperactivity factor were significantly correlated with its corresponding Hyperactivity dimension in the chart ratings and *not* significantly correlated with the Aggression dimension. Pearson correlations between the relevant factors of the Conners Teacher's Rating Scale and the Hyperactivity and Aggression factors derived from the charts are presented in Table 1. Clearly, none of the existing Conners factors correlated with only one criterion factor. Therefore, none of the existing Conners factors could form the basis for a practical and discriminating operational measure of one of the criterion factors.

We therefore set about constructing measures of our Hyperactivity and Aggression dimensions using individual items from the Conners Teacher's Rating Scale.[5] We did this by correlating each Conners item with both chart rating factors. For our potential hyperactivity subscale, we retained those items that correlated significantly ($p < .05$) with the Hyperactivity factor but not with the Aggression factor; for the potential aggression subscale, we retained items that

*Table 1.*   Pearson Correlations\* between Factor Scores from Chart Ratings
and Scores on the Conners Teacher's Rating Scale in a Sample of Clinic Boys
($N = 50$)

| Factors from the Conners Teacher's Rating Scale | Factors from Chart Ratings | |
|---|---|---|
| | Hyperactivity | Aggression |
| Conduct Problem Factor | .32 | .56 |
| Hyperactivity Factor | .54 | .44 |
| Inattentive-Passive Factor | ns | ns |

*Note*:
\*All reported correlations are different from zero at or beyond the $p < .05$ level of significance.

correlated significantly with the Aggression factor but not with the Hyperactivity factor. Although more potential aggression items were identified than potential hyperactivity items, each of the potential subscales was reduced to five items so that the hyperactivity and aggression subscales would be short and of equal length.[6]

The 10 items that were retained as potential measures of the Hyperactivity and Aggression dimensions are presented in Table 2, along with all of the items that are included in (1) the existing 6-item Conners Hyperactivity factor and (2) the existing 10-item Conners Abbreviated Teacher's Rating Scale (ATRS) or Hyperkinesis Index (HI). The correlations between items from these existing factors or scales and the criterion chart ratings provide evidence that many so-called hyperactivity items may measure aggression as well as (e.g., item 5) or instead of (e.g., item 3) hyperactivity. Using data from the present study, the existing 6-item Conners Hyperactivity factor contains only two items that actually correlated with hyperactivity but not aggression, and the existing 10-item Hyperkinesis Index contains only three such discriminating items.

The Pearson correlations between the two 5-item subscales that resulted and the two criterion measures are presented in Table 3. The derived hyperactivity subscale correlated significantly with the Hyperactivity dimension but not with the Aggression dimension; for the derived aggression subscale, the converse was true. In order to describe clearly the content of the derived 5-item hyperactivity subscale, we call it the Inattention-Overactivity or IO subscale. The derived 5-item aggression subscale is called the Aggression or A subscale. To distinguish the 10-item Conners scale which results when these two 5-item subscales are combined (Figure 1) from the original 10-item Conners ATRS or HI, we will refer to the new 10-item version as the IOWA Conners Teacher's Rating Scale.[7] In this instance, the letters in IOWA are an acronym for *I*nattention-*O*veractivity *W*ith *A*ggression.

*Table 2.* Pearson Correlations* between Factors Scores from Chart Ratings and Selected Items on the Conners Teacher's Rating Scale in a Sample of Clinic Boys ($N = 50$)

| Original Item No. | Item | Factors from Chart Ratings | |
|---|---|---|---|
| | | Hyperactivity | Aggression |
| 1 | Fidgeting[a,b,c] | .44 | ns |
| 2 | Hums and makes other odd noises[a,c] | .38 | ns |
| 3 | Demands must be met immediately[b] (easily frustrated) | ns | .40 |
| 5 | Restless or overactive[a,b] | .54 | .47 |
| 6 | Excitable, impulsive[a,b,c] | .43 | .28 |
| 7 | Inattentive, distractible[b,c] | .27 | ns |
| 8 | Fails to finish things he starts[b,c] | .35 | ns |
| 13 | Cries often and easily[b] | ns | ns |
| 14 | Disturbs other children[a,b] | .45 | .39 |
| 15 | Quarrelsome[d] | ns | .45 |
| 16 | Mood changes quickly and drastically[b] | .33 | .42 |
| 17 | Acts "smart"[d] | ns | .30 |
| 21 | Temper outbursts[b,d] (explosive and unpredictable behavior) | ns | .39 |
| 29 | Teases other children and interferes with their activities[a] | .36 | .26 |
| 31 | Defiant[d] | ns | .51 |
| 38 | Uncooperative[d] | ns | .36 |

*Notes*:

*All reported correlations are different from zero at or beyond the .05 level of significance.

[a]Item included on original Conners Hyperactivity factor.

[b]Item included on original 10-item Hyperkinesis Index.

[c]Item selected for IOWA Conners Inattention-Hyperactivity (IO) subscale.

[d]Item selected for IOWA Conners Aggression (A) subscale.


*Table 3.* Pearson Correlations* between Factor Scores from Chart Ratings and Subscales derived from the Conners Teacher's Rating Scale in a Sample of Clinic Boys ($N = 50$)

| Subscales from the IOWA Conners Teacher's Rating Scale | Factors from Chart Ratings | |
|---|---|---|
| | Hyperactivity | Aggression |
| Inattention-Overactivity (IO) | .50 | ns |
| Aggression (A) | ns | .51 |

*Note*:

*All reported correlations are different from zero at or beyond the .05 level of significance.

**Check the column which best describes this child.**

| | Not at All | Just a little | Pretty Much | Very Much |
|---|---|---|---|---|
| 1. **Fidgeting** | | | | |
| 2. **Hums and makes other odd noises** | | | | |
| 3. **Excitable, impulsive** | | | | |
| 4. **Inattentive, easily distracted** | | | | |
| 5. **Fails to finish things he starts (short attention span)** | | | | |
| 6. **Quarrelsome** | | | | |
| 7. **Acts "smart"** | | | | |
| 8. **Temper outbursts (explosive and unpredictable behavior)** | | | | |
| 9. **Defiant** | | | | |
| 10. **Uncooperative** | | | | |

*Figure 1.* The IOWA Conners Teacher's Rating Scale.

Items 1 through 5 are summed to provide a score on the Inattention-Overactivity (10) subscale; items 6 through 10 are summed to provide a score on the Aggression (A) subscale. For both subscales, items checked *not at all* are scored 0, those checked *just a little* are scored 1, those checked *pretty much* are scored 2, and those checked *very much* are scored 3.

# THE IOWA CONNERS TEACHER'S RATING SCALE

*Some Preliminary Data*

Our first step in investigating the properties of the 10-item IOWA Conners Teacher's Rating Scale was to determine whether the new subscales correlated differentially with various other measures collected on the 50 boys in the clinical sample. This was important because, while the original Hyperactivity and Aggression factors derived from the chart ratings correlated a modest .35 with each other, the derived Conners IO and A subscales intercorrelated .63. Although a correlation of .63 represents only 40% common variation, it was clear that the size of the correlation between the two subscales posed a potential threat to differential diagnosis. We discovered that neither the IOWA Conners IO subscale nor the IOWA Conners A subscale correlated significantly ($p < .05$) with the clinic boys' age, IQ, or socioeconomic status.

We then correlated the two IOWA Conners subscales with available measures of the children's observed behavior in a clinic playroom during a Free Play and a Restricted Academic situation. In the Free Play situation, the child was invited into a room with four identical sets of toys at each of four tables and chairs and told to play alone as he wished for 15 minutes. In the Restricted Academic situation, the child was returned to the playroom after a brief absence. At one table, several new and distracting toys were arranged, including a large Space Station. The child was instructed to work at an adjacent table on a digit-to-symbol coding task for 15 minutes while the examiner was out of the room (see Roberts, 1979, for additional details). Trained observers recorded the children's behaviors during these periods through a one-way mirror. Observer reliabilities exceeded .95 for all but one type of behavior (see Milich et al., 1980).

In the Free Play situation, three "activity" measures correlated significantly with the IO subscale, but not with the A subscale. Boys higher on IO (but not boys higher on A) crossed more times across the grids than had been marked in tape on the floor, spent more time out of their seats, and ran up higher readings on their ankle actometers. In contrast, two "inattention" measures correlated with the A subscale, but not with the IO subscale. Boys higher on A (but not boys higher on IO) spent more time "off-task" (not playing with the toys) and shifted their attention more often (from a toy to something other than a toy or from one toy to another).

In the Restricted Academic situation, none of the three previously significant activity measures correlated with either of the IOWA Conners subscales. In contrast to the Free Play situation, during the Restricted Academic situation, the off-task measure correlated with the IO subscale, but not with the A subscale. Boys higher on IO (but not boys higher on A) now spent more time "off-task" (not working on the coding task). Although this pattern of differential correlations does not provide a complete test of the fourfold model, it encouraged us to proceed with further investigations of the properties of the 10-item IOWA Conners Teacher's Rating Scale.

Our next step was to compare the scores of our clinic-referred boys with scores of unselected[8] elementary school boys. For this purpose we used Conners Teacher's Rating Scale data collected during a previous study (Roberts, Milich, Loney, & Caputo, 1981). Like the clinic boys, these 120 subjects were Iowa school children in grades one through six. The means and standard deviations of the IO and A subscales in the two samples are shown in Table 4. The means of

*Table 4.* The 10-Item IOWA Conners Teacher's Rating Scale: Means and Standard Deviations of the 5-Item IO and A Subscales in two Samples

|  | Clinic Boys (N = 50) | | Classroom Boys (N = 120) | |
|---|---|---|---|---|
| Subscale | Mean | SD | Mean | SD |
| Inattention-Overactivity (IO) | 8.54* | 3.93 | 4.30* | 3.78 |
| Aggression (A) | 6.18* | 4.60 | 2.29* | 2.89 |

*Note:*
*Means of clinic and classroom groups different at $p < .0001$ level of significance.

**TEST DECISIONS**

|  |  | NOT HYPERACTIVE | HYPERACTIVE |  |
|---|---|---|---|---|
| **ACTUAL** | **NOT HYPERACTIVE** | true negatives a | false positives b | **Actual Negatives** |
| **PLACEMENTS** | **HYPERACTIVE** | false negatives c | true positives d | **Actual Positives** |
|  |  | **Test Negatives** | **Test Positives** |  |

*Figure 2.* A two-by-two decision table for hyperactivity.

the clinic and the classroom boys are different at a highly significant level for both the IO and A subscales, despite the fact that the consecutive clinic sample included boys who were neither hyperactive nor aggressive and that 10% of the boys in the classroom sample were considered by their teacher to require referral by the average teacher for outside help because of hyperactivity.

Within the classroom sample, the intercorrelation of the IO and the A subscales was once again .63. Neither subscale correlated significantly with either the grade or the age of these unselected elementary school boys.[9] The internal consistency ($\alpha$) within the classroom sample was .87 for the IO subscale and .85 for the A subscale; comparable internal consistency figures within the clinic sample were .80 and .87.

The teachers of the 120 boys in the classroom sample rerated their students one week later, thus allowing us to calculate one-week rater reliabilities. These stability coefficients were .89 for the IO subscale and .86 for the A subscale. The mean of the IO scale did not drop significantly from the first to the second rating, but the mean of the A scale was significantly lower at the second rating ($p$ < .01), indicating that care should be exercised in interpreting data from the first as opposed to the second and subsequent ratings of the A subscale.

## Decision Tables and Screening Scores

A hypothetical 2 × 2 decision table is shown in Figure 2, where the decisions made by a test at a given cutoff point or screening score are tabulated against an actual placement or diagnosis. In this case we wanted to compare test decisions based on scores from the IO subscale of the IOWA Conners Teacher's Rating Scale with teachers' judgments as to whether or not a child was both hyperactive and referable.[10] If the child obtained a score above the screening score on the IO subscale, the child is a *test positive*. If the child obtained an IO score at or below the screening score, the child is a *test negative*. Similarly, if a child's teacher considered the child to be both hyperactive and referable, the child is an *actual positive;* if the teacher did not consider the child hyperactive and referable, the child is an *actual negative.* There are four resulting possibilities: *true positives* (children who are actually hyperactive and who are identified as hyperactive by the test); *false positives* (children who are actually normal but were identified as hyperactive by the test); *false negatives* (children who are actually hyperactive but who were called normal by the test); and, finally, *true negatives* (children who are actually normal and were called normal by the test).

The line separating actual positives from actual negatives was set by the teachers and is not subject to change by the test developers. However, the line separating test positives from test negatives is subject to change; we can place that line or screening score in any location we choose. If it is set very high (if children need to obtain a very high score to be called hyperactive), there will be relatively few test positives and relatively many test negatives in a given sample. This will have the desirable effect of decreasing the number of false positives and increasing the number of true negatives. However, it will also have the undesirable effect of increasing the number of false negatives and decreasing the number of true positives. These proportions are reciprocal; decreasing the number of false positives will simultaneously increase the number of false negatives, and vice versa. Therefore, if we change the screening score in order to make less of one kind of error, we necessarily make more of the other kind of error.

In general terms, there is a particular screening score that minimizes total errors, and that would be the optimal cutoff point if it were assumed that false positives and false negatives were of equal importance. In specific terms, however, much depends upon the costs and benefits in the particular situation, because they will determine what kinds of errors one most wants to avoid making. Estimates of these costs and benefits often vary from one person using the test to another.

In the case of the present IOWA Conners Teacher's Rating Scale, we examined the performance of the Inattention-Overactivity (IO) subscale against teachers' judgments of whether a child was hyperactive enough to require referral for outside help by the average teacher. A series of 2 × 2 decision tables of the kind represented in Figure 2 was constructed, using data from 120 unselected elementary school boys. Table 5 presents a summary of the results of examining 2 × 2 tables for five illustrative screening scores.

The percentages of true positives, true negatives, false positives, and false negatives are shown first in Table 5. The proportions of both kinds of positives decreased as screening scores increased, while the proportions of both kinds of negatives increased. At a screening score of 5, 10% of the current sample were correctly called hyperactive, and 21% were incorrectly called hyperactive; at a screening score of 12, only 3% were correctly called hyperactive, and none was incorrectly called hyperactive. Comparably, at a screening score of 5, 69% of the sample were correctly called normal, and none was incorrectly called normal;

*Table 5.* Comparisons of Different Screening Scores in the Classroom Sample

| Percentages | Screening Score | | | | |
|---|---|---|---|---|---|
| | 5 | 7 | 10 | 11 | 12 |
| True Positives in Total Sample $\left(\dfrac{d}{a+b+c+d}\right)$ | 10 | 8 | 5 | 4 | 3 |
| True Negatives in Total Sample $\left(\dfrac{a}{a+b+c+d}\right)$ | 69 | 77 | 86 | 88 | 90 |
| False Positives in Total Sample $\left(\dfrac{b}{a+b+c+d}\right)$ | 21 | 13 | 4 | 2 | 0 |
| False Negatives in Total Sample $\left(\dfrac{c}{a+b+c+d}\right)$ | 0 | 2 | 5 | 6 | 7 |
| Actual Positives in Total Sample $\left(\dfrac{c+d}{a+b+c+d}\right)$ | 10 | 10 | 10 | 10 | 10 |
| Test Positives in Total Sample $\left(\dfrac{b+d}{a+b+c+d}\right)$ | 31 | 21 | 9 | 6 | 3 |
| Correct Classifications in Total Sample $\left(\dfrac{a+d}{a+b+c+d}\right)$ | 79 | 86 | 91 | 92 | 93 |
| True Positives among Test Positives $\left(\dfrac{d}{b+d}\right)$ | 32 | 40 | 54 | 71 | 100 |
| True Positives among Actual Positives $\left(\dfrac{d}{c+d}\right)$ | 100 | 83 | 50 | 42 | 33 |

at a screening score of 12, 90% were correctly called normal, and 7% were incorrectly called normal. The proportions of both kinds of correct or true decisions were similarly reciprocal. At a screening score of 5, 10% of the sample were true positives, and 69% were true negatives; at a screening score of 12, only 3% of the sample were true positives, but 90% were true negatives.

The percentage of actual positives in the total sample is commonly called the *base rate* for positives. Its converse is the base rate for negatives. The base rates in a given sample are constant, regardless of the screening score used. The larger of the two base rate figures indicates how well one could predict by chance in the given sample. In the present classroom sample, 90% of our decisions would be correct if we simply called all children nonhyperactive or normal.

The percentage of test positives in the total sample, irrespective of accuracy, is simply the sum of true and false positives. This value can be called the *test prevalence*. Test prevalence, or the proportion of the sample called hyperactive, falls as the screening score rises. The percentage of *correct classifications* in the total sample is the sum of true positives and true negatives. In the present instance, this percentage increased as the screening score increased.

Numerous indices have been proposed for summarizing a test's effectiveness for a particular purpose at a given screening score. Two of these indices are also presented in Table 5. The percentage of true positives among all of the test positives (those identified by the IO subscale) has been called the predictive utility for positives or the *homogeneity* of the test group. A second summary index is the percentage of true positives among all of the actual positives (those identified by the teachers). This index has been called the *sensitivity* of the test. In the present case, at a screening score of 5, the homogeneity of the test group was only 32%, but the sensitivity of the test was 100%. At a screening score of 12, the homogeneity of the test group rose to 100%, but the sensitivity of the test fell to 33%. A screening score of 10 achieved the closest match between test prevalence (9%) and base rate (10%), but at that screening score the homogeneity of the test group was a modest 54%, and the sensitivity of the test was an equally unappealing 50%. At the screening score that matched the base rate in this sample, the test did neither of its possible jobs well.

So far, we have been considering the situation where the screening is being done in an essentially unselected school sample, and perhaps 10% of the boys are hyperactive. The situation where one is screening referrals to a clinic practice or agency is quite different, because the proportion of actual hyperactives among clinical referrals is apt to be closer to 50%. We know from the classic work of Meehl and Rosen (1955) that the usefulness of a diagnostic instrument varies with the base rate of the diagnosis in the samples to which the instrument is applied. However, the essentail barrier to doing a parallel decision analysis within one of our clinic samples was that all potential criteria for "actual diagnosis" were even less satisfactory than they had been in the elementary school sample, where we used teachers' global judgments about hyperactivity and referability. We therefore estimated the necessary percentages by assuming that the base rate had risen from 10% to 50% and that the sensitivity of the IO scale remained stable, identifying 83% of the actual positives at a screening score of 7 and 42% of actual positives at a screening score of 11.

In this hypothetical "clinic" sample, a screening score of 7 produced 42% true positives (compared to 8% in the school sample), 43% true negatives (compared to 77%), 7% false positives (cf. 13%), and 8% false negatives (cf. 2%). Thus, at a screening score of 7, 49% of the clinic sample were considered hyperactive, 85% of the test decisions were correct, and the homogeneity of the test group was 86%. A screening score of 11 in this "clinic" group produced 21% true positives (compared to 4% in the school sample), 49% true negatives (compared to 88%), 1% false positives (cf. 2%), and 29% false negatives (cf. 6%). Therefore, at a screening score of 11, 22% of the clinic sample were considered hyperactive, 70% of the test decisions were correct, and the homogeneity of the test group was 95%.

Examination and comparisons of all of these percentages and estimates leads us to suggest (1) the use of an IO subscale screening score of at least 11 for research purposes (where the central goal is to maximize the homogeneity of the test group by minimizing false positives)[11] and (2) the use of an IO subscale screening score of 7 for clinical purposes (where the central goal is to diagnose hyperactive children[12] while not diagnosing normal ones[13]).

The recommended research screening score identified 6% of the classroom sample as hyperactive; the more lenient clinical screening score identified 21% of the classroom sample as hyperactive. Because we unfortunately did not ask the teachers in the classroom sample to identify boys whom they considered referable for *aggressive* behavior, we could not carry out decision analysis using teachers' judgments about aggression. Therefore, we arbitrarily selected for the A subscale a research screening score (7) that would identify a comparable percentage (6%) as aggressive and a clinical screening score (4) that would identify a comparable percentage (21%) as aggressive.

## THE FOURFOLD MODEL

### Incidence in Classroom and Clinic Samples

When the entire classroom sample was categorized on both the IO and the A subscales according to the lower (clinical) screening scores (Table 6), 9% of the sample were aggressive but not hyperactive (A), 12% were aggressive *and* hyperactive (AH), 9% were hyperactive but not aggressive (H), and 70% were neither hyperactive nor aggressive (classmate control or CC). Thus 30% of the unselected classroom boys were identified as deviant on hyperactivity and/or aggression in terms of the lenient (21%) clinical screening scores. When these 21% screening levels were applied to the consecutive clinic sample, 14% of clinic boys were placed in the A group, 46% in the AH group, 12% in the H group, and 28% in the psychiatric control (PC) group. (This 28% of the sample should include those clinic children who were primarily anxious, withdrawn, learning-disabled, encopretic, undiagnosed, etc.). Thus 72% of the unselected clinic boys were identified as deviant on hyperactivity and/or aggression in terms of the lenient (21%) clinic screening scores.

When the entire classroom sample was categorized on the IO and A subscales according to the higher (research) screening scores (Table 6), 5% of the sample fell into the A group, 1% into the AH group, 5% into the H group, and 89% into the CC group. Thus 11% of the unselected classroom boys were identified as deviant on hyperactivity and/or aggression in terms of the stringent (6%) research screening scores. When these 6% screening levels were applied to the consecu-

*Table 6.*   Percentage of Classroom and Clinic Samples Placed in Four
Diagnostic Groups by Each of Two Levels of Screening Scores on the IO and
A Subscales of the IOWA Conners Teacher's Rating Scale

|  | *Lower Screening Scores[a]* | | *Higher Screening Scores[b]* | |
|---|---|---|---|---|
| *Diagnostic Group* | *Unselected[c] Classroom Boys (N = 120)* | *Unselected[d] Clinic Boys (N = 50)* | *Unselected[c] Classroom Boys (N = 120)* | *Unselected[d] Clinic Boys (N = 50)* |
| Exclusive Aggressive (A) | 9 | 14 | 5 | 16 |
| Aggressive and Hyperactive (AH) | 12 | 46 | 1 | 20 |
| Exclusive Hyperactive (H) | 9 | 12 | 5 | 8 |
| Neither Aggressive nor Hyperactive | 70 | 28 | 89 | 56 |

*Notes*:

[a]The lower screening scores were those integer values on the IO or A subscales that identified closest to 20% of the
sample of unselected classroom boys as Hyperactive or Aggressive (>7 for the IO subscale and >4 for the A
subscale).

[b]The higher screening scores were those integer values on the IO or A subscales that identified closest to 5% of the
sample of unselected classroom boys as Hyperactive or Aggressive (>11 for the IO subscale and >7 for the A
subscale).

[c]The classroom sample consisted of all boys in grades 1 through 6 whose parents gave permission for them to
participate, including those whose teachers considered them hyperactive and/or aggressive.

[d]The clinic sample consisted of all nonretarded referred boys in grades 1 through 6 who were not excluded because
of overt brain damage or psychosis, including those whom no one considered either hyperactive or aggressive.

tive clinic sample, 16% of the clinic boys were placed in the A group, 20% in the
AH group, 8% in the H group, and 56% in the PC group. Thus 44% of the
unselected clinic boys were identified as deviant on hyperactivity and/or aggression in terms of the stringent (6%) research screening scores.

These data not only allow us to state the proportion of clinic-referred boys who
fell into the four groups (A, AH, H, and PC) at the two screening levels, but they
also allow us to estimate the proportion of AH and H boys in subgroups identified
solely on the basis of high scores on the Inattention-Overactivity (IO) subscale.
Using the stringent (6%) screening score, only 29% of boys considered hyperactive will be *exclusively* hyperactive; 71% will be *both* hyperactive and aggressive. Using the lenient (21%) screening score, only 21% of boys considered
hyperactive will be *exclusively* hyperactive; 79% will be *both* hyperactive and
aggressive. Therefore, even a clinic subgroup that is screened on a relatively
unidimensional hyperactivity scale can be expected to consist preponderantly of
aggressive boys, so long as the hyperactivity scale is correlated with measures of
aggression.

# SOME DIFFERENCES AMONG THE FOUR GROUPS

Our next step was to group boys on the basis of their scores on the two subscales of the IOWA Conners Teacher's Rating Scale and then to investigate possible differences among the four groups across a number of dependent variables. For these validating analyses, we used a sample of 37 clinic boys different from the 50 on whom the IOWA Conners subscales were originally derived; this validation sample had been referred to our clinic the year before the derivation sample, but all selection criteria were the same. Within this new clinic sample, groups were formed using the clinical (lenient) screening scores ($> 7$ on the IO subscale and $> 4$ on the A subscale) in order to have sufficient numbers in all groups. We then did a series of one-way analyses of variance, testing on each dependent variable for overall differences among the four groups. If an overall $F$-test was significant,[14] post hoc analyses were done to identify which pairs of groups were significantly different on that variable.

The four groups (A, AH, H, and PC) did not differ in age or socioeconomic status. Likewise, no group differences were found in WISC-R (Full Scale, Verbal, Performance, or any subtest) or on the Wide Range Achievement Test (Reading Recognition, Arithmetic, or Spelling).

The AH boys made more errors than the A or PC boys on the Kagan Matching Familiar Figures (MFF) Test, but the groups did not differ significantly in the average time they took to respond. Because these MFF analyses involve differences within the clinic sample, they can be discussed only in relative, rather than absolute, terms. However, comparisons of the total errors and mean response latency of the AH group (20 and 8 respectively) with data from a group of Iowa volunteer boys of the same age (8 errors and 16 seconds), and with data from other studies of the MFF, suggest that the AH boys are in fact very impulsive on this test.

Each boy in this clinic validation sample also completed a 25-item self-report questionnaire (the Student Off-Task Scale or SOTS) which asked how much of the time (none, some, most, or all) he did a list of off-task (e.g., "disobeys and talks back to the teacher") and on-task (e.g., "does his work silently") behaviors while in his classroom. A previous factor analysis of the SOTS responses of a group of unselected elementary school boys yielded three factors: Aggression, Hyperactivity, and Inattention. On the SOTS, the clinic AH boys described themselves as more aggressive than the PC boys. There were no self-report differences on either the Hyperactivity or the Inattention factor of the SOTS.

The teacher of each boy in the clinic validation sample completed a 25-item questionnaire (the Teacher Off-Task Scale or TOTS) that paralleled the SOTS; the item content, response format, and factor scoring were identical. On the TOTS, the AH boys were described by their teachers as more aggressive and hyperactive than the other three groups, the H boys were described as more hyperactive than the A and PC boys, while the A boys were described as more aggressive than the H and PC boys. Since the teacher's rating scale responses had been used to assign the boys to their respective groups, these corresponding TOTS findings are not surprising; however, it is worth noting that the TOTS Inattention factor did not distinguish among the A, AH, and H groups. Instead, teachers described all three symptom groups as less attentive than psychiatric controls.

The mother of each boy in the clinic validation sample completed a parent version of the off-task instrument (the Parent Off-Task Scale or POTS). The item content was modified slightly to be suitable for describing behavior in the home, rather than the classroom; the response format and factor scoring remained virtually identical. On the POTS, the mothers of the A boys rated them as more aggressive and tended ($p < .09$) to rate them as less attentive than did mothers of controls. Mothers of the AH boys rated them as more hyperactive, but mothers of the H boys rated their sons as no different from controls on aggression, inattention, or hyperactivity.

On the traditional factors of the Conners Mother's Rating Scale, the H and AH groups were rated higher than the A and the PC groups on the Impulsive-Hyperactive factor. All three symptom groups (A, AH, and H) were rated higher by their mothers than the PC group on the Conduct Problem (aggression) factor, but there were no differences among these three groups on the Conduct Problem factor. There were no group differences at all on the Anxiety, Learning Problem, Psychosomatic, Perfectionism, Antisocial, or Muscular Tension factors of the Conners Mother's Rating Scale.

Because the groups were formed on the basis of teachers' responses to 10 items from the Conners Teacher's Rating Scale, they of course differ in expected ways on some of the traditional Conners factors. For example, the AH group was rated highest on both the Conduct Problem (aggression) and Hyperactivity factors. The A group was rated significantly lower than the AH group on the Conduct Problem factor, but the A group was in turn rated significantly higher on the Conduct Problem factor than the H and the PC groups. Similarly, the H group was rated lower than the AH group, but higher than the A and the PC groups, on the Hyperactivity factor. The A group did not differ from the PC group on the Hyperactivity factor, nor did the H group differ from the PC group on the Conduct Problem factor. There were no group differences at all on the Inattentive-Passive, Tension-Anxiety, or Sociability factors of the Conners Teacher's Rating Scale.

As noted above, comparisons between any two kinds of teacher data (e.g., Teacher Off-Task Scale factor scores and the four groups formed on the basis of scores on the IOWA Conners Teacher's Rating Scale) tend merely to demonstrate that teachers are consistent across different sorts of items. And, where the two data sets involve overlapping items (e.g. Conners Teacher's Rating Scale factor scores and the four groups formed from the IOWA Conners), the comparisons are actually contaminated. However, the scores of the four groups on the original Conners Abbreviated Teacher's Rating Scale (ATRS) or Hyperkinesis Index (HI) are interesting in light of the frequent use of this scale for diagnostic assessments. In the clinic validation sample, the four groups were rated very differently ($p < .0001$) on the original 10-item HI: the AH boys were significantly higher (mean = 23.0) than the remaining three groups; and, while the A and H groups did not differ from each other (means = 13.5 and 16.3), they both differed from the PC group (mean = 7.3). Identical findings were obtained in the original clinical sample in which the IOWA Conners subscales were derived and in the unselected classroom sample in which potential screening scores were compared.

Such findings make it clear that samples selected on the basis of scores on the Conners HI will consist disproportionately of boys who are *both* hyperactive and aggressive. They further suggest that boys who are only hyperactive will not be selected for research samples or for clinic intervention any more frequently than will boys who are only aggressive. This occurs partly because teachers' judgments of hyperactivity and aggression are moderately correlated. But it also occurs because the HI is actually a scale of externalizing behaviors (cf. Table 2), which was apparently originally developed (Conners, 1973) mainly to provide a shorter version of the 39-item Conners Teacher's Rating Scale and not to measure hyperactivity per se.

Boys from the four groups in the clinic validation sample were also observed in the two playroom settings that were previously described. In the Free Play situation, it was motor behaviors that discriminated the groups. The H and AH boys tended to accumulate higher ($p < .07$) wrist actometer readings than did the A boys, and the H boys tended ($p < .08$) to be out of their seats more than the A and PC groups. In the Restricted Academic situation, the AH boys again accumulated higher ($p < .05$) wrist actometer readings than the A and PC boys, but inattentive behaviors also discriminated the groups. Both the H and the AH boys tended ($p < .07$) to be off-task more and both finished fewer items on their coding worksheets ($p < .05$) than the A and PC boys. The H boys showed a trend toward more attention shifts ($p < .09$) than the A boys. In both of the playroom situations, the A boys showed less deviant behavior than either of the hyperactive groups (H and AH); in fact, none of their observed behaviors distinguished them from the psychiatric control (PC) group (cf. Roberts, 1979). This finding is consistent with the belief that exclusive aggressive boys *can* control themselves and that in situations like the clinic evaluation, where it is to their advantage to conform, they in fact do so. Since the AH group was often deviant in the playroom, there is little doubt that these two kinds of aggressive conduct-problem boys (A and AH) do differ in their behavior. The fact that the H and AH groups were repeatedly different from the A and PC groups on these dependent variables suggests that hyperactivity is an important determinant of behavior at referral. Our previous work with an older sample (Loney et al., 1981) suggests that aggression plays a major role in behavior at 5-year follow-up. If so, the most frequent differences in adolescent behavior might be between the A and AH boys as contrasted with the H and PC boys.

Analyses similar to these have been carried out in two previous studies of new referrals to the University of Iowa child psychiatry outpatient clinic. The first study (Roberts, 1979) used the same (validation) sample and divided it into three groups (A, AH, and H) on the basis of chart ratings of hyperactivity and aggression, extreme scores on the traditional Hyperactivity factor of the Conners Teacher's Rating Scale, and extreme scores on the traditional Conduct Problem (aggression) factor of the Conners Mother's Rating Scale. Assignment to a symptom group in the Roberts study required agreement between two sources (clinic rater and teacher in the case of hyperactivity; clinic rater and mother in the case of aggression). The second study (Milich et al., 1980) used the 50 boys of the original (derivation) sample and divided them into three groups (A, AH, and H) on the basis of median splits on Hyperactivity and Aggression factor scores derived from chart ratings.

In both of these studies, the boys' behaviors in a Free Play and a Restricted Academic situation were analyzed. Five "activity" measures were obtained in both situations: number of grid crossings, percent of time spent out-of-seat, ankle actometer reading, wrist actometer reading, and percent of time spent fidgeting. Two "inattention" measures were obtained in both situations: percent of time off-task and number of attention shifts. An additional measure of number of correct worksheet items on a coding task was also obtained during the Restricted Academic period. Therefore, a total of 15 different measures of active or inattentive playroom behaviors were obtained in both studies.

Six of the 15 core measures tended to differentiate ($p < .10$) the four groups (A, AH, H, and PC) in the above validation analyses. Five of those six measures were significant in the Roberts (1979) study using the same sample; four of the six were also significant in the Milich et al. (1980) study using a different sample. All six currently differentiating measures (Free Play out-of-seat and wrist-actometer; Restricted Academic wrist actometer, off-task, attention shifts, and worksheet items) were replicates of significant measures in one or both of the previous studies.

Nine of the core playroom measures did *not* differentiate the four groups in the above validation analyses. Four of those nine measures were not significant in either the Roberts (1979) or the Milich et al. (1980) studies. These consistently nondiscriminating measures were: fidgeting and attention shifts in the Free Play situation and fidgeting and ankle actometer in the Restricted Academic situation.

## Five Children in the Clinic Playroom

In order to illustrate individual behavioral differences associated with the four identified groups, four of the 50 referred boys in the original derivation sample were chosen on the basis of their IOWA Conners scores to represent examples of the groups: exclusive aggressive, aggressive hyperactive, exclusive hyperactive, and neither hyperactive nor aggressive (psychiatric control). The research level screening scores ($> 11$ for the IO subscale and $> 7$ for the A subscale) were used. An additional classmate control boy was similarly chosen from a group of 35 volunteer classmates of the 50 clinic-referred boys. The five boys (Table 7) were equated as closely as possible on age, grade, and WISC-R IQ, but other test scores, descriptions, ratings, and data on their behavior in the playroom were not tabulated until after their selection.[15]

Jay was placed in the exclusive aggressive group on the basis of his scores on the IOWA Conners IO and A subscales. He was an 11-year-old fourth grader and had a WISC-R Full Scale IQ of 83 (Verbal IQ 77, Performance IQ 92). Jay's teacher described him as showing low achievement with only a few exceptions. On the intake form, she wrote about his hostile behavior, occasional dangerousness to peers, disobedience, chronic lying, and exhibitions of hate and vengefulness. She wrote that she believed him to be beyond remediation, but she noted that during the few weeks before the outpatient evaluation his behavior had improved to the point that he was a "different child." Jay's mother said that he liked to act stupid, and she complained that he lied all the time, was lazy, and picked up money left around the house. He had a tendency to disappear from home periodically and had to be looked for. On the day of the outpatient evaluation, Jay's behavior in the playroom was exemplary. During the Free Play situation, he crossed only one of the grids that were marked on the floor, was out of his seat only 4% of the time, and fidgeted or made noise only 14 of the time. He was off-task (not playing) only 8% of the time, but he made 22 attention shifts (from toy to nontoy or from one toy to another). In the Restricted Academic situation, Jay crossed no grids and was never out of his seat, but he fidgeted 16% of the time. He made no noise and was off-task (not working) only 10% of the time, but he shifted attention 18 times (from coding task to something else). He did not play with any of the forbidden toys on an adjacent table. Jay correctly completed 255 worksheet items.

John, the boy who was selected to represent the aggressive hyperactive group, was a 10-year-old third grader. His WISC-R Full Scale IQ was 81 (Verbal IQ 78, Performance IQ 87). John's teacher described him as unable to pay attention, unwilling to try difficult work, daydreaming, disruptive, and as sometimes defiant and belligerent. She said John lost his temper quickly, fought easily, and did not play by the rules. His mother described him as very active and unsettled, and as misbehaving and fighting. In the clinic playroom, John behaved well when allowed to play as he wished, but he did not comply when asked to work. In the Free Play situation, John crossed 15 grids and was out of his seat 52% of the time, but he did not fidget and made noise only 2% of the time. He was off-task only 5% of the time in the Free Play situation, and he made 15 attention shifts. In the Restricted Academic Situation, John crossed 5 grids, was out of his

## Table 7.  Performance of Five Boys in Two Playroom Situations

| Child's Name* | Diagnostic Group** | Number of Grids Crossed | Percent Out-of-Seat | Percent Fidgeting | Percent Noise | Number of Attention Shifts | Percent Off-Task | Forbidden Toy | Number of Correct Worksheet Items |
|---|---|---|---|---|---|---|---|---|---|
| | | | | Behavior | | | | | |
| | | | | *Free Play Situation* | | | | | |
| Jay | A | 1 | 4 | 1 | 1 | 22 | 8 | — | — |
| John | AH | 15 | 52 | 0 | 2 | 15 | 5 | — | — |
| Jeff | H | 24 | 100 | 0 | 12 | 8 | 53 | — | — |
| Barry | PC | 2 | 2 | 0 | 0 | 12 | 2 | — | — |
| Todd | CC | 25 | 79 | 2 | 1 | 15 | 3 | — | — |
| | | | | *Restricted Academic Situation* | | | | | |
| Jay | A | 0 | 0 | 16 | 0 | 18 | 10 | No | 255 |
| John | AH | 5 | 11 | 59 | 26 | 14 | 85 | Yes | 45 |
| Jeff | H | 4 | 4 | 13 | 1 | 11 | 42 | Yes | 160 |
| Barry | PC | 0 | 0 | 4 | 0 | 12 | 5 | No | 268 |
| Todd | CC | 0 | 0 | 3 | 0 | 9 | 2 | No | 328 |

Notes:

*Children's names are pseudonyms.

**Children were assigned to groups based on their scores on the IOWA Conners Teacher's Rating Scale: A = Exclusive Aggressive; AH = Aggressive Hyperactive; H = Exclusive Hyperactive; PC = Psychiatric Control; and CC = Classmate Control.

seat 11% of the time, and fidgeted 59% of the time. He made noise 26% of the time, was off-task 85% of the time, and made 14 attention shifts. John played with one of the forbidden toys during the examiner's absence, and he correctly completed only 45 worksheet items.

Jeff, the boy selected to exemplify exclusive hyperactivity, was an 11-year-old fourth grader at the time of his psychiatric evaluation, with a WISC-R Full Scale IQ of 88 (Verbal IQ 87, Performance IQ 91). Jeff's teacher described him as a slow worker who was easily distracted, did not complete assignments, made excuses, and demanded a great deal of attention. The aunt who was raising him complained mostly of Jeff's problems in minding, completing chores, and helping around the house. She indicated that when Jeff was alone he did things better than when other family members were around. During his evaluation, Jeff had trouble with both playroom settings. In the Free Play situation, Jeff crossed 24 grids, was out of his seat 100% of the time, and was off-task 53% of the time. He did not fidget at all, was involved in noisy behavior 12% of the time, and made 8 attention shifts. In the Restricted Academic situation, Jeff crossed only 4 grids and was out of his seat only 4% of the time, but he was off-task 42% of the time. He fidgeted 13% of the time, was involved in noisy behavior 1% of the time, and made 11 attention shifts. Jeff played with one of the forbidden toys and finished 160 worksheet items.

Barry, the control boy from the clinic-referred group, was a 10-year-old third grader whose WISC-R Full Scale IQ was 83 (Verbal IQ 75, Performance IQ 93). The fact that English was not spoken in his home and that Barry himself was depressed may have contributed to the WISC-R score discrepancy. Barry's teacher said that he did not make efficient use of time and that he handed his work in late, but when he did it was acceptably done. She considered Barry to be no discipline problem, and she had observed no problems in his relationships with other children. Barry's mother described him as depressed and occasionally irritable. Barry performed well in both playroom settings. In the Free Play situation, Barry crossed two grids, was out of his seat only 2% of the time, and did not fidget at all. He made no noise, was off-task only 2% of the time, and shifted attention 12 times. In the Restricted Academic situation, Barry crossed no grids, was never out of his seat, and fidgeted 4% of the time. He again made no noise, was off-task only 5% of the time, and shifted attention 12 times. Barry did not approach the forbidden toys, and he correctly completed 268 worksheet items.

Todd was chosen from the group of classmate controls who were involved in the clinic study. He was a 10-year-old fourth grader with a WISC-R Full Scale IQ of 91 (Verbal IQ 81, Performance IQ 104). On the day of his clinic visit, he was active and involved when he played alone, and he did very well when asked to work. In the Free Play situation, Todd crossed 25 grids and was out of his seat 79% of the time, but he was off-task (not playing) only 3% of the time. He fidgeted only 2% of the time, made noise only 1% of the time, and made 15 attention shifts. In the Restricted Academic situation, Todd crossed no grids and never left his seat. He was off-task (not working) only 2% of the time, fidgeted only 3% of the time, made no noise, and 9 attention shifts. Todd did not approach the forbidden toys, and he correctly completed 328 worksheet items.

In the Free Play situation, both the H boy and the AH boy crossed more grids and were out of their seats more than were either the A or the PC boy.[16] Therefore, within the clinic sample, the two hyperactive boys appeared to be "overactive" in their locomotor behavior. However, the nonreferred classmate control (CC) boy also showed a great deal of locomotor activity in the Free Play situation. To the extent that the CC boy is representative, it may thus be more accurate to speak of the A boy and the PC boy (who was depressed) as having shown locomotor "underactivity." There was almost no fidgeting in the Free Play situation, even though the A and the PC boys were seldom out of their seats. The H boy was off-task much more than any of the other boys, and he tended to be more noisy. However, it was the A boy who most often shifted his attention.

When the circumstances were changed from Free Play to Restricted Academic, all boys showed less locomotor behavior and correspondingly more fidgetiness. Changes in attention shifts were minimal; the A boy made the most attention shifts in both settings. Similarly, there were minimal changes across settings in off-task behavior for four ot the five boys. The A, PC, and CC boys were seldom off-task in either situation, and the H boy was frequently off-task in both situations. In contrast, the AH boy was off-task very little in the Free Play situation and almost all of the time in the Restricted Academic situation. This suggests that the H boy may have a general problem *sustaining his attention,* while the AH boy may have a problem with *adapting to external demands.*

Whatever the reason for these differences, they are in fact typical of the diagnostic groups that these individual boys represent. In Roberts' (1979) study of previously referred boys from the validation sample, the H group was off-task significantly more often than the other groups in the Free Play situation (18% of the time, compared to 7% for the A and AH groups); in the Restricted Academic situation, the AH group was off-task more often (66% of the time, compared to 40% for the H group and 12% for the A group).

It is easy to see that "hyperactive" groups with different ratios of H to AH boys could behave differently, and that differences in the specific situations in which their behavior is observed might easily interact with differences in the diagnostic composition of the groups to produce widely divergent average behavior. And, since A boys are indistinguishable from psychiatric controls on these playroom variables, it is obvious that if one considers H, AH, *and* A boys to be alternative and indistinguishable representatives of a generalized *conduct disorder,* the results of observational studies will be even more perplexing. The fact that most research has been done on groups in which AH boys predominate perhaps accounts for the commonly reported finding that "hyperactive" children do not differ from normals in free play settings, but that differences appear under conditions of external constraint and pacing.

Likewise, the variations in these playroom data are reminiscent of the behavioral discrepancies that are typically reported between what clinicians see in their clinics and what teachers and parents see in school and at home. Rather fine-grained diagnostic distinctions may be related to relatively distinct patterns of child behavior in different situations. If so, a belief in either "true" (cross-situationally invariant) hyperactivity or generalized conduct disorder will tend to be accompanied by a belief in the inexplicable variability of children with behavior problems.

Within the Restricted Academic situation, only the H and the AH boys left their assigned seats at all. Not surprisingly, they showed markedly more off-task behavior and did much less assigned work than the A, PC, and CC boys. When they were out of their seats, they both interacted with the forbidden or "distractor" toys. Only the H and the AH boys made any noise in the Restricted Academic situation. For all of the six variables involved in the above description (number of grids crossed, percent out-of-seat, percent noise, percent off-task, forbidden toy, and number of correct worksheet items), the AH boy was relatively more active, off-task, and noncompliant than the H boy, suggesting once again that the AH boy had more problems than the H boy in adapting to external demands. The AH boy also fidgeted over half of the time in the Restricted Academic situation, while the H boy fidgeted relatively little. (In contrast, within the Free Play situation, it was the H boy who crossed more grids, spent more time out of his seat, made more noise, and was more off-task). It should be noted that greater locomotor activity does not completely account for the lack of attention paid to the coding task by the H and AH boys in the Restricted Academic situation; even the AH boy was *in* his seat 89% of the time, but he was *off*-task 85% of the time.

# USING THE IOWA CONNERS TEACHER'S RATING SCALE

## General Considerations

The IOWA Conners Teacher's Rating Scale is essentially an empirically derived method for achieving greater control over subjective teacher judgments by making them conform more closely to external ratings of two important symptom dimensions: hyperactivity and aggression. Using the IOWA Conners subscales to assign children to one of the four diagnostic groups suggested by the fourfold model is almost completely operational and objective from the clinician's standpoint, but it still relies on the judgments of individual teachers as to what is or is not problematic behavior. One might argue that we have simply exchanged

The teacher's subjective judgments for our own, and there is room for considerable debate as to whether teachers' judgments should play a central role in diagnosis.[17] However, there is little evidence that clinicians' judgments of hyperactivity are better than teachers'—and there is considerable evidence that parents' judgments are worse (e.g., Sprague & Sleator, 1973). Direct playroom (e.g., Roberts, 1979) or classroom (e.g., Abikoff, Gittelman-Klein, & Klein, 1977) observations can provide valid information about hyperactivity, but they are less practical, and they seldom provide ample data on aggression.

An important factor in the perpetuation of such controversies is that both sides are right: those who correctly point out that teacher judgments are not sufficiently reliable or valid and that they can lead in individual cases to blatant errors, *and* those who maintain that teacher judgments are demonstrably the most reliable and valid of the easily available alternatives. In some respects, the end result of requiring that newly introduced diagnostic instruments be accompanied by evidence of high reliability and validity has been that inadequate, but traditional, methods have not been replaced with better, albeit imperfect, new methods. To argue that teachers can be biased and unfair is to be correct; but to ignore teachers' input in favor of a parent or child interview, psychological or educational tests, and/or electroencephalographic or neurological studies is to base diagnoses on information of even more questionable value.[18] In both psychiatric and medical sources (DSM-III, American Psychiatric Association, 1980; Sleator, in press), increasing emphasis is being placed on teacher reports as necessary and sufficient in the assessment of childhood hyperactivity. Therefore, an assessment method using teacher data should provide a good foundation upon which to construct what might eventually become a truly complete diagnostic system (i.e., one that uses information from different sources, situations, and occasions to produce its assessments).

In the meantime, we view the new fourfold method as having been derived from a statistical decision model, rather than a medical syndrome model. We have moved from a method that placed descriptors into arbitrary conceptual categories, that depended upon complex ratings of secondary materials, and that was anchored within a single sample of boys with "minimal brain dysfunction" (Langhorne & Loney, 1979) to a method where each of the individual descriptors has been empirically validated, where decisions are based on raw scores from easily obtained teacher ratings, and where some validity has been shown for several heterogeneous samples.[19]

## Exclusion Criteria and Additional Information

There are only some children to whom these subscales and screening scores can be applied. Naturally, the children should be attending more-or-less conventional schools in order to be appropriate subjects for the Conners Teacher's Rating Scale. In the interests of increasing homogeneity, our validating studies have excluded girls, preschoolers, teenagers, and children with IQs below 70 or with unequivocal brain damage, sensory loss, or psychosis; the applicability of the IOWA Conners subscales to such children is therefore unknown.

It is hoped that the present operational definition will adequately handle the most frequent form of childhood hyperactivity: that which causes serious problems in school. Data from a previous study suggest that only 5% of cases will involve a parent-identified hyperactive child whose current teacher does *not* see a problem at school, and in at least some of those cases, one will be dealing with an essentially aggressive child rather than a hyperactive one.

Supplementary information is often sought from parents and/or clinic personnel (e.g., examining physician, psychologist) in order to confirm the presence of cross-situational ("true") hyperactivity, as opposed to "mere" situational or psychogenic hyperactivity. Some diagnosticians and researchers refuse to call children from "chaotic" or "disadvantaged" homes hyperactive on similar etiological grounds: the child's hyperactivity presumably has an environmental component. Likewise, data on age of onset (i.e., duration of problem) can be collected in order to demonstrate that one is dealing with "genuine" (i.e., lifelong or chronic) hyperactivity, conceived of as organic, temperamental, and/or genetic.

Most of these etiological distinctions are actually made because people want to avoid medicating children who do not have a medical condition. However, none of them can be made with confidence. Few children are unceasingly overactive, and those few are not inevitably more responsive to CNS stimulants (Klein & Gittelman-Klein, 1974). Chaotic or disadvantaged parents may themselves be suffering from residual forms of a life-long hyperkinetic disorder. Distinguishing typical activity level and age-appropriate disciplinary dramas from atypical patterns in 2- to 4-year-olds is no easy feat. And attempts to pinpoint retrospectively the onset of a child's behavior problems are notoriously apt to miss their mark, especially since parents' attitudes and reactions interact with children's behaviors. It seems especially paradoxical to require for a definitive diagnosis that parents recall an early onset of behaviors, if one is willing to disregard those same parents' report about current behaviors when they conflict with teachers' reports (DSM-III).

Moreover, there is no easy link between symptom descriptions and causation or etiology—and, perhaps fortunately, the kind, severity, extent, or chronicity of symptoms do not necessarily imply what treatment should be used. "Organic" problems can respond to "psychological" treatments, and vice versa; both stimulant medication and behavior modification change behaviors across wide ranges of known and unknown etiology. Rapoport's work (Rapoport, Buchsbaum, Zahn, Ludlow, & Mikkelsen, 1978) suggests that even normal children are affected by stimulant medication.

The central questions for those who diagnose childhood hyperactivity on the basis of symptoms should be: (1) Are this child's symptoms sufficiently severe (atypical) to require intervention? (2) What influences are maintaining or exacerbating the symptoms? (3) Will any of those influences respond to simple environmental change? And, finally, (4) what is the *least drastic intervention* that is apt to reduce the atypicality of the remaining symptoms? The therapeutic principle here is that one wants to approach flies with a flyswatter and save the elephant gun for elephants.

*Secondary Screening*

When test decisions are not considered accurate enough, the suggestion to apply a secondary screening device is sometimes made. In the case of the Iowa IO subscale, for example, one might call children hyperactive who scored above 11 (95% of whom should actually be hyperactive) and apply a secondary screen to those who scored at or below 11 (37% of whom should also be hyperactive). However, in these circumstances, it is difficult to make any recommendations for a potential secondary screening device. One's own observations of the child in the clinic, either in interview or in unstandardized play situations, are apt to lead to the conclusion that a child who has genuine problems in his or her customary environments does not have a problem. Existing parent rating scales are not sufficiently discriminating and may identify a different subset of children as hyperactive, rather than "corroborate" the existence of hyperactivity in a subset already identified by teachers (Glow, 1981). Many believe that parent interviews are useful, but at present there is no widely used structured interview and very little empirical evidence to substantiate these beliefs.

One *can* defend gathering additional information in the school in order to improve the diagnostic process. Where possible, independent ratings from several teachers should be collected. The child's teacher from a previous year is perhaps the best source of historical data. A substitute teacher, student teacher, or teacher's aide can provide useful information to clarify or confirm the ratings of the child's primary teacher. There will be occasions when a school nurse, librarian, or art or music teacher will be able to rate the child accurately. Observations by a school psychologist, using if at all possible one of the validated observational methods (e.g., Abikoff, Gittelman-Klein, & Klein, 1977) can be invaluable in decision making. And, for the future, a structured telephone interview with teachers could be developed in order to allow teachers to amplify and qualify their input in ways similar to those that make interviews with parents better than parent rating scales.

# SUMMARY

Children placed in the different symptom groups by the IOWA Conners subscales should behave differently in important respects; if they do not, the groupings (and/or the methods used to form them) can be abandoned without either difficulty or regret. The fact that the subscales will surely not be as good as they should be—and that they might simultaneously be as good as most alternatives—is an unfortunate commentary on our current level of understanding of childhood hyperactivity.

If the IOWA Conners subscales prove to be of little utility, the data presented here should still convey a message to those of us involved in diagnosing childhood hyperactivity for either clinical or research purposes. That message is: We do not have a literature about childhood hyperactivity as such; instead, we have a literature about childhood externalizing behavior problems (hyperactivity *and* aggression) that we *call* a literature about childhood hyperactivity. This is true because hyperactivity and aggression are typically correlated (especially in the teacher's scales on which we have increasingly relied for diagnosis) and because we have applied few methods with discriminant, as opposed to convergent, validity. Since existing hyperactivity scales include both hyperactive and aggressive descriptors, they naturally overselect children who have both kinds of symptoms.

It is apparent that definitions of childhood hyperactivity which mix *both* hyperactive and aggressive descriptors will produce heterogeneous samples, as will exclusion criteria or sampling biases that favor the selection of aggressive youngsters. The data that we have presented in this chapter make it obvious that definitions and scales which use *only* hyperactivity descriptors (including the IOWA Conners IO subscale) also produce heterogeneous samples of hyperactive and aggressive youngsters. Although numerous others have pointed out these problems, the current data make it possible to estimate precisely how mixed our samples may typically have been. Using data from our clinic validation sample, it is possible to determine that 93% of the boys placed in the aggressive hyperactive group by the clinical screening scores of the empirically derived IOWA Conners obtained scores at or above the conventional cutoff of 15 on the original Conners Abbreviated Teacher's Rating Scale or Hyperkinesis Index (HI). Similarly, 57% of the exclusive hyperactive group and 50% of the exclusive aggressive group obtained "hyperactive" scores on the original Conners HI. If a new sample were formed consisting only of those boys who were identified by the original Conners HI as hyperactive, 65% of that "hyperactive" sample would be aggressive *and* hyperactive according to their scores on the IOWA Conners, and 18% would be exclusively aggressive. Only *17%* of a hyperactive sample formed using the customary cutoff score of 15 on the original 10-item Conners Hyperkinesis Index would actually be *exclusively* hyperactive, using boys referred to our clinic and the clinical level screening scores on the IO and A subscales of the IOWA Conners Teacher's Rating Scale. Adding to our diagnostic procedures in the typical ways (e.g., by getting parent input) might easily make the situation worse instead of better, because parents' ratings of hyperactivity are even more contaminated with aggression than teachers' ratings are.

These sorts of findings make it easy to argue that it is necessary to apply an exclusionary criterion for aggression when studying childhood hyperactivity (and vice versa). The IOWA Conners provides a means for studying *only* exclusively hyperactive children—or, preferably, for studying exclusively hyperactive, aggressive hyperactive, and exclusively aggressive children *separately*. It is hoped that subsequent studies of the three symptom groups may explain some part of the variability that is the central characteristic of hyperactive children.

## ACKNOWLEDGMENTS

Some of the findings reported in this chapter were presented in a symposium at the American Psychological Association meeting in Montreal, 1980. Collection of the data in the clinical derivation sample was supported by NIMH grant MH-32992. The contributions of James Caputo, Mary Ann Roberts, and Paul Whitten to the final shape of this work are gratefully acknowledged.

## NOTES

1.  Large motor hyperactivity (locomotor restlessness) and small motor hyperactivity (fidgetiness) originally loaded on two different factors, but in our subsequent studies of more heterogeneous clinic groups, they occupied the same factor and are therefore both considered part of the general Hyperactivity dimension.

2.  To date, our studies have not led us to separate inattention from overactivity, or to consider either one as central to diagnosis in the way that is proposed by DSM-III. This may be because most attention-deficit children referred to a tertiary clinic such as ours have the combined form of the disorder.

3.  We have not found it necessary to distinguish between socialized and unsocialized forms of aggression, or between instrumental and hostile aggression.

4.  A similar distinction has been made between learning disabled and hyperactive children by Dykman, Ackerman, and Oglesby (1980).

5.  Both the mothers' and the teachers' scales were originally included in our analyses, but it proved impossible to derive a mother's hyperactivity scale that did not correlate with *both* the Hyperactivity and the Aggression factors.

6.  Decisions to include or exclude an item were based on examination of both the present correlations and the correlations between the item and the two factors in previous studies. Items that loaded negatively on a factor were excluded for the sake of scoring convenience. Items were excluded that did not describe the child's symptom behavior, but instead described the reactions to it of adults or peers, or that seemed to involve either illegal or norm-violating outcomes of the child's symptom behavior. The item "excitable, impulsive" was included because it was the remaining potential hyperactivity item that correlated highest with the Hyperactivity factor and lowest (although significantly) with the Aggression factor.

7.  The Conners Teacher's Rating Scale has undergone several revisions in which items have been added, eliminated, or changed in wording. All of these revisions yield similar factor structures and are considered essentially equivalent. The IOWA Conners was derived from the 39-item version described by Conners in 1973 and later incorporated into the child assessment battery of the NIMH Early Clinical Drug Evaluation Unit (Guy, 1976). In the earlier 39-item version (Conners, 1969), the IOWA Conners IO subscale would consist of the following 5 items: sits fiddling with small objects, hums and makes other odd noises, excitable, inattentive, and difficulty in concentrating; the A subscale would consist of: quarrelsome, acts "smart," temper outbursts, defiant, and uncooperative. In the most recent 28-item version (Goyette, Conners, & Ulrich, 1978), the IOWA Conners IO subscale would consist of items 1, 2, 7, 15, and 21, and the A subscale would consist of items 4, 5, 10, 12, and 27.

8.   By "unselected," we mean that all boys in six schools of a rural school district whose teachers and parents consented were included; the term is used to emphasize that inclusion in the sample was not random or stratified, nor was it based on any particular selection criterion.

9.   The failure of the IO subscale to show the common decrease with age is perhaps due to the fact that the subscale reflects primarily inattentive, impulsive, and small motor behavior, rather than large motor behavior (Weiss, Minde, Werry, Douglas, & Nemeth, 1971).

10.   After all rating scales had been completed, each teacher was asked to identify any boy(s) on her/his class list who was "on the go, excitable, inattentive, into everything, and unable to keep his mind on one thing" and to indicate any of those boys who would need to be referred by the average teacher for outside help because of their activity level.

11.   The central problem for the researcher is that, in order to insure that homogeneous diagnostic groups are studied, the majority of truly hyperactive children will be excluded. This will sometimes make it difficult to find enough "diagnosed" hyperactive children to carry out a study.

12.   If one believes that hyperactive children should be *spared* diagnosis and treatment (e.g., that diagnosis is stigmatizing, that the side effects of treatment are inevitable and deleterious, and that the long-term efficacy of treatment is negligible), then no test is necessary.

13.   If one believes that treatment is necessary (i.e., that it is both safe and effective, that there are no effective alternatives, that there are no means for predicting beforehand which children will respond, but that normal children will *not* respond), then the overriding concern should be to avoid *depriving* hyperactive children of treatment, and no test is necessary.

14.   When we speak of differences among any of these groups, we are talking about differences that reached a two-tailed $p = .05$ level of significance; if the comparison resulted in a larger $p$ value, that value is specifically mentioned (e.g., $p < .06$). When the $p$ value exceeded .10, we describe the groups as equivalent on the given variable, regardless of the existence or size of numerical differences.

15.   Wrist and ankle actometer scores are not tabulated for these boys; their patterns generally paralleled those of the grid crossing and out-of-seat observations.

16.   Throughout the discussion of individual cases, we are obviously speaking of numerical, rather than statistical, differences between individual boys. However, we have tried to avoid emphasizing differences that are numerically small or that do not correspond to statistical findings in group comparisons.

17.   The IOWA subscales are simply 10 items completed by individual teachers, and the "actual diagnoses" used in the decision tables were merely global judgments by the *same* teachers. These appear to be extremely flimsy data on which to erect even a preliminary assessment method. However, we have demonstrated using a multitrait ANOVA (Roberts et al., 1981) that these same teachers can reliably differentiate among the traits involved, and their ratings are correlated with children's observed off-task behavior in the classroom. The teachers in the present classroom sample considered 36% of the AH boys and 45% of the H boys identified by their IOWA subscale ratings to be hyperactive enough to require referral, but they considered only 9% of the A group and 1% of the CC group to be hyperactive and referable ($p < .0001$). These differences indicate that teachers do not confuse hyperactivity and aggression in their global identifications. In another sample of rural Iowa elementary school children (Jones, Loney, Weissenburger, & Fleischmann, 1975), the 12% of unselected boys considered hyperactive and referable by their teachers spent as much time off-task as clinic-diagnosed hyperkinetic boys when observed in their respective classrooms. Moreover, these teacher-identified hyperactive boys were off-task more often than were teacher-identified average boys. Finally, the playroom and test data presented in this chapter for boys placed in groups solely on the basis of ratings on these 10 items by their classroom teachers suggest that these subjective ratings may possess considerable validity.

18.   Wender (1971) was an early advocate of the excellent notion that only demonstrably useful tests should be used in diagnosing minimal brain dysfunction/hyperkinesis, and Sleator (1982) employed the same principle, with wonderfully parsimonious results.

19.  O'Leary and Steen (1980) have also developed a method for operationalizing the hyperactivity and aggression dimensions. They assigned items from both the Conners and the Quay teacher rating scales to apparently appropriate individual symptom categories and then replicated and cross-validated the Loney et al. (1978) factor structure in two groups of youngsters high on the Conners Hyperactivity factor. (They failed to replicate the factor structure in a more heterogeneous group). As yet they have presented no screening scores or validity data for their method. Because their subscales are lengthy and require an administration of two different questionnaires (a total of 94 items), they are perhaps more reliable *and* more redundant than the subscales that we have developed. To date, the exact price that each method pays for its particular trade-off between reliability and convenience has not been assessed.

# REFERENCES

Abikoff, H., Gittelman-Klein, R., & Klein, D. Validation of a classroom observation code for hyperactive children. *Journal of Consulting and Clinical Psychology*, 1977, *45*, 772–783.

Achenbach, T. A., & Edelbrock, C. S. The classification of child psychopathology: A review and analysis of empirical efforts. *Psychological Bulletin*, 1978, *85*, 1275–1301.

American Psychiatric Association. *DSM-II: Diagnostic and statistical manual of mental disorders.* 2nd ed. Washington, D.C.: APA, 1968.

American Psychiatric Association. *DSM-III: Diagnostic and statistical manual of mental disorders.* 3rd ed. Washington, D.C.: APA, 1980.

Barkley, R. Hyperactivity. In E. Mash & L. Terdal (Eds.), *Behavioral assessment of childhood disorders*. New York: Guilford Press, 1981.

Cantwell, D., Russell, A., Mattison, R., & Will, L. A comparison of DSM-II and DSM-III in the diagnosis of childhood psychiatric disorders: I. Agreement with expected diagnosis. *Archives of General Psychiatry*, 1979, *36*, 1208–1213.

Conners, C.K. A teacher rating scale for use in drug studies with children. *American Journal of Psychiatry*, 1969, *126*, 152–156.

Conners, C. K. Rating scales for use in drug studies with children. *Psychopharmacology Bulletin* (Special Issue—Pharmacology of Children), 1973, 35–42.

Dykman, R. A., Ackerman, P. T., & Oglesby, D. M. Correlates of problem solving in hyperactive, learning disabled, and control boys. *Journal of Learning Disabilities*, 1980, *13*, 309–318.

Glow, R. Cross-validity and normative data on the Conners' parent and teacher rating scales. In K. Gadow & J. Loney (Eds.), *Psychosocial aspects of drug treatment for hyperactivity*. Boulder, Colorado, Westview Press, 1981.

Goyette, C. H., Conners, C. K., & Ulrich, R. F. Normative data on revised Conners parent and teacher rating scales. *Journal of Abnormal Child Psychology*, 1978, *6*, 221–236.

Guy, W. *ECDEU assessment manual for psychopharmacology*. Washington, D.C.: U.S. Government Printing Office, 1976. (Department of H.E.W. publication No. 76-3381)

Jones, N. M., Loney, J., Weissenburger, F. E., & Fleischmann, D. J. The hyperkinetic child: What do teachers know? *Psychology in the Schools*, 1975, *12*, 388–392.

Klein, D. F., & Gittelman-Klein, R. Diagnosis of minimal brain dysfunction and the hyperkinetic syndrome. In C. K. Conners (Ed.), *Clinical use of stimulant drugs in children*. New York: American Elsevier, 1974.

Langhorne, J. E., & Loney, J. A four-fold model for subgrouping the hyperkinetic/MBD syndrome. *Child Psychiatry and Human Development*, 1979, *9*, 153–159.

Loney, J. Hyperkinesis comes of age: What do we know and where should we go? *American Journal of Orthopsychiatry*, 1980, *50*, 28–42.

Loney, J., Kramer, J., & Milich, R. The hyperkinetic child grows up: Predictors of symptoms, delinquency, and achievement at follow-up. In K. Gadow & J. Loney (Eds.), *Psychosocial aspects of drug treatment for hyperactivity*. Boulder, Colorado: Westview Press, 1981.

Loney, J., Langhorne, J. E., Jr., & Paternite, C. E. An empirical basis for subgrouping the hyperkinetic/minimal brain dysfunction syndrome. *Journal of Abnormal Psychology*, 1978, *87*, 431-441.

Mattison, R., Cantwell, D., Russell, A., & Will, L. A comparison of DSM-II and DSM-III in the diagnosis of childhood psychiatric disorders: II. Interrater reliability. *Archives of General Psychiatry*, 1979, *36*, 1217-1222.

Meehl, P. *Clinical versus statistical prediction: A theoretical analysis and a review of the evidence.* Minneapolis: University of Minnesota Press, 1954.

Meehl, P., & Rosen, A. Antecedent probability and the efficiency of psychometric signs, patterns, or cutting scores. *Psychological Bulletin*, 1955, *52*, 194-216.

Milich, R., & Loney, J. The role of hyperactive and aggressive symptomatology in predicting adolescent outcome among hyperactive children. *Journal of Pediatric Psychology*, 1979, *4*, 93-112.

Milich, R., Loney, J., & Landau, S. *The independent dimensions of hyperactivity and aggression: A replication and further validation.* Unpublished manuscript, University of Iowa, 1980.

O'Leary, S. G., & Steen, P. *Independent assessment of hyperactivity and aggression in hyperactive children.* Paper presented at the meeting of the American Psychological Association, Montreal, September, 1980.

Quay, H. Classification. In H. Quay & J. Werry (Eds.), *Psychopathological disorders of childhood.* 2nd ed. New York: Wiley, 1979.

Rapoport, J., Buchsbaum, M., Zahn, T., Ludlow, C., & Mikkelsen, E. J. Dextroamphetamine: Cognitive and behavioral effects in normal prepubertal boys. *Science*, 1978, *199*, 560-563.

Roberts, M. A. *A behavioral method for differentiating hyperactive, aggressive, and hyperactive plus aggressive children.* Unpublished doctoral dissertation, University of Wisconsin, Madison, 1979.

Roberts, M. A., Milich, R., Loney, J., & Caputo, J. A multitrait-multimethod analysis of variance of teachers' ratings of aggression, hyperactivity, and inattention. *Journal of Abnormal Child Psychology*, 1981, *9*, 371-380.

Rosenthal, R. Estimating effective reliabilities in studies that employ judges' ratings. *Journal of Clinical Psychology*, 1973, *29*, 342-345.

Routh, D. K., & Schroeder, C. S. Standardized playroom measures as indices of hyperactivity. *Journal of Abnormal Child Psychology*, 1976, *4*, 199-207.

Sandberg, S. T., Rutter, M., & Taylor, E. Hyperkinetic disorder in psychiatric clinic attenders. *Developmental Medicine and Child Neurology*, 1978, *20*, 279-299.

Sleator, E. Office diagnosis of hyperactivity by the physician. In K. Gadow & I. Bialer (Ed.), *Advances in learning and behavioral disabilities.* Greenwich, Connecticut: JAI Press, 1982.

Sprague, R. L., & Sleator, E. K. Effects of psychopharmacological agents on learning disorders. *Pediatric Clinics of North America*, 1973, *20*, 719-735.

Weiss, G., Minde, K., Werry, J., Douglas, V., & Nemeth, E. The hyperactive child. VIII. Five year follow-up. *Archives of General Psychiatry*, 1971, *24*, 409-414.

Wender, P. *Minimal brain dysfunction in children.* New York: Wiley, 1971.

Werry, J. S., Sprague, R. L., & Cohen, M. N. Conners' teacher rating scale for use in drug studies with children: An empirical study. *Journal of Abnormal Child Psychology*, 1975, *3*, 217-229.

# THE EFFECT OF ALCOHOL ON FETAL GROWTH AND DEVELOPMENT AND IMPLICATIONS FOR COGNITIVE FUNCTION

James W. Hanson

The effects of ethanol on human behavior have been the subject of social commentary and scientific interest since the advent of recorded history (Warner & Rosett, 1975). Throughout most of this period, attention was directed to the acute and chronic consequences of ethanol abuse in adults. During the past decade, however, a rapidly growing body of data has reminded the medical and scientific communities and general public of the biological consequences of maternal prenatal ethanol use for the fetus. The effects have been demonstrated to extend over a spectrum, apparently dose-related, ranging from mild growth deficiency to a

Advances in Developmental and Behavioral Pediatrics, vol. 3, pages 149–162
Copyright © 1982 by JAI Press Inc.
All rights of reproduction in any form reserved.
ISBN: 0-89232-223-3

pattern of severe alterations of growth, morphogenesis and behavior clinically recognizable as the fetal alcohol syndrome (FAS) (Clarren et al., 1978).

The clinical delineation of the FAS has included attempts to investigate the behavioral correlates of observed neuropathologic changes in man and animals. However, many important questions remain unresolved. This is a matter of more than abstract interest, as several epidemiological studies (Jones et al., 1974; Hanson et al., 1976; Majewski et al., 1976; Dehaene et al., 1977a) suggest that ethanol use during pregnancy may be one of the most common recognizable causes of mental deficiency in this country today. Furthermore, the behavioral alterations frequently described in FAS children may also represent a considerable burden to our educational system as well as a substantial barrier to the habilitation of affected individuals. A fuller understanding of these aspects is necessary if we are to cope with needs of FAS children in the home, in the school, or in the community.

## CLINICAL FEATURES OF THE FETAL ALCOHOL SYNDROME

Although concern over the effects of ethanol on the developing fetus was expressed by ancient writers (Warner et al., 1975) it was not until the pioneering reports of Jones et al. (1973); Jones and Smith (1973); and Jones et al. (1976) in the early 1970s that sufficient attention was focused on specific clinical outcomes including behavior and other aspects of neurological performance. In 1973, these authors first reported recognizing a pattern of altered fetal growth, performance, and morphogenesis associated with maternal prenatal ethanol abuse which they termed FAS (Jones et al., 1973). They and subsequent authors have continued to explore the confines of this syndrome, which can be recognized clinically in many instances by the following features: (1) prenatal-onset growth deficiency; (2) a characteristic facial appearance; (3) an increase in the likelihood of major and minor congenital anomalies; and (4) alterations of nervous system function.

Children with FAS are usually small at birth and grow poorly thereafter (Kaminski et al., 1978; Little, 1977). Although in the neonatal period linear growth appears to be disproportionately reduced in comparison to weight, during postnatal life these children may display striking failure to thrive particularly with regard to weight gain. Thus, they often present to the clinician as short, slender children. Furthermore, recent evidence (Kaminski et al., 1978; Harlap et al., 1979; Kline, 1980) suggests a relationship between maternal prenatal alcohol consumption and abortion and stillbirth, even when controlled for other maternal variables, including socioeconomic status and smoking behavior.

The facial characteristics of children with FAS include narrow palpebral fissures, a short nose with low nasal bridge, epicanthic folds, a long smooth philtrum with narrow vermilion border of the upper lip, a rather hypoplastic midface and micrognathia (Jones et al., 1976). Other ocular abnormalities such as ptosis and strabismus are often noted, and minor malformations of the external ear may be present. These facial features when present in affected children, may be sufficiently striking to suggest the diagnosis in situations where the maternal history has not been available. These features have been well reviewed by Clarren and Smith (1978).

Children with the FAS also have an increased frequency of major congenital abnormalities (Clarren & Smith, 1978). Of particular importance is the increased frequency of cardiac malformations. However, cleft palate, ocular malformations, minor joint anomalies, aberrant palmar crease patterns, and minor genitourinary abnormalities have all been described with increased frequency. Malformations of the central nervous system are of particular concern. Among seven autopsied cases described by Clarren et al. (1978) microencephaly and abnormalities of neuroglial migration resulting in heterotopias have been among the most consistent findings. These observations have been confirmed by Majewski et al. (1978).

Alterations of central nervous system function have also been an outstanding feature of children damaged prenatally by maternal ethanol ingestion. These effects have been reported to include mental retardation as well as early developmental delay, tremulousness, hyperactivity, short attention span, and electroencephalographic alterations. These abnormalities, which are of primary interest for this report, will be discussed later. However, it is of particular importance to note that the frequency and severity of these effects can be related to the timing and amount of maternal alcohol ingestion during pregnancy and appear to be permanent in at least the more severely affected children. Furthermore, other functional abnormalities including neonatal hypotonia, hyperacusis, poor suck, and feeding difficulties have been described during the first year of life (Jones & Smith, 1973; Pierog et al., 1977; Streissguth et al., 1978b).

Not all children born to chronic alcoholic mothers have FAS. Indeed it is not possible at the present time to accurately estimate the prevalence of FAS among such children or to completely separate the effects of socioeconomic and other environmental and genetic factors which may contribute to the likelihood of occurrence of FAS. Furthermore, although a significant risk for the offspring of chronic alcoholic mothers clearly exists, a much larger group of women drink at more moderate levels during pregnancy. Thus, there has been considerable concern about the possibility of a dose-response relationship between amount and timing of ethanol consumption and the frequency and severity of effects on the fetus. Clinicians are frequently asked if there is a safe level of alcohol consumption during pregnancy, or in other situations are asked to quantitate the risk to a particular level of alcohol consumption because of maternal concern for fetal welfare. At the present time, no entirely satisfactory answer can be presented to such questions. However, a variety of animal and human epidemiologic studies have suggested that more moderate levels of alcohol consumption may also present a hazard to the fetus.

Perhaps the most convincing animal studies which point to a dose-response relationship have been carried out by Chernoff (1977). However, extrapolation of these results to humans is open to challenge on a variety of grounds. The studies of Little (1977) and Kaminski et al. (1976) suggest a dose-response relationship in man between maternal alcohol consumption and fetal growth which extends at least down to moderate levels of alcohol consumption if not lower. Similar results linking low to moderate levels of alcohol consumption to increased abortion rates have also been presented as mentioned above (Harlap et al., 1979; Kline et al., 1980). Furthermore, Ouellette et al. (1977) have presented data suggesting that increasing levels of maternal alcohol intake during pregnancy are related to increased risks for congenital anomalies in the fetus.

Up to the present time, a single prospective study has evaluated and categorized newborns according to maternal prenatal ethanol intake and FAS characteristics at the time of birth. Hanson et al. (1978) studied the effects of moderate alcohol consumption during pregnancy on fetal growth and morphogenesis. The subjects of this investigation were selected from 1,529 offspring of mothers participating in a larger study of pregnancy and health at two Seattle hospitals. All pregnant women in prenatal care by the fifth month of pregnancy at either hospital during a one-year period were eligible for the study. Eighty-five percent of those eligible agreed to participate. These mothers were interviewed during the fifth month of pregnancy regarding their alcohol and caffeine ingestion during and in the month prior to recognition of pregnancy. Also determined was their use of nicotine, drugs, and their diet during pregnancy. Alcohol use was determined by self-report from a quantity-frequency-variability interview and scored according to average ounces of absolute alcohol consumed daily.

The mothers were predominately white, middle-class, and well educated. Two-thirds were receiving prenatal care through a prepaid medical cooperative and one-third through the University of Washington Hospitals and Clinics which serve a wide variety of socioeconomic classes. The methodology of this study has been carefully described elsewhere (Streissguth et al., 1978c).

At the time of delivery, pairs of high risk and control infants were examined without knowledge of maternal drinking history. Infants were evaluated for abnormalities of growth, development, and morphogenesis using a standard procedure. Particular attention was paid to major and minor alterations of morphogenesis characteristic of the fetal alcohol syndrome.

Of 163 infants examined, 11 were judged clinically to show signs compatible with the prenatal effects of alcohol on growth and morphogenesis. Nine of the 11 came from the highest risk drinking group. Two of these infants were classified as having the full FAS and each of the mothers were subsequently identified as being a very heavy drinker. The other seven infants who showed lesser alterations of growth and morphogenesis were born to women who were reported to drink an average of one ounce or more of absolute alcohol per day in the month prior to recognition of pregnancy. Nicotine and caffeine use were also evaluated but neither was found to be as strongly related to neonatal abnormality as was alcohol. Likewise, no other clear effects related to the intake of other drugs could be identified.

These results were interpreted as indicating that both moderate and high levels of alcohol intake during early pregnancy may result in alterations of growth and morphogenesis in the fetus. Although at the time of completion of the study, little was known about the predictive validity of the partial FAS manifestations identified in some of the studied children, subsequent follow-up has begun to suggest that this population of children may be at an increased risk for behavioral and cognitive difficulties.

From these animal and human investigations, it has been concluded that no safe threshold of maternal alcohol consumption during pregnancy has yet been identified. For this reason, as a matter of prudence, it has been recommended by the Food and Drug Administration (Fetal Alcohol Syndrome, 1977) that maternal ethanol consumption during pregnancy not exceed two drinks per day.

In summary, the FAS is a unique and easily recognizable pattern of altered growth and development. However, it has become increasingly apparent that prenatal intrauterine alcohol exposures can result in a spectrum of effects of which FAS is only the most severe end. This is important to emphasize since behavioral effects may be found in children who lack many of the characteristic physical features of FAS (Streissguth et al., 1978b).

## BEHAVIORAL AND COGNITIVE FINDINGS IN THE FETAL ALCOHOL SYNDROME

As mentioned earlier, numerous behavioral abnormalities and other abnormalities of central nervous system function have been described in the FAS. These abnormalities are perhaps the most debilitating aspect of this condition. Thus, an increasing emphasis has been placed on the clinical description and investigation of the pathogenesis of these problems in the hope that this would lead to improved care of affected children.

Unfortunately, although increasing numbers of children affected with FAS are being identified in virtually all communities, the range of effects on children, the lack of familiarity of medical, educational, and other health care personnel with this condition, and as of yet relatively small numbers of affected children in individual centers have resulted in considerable confusion over the nature and significance of such findings. Furthermore, as is true in other situations where human outcomes are being investigated, carefully controlled studies are extremely difficult and many kinds of direct intervention studies are not possible.

Thus, a substantial amount of emphasis has been placed on epidemiologic approaches and upon the development of animal model test systems. Although many points of confusion still remain, a sufficient amount of data has now been generated for the overall nature of the problem to be discerned.

Perhaps the most obvious behavioral abnormality identified in children damaged by prenatal exposure to ethanol is a frank mental deficiency. Although a wide range of mental disability has been seen in association with FAS, ranging from apparently normal mental abilities to severe degrees of handicap, typical IQ scores of FAS children reported in the medical literature would place these individuals in the mildly retarded range of intellectual functioning. Studies throughout the world, (Majewski et al., 1978; Dehaene et al., 1977a; Streissguth et al., 1978b) have produced similar psychometric findings despite differences in tests administered. However, to suggest that children with facial and other characteristics of the FAS invariably display frank mental deficiency would be misleading. Some such children have been observed to have normal or near normal intellectual functioning, though these children generally appear to be among the most mildly affected patients in other respects. Indeed, it is not possible at the present time to quote a specific incidence of mental deficiency among children recognizable as having FAS, though it is clearly high among those children having the most numerous features of this disorder.

This variability becomes more understandable when it is recalled that FAS appears to represent a point near the severe end of a continuum relating maternal ethanol consumption to fetal outcome. Under this circumstance, one would expect to see a continuous range of outcomes representing fetal alcohol effects. The specific prevalence of any abnormality of nervous system performance among FAS children becomes a function of tests utilized, of the methods of ascertainment, and of criteria for accepting children into a particular study. The scattering of results found in available literature reflects this problem. These conflicting reports will not be easily resolvable until standardized procedures are utilized. Nevertheless, it is becoming increasingly clear that a broader population of children exists who display qualitatively and quantitatively different signs of central nervous system dysfunction for whom the problems may be ascribable to maternal prenatal ethanol use. As these children may also display milder physical abnormalities, it is correspondingly more difficult to establish a causal relationship. Nevertheless, observations on apparently more mildly affected offspring of alcoholic mothers and some epidemiologic data suggest that milder degrees of mental impairment may be even more pervasive among the offspring of drinking mothers and that such abnormalities may be sufficiently frequent to represent a substantial public health and educational problem.

Shaywitz et al. (1978) have described a syndrome of minimal brain dysfunction in offspring of alcoholic mothers with generally normal intelligence. This observation has raised the question as to whether these effects are due to maternal ethanol exposure or to the effect of some postnatal factor present in the homes of alcoholic mothers such as child abuse and neglect, marital stress, or factors relating to lower socioeconomic status. In this regard, the studies of Jones et al. (1974) showed that offspring of alcoholic mothers have significantly lower overall IQ scores than do controls matched on a variety of relevant variables, suggesting a specific effect of prenatal ethanol abuse. Subsequent studies by Streissguth et al., (1980) have confirmed and extended these observations in a different sample of alcoholic mothers and matched controls from better socioeconomic backgrounds. Furthermore, the observations of Havlicek et al. (1977) and Root et al. (1975) describing electroencephalographic abnormalities in FAS children as well as the neuroanatomical studies of Clarren et al. (1978) point to specific neuropathological alterations which could have only occurred during prenatal life and which would be expected to have a significant effect on central nervous system function during postnatal life. Finally, the persistence of functional abnormalities in FAS infants reared in good adoptive or foster homes (Streissguth et al., 1978b), as well as the stability of IQ scores on follow-up in these children (Streissguth et al., 1979), do point to a specific role for alcohol in the pathogenesis of these functional deficits. Nevertheless, well-controlled studies comparing more mildly affected children raised in and outside alcoholic homes have not been carried out. At least one study, (Streissguth et al., 1978c) does suggest that more mildly affected children may show some improvement in IQ scores later in life, which could be related to improved living circumstances.

An additional problem posed by behavioral research on the effects of antenatal alcohol use on the fetus surrounds the problem of identification of behavioral and other functional abnormalities in newborns and young children and their long-term clinical significance. At present, a neonatal diagnosis of FAS would appear to be predictive of a long-term increased risk for significant central nervous system dysfunction, as well as for other problems of growth and for certain congenital malformations. However, more subtly impaired children may also have alterations in long-term prognosis. It would be important to identify those factors in the neonatal period, which are truly predictive of such a long-term outcome, particularly in the offspring of women who drink at more moderate levels during pregnancy.

The Seattle study (Streissguth et al., 1978c) has attempted to examine this problem in a prospective fashion. A cohort of offspring whose mothers drank alcohol infrequently or not at all, were selected for detailed behavioral evaluation. All outcome studies were conducted without knowledge of parental drinking history, medical diagnosis, or infant performance on other tests. Independent teams of examiners used standardized conditions, and data were analyzed using multiple regression techniques to adjust for the effects of nicotine, caffeine, parity, and other relevant variables. Brazelton neonatal assessments, naturalistic observations, operant learning studies and neonatal sucking evaluations were all carried out. Taken together, these data suggest an effect of even moderate levels of alcohol consumption during pregnancy on neonatal behavior.

Data collected from the Brazelton evaluations carried out on the first day of life (Streissguth et al., 1977) revealed significant differences in habituation and arousal characteristics. Infants of the heavier drinking mothers were unable to tune out redundant stimuli as readily as did infants of control mothers. This is particularly interesting in view of the apparent hyperacusis described clinically in FAS infants (Pierog et al., 1977).

Operant learning studies (Martin et al., 1977a) revealed that infants whose mothers both smoked and drank heavily during pregnancy performed significantly more poorly on both head turning and sucking learning tasks. However, neither smoking nor drinking alone were significantly related to these learning decrements. Other studies of sucking parameters (Martin et al., 1979) obtained on the second day of life revealed that infants of heavier drinking mothers had significantly weaker sucking pressure than control infants. This corresponds to the clinical observation of feeding difficulties in FAS infants.

A variety of naturalistic observations were also obtained on 124 infants from this group during the first day of life (Landesman-Dwyer et al., 1978). Among the sixteen behaviors examined, higher alcohol consumption was positively correlated with an increase in body tremors, increase with time eyes were opened, increased head orientation in atypical positions, increased hand to mouth behavior, and decreased vigorous body activity. Furthermore, significantly more infants born to heavier drinking mothers had one-minute Apgar scores of three or below, and five-minute Apgar scores of eight and below. Significantly more of these infants also required ventilatory resuscitation and displayed heart rate abnormalities (Streissguth et al., 1978a).

Similar data revealing adverse effects in offspring of drinking mothers has been reported from Boston. Sander et al., (1977) studied 31 newborns. Computerized analysis of continuously monitored 24-hour respiratory and activity functions revealed alterations in state regulation in the offspring of heavy drinking mothers. This seemed to correlate well with the study of Ouellette et al. (1977) in which significantly more jitteriness in neonates of heavy drinking mothers was found.

Two recent papers suggest that some or all of these observations may be related to permanent significant changes in mental and motor development (Streissguth et al., 1980; Landesman-Dwyer et al., 1979). In these studies, follow-up on the children in the Seattle study revealed significant decreases in mental and motor development at eight months of age in infants of drinking mothers; and four-year-old children displayed decreased attentiveness. These studies were statistically adjusted for several other variables including maternal smoking and gestational age. Finally, the two children from the Seattle study in whom the neonatal diagnosis of fetal alcohol syndrome was made have been recently reevaluated at the approximate chronological age of four years. These children have IQs in the mild range of mental deficiency.

Animal models of the teratogenic affects of alcohol have also been developed, utilizing several different animals, including the mouse, guinea pig, beagle dog, rat, and pig-tailed macaque. These animal models allow investigators to control timing and dose of alcoholic exposure, postnatal environmental factors, and to make comparisons of genetic differences in metabolism. They also allow direct pathological and biochemical examination of tissues which cannot be carried out in human investigations.

In addition to growth retardation, fetal wastage, and morphological effects, behavioral alterations have been described in experimental animals. An extensive review of these findings have been presented by Abel (1980). In the guinea pig (Papara-Nicholson & Telford, 1957) cortical and basal ganglia lesions were found as an outcome of maternal ethanol administration during pregnancy. In the mouse, a variety of neural abnormalities have been described (Chernoff, 1977; Randall et al., 1977). Observations by West et al. (1981) suggest that in the rat, prenatal ethanol ingestion at a time period equivalent to the first two trimesters of pregnancy in man, results in aberrant development of mossy fibers in the temporal regions of the hippocampus. These alterations in the neural connections could have a profound effect on the area of the brain which is thought to play an important role in memory, whereas other changes in neuronal architecture could be responsible for other serious mental impairments. These authors note that these abnormalities were found in animals lacking other conspicuous malformations.

Neurochemical studies in animal models have found evidence of reduced protein synthesis (Rawat, 1975) reduced brain serotonin levels (Krsiak et al., 1977) and delayed myelinization in fetal brain (Rosman & Malone, 1976).

Developmental effects are also described in various animal models. Papara-Nicholson and Telford (1957) described poor locomotion, poor sucking and feeding, and increased incoordination, as well as poor growth in guinea pig offspring. Of particular interest are observations suggesting an increase in hyperactivity in offspring of alcohol treated mothers. This observation supports clinical reports of hyperactivity in FAS humans (Streissguth et al., 1978b). Krsiak et al. (1977) also noted increased aggressiveness in the offspring of mice treated with alcohol during pregnancy and related this to reduced levels of brain serotonin. It has been suggested that reduced activity of the serotonergic system in humans is related to hyperactivity as well (Brase & Loh, 1975).

Other learning effects have also been reported in animal models (Riley et al., 1979a). Riley et al. (1979b) report difficulties with response inhibition and reversal learning, while Bond and DiGuisto (1977, 1978) noted that prenatal alcohol exposure impaired the ability of offspring to learn to avoid noxious stimuli. Vincent (1958) reported reduced learning ability and greater emotionality in offspring of alcohol-treated rats, and Phillips and Stainbrook (1978) present evidence that alcohol-exposed offspring are inferior in "conceptualization" of tasks. Finally, operant studies carried out by Martin et al.(1977b) also indicated a reduced ability to learn various tasks.

In summary then, clinical observations of FAS children and epidemiologic studies of alcohol-exposed human infants and children suggest a wide range of neurological and cognitive impairments. Animal models designed to examine the teratogenic effects of alcohol tend to confirm these observations and suggest specific pathogenetic hypotheses. However, many problems remain. It must be remembered that the human studies are subject to a variety of problems in interpretation. Most reports are based on self-report of maternal alcohol intake. Furthermore, it is difficult to collect large numbers of children with similar alcohol exposures for systematic investigation. Finally, it has been difficult to control for other associated characteristics such as maternal smoking, nutrition, socioeconomic class, and exposure to other hazardous environmental agents.

## CLINICAL IMPLICATIONS OF THE FAS

Although many important questions remain to be answered in regard to the effects of alcohol on fetal growth, development, and cognitive function, the body of research just described has important clinical implications for physicians and other health care personnel, educators, psychologists, public health officials, and the general public. Current knowledge suggests that FAS may have an incidence somewhere between 1:750 and 1:1000 newborns, making FAS one of the most common patterns of altered growth and development known at the present time. Furthermore, present data would indicate that milder effects of alcohol on fetal growth and cognitive function may be substantially more frequent in the general population and may account for a significant proportion of children presently identified with cognitive and behavioral problems in school settings. Accordingly, it is imperative that physicians and other individuals who care for pregnant or potentially pregnant women come to recognize that alcohol is a dangerous drug, not only for the mother but for her offspring as well. Thus, a careful history of maternal alcohol intake should be a part of every prenatal evaluation. Mothers should be cautioned against excessive alcohol consumption at any time in pregnancy and those who are found to be drinking heavily should be warned of the risks to their infants. In some cases, the risk may be sufficiently high to warrant consideration of termination of pregnancy.

Pediatricians and other physicians who care for children should appreciate that FAS may be one of the most frequent recognizable causes of mental deficiency. Identification of affected children has many potential advantages including more appropriate use of medical facilities in the evaluation of problems of growth and development, early recognition of infants at high risk for serious congenital anomalies, and recognition of a mother at substantial risk for problems in her other or future offspring.

Third, psychologists, educators, and other school personnel should become familiar with the effects of prenatal ethanol exposure on cognitive function and physical health in order that high risk children be more readily identified. This should lead to improved educational planning as well as maternal therapy. Furthermore, programs for the appropriate educational, psychological and health care of FAS children and other children displaying milder effects of prenatal ethanol exposure should be developed. The frequency of this problem may be sufficiently high to warrant the establishment of specific programs for targeted populations in larger school districts.

Fourth, researchers including physicians, psychologists, educators, and teratologists need to expand their investigations concerning the effects of alcohol on fetal growth and development. Mechanisms through which these effects are produced remain unclear. Furthermore, the interaction between alcohol and other potential risk factors which might exacerbate or ameliorate alcohol effects should be further studied. Particular attention should be paid to the behavioral and cognitive effects of prenatal ethanol exposure. Special attention also needs to be directed to the timing of exposure during pregnancy and the effects of binges of alcohol consumption on fetal growth and performance.

Finally, current findings suggest that drinking behavior in the earliest parts of pregnancy may be a special hazard. This is of course a period during which women may be unaware of their pregnancy. This is particularly true of teenagers. Thus, current trends in social drinking, which indicate that an increasing number of young women and children are being exposed to alcohol, lead to the conclusion that the frequency of fetal damage from prenatal ethanol exposures are likely to increase. One may conclude from these observations that the most important mode for controlling this avoidable tragedy is early education of school-age children with regards to the hazards of alcohol and other dangerous drugs. Public health, medical, and school personnel should collaborate in developing programs to meet this need.

## SUMMARY

In conclusion, current data clearly point to an association between maternal prenatal ethanol abuse and serious problems of growth, morphogenesis, behavior, and cognition in the fetus and child. At the severe end of the spectrum, this condition is recognizable as the fetal alcohol syndrome. However, it would appear that this represents only the most severe end of a spectrum of abnormalities which may be found to a lesser degree in some infants exposed to smaller amounts of alcohol during pregnancy.

The most debilitating effect of the damage from ethanol is mental deficiency. However, other behavioral and cognitive deficits including hyperactivity, short attention span, and poor coordination also appear to be frequent. A great deal more needs to be learned about the pathogenesis, treatment, and prevention of these problems, but sufficient evidence is already available indicating the need for special efforts to control this problem. Alcohol is an avoidable hazard for the fetus, but increased awareness by the medical community, and improved education for the lay public is urgently needed.

# REFERENCES

Abel, E. L. Fetal alcohol syndrome: Behavioral teratology. *Psychological Bulletin*, 1980, *87*, 29–50.

Bond, N. W., & DiGiusto, E. L. Effects of prenatal alcohol consumption on shock avoidance learning in rats. *Psychological Reports*, 1977, *41*, 1269–1270.

Bond, N. W., & DiGiusto, E. L. Avoidance conditioning and Hebb-Williams maze performance in rats treated prenatally with alcohol. *Psychopharmacology*, 1978, *58*, 69–71.

Brase, D. A., & Loh, H. H. Possible role of S-hydroxytryptamine in minimal brain dysfunction. *Life Sciences*, 1975, *16*, 1005.

Chernoff, G. F. The fetal alcohol syndrome in mice: An animal model. *Teratology*, 1977, *13*, 223–230.

Clarren, S. K., Alvord, E. C., Sumi, S. M., Streissguth, A. P., & Smith, D. W. Brain malformations related to prenatal exposure to ethanol. *Journal of Pediatrics*, 1978, *92*, 64–67.

Clarren, S. K., & Smith, D. W. The fetal alcohol syndrome. *New England Journal of Medicine*, 1978, *298*, 1063–1067.

Dehaene, P., Titran, M., Samaille-Villette, C., Samaille, P., Crepin, G., Delahousse, G., Walbaum, R., & Fasquelle, P. Frequence du syndrome d'alcoolisme foetal. *Nouvelle presse medicale*, 1977a, *6*, 1763.

Dehaene, P., Walbaum, R., Titran, M. Samaille-Villette, C., Samaille, P. Crepin, G., Delahousse, G., Decocq, J., Delcroix, M., Caquant, F., & Querleu, D. La descendance des meres alcooliques chroniques, a propos de 16 case d'alcoolisme foetal. *Revue Francaise de Gynecologie et Obstetrique*, 1977, *72*, 492–498.

Fetal Alcohol Syndrome. *FDA Drug Bulletin*, 1977, *7*, 18.

Hanson, J. W., Jones, K. L., & Smith, D. W. Fetal alcohol syndrome: Experience with 41 patients. *Journal of the American Medical Association*, 1976, *235*, 1458–1460.

Hanson, J. W., Streissguth, A. P., & Smith, D. W. The effects of moderate alcohol consumption during pregnancy on fetal growth and morphogenesis. *Journal of Pediatrics*, 1978, *92*, 457–460.

Harlap, S., Shiono, P. H., & Ramcharan, S. Alcohol and spontaneous abortions (abstract). *American Journal of Epidemiology*, 1979, *110*, 372.

Harlap, S., & Shiono, P. H. Alcohol, smoking and incidences to spontaneous abortions in the first and second trimester. *Lancet*, 1980, *2*, 173.

Havlicek, V., Childiaeva, R., & Chernick, V. EEG frequency spectrum characteristics of sleep states in infants of alcoholic mothers. *Neuropaediatrie*, 1977, *8*, 360–373.

Jones, K. L., & Smith, D. W. Recognition of the fetal alcohol syndrome in early infancy. *Lancet*, 1973, *2*, 999–1001.

Jones, K. L., Smith, D. W., Ulleland, N., & Streissguth, A. P. Pattern of malformation in offspring of chronic alcoholic mothers. *Lancet*, 1973, *1*, 1267–1271.

Jones, K. L., Smith, D. W., Hanson, J. W., Streissguth, A. P., & Myrianthopoulos, N. C. Outcome in offspring of chronic alcoholic women, *Lancet*, 1974, *1*, 1076–1078.

Jones, K. L., Smith, D. W., & Hanson, J. W. The fetal alcohol syndrome: Clinical delineation. *Annals of the New York Academy of Sciences*, 1976, *273*, 130–139.

Kaminski, M., Rumeau-Rouquette, C., & Schwartz, D. Consommation d'alcool chez les femmes enceintes et issue de la grossesse. *Revue d'Epidemiologie et de Sante Publique*, 24:27–40,

1976. English translation by Little, R. E. and Schinzel, A. Alcohol consumption in pregnant women and the outcome of pregnancy. *Alcoholism: Clinical and Epxerimental Research,* 1978, *2,* 155-163.

Kline, J., Schrout, P., Stein, Z., Susser, M., & Warburton, D. Drinking during pregnancy and spontaneous abortions. *Lancet,* 1980, *2,* 176.

Krsiak, M., Elis, J., Poscholova, N., & Masek, K. Increased aggressiveness and lower brain serotonin levels of offspring of mice given alcohol during gestation. *Journal of Studies of Alcohol,* 1977, *38,* 1696-1704.

Landesman-Dwyer, S., Keller, L. S., Streissguth, A. P. Naturalistic observations of newborns: Effects of maternal alcohol intake. *Alcoholism: Clinical and Experimental Research,* 1978, *2,* 171-177.

Landesman-Dwyer, S., Ragazon, Little, R. E. Behavior correlates of prenatal alcohol exposure: A 4-year followup study. *Neurobehavioral Toxicology and Teratology,* 1981, *3,* In press.

Little, R. E. Moderate alcohol use during pregnancy and decreased infant birthweight. *American Journal of Public Health,* 1977, *67,* 1154-1156.

Majewski, F., Bierich, J. R., Loser, H., Michaelis, R., & Leiber, B. Zur Klinik and Pathogenese der Alkohol-Embryopathie. Bericht uber 68 Falle. *Muenchener Medizinisiche Wochenschrift,* 1976, *118,* 1635-1642.

Majewski, F., Fischbach, H., Peiffer, J., & Beirich, J. R. Zur frage der interrputic alkohol-kranken frauen. (interruption of pregnancy in alcoholic women). *Duetsche Medizinische Wochenschrift,* 1978, *103,* 885-893.

Martin, J. C., Martin, D. C., Lund, C. A., & Streissguth, A. P. Maternal alcohol ingestion and cigarette smoking and their effects upon newborn conditioning. *Alcoholism: Clinical and Experimental Research,* 1977a, *1,* 243-247.

Martin, J. C., Martin, D. C., Sigman, G., & Radow, B. Offspring survival, development and operant performance following maternal ethanol consumption. *Developmental Psychobiology,* 1977b, *10,* 435-446.

Martin, J. C., Martin, D. C., Sigman, G., & Radow, B. Maternal ethanol consumption and hyperactivity in cross-fostered offspring. *Physiological Psychology,* 1978, *6,* 362-365.

Martin, D. C., Martin, J. C., Streissguth, A. P., & Lund, C. A. Sucking frequency and amplitude in newborns as a function of maternal drinking and smoking. In M. Galanter (Ed.), *Currents in Alcoholism.* Vol. 5. New York: Grune & Stratton, 1979, 359-366.

Ouellette, E. M., Rosett, H. L., Rosman, N. P., & Weiner, L. Adverse effects on offspring of maternal alcohol abuse during pregnancy. *New England Journal of Medicine,* 1977, *297,* 528-530.

Papara-Nicholson, D., & Telford, I. R. Effects of alcohol on reproduction and fetal development in the guinea pig. *Anatomical Record,* 1957, *127,* 438-494.

Phillips, D. S., & Stainbrook, G. L. Fecundity, natality and weight as a function of prenatal alcohol consumption and age of mother. *Physiologic Psychology,* 1978, *6,* 75-77.

Pierog, S., Chandavasu, O., & Wexler, I. Withdrawal symptoms in infants with the fetal alcohol syndrome. *Journal of Pediatrics,* 1977, *90,* 630-633.

Randall, C. L. Teratogenic effects of in utero ethanol exposure. In K. Blum (Ed.), *Alcohol and Opiates: Neurochemical and Behavioral Mechanisms.* New York: Academic Press, 1977, 91-107.

Randall, C. L., Taylor, W. J., & Walker, D. Ethanol induced malformations in mice. *Alcoholism: Clinical and Experimental Research,* 1977, *1,* 219-223.

Rawat, A. K. Ribosomal protein synthesis in the fetal and neonatal rat brain as influenced by maternal ethanol consumption. *Research Communications in Chemical Pathology and Pharmacology,* 1975, *12,* 723-732.

Riley, E. P., Lochry, E. A., Shapiro, N. R., & Baldwin, J. Response preservation in rats exposed to alcohol prenatally. *Pharmacology, Biochemistry, and Behavior,* 1979a, *10,* 255-259.

Riley, E. P., Lochry, E. A., & Shapiro, N. R. Lack of response inhibition in rats prenatally exposed to alcohol. *Psychopharmacology*, 1979b, *62*, 47–52.

Rott, A. W., Reiter, E. O., Andriola, M., & Duckett, G. Hypothalmaicpituitary function in the fetal alcohol syndrome. *Journal of Pediatrics*, 1975, *87*, 585–588.

Rosman, N. P., & Malone, M. J. An experimental study of the fetal alcohol syndrome. *Neurology*, 1976, *26*, 365.

Sander, L. W., Snyder, P., Rosette, H. L., Lee, A., Gould, J. B., & Ouellette, E. Effects of alcohol intake during pregnancy on newborn state regulation; a progress report. *Alcoholism: Clinical and Experimental Research*, 1977, *1*, 233–241.

Shaywitz, S. E., Cohen, D. J., & Shaywitz, B. A. The expanded fetal alcohol syndrome (EFAS). Behavioral and learning deficits in children with normal intelligence (abstract). *Pediatric Research*, 1978, *12*, 375.

Streissguth, A. P., Martin, D. C., & Barr, H. M. Neonatal Brazelton assessment and relationship to maternal alcohol intake. Fifth International Congress on Birth Defects. *International Congress Series*, 1977, *426*, 62.

Streissguth, A. P. Fetal alcohol syndrome: An epidemiological perspective. *American Journal of Epidemiology*, 1978, *107*, 467–478.

Streissguth, A. P., Barr, H. M., Martin, D. C., & Woodell, S. Effects of social drinking on Apgar scores and neonatal states (abstract). *Alcoholism: Clinical and Experimental Research*, 1978a, *2*, 215.

Streissguth, A. P., Herman, C. S., & Smith, D. W. Intelligence, behavior, and dysmorphogenesis in the fetal alcohol syndrome: A report on 20 patients. *Journal of Pediatrics*, 1978b, *92*, 363–367.

Streissguth, A. P., Martin, J. C., & Martin, D. C. Experimental design considerations and methodological problems in the study of the effects of social drinking on the outcome of pregnancy. *Alcoholism and Drug Abuse Institute Technical Report*, #78-01, University of Washington, Seattle, WA.: 1978c.

Streissguth, A. P., Barr, H. M., Martin, D. C., & Herman, C. S. Effects of maternal alcohol, nicotine and caffeine use during pregnancy on infant mental and motor development at 8 months. *Alcoholism: Clinical and Experimental Research*, 1980, *4*, 152–164.

Streissguth, A. P., Little, R. E., Herman, C., & Woodell, S. IQ in children of recovered alcoholic mothers compared to matched controls (abstract). *Alcoholism: Clinical and Experimental Research*, 1979, *3*, 197.

Vincent, N. M. The effects of prenatal alcoholism upon motivation, emotionally and learning in the rat. *American Psychologist*, 1958, *13*, 401.

Warner, R. H., & Rosett, H. L. The effects of drinking on offspring: An historical survey of the American and British literature. *Journal of Studies on Alcohol*, 1975, *36*, 1395–1420.

West, J. R., Hodges, C. A., & Black, A. C. Prenatal ethanol exposure alters the organization of hippocampal mossy fibers. *Science*, 1981, *211*, 957–959.

# CHILDREN'S UNDERSTANDING OF ILLNESS:

## DEVELOPMENTAL CONSIDERATIONS AND PEDIATRIC INTERVENTION

J. Kenneth Whitt

"Having a seizure is like going off into outer space. I feel like a shooting star that falls to the ground and burns out." The metaphor of this 11-year-old boy's description of his epilepsy reflects the complex interplay of cognitive, affective, and experiential factors which influence children's concepts of health phenomena. Like comprehension of birth (Bernstein & Cowan, 1975), death (Childers & Wimmer, 1971; Koocher, 1973), religion (Elkind, 1962), and humor (McGhee, 1964; Schultz, 1974; Whitt & Prentice, 1977), children's views of bodily functions, illness, and hospitalization not only differ qualitatively from adult perspectives but also vary substantially according to the child's stage of development (Whitt, Dykstra, & Taylor, 1979). Due to inconsistencies with adult logic, communica-

Advances in Developmental and Behavioral Pediatrics, vol. 3, pages 163–201
Copyright © 1982 by JAI Press Inc.
All rights of reproduction in any form reserved.
ISBN: 0-89232-223-3

tion of disease concepts and medical treatment procedures to the child is at best a difficult process (Korsch, 1973; MacCarthy, 1974). Yet the efficacy of pediatric care may depend at times upon the child's understanding of illness, acceptance of hospitalization, and active participation in ongoing treatment.

Research defining the characteristics of children's changing conceptions of health, illness, and medical procedures may play a dual catalytic role in facilitating physician-child communication. First, a developmental framework of cognitive and emotional constructs related to illness understanding will afford an empirical basis for childhood health care education. In addition, pediatric awareness of this theoretical structure should foster improved explanations of bodily phenomena to both acutely and chronically ill children, promoting child and family adaptation to disease, and encouraging children's compliance with therapeutic injunctions (Perrin & Gerrity, 1981). The present chapter reviews contemporary clinical and research findings pertaining to children's understanding of illness and draws practical conclusions regarding the implications for pediatric practitioners.

## CHILDREN'S EMOTIONAL REACTIONS TO ILLNESS AND HOSPITALIZATION

The onset of childhood illness and ensuing hospitalization creates a precipitous series of challenges to child and family adaptation. Just going for an outpatient appointment with a physician may provoke considerable apprehension. Stimson (1974) reported on 151 essays written by healthy school children between the ages of 12 and 16 years. Although asked to write about "Going to the Doctor," the children generally gave evaluative comments. References to aversion and anxiety outnumbered positive appraisals by four to one. Worried anticipation found in half of the essays focused on what the doctor would do, injections, diagnosis of illness, treatment procedures, and referral to the hospital.

Hospital admission frequently is associated with affective and behavioral changes. In many a child's memory, the hospital has been the final stop for now deceased grandparents or family friends, rather than a safe place to receive medical care. Children manifest the untoward effects of hospitalization (and accompanying separation from familiar family, school, and peer routines) in a number of ways. As Gellert (1958) observed:

> Children cry, whine, and scream; they cling tenaciously to their parents; they eat or sleep poorly; they struggle against treatment and resist taking medications; they are tense and fearful; they become silent, sad, and withdrawn. They may show an increase in regressive or compulsive behavior; they may become destructive of their environment or even themselves (p. 125).

Chapman, Loeb, and Gibbons (1956) provided a similarly comprehensive list of symptoms and problems which may follow traumatic hospital experiences. They include (1) eating problems; (2) sleep disturbances, such as insomnia, night-mares, or phobias of the dark; (3) enuresis or encopresis; (4) regression to more immature levels of behavioral and social functioning; (5) tics; (6) depression, restlessness, and anxiety; (7) terror of hospitals, medical personnel, hypodermic needles, and so on; (8) fears of death; (9) mute or autistic regression to uncom-municative states or frightened withdrawal from interpersonal contact; (10) hypochondriacal concerns or delusions regarding body functions; and (11) hys-terical symptomatology.

The literature of clinical pediatrics and psychiatry that reports these childhood encounters with illness historically has described numerous factors, generally from the perspective of dynamic psychology, which contribute to the distress of sick children. (See, for example, Belmont, 1970; Blom, 1958; Freud, 1952; Geist, 1979; Langford, 1961; Prugh, 1971; Robertson, 1958; Van der Veer, 1949.) A comprehensive review of the psychodynamic aspects of children's adjustment to illness and hospitalization is beyond the scope of the present chapter. However, reviews by Mattsson (1972), Nagera (1978), Prugh and Eck-hardt (1974), and Vernon, Foley, Sipowicz, and Schulman (1965), among others, conclude that whether illness produces a deleterious effect on a child's adaptation or family equilibrium depends on multiple individual and family determinants. Essential factors include the child's level of psychosocial de-velopment and previous adaptive capacities, the prevailing parent-child rela-tionship, current family homeostasis, and the nature and meaning of the specific illness. From this perspective, individual emotional reactions depend as much upon the child's current development and affective challenges as the realities of the illness. Thus, illness phenomena are thought to variously evoke separation anxiety in the older infant and toddler, fears of bodily mutilation in the older preschool youngster, fear of loss of control of feelings or impulses in the school-aged child, and concerns regarding independence and identity for the adolescent patient (Prugh, 1971; Prugh & Eckhardt, 1980).

The concept of developmental stage-related stresses may be illustrated by the young child's difficulty coping with the hospital milieu. One of the most dis-cussed factors influencing children's reactions to hospitalization is separation from parents. Some authors (e.g., Bowlby, 1953, 1960; Robertson & Bowlby, 1952; Robertson, 1958) have described phases of response to the experience of hospitalization characteristic of children under four years of age, a developmen-tal period when separation from one's primary caregiver is the most stressful aspect of adaptation (Mahler, Pine, & Bergman, 1975). In the parents' absence, hospitalized children were observed to proceed through behavioral sequences of (1) *protest,* characterized by crying and somewhat angry demands for the mother's presence, often coupled with rejection of alternative caregivers; (2) *despair,* during which the child exhibits increasing helplessness, diminished physical activity, and develops misconceptions, such as punishment, to explain the parents' absence; and (3) *detachment,* in which children withdraw and distance themselves emotionally from adults. According to Prugh and Eckhardt (1980), the latter phase was frequently welcomed and often misunderstood as "settling in," although there existed a striking absence of behavior characteristic of the strong attachment normal at this age.

Subsequent writings have questioned the idea of "maternal deprivation" as the most relevant construct in understanding the child's reactions to hospitalization (Rutter, 1972, 1979; Seagull, 1980). Recent studies (Brain & Maclay, 1968; Douglas, 1975; Goslin, 1978; Skipper & Leonard, 1968; Vernon, Foley, & Schulman, 1967) indicate that the positive effect of the child's mother, or other familiar caregiver, is helpful not only in a global fashion, to give comfort to an anxious child, but also specifically by helping the child to impose cognitive structure on the experience in terms he or she can understand (Seagull, 1980). These empirical clarifications notwithstanding, it was the widespread acceptance of the descriptive efforts of authors including Bowlby (1953, 1960), Heinicke (1956), Robertson (1958), Spitz and Wolf (1946), among others, as well as the Platt Committee Report (Ministry of Health and Central Health Services Council, 1959) in Britain and the publication of *Red is the Color of Hurting* (Shore, 1971) in the United States which stimulated the liberalization of visitation policies and introduction of parental rooming-in at many pediatric hospitals, arrangements which have altered patterns of parent absence and distress for both hospitalized children and infants requiring extended medical care (cf. Klaus & Kennell, 1976).

Recognition of the demands for adjustment to the hospital environment, confusing teams of health care specialists, and painful medical procedures, which compound the child's initial feelings about being sick or physically injured, also has led to improvements in the quality of pediatric care. Procedures requiring immobilization or restriction of activity are a particularly distressing deviation from children's normal use of freedom of movement to discharge tension, to express dissatisfaction, and to master novel situations (Bergmann, 1965; Freud, 1952; Levy, 1944). The hospitalized child, dependent on nurses and parents for care previously performed autonomously, may also experience conflict regarding his or her desires to express feelings of helplessness, embarrassment, and irritation at being treated "like a child." Rather than comfort, security, and gratitude regarding medical care, the hospitalized child may feel humiliation, guilt, and anxiety in the face of regression from prior developmental achievements to the dependency implicit in medical treatment. Revised management practices; altered staff attitudes regarding uniforms, education, visitation, and "child life" activities (Association for the Care of Children in Hospitals, 1979); interpersonal strategies for facilitating child and family coping (Melamed & Siegel, 1975; Melamed, Meyer, Gee, & Soule, 1976; Wolfer & Visintainer, 1979); and even pediatric hospital design (cf. Kennedy, 1971; Wines, 1971) owe to the awareness brought by early anecdotal recountings of children's emotional responses and psychodynamic explanations of age-linked behavioral reactions.

Despite these continuing inroads into hospital procedures and policies, the historical pattern of clinical descriptions stimulating both changes in pediatric management practice and further empirical clarification has not been as evident for early psychoanalytic notions of childhood illness misconceptions. Mattsson's (1972) thoughtful clinical review noted that in contrast to the younger child's vulnerability to separation, the psychological and symbolic significance of hospitalization, illness, and medical treatment have traumatic potential beyond the scope of actual pain and discomfort for youngsters between the ages of 5 and 10 years. Stimulation of common childhood apprehensions of body mutilation was thought by many psychoanalytic observers (e.g., Blom, 1958; Freud, 1952; Miller, 1951) to underlie these invariant fears, anxious fantasies, and frequent distortions of the illness and treatment process. For example, on the basis of their survey of 200 children between the ages of 2 and 12 years of age, Prugh, Staub, Sands, Kirschbaum, and Lenihan (1953) argued that:

> reality factors, inviting misinterpretation and fears of mutilation or death, appeared to combine with unconscious anxieties and fantasies to invest various treatment or diagnostic procedures with punitive significance, reviving or intensifying castration fears in the boy and helping to fixate in the girl fantasies that her genital configuration arose through mutilation (pp. 101–102).

Although these conclusions benefited the general understanding of children's emotional reactions to hospital procedures, and highlighted the limited opportunity afforded children for resolving distorted views of illness, guidance for the prevention of childhood misconceptions of illness is rare in pediatric circles. Moreover, the historical emphasis on problem behavior fails to capture adequately the struggles for understanding of the (many) children who exhibit no adverse behavioral reactions or emotional sequelae to medical encounters. In the absence of clearly defined preventive or ameliorative practice, many contemporary clinicians anticipate that children will "get used to" treatment procedures. However, empirical evidence does not support this conclusion (Katz, Kellerman, & Siegel, 1980; Patenaude, Szymanski, & Rappeport, 1979; Powazek, Goff, Schyving, & Paulson, 1978). Indeed, adverse behavioral reactions may increase with the child's continued interpretation of illness and hospitalization as punishment for past transgressions, the construct most often offered to explain the common childhood view that diagnostic and treatment procedures are punitive and hostile (Freud, 1952). In light of the evidence for informational needs by sick children and their families (Reddihough, Landau, Jones, & Rickards, 1977; Visintainer & Wolfer, 1975), a combination of both cognitive and emotional constructs seems necessary to advance pediatric practice in this area. However, until recently, few systematic attempts had been made to define the influence of cognitive developmental changes on children's conceptions of illness. This neglect is perhaps best addressed by looking first at the complex cognitive and emotional task of understanding an illness experience from the knee-high perspective of a young child.

## EXPERIENTIAL ASPECTS OF CHILDREN'S PERCEPTIONS OF ILLNESS

While acknowledging the multiple affective responses and deviations in emotional development emphasized in early clinical papers on childhood illness, recent accounts have recast much of the behavioral and emotional disturbance reported by pediatric professionals as the child's wayward attempts to solve the cognitive dilemmas and discrepancies introduced by illness, hospitalization, and medical procedures (Steward & Steward, in press; Whitt, Dykstra, & Taylor, 1979). Consider, for example, the determinants of the child's response to the onset of epilepsy. As described by Bridge (1947) the initial seizure may be associated with intense alarm and excitement. The world of a normally playing child suddenly goes dark, preceded only by feelings of vague anxiety or an unfamiliar sensory aura. The child awakens to find his or her family in a state of terror and is taken to the nearest doctor, who subsequently prescribes daily medication. Although the child may not be told what has happened, the attendant circumstances and attitudes make it clear that whatever transpired must have been serious.

For the physician, a diagnosis is indicated on the basis of extensive training and experience interpreting fragments of information that fit together like interlocking pieces of a puzzle. However, the defining clinical history, physical symptomatology, and laboratory data which lead to physician certainty (and, therefore, security) may not be evident, or ambiguous to the child with epilepsy. Alterations in consciousness may becloud the physical symptoms of the seizure or mask these happenings from the child's awareness. If described to the child at all, these bodily events may be colored by the observer's feelings of anxiety and fright, not infrequently voiced as, "It was like the devil was in you!" Neurological examination, electroencephalography, and computerized axial tomography may add little to the child's understanding. Indeed, for the four-year-old youngster to whom the body may appear nothing more than a bag of bones and blood, the emphasis on the brain and its "waves" may contribute to the confusion. Even for the older child, exploration into the adequacy of the organ system which, as all school children know, "makes you think smart" raises significant apprehensions. Thus, the child with epilepsy may find little of comfort (or even comprehensible) to be revealed by the diagnostic or treatment process.

In looking to other significant persons for clarification, the child may find only confirmation of his or her concerns regarding the seriousness of the incident. Parents' fears, anxieties, and guilt feelings often lead to alterations in their approach toward the "sick" child. Fortunately, parental attitudidinal and behavioral changes more frequently occur in the direction of becoming protective and indulgent rather than the opposite tendency toward rejection of the ill child, blame for financial inconvenience, and neglect of medical care. However, any amendment to time-honored patterns of interaction, discipline, and family routine puzzles the child, giving rise to questions of causality which, like the illness itself, require explanation. Children with chronic illness uniformly comment, "I know that I'm *very* sick (or dying) because everyone treats me differently. Before I was sick, my parents would have never let me get away with.... Now, I can even hit my little sister without being punished."

Classroom reactions may be equally perplexing to the child struggling to define the parameters of his or her own illness. the child with a seizure disorder may become the object of considerable attention, be considered "retarded" or "crazy" due to this illness, or find himself or herself rejected from group games because "epilepsy is contagious." Teachers are not immune to caregiving anxieties. Having a chronically ill child in the classroom often evokes affective responses similar to those seen in parents—either the extreme of overconcern and solicitous treatment or "resolution" through rejection of the child, sometimes expressed as recognition that this child needs special care best given by a homebound teacher.

For the child looking for determinants with which to define the illness experience, the findings can be bewildering. Faced with changes in the family system, adults who become increasingly solicitous regarding minor details of the child's life, limitations on previously enjoyed activities, and distinction by treatment from peers and siblings, children's fears may spiral with increasing apprehension about what it is that could provoke such change and chaos. In the absence of adequate information, unwilling merely to accept the confusing gaps in their knowledge created by developmental limitations and voids in adult communication, children often complete their "understanding" with idiosyncratic interpretations of illness.

The illness experience of a child is projected onto a psychological substrate of limited cognitive and language abilities and heightened concerns about body integrity. In this context, it is not surprising that children frequently conclude that sickness is a punishment for past transgressions (cf. Beverly, 1936; Langford, 1948). Piaget (1963/1947) emphasized the adaptive role of play, first seen in the two-to-four year-old-child, as a means of adjustment to reality which cannot yet be assimilated into more logical cognitions. Play provides children an opportunity to shape reality to their own needs and act out, in fantasy, otherwise incomprehensible experiences. This capacity to intertwine fantasy with reality enables the child to use symbolic play cathartically, for example, by stabbing a doll with a pencil in an effort to master the trauma of an injection given during pediatric care. Such leanings toward fantasy, along with the vagaries of logic which allow the child to accept unquestioningly the Santa Claus legend (Prentice, Manosevitz, & Hubbs, 1978) also lead the young child to draw conclusions based on temporal (rather than causal) associations between events, omnipotent or egocentric feelings, and fantasied "reasons" for illness which distort the content of verbalization from persons "in the know." Thus, even at age seven, the child hearing "there is edema in your belly" may find it quite reasonable to wonder only about which wrongdoing the demon was sent there to punish (Perrin & Gerrity, 1981).

Clearly, as Freud (1952) emphasized, distortions and fantasies aroused by illness may undermine the youngster's cooperation with medical regime, maintenance of self-esteem, and successful adjustment to the stresses of both acute and chronic disease. However, despite the richness of early clinical reports, there has been little empirical basis for guiding pediatricians, nurses, and parents who seek to address childhood misconceptions of illness. Until recently, systematic attempts to ascertain the normal developmental correlates of children's views of health phenomena resulted in reports that younger children are more concrete and egocentric, while older children's perceptions have a more abstract and adultlike character. Normative data on children's views of health and illness with emphasis on the cognitive processes that underlie developmental changes in these conceptions were lacking. Inspection of the available, more carefully designed developmental investigations may add historical clarity to what many professionals view as the infinitely varied, "quaint" character of children's perceptions of illness (Bibace & Walsh, 1979).

## COGNITIVE-DEVELOPMENTAL FACTORS IN CHILDREN'S UNDERSTANDING OF ILLNESS

The results of attempts to detect the effects of cognitive-developmental changes on children's comprehension of health and illness have depended heavily upon the theoretical perspective, the specific questions employed, and the methodology utilized for data analysis. (A summary of methodological aspects of illness interview procedures is presented for relevant studies in Table 1). The exploratory efforts of Beverly (1936) and Langford (1948) were among the first to sample populations of children using a structured interview format. In the absence of an expository cognitive framework for interpreting the *structure* of children's verbalizations, initial investigations tended to report the *content* of childhood conceptions, often invoking psychoanalytic constructs (e.g., castration anxiety) to account for the distortions found in children's views of illness.

Although accepting the implicit necessity to recognize the multiple meanings illness holds for the average child, many pediatric practitioners found limited practical utility in psychoanalytic explanations of childhood anxieties. However, inquiries into the specific content of children's illness fantasies underscored the probability of underestimating the cognitive immaturity even of school-age children. Take, for example, the tangle of prelogical, magical, and otherwise erroneous concepts children hold regarding bandages. Howe (1968) presented hospitalized and well children between 7 and 10 years of age with pictures of

*Table 1.* Methodological Summary of Major Studies of Children's Understanding of Illness

| Study | Sample/Design Characteristics | Interview Format | Explanatory Taxonomy | Reliability |
|---|---|---|---|---|
| Bibace & Walsh (1979) | 24 healthy boys and girls in each of three age groups: 4, 7, and 11-year-olds assumed to represent preoperational, concrete operational, and formal operational thinking | 1. What does it mean to be healthy? <br> 2. Do you remember anyone who was sick? What was wrong? How did he or she get sick? How did he or she get better? <br> 3. Were you ever sick? Why did you get sick? How did you get better? <br> 4. What is the worst sickness to have? Why? What is the best sickness to have? Why? <br> 5. What happens to people when they are sick? What happens to people when they are very sick? <br> 6. What is a cold? How do people get colds? Where do colds come from? What makes colds go away? <br> 7. What are the measles?..... <br> 8. What is a heart attack?..... <br> 9. What is cancer?..... <br> 10. What is a headache?..... <br> 11. Have you ever had a pain? Where? What is pain? Why does it come? Where does it come from? | 1. Incomprehension <br> 2. Phenomenism: illness in terms of single external symptom, usually sensory <br> 3. Contagion: proximity, temporal or spatial causes <br> 4. Contamination: external cause <br> 5. Internalization: recognize process of external cause linking internal effect <br> 6. Physiological: illness in terms of internal bodily organs and functions <br> 7. Psychophysiological: as in physiological, but includes psychological causes | .88 (agreement for protocal) |

*(continued)*

*Table 1.—Continued*

| Study | Sample/Design Characteristics | Interview Format | Explanatory Taxonomy | Reliability |
|---|---|---|---|---|
| | | 12. What are germs? What do they look like? Can you draw germs? Where do they come from? | | .83 (agreement for protocol) |
| Bibace & Walsh (1980) | 24 healthy boys and girls in each of three age groups: 4, 7, and 11-year-olds assumed to represent preoperational, concrete operational, and formal operational thinking | Same as Bibace & Walsh (1979) | Same as Bibace & Walsh (1979) | |
| Campbell (1975) | 132 hospitalized boys and girls in each of two age ranges: 6 to 9-6 and 9-6 to 12-11 years; No Piagetian stage assessment | Now I'm wondering how you know when you're sick. When you say you are sick, what do you mean? On one day you know you are well; on another you know you are sick. OK, what's the difference? | 1. Nonlocalized, nonspecific feeling states<br>2. Nonlocalized, but specific feeling states<br>3. Specific and localized somatic feelings<br>4. Visible external signs<br>5. Objective signs not immediately visible<br>6. Disease concept or specific diagnosis<br>7. Mood, motivational, attitude states<br>8. Increase in sick role behavior<br>9. Altered conventional role<br>10. Behavior or intentions of others<br>11. Explicit restriction of illness concept | .89 (median intercoder $r$ per theme) |

| | | | |
|---|---|---|---|
| Carandang, Folkins, Hines & Steward (1979) | 36 siblings of children with diabetes and 36 matched siblings of healthy controls assessed using conservation tasks as concrete operational (6-6 to 8 year), transitional (9 to 14 years), or formal operational (10-6 to 15 year) thinking | 1. How do people get sick?<br>2. How do doctors help make people get well? | 1. Concrete operational<br>2. Transitional operational<br>3. Formal operational | .92 (Pearson interrater $r$) |
| Myers-Vando, Steward, Folkins & Hines (1979) | 12 chronically ill outpatient and 12 matched control children (8 to 16 years); Conservation task performance as dependent variable | Questioned children directly about their own experiences with illness, its causes, and their recovery; specific interview questions not reported | Same as Bibace & Walsh (1979) | .87 (agreement for protocol) |
| Neuhauser, Amsterdam, Hines & Steward (1978) | 12 healthy boys and girls in each of two groups evincing either preoperational (4 to 5 years) or concrete operational (8 to 9 years) thought | 1. How did you know when you were hurt (sick)?<br>2. When you were hurt (sick), how did you heal (get better)? How did that work to help you heal (get better)?<br>3. What was going on inside your body that helped you heal (get better)? How does that work? Can you show me?<br>4. Control over healing ladder diagram: Show me how much you have to do with healing your cut (getting well)? Now show me how much somebody, like your parents, or something else, like medicine, has to do with healing your cut (getting you well)?<br>5. How did you know when you were all healed (all better)? | 1. "I don't know" answer<br>2. A listing of body parts or causally inaccurate response<br>3. Accurate statement of causality and of something inside the body that aids healing | No report |

173

*(continued)*

*Table 1.—Continued*

| Study | Sample/Design Characteristics | Interview Format | Explanatory Taxonomy | Reliability |
|---|---|---|---|---|
| Perrin & Gerrity (1981) | 128 healthy kindergarten, second, fourth, sixth, and eighth grade children; conservation tasks given but not reported separately | 1. All children get sick once in a while. How do kids know when they are sick?<br>2. How do children get sick?<br>3. How can children keep from getting sick?<br>4. Some children get stomach aches when they are sick. How do they get stomach aches?<br>5. Sometimes when children get sick they get little bumps or spots on their skin. How do children get those bumps or spots?<br>6. Sometimes when children get sick they have to stay in the hospital. What would be wrong with them that would make them have to stay in a hospital?<br>7. When children are sick, how can they get better again?<br>8. Sometimes when children are sick they have to take medicine. How does medicine work? | 0. No response<br>1. Don't know<br>2. Circular, magical, or global response<br>3. Concrete, rigid response with enumeration of symptoms, actions, or situations associated with illness<br>4. More generalized response with quality of invariant causation<br>5. Beginning use of underlying principle and causal agents<br>6. Organized description of the mechanism underlying illness and recovery; abstract system | .84 (overall *r*) |
| Simeonsson, Buckley & Monson (1979) | 20 hospitalized children in each of three age ranges: 4 to 5-11, 6 to 7-11, and 8 to 9-11 years; conservation tasks administered with only correlations reported | 1. How can children keep from getting sick?<br>2. What does medicine do?<br>3. How do children get sick?<br>4. How do children get stomach aches?<br>5. How do children get bumps or spots? | 1. Global or undifferentiated responses<br>2. Concrete, specific responses reflecting rule breaking, rule keeping, and/or specific acts and events<br>3. Abstract verbalizations or expressions of principle | .86 (interater agreement) |

Whitt, Johnson, Dykstra & Taylor (1981)

119 hospitalized children (age range 5 to 16 years) and 44 healthy kindergarten, second, fourth, and sixth grade controls assessed using conservation and/or pendulum tasks as evincing preoperational, concrete operational, or formal operational thinking

Revision in preparation

6. When children are sick, how do they get better again?

1. When children say they're sick, what do they mean?

2. How do children usually know they are sick?

3. How come children get sick?

4. When children are sick, how do they get better again?

5. How can children keep from getting sick?

6. When you say you're sick, what do *you* mean?

(*Additional questions for hospitalized children*)

7. Are you sick now? (If yes) How do you know you're sick? (If no) How come you're in the hospital?

8. What do you have?

9. What do you think made you get sick? How do children get sick? _____ (child's term)?

10. (If diagnosis is different) The doctor says you have $\underline{X}$. How do children get $\underline{X}$?

11. How often do you get sick? How often do you get $\underline{X}$? How long have you had $\underline{X}$?

12. When a child has $\underline{X}$, how does he or she get better?

13. What can you do to make yourself better?

14. How can you keep from getting $\underline{X}$ again?

bandaged school children posing in pajamas. Each child was questioned regarding causation of the injury, reasons for the bandage, appearance of the wound beneath the bandage, and ultimate treatment outcome. The children revealed that they thought bandages were applied because they "keep the sore place from getting cold," or to "take the place of the leg so he can walk, and get places uninfected." These perceptions were paralleled by children's images of wounds concealed by the bandage. Some denied any trauma or indicated the presence of black and blue spots, scratches, little scars, bumps, and so on. Other children visualized evidence of extensive damage: "the arm would be cut in half and just hanging with rows and rows of stitches and lots of dried blood"; "bones would be poking up under the skin like the top of a circus tent." Howe concluded that the identification of fantasies is an initial step toward correcting misconceptions that contribute to poor adjustment.

Several investigators, recognizing limitations in children's verbal abilities, paired doll play or projective assessment techniques with structured interviews in exploring childhood concepts of illness causality. In a study contrasting children with rheumatic fever and those having an acute transitory illness (Lynn, Glaser, & Harrison, 1962), nearly half of the children failed to acknowledge a cause for their illnesses. However, most responded to the more general inquiry about the origins of "other children's" illnesses. The absence of direct articulation of personal anxieties and guilt feelings provided no guarantee of their nonexistence. Indeed, twice as many children attributed illness causality to the ill child's actions as perceived sickness as a result of circumstances beyond one's control, a conclusion also reached by Peters (1975). According to Lynn, Glaser, and Harrison, children with rheumatic heart disease were significantly more likely to consider illness as self-caused and more frequently expressed anxiety about injections, medication, hospitalization, and surgery than the children with acute transitory illness. Doll play responses indicated that children with rheumatic fever associated illness with pain, physical restrictions, social handicap, heart disease, crippling, and death, despite a medical regime that encouraged activity and the marked absence of surgical procedures in these youngsters' medical histories.

Rashkis (1965) used a similar combination of structured interview and concurrent doll play to investigate the meaning of health to kindergarten through third grade children. Children below seven years of age failed to ascribe any positive feeling to being well. Rather, health was perceived as the absence of sickness. As a group, children recognized limitations in their capacity to keep themselves well and viewed the adult's role as one of protection of the child against illness. It was not until the age of 8 to 9 years that children expressed confidence in the physician more frequently than other adults as a health protector. This milestone may be fundamental as a determinant of the format of pediatric health care. Prior to this age, physician interpersonal communication and explanations of childhood illness may require mediation through the security of parental interactions.

Nagy (1951) was one of the first to study developmental characteristics of well children's illness theories. Although generally descriptive, her findings suggest four identified stages of illness causality beliefs. The youngest children in her sample tended to relate illness cause and effect to events contiguous in time. At 6 to 7 years of age, children indicated that illness is caused by an unspecified infection, defined as microorganisms by her 8 to 10 year-old subjects. Few children, even between the ages of 8 and 12 years, had a conceptualization of illness that embraced the multitude of factors associated in disease etiology. However, around 11 years of age children discovered that different diseases originated with different organisms. In subsequent research on children's ideas of germs, Nagy (1953b) concluded that children from 5 to 10 years of age fail to consider either the degree of infestation or the resistance of the body—if germs get inside the human body, one necessarily becomes ill. Medicine, in a similar reflexive fashion, was thought by these children to promote instantaneous healing.

Blos (1956, 1978), in a study of healthy children using stimulus pictures to depict a variety of illness situations, found a distinct difference between his oldest group (9–10 years of age) and two younger groups (5–6 years; 7–8 years of age) in their capacity to understand respiratory illness transmission. Similar to Nagy, Blos described three stages of illness causality concepts (descriptive, exploratory, causitive) ranging from contiguous events as explanatory causes through childhood descriptions of disease that postulate a multistep causal mechanism. In contrast to Nagy, Blos suggested that the older children in his sample comprehended health and vulnerability concepts when they implied that children may catch cold in more than one way, and do not always become ill when exposed.

To determine whether children's illness ideas show developmental progression towards the concepts characteristic of adults and to examine age-linked themes in illness definitions, Campbell (1975) studied the themes evident in 264 children's and mothers' definitions of illness using 11 content categories as listed in Table 1. Children aged 6 through 12 years who were short-term patients in a pediatric hospital were independently asked: "Now, I'm wondering about how you know you are sick. When you say you are sick, what do you mean? On one day you know you are well; on another you know you are sick. OK, what's the difference?"

Campbell's findings support the view that acquisition of illness perspective is a developmental phenomenon. He argued that the trends in thematic content used in childhood conceptions of illness develop from reliance on feeling states toward definitions that, while not ignoring this aspect, extend the meaning in two principal ways. First, there was an age-linked increase in the precision of illness definitions. Younger children were more apt to mention vague, nonlocalized feelings ("hurts," "feels bad") as the major feature of their explanations. Older children gave more definitional attention to specific disease or diagnostic concepts ("appendicitis," "chicken pox"). In addition, their views of illness encompassed a broader range of illness factors including recognition of altered role performance ("don't go to school") and explicit restrictions of the illness concept ("if I just have a cold, I'm not sick").

Contrasts between maternal and child responses evidenced continued maturation of illness concepts. Mothers' definitions of illness showed significantly greater relative frequency of unseen objective indicators ("sugar in urine"), specific disease concepts, mood and motivational states ("grouchy," "unhappy"), increase in sick role ("let housework go"), and restriction of the illness concept.

Perhaps most provocative is Campbell's finding that children's health history influenced their conceptualizations of illness in an interaction with age. The younger child with a history of poor health may be at a disadvantage. Despite the early vested interest in health care phenomena, younger children were unable to assimilate their experience to the fullest. In contrast, older children having recent poor health demonstrated greater sophistication in their illness concepts than their healthier peers. Thus, at least in the domain of illness concepts, Campbell concluded that children's capacity to profit from illness experiences may be contingent upon their attainment of a requisite level of cognitive development.

The methodological refinements adopted by Campbell (1975) heralded substantial progress in the empirical status of research into children's conceptions of illness. Objectively gathered and defined explanations of illness, emphasis on interrater reliability, and statistical rather than purely clinical analysis of data revealed new dimensions in the content of developing illness concepts. However, to professionals faced with the clinical task of providing cognitively and effectively appropriate explanations of illness, the need was apparent for continued investigation of the logical structure of children's conceptions. In particular, identification of cognitive developmental factors independent of age was needed to allow assessment of children's understanding of health care phenomena.

Recently, several investigators (e.g., Bibace & Walsh, 1979, 1980; Perrin & Gerrity, 1981; Steward & Steward, in press; Whitt, Dykstra, & Taylor, 1979; Whitt, Johnson, Dykstra, & Taylor, 1981) have attempted to validate a conceptual framework which may guide professionals in providing explanations of illness that are both accurate and within the child's cognitive capacity for understanding. These investigators have postulated that the theory of intellectual development advanced by Piaget (cf. 1963/1947) indexes the structural characteristics of illness explanations that are appropriately "concrete" for children of various ages. Although alternative views of cognitive development exist (see e.g., studies by Anderson & Cuneo, 1978; Cuneo, 1980; Shaklee, 1979; Tomlinson-Keasy, Eisert, Kahle, Hardy, & Keasy, 1979; Wilkening, 1979), the Piagetian concepts influencing contemporary illness-conceptions research warrant more detailed elaboration.

# PIAGET'S THEORY OF COGNITIVE DEVELOPMENT

Piaget's observations about childhood intellectual development are organized around a number of unifying principles (Ginsberg & Opper, 1969). Central among these constructs is the idea that interaction of humans with their environment is part of an organized process that tends toward adaptation. As children grow, they assimilate novel features of their experience in terms of their existing structure of cognition. In turn, the cognitive challenge of complex experiences leads to accomodation, the modification of cognitive structures which increases the child's adaptation potential. According to Piaget, this dynamic, nonstop process leads children's thinking through an invariant series of four major stages, each characterized by a qualitatively different structure of cognition. Each stage is a transformation—the evolution of a more complex, integrated version of the mode of thought that preceded it (Breger, 1974). Although obscured at times by the gradual and continuous nature of development, the often imperceptible steps between stages represent giant leaps forward in the child's capacity to understand new and more complex illness concepts (Papalia & Olds, 1975).

The principal stages of cognitive development described by Piaget (1952/1936; 1963/1947) are: (ages are approximate) te sensorimotor stage, covering the first 18 to 24 months of a child's life; the stage of preoperational thinking, from about 1½ to 6 years; concrete operations, from 6 or 7 to 11; and formal operations, from early adolescence through adulthood. Roughly speaking, the person passes from an undifferentiated state of sensations and reflexes; to a physical (sensory and motor) apprehension of functioning in the world; to crude symbolic (intuitive) thinking; to a more differentiated—but still literal or concrete—mode of thought; to, finally, the ability to manipulate logical abstractions (Breger, 1974).

## Sensorimotor Stage

As Piaget's term sensorimotor intelligence implies, this remarkable period of infant development is indexed by changes from newborn dependency on reflexes for interaction with the environment, to an increasing capacity for organized patterns of sensory and motor action. "Thinking" during this stage is exemplified by infant recognition or anticipation of familiar objects and events, which is demonstrated behaviorally with the mouth, hands, eyes, and other "sensorimotor" tools in a predictable, organized, and often adaptive fashion (Flavell, 1977).

In the course of trial and error exploration of the properties of objects, the infant discovers their quality of permanence—items exist even when they are not perceived (seen, felt, heard, smelled, or tasted). Discovery of object permanence is not without its complications for the young infant who then begins to recognize the mother's departure with a new "separation anxiety," possible only with the realization that when Mom is not here, she *is* somewhere. Prior to this understanding, "out of sight" not only meant "out of mind," but also "out of existence." The sensorimotor stage ends around 18 months of age as the infant begins to acquire the capacity to represent the objects of his or her cognition with mental symbols and reflect on inner, symbolized reality rather than merely act upon outer, perceived reality.

## Stage of Preoperational Thinking

As the ability to use symbolic mental representations to stand for objects not immediately present is acquired, new avenues of thought free the preoperational child from the immediate here and now action of "sensorimotor" thinking. Symbolic thought manifests itself in many ways. Deferred imitation, made possible by the recall of previous mental representations, allows the child to reenact situations as "pretend." Through symbolic play, realities including hospital trauma can be mastered at a safer pace and a less stressful time. Symbolic play has an important role in emotional development, allowing the child to shape reality to his or her own requirements. Thus, the child can become the doctor; a pencil can become a syringe; and a doll can assume the child's previously passive role in the acting out of a painful, although necessary, injection procedure. In brief, symbolic play, serving a crucial cathartic purpose, is essential for the child's emotional stability and adjustment to otherwise incomprehensible realities (Ginsberg & Opper, 1969). A third aspect of the symbolic function of the preoperational child is, of course, the acquisition of language. During this early period, the child learns the language spoken in his or her culture, managing this symbol system with considerable skill by age four or five.

The emergence of language and symbolic competence during this stage is such a leap forward that it is easy to overestimate the conceptual ability of the child. However powerful these symbolic representations appear, preschool children's thoughts remain empirical rather than logical in nature and are dominated by associations to static, perceptual characteristics of events. Egocentrism characterizes the child's thought. The child does not differentiate his or her own intuitive point of view from the perspectives of other people. The only viewpoint that exists is that of a child. Time is similarly present-centered, consisting of a series of succeeding "nows." The preoperational child also tends to center, or focus, on a single aspect of the situation, neglecting the importance of other features and thus making patently illogical deductions.

The role of perception in children's cognitions at this stage and the lack of logic in their thinking is illustrated by Piaget's classical experiments on conservation. For example, if presented with two identical tall, thin glasses filled with equal amounts of water, a five-year-old child will acknowledge that they contain equal amounts to drink. If the water from one glass is then poured into a short, wide glass, the preoperational child is likely to say the original glass has more because it is "taller," or has less because it is "thinner" than the short, wide glass. Preoperational children are mislead by centering on a single perceptual feature of their experience.

Nor do these children apply the logical operations that will characterize their later thought. Logical reasoning is basically of two types, deductive and inductive. Deductive reasoning, which goes from the general to the particular, is expressed in the syllogism: "All people are mammals. I am a person. Therefore, I am a mammal." Inductive reasoning moves from the particular to the general: "Investigation has shown that the red blood cells of horses, porpoises, tree shrews, people, and other mammals lack nuclei. Therefore, we can probably assume that the red blood cells of all mammals lack nuclei." The judgments of preoperational children follow neither of these logical lines (Papalia & Olds, 1975). Instead, the child proceeds from one particular to another without taking into account the general. Thus, the preschool child can observe Santa Claus in several different stores on the same day and not suspect for a moment that there might be more than one Santa Claus. For these children, reality is without question as it is perceived. Along with the belief that the world is purposive (everything has a reason or cause; nothing is arbitrary or by chance), transductive reasoning explains the preschooler's penchant towards phenomenalistic causality—the belief that when two events occur in succession, the first "causes" the second. Given these underpinnings, it is not surprising that the child ascribes cause and effect linkage to totally unrelated events. "I had mean thoughts about my brother. I got sick. Therefore, my mean thoughts made me sick."

## Stage of Concrete Operations

With the acquisition of concrete operational thinking, around the age of seven, the child's imagery becomes less static and perceptually bound. In contrast to the younger child who centers attention exclusively on a single feature of his or her experience, the concrete operational child accomplishes a more balanced "decentered" analysis of the data at hand. While thought remains limited to the youngster's concrete experience, children between 7 and 11 years of age are able to focus simultaneously on several dimensions of a situation, recognize the sequence of actions involved in the transformation between apparent perceptual changes, and can reverse the direction of their thinking to verify their logical judgments. These abilities allow the child to understand that, regardless of perceptual alterations in height or width, quantities do not change as long as nothing is added or taken away. Reality testing is well served by this attainment. The child now has available a more accurate and detailed rendering of the events on which to base reasoning and logical judgments (Ginsberg & Opper, 1969).

Changes in the structure of a child's thought beginning around 6 or 7 years of age are particularly robust and significant. It is not merely coincidental that as children's cognitive processes change from primitive egocentric judgments to more abstract and concretely logical thinking, formal education is initiated, belief in Santa Claus and his imaginary colleagues comes to an end (Prentice, Schmechel, & Manosevitz, 1979), and spontaneous symbolic play is replaced by rule-guided games with peers.

Harter (1977) has applied these principles to the child's developing sense of emotional concepts. She postulates a parallel between the preoperational child's centering on one perceptual dimension and children's difficulty focusing on more than one emotion at a time. If the preoperational child has difficulty understanding both the concept of "mixed feelings" and views which hold one's self as good and bad simultaneously, transductive thinking may provide "proof" that "I am ill because I am bad." Similarly, only with the concrete operational capacity to decenter from a single perceptual feature is the child likely to understand even the most rudimentary explanation of physiological functioning of organ systems which fall outside the child's perceptual awareness.

*Stage of Formal Operations*

The final period of cognitive development described by Piaget, the stage of formal operations, begins around age 11 or 12 years and is consolidated throughout adolescence. During this stage, the adolescent begins to transcend concrete here and now experiences and thinks abstractly about thought itself, including concepts such as democracy, honesty, love, and justice. For the first time, the child is capable of hypothetical deduction. Faced with a perplexing situation, the adolescent can develop hypotheses concerning what might have happened, construct scientifically sound tests of these possibilities, and deduce whether the hypothesis is true. Like the exercise of logic seen in children's humor in second and third grades (Whitt & Prentice, in press), adolescent idealism seems to represent a flexing of new intellectual muscles during this later stage. Although in the process of exploring these new abilities the adolescent may sometimes feel that goals can be accomplished by thought alone, these advances of age and cognitive development occasion new attainments in abstract understanding of health and disease concepts.

# RESEARCH BASED ON PIAGETIAN THEORY

In an attempt to define, empirically, the association of illness and health causality with other cognitive growth parameters in young hospitalized children, Simeonsson, Buckley, and Monson (1979) emphasized the transition from pre-operational to concrete operational stages which, according to Piaget, marks the shift from magical and egocentric cognition to more decentered and logical thought processes. Sixty subjects hospitalized at a university teaching center for a variety of elective admissions, accidents, chronic conditions, and acute illnesses were selected to constitute three age groups (4-0 to 5-11 years; 6-0 to 7-11 years; and 8-0 to 9-11 years) of approximately equal numbers of boys and girls. All children were individually administered measures of conservation, role-taking skills, and conceptualization regarding causality (i.e., "What makes clouds move?"). Responses to six additional questions (see Table 1) constructed to assess causality of illness were scored by applying specific criteria to children's explanations. Stage I conceptions of illness causality were undifferentiated, magical, superstitious, and/or reflected circularity of reasoning in which cause and effect are confused. For example, children may become sick "when you kiss old people and women" or "when they need pills." Stage II responses were scored according to the presence of concrete and specific conceptions of illness. The violation and/or observation of specific rules and enumeration of acts or events in the absence of an organizing or generalizing principle characterized explanations at this stage. For example, childhood illness occurs when, "peanuts go in the wrong pipe, getting finger cut, getting electrocuted," or if you "go to the medicine cabinet and take medicine you are not supposed to, eat poison." Stage III responses showed evidence of an abstract and/or generalizing principle. Thus, children get sick because "you catch it from other people from germs," illustrating a relative understanding of disease and causal factors of illness which extend beyond specific acts, events, and/or violations of rules.

The findings of Simeonsson, Buckley, and Monson (1979) evidenced a significant developmental progression of illness causality stages by age groups, with conceptions having some uniformity at each developmental level and progressing with age toward a more abstract view. Stage I responses characterized 39% of all responses of five-year-olds but dropped to 20% and 10% of responses for the two older age groups. Stage II reasoning accounted for 61%, 74%, and 84% of all responses for the 5, 7, and 9 year age groups, respectively. Stage III responses, on the other hand, were nonexistent for the youngest population and represented only a small percentage (6%) in each of the middle and oldest age groups. Mean illness causality scores correlated significantly with measures of conservation ($r = .53$), egocentrism ($r = .56$), and chronological age ($r = .49$). This study provided evidence that the structure of children's conceptions of illness from ages 4 through 11 parallels the cognitive developmental changes reported by Piaget. While it cannot be concluded that these changes are caused by cognitive developmental advances per se, since age and Piagetian stages are confounded in the study, the rarity of Stage III responses in the Simeonsson et al. study is consistent with expectations derived from Piaget. Only with the onset of formal operational thinking around age 11 or 12, an age not sampled in this study, would children's illness conceptions be expected to encompass the abstract phenomena defined by Stage III conceptualizations.

Perrin and Gerrity (1981) sampled 128 kindergarten, second, fourth, sixth, and eighth grade children in an attempt to expand the separation of responses into discrete scoring categories representing preoperational, concrete operational, and formal operational cognitive structures. They added transitional stages to create a seven-point coding scale illustrated in Table 1. No score was given if the child refused to answer the question or answered with clearly inappropriate content. A score of 1 designated the response, "I don't know." A score of 2 was assigned to circular and magical responses, when illness was defined solely by associations with external events or sensory phenomena without articulation of the causal link between the event and illness. Explanation of concrete rules and prohibitions associated with illness received a score of 3. These responses typically included only an external causal agent, failing to discuss any notion of taking in the contaminant or the process by which the illness occurs. Four points were assigned to those explanations which included not only the illness causal agent but also the method of internalizing the agent, thus demonstrating an initial understanding of the process of getting sick. Five-point responses reflected appreciation of the relativity of illness causation, and the role of an active host as well as an agent in causing illness. These responses described the etiologic interaction of an underlying body process with a causative agent. Six points were assigned to responses which discussed a coherent mechanism operating with the body to cause illness. Although triggered by external events, these descriptions captured the dysfunction of internal body organs or systems which were manifested by various externally visible symptoms of illness.

The overall mean scores for questions regarding illness causality increased significantly with grade, demonstrating a positive linear trend. As seen in other categorical data, the use of more abstract and complex illness-related concepts increased systematically with age. Perrin and Gerrity found that two and three-point responses characterized 75% of the kindergarten children's scores, and the percentage decreased with increasing grade. On the other hand, only by sixth grade did children receive scores of 5 or 6, a level which accounted for 47% of the eighth graders' responses. Rarely did any children achieve a score of 6 on any question. The ability to describe illness mechanisms was demonstrated by only 6% of the sixth graders and only 10% of the eighth grade children.

Bibace and Walsh (1979) also reported a developmental taxonomy of children's explanations of health and illness. They employed 24 subjects in each of three age groups: four, seven, and 11-year-olds assumed to be in the stages of preoperational, concrete operational, and formal operational thinking, respectively. A protocol containing 12 sets of questions was utilized in a school setting to probe each child's cognitive understanding of illness (Table 1). Seven categories were defined which, according to Bibace and Walsh, reflect the three major Piagetian stages. Incomprehension (Type 0), Phenomenism (Type 1), and Contagion (Type 2) indicate preoperational modes of thinking. Contamination (Type 3) and Internalization (Type 4) evidence concrete operational thinking, while Physiological (Type 5) and Psychophysiological (Type 6) demonstrate explanations within the formal operational stage of development. Looking first at the youngest group of children sampled, 12.5% gave phenomenalistic explanations (Type 1), 70.8% were categorized as giving contagion explanations (Type 2), while 16.7% gave contamination explanations (Type 3). Among the 7-year-olds, 16.7% told contagion explanations (Type 2), 75% gave contamination explanations (Type 3), and 8.3% gave internalization explanations (Type 4). Of the 11-year-old children, 25% offered internalization explanations (Type 4), 70.8% gave physiological explanations, and 4.2% gave psychophysiological explanations (Type 6).

The significance of this developmental progression (recently replicated by Bibace & Walsh, 1980) is seen by examination of the following categories and examples of Bibace and Walsh (1979, 1980):

*Incomprehension (Type 0)*: The child evades the what, why, and how of the question and gives answers that appear irrelevant;

*Phenomenism (Type 1)*: Illness is defined in terms of external sensory experience which is associated with the illness via spatial or temporal contiguity. The source is at best a magical and inappropriate cause of the illness (e.g., "Headache is from the wind." "Pain is because it's red.");

*Contagion (Type 2)*: While the child continues to explain illness in terms of externally perceived persons, objects, or events, and fails to articulate the link between these phenomena and the illness, the causes invoked are both more proximal to the person and appropriate to the domain of illness. The source of illness is usually a person or objective spatially near, but not touching, the ill person, or an activity or event which is temporally prior to, but not simultaneous with, the occurrence of the illness (e.g., "Measles are from other people. When you walk near them." "A headache is from leaning against something.");

*Contamination (Type 3)*: The child's definition of illness no longer centers on a single feature but encompasses multiple symptoms. Although the locus of illness is at the surface of the body, externally visible bodily processes such as breathing may also be mentioned. The child now perceives a concrete causal link between the still external source of the illness and its effect through poor hygiene or dirt, or moral contamination via bad or immoral overt behavior (e.g., "Germs are kissing someone." "Cancer is smoking without your mother's permission." "Measles are little bumps on your stomach.");

*Internalization (Type 4)*: For the first time, with this type of explanation, the child locates illness, in a global way, inside the body. However, the child's emphasis is not on what occurs within the body, but on the internalization process by which "bugs" get from outside to inside. Internal organ systems may be introduced using concrete analogies, that is, descriptions in terms of externally perceived objects or events (for example, the heart is a pump, or the stomach as a bag of food). However, the child's emphasis is not on what occurs within the body, but on the visible events (e.g., swallowing, inhaling) by which external contaminants (e.g., smoke, dirt, germs) are internalized, or unhealthy body conditions (obesity, old age) have an effect on internal organs (e.g.,

"Colds are from germs in the air, you breathe them in." "A heart attack is when your heart stops, like a pump shuts off. It happens from lifting heavy stuff, your arms hurt and the hurt goes up your arms into your heart.");

*Physiological (Type 5)*: Children using this type of explanation define illness in terms of internal physiological structures and functions whose malfunctioning manifests itself in multiple external symptoms. Recognizing the triggering effect of external factors in illness causality, the child departs from concrete experience and makes hypotheses about the relationship between physical environmental events and internal organ systems (e.g., "Pain is from an injury to a muscle." "Cancer is when there's too many cells. Some people think air pollution or chemicals . . . cause the cells to start growing.");

*Psychophysiological (Type 6)*: Illness continues to be explained in terms of internal physiological functioning. However, the child additionally is aware of an alternative illness etiology, that is, psychogenic factors linked to a person's thoughts or feelings (e.g., "A headache is pressure inside your head. They worry too much. It's from problems and aggravations.").

As noted above, the categories of Bibace and Walsh draw heavily on expectations from Piagetian theory. Their proposed developmental sequence of childhood understanding progresses from magical preoperational concepts which focus solely on a single sensory aspect of the illness experience, to concrete operational emphasis on multiple external perceived cues and transpositions between these events, to the abstract logic and hypotheses regarding internal phenomena outside the child's concrete perceptual awareness expected of persons attaining formal operational thought. Unfortunately, the role of Piagetian cognitive structures can only be inferred from age groupings, since Bibace and Walsh (1979, 1980) did not report the cognitive stage of children in their sample.

Bibace and Walsh (1979) also discuss the construct of locus of control as reflected in the children's comprehension of illness. Internal-external locus of control expectancies refer to the degree to which an individual perceives the events which happen as dependent on his or her own behavior (internal control) or as a result of luck, chance, fate, or powers beyond one's personal control (Strickland, 1978). For example, as a child's understanding develops from phenomenism to contamination, Bibace and Walsh suggest that the child acquires a sense of control over illness acquisition through avoidance of agents that contact the body surface. Internalization-type conceptualizations and the concurrent focus on the process by which external agents are taken into the body allows even greater internal control, invoking an aggregation of regularly occurring events (e.g., eating habits) as relevant to health and illness prevention. Finally, they argue that physiological and psychophysiological conceptions allow the child to perceive multiple causes for illness, therefore enhancing the child's sense of control further by the diversity of personal actions which contribute to health or illness.

Although Bibace and Walsh (1979) report no date in support of their hypotheses, data from Neuhauser, Amsterdam, Hines, and Steward (1978) provide empirical grounding for conclusions regarding the association of cognitive development and locus of control in children's views of illness and perception of influence upon the healing process. They verbally administered a locus of control scale and a questionnaire on concepts of the healing process to each of 24 healthy children, 12 functioning cognitively at the concrete operational state (age range of 8 to 9 years) and 12 children (age range of 4 to 5 years) who performed at the preoperational stage of cognitive development. No group difference in internal control—the perception of an individual's influence on life experiences—was found between the younger preoperational and older concrete operational children. Although children in both groups frequently responded to inquiries with "I don't know," concrete operational children were much more likely than the preoperational group to have an accurate understanding of what goes on inside their bodies during healing. Concrete operational children indicated more control over healing and used more internal cues (e.g., "My finger or stomach hurts." "I feel like jumping again.") for knowing when they are ill and well again, in contrast to preoperational children's dependence on external indicators (e.g., "My friend told me I was cut.").

Since the degree to which a child was internal in his or her locus of control correlated with the use of internal health cues only for older children, Neuhauser et al. hypothesized that children's thoughts about illness and health have both a cognitive-developmental and personality dimension. The extent to which these factors come into play depends upon the abstractness of the concept involved. Both groups respond similarly when asked about a tangible injury (a cut finger). However, the more abstract concepts of internal bodily illness and healing provide few concrete, external cues, thus presenting too difficult a task for comprehension by younger children. Furthermore, the personality factor of locus of control only influenced the concrete operational children's use of internal cues in describing abstract illness phenomena. The more internal children not only felt they had more control over the healing process, they also had more apparent access to internal cues for knowing they were ill in the first place. These data support a hypothesis that this personality dimension becomes a factor in children's differential understanding of illness only when the task of comprehension is at the upper limits of their cognitive ability. If the task is too easy or too difficult, locus of control makes no difference.

Our own developmental research on cognitive processes and children's understanding of illness and health care phenomena (cf. Whitt, Dykstra, & Taylor, 1979) explores the additional "cues" or perceptual referents of body functioning and symptoms provided by various illnesses. Thus, organ systems without concrete external indicators (e.g., "nerves") or illnesses which allow no overt sensory experience for a child (e.g., epilepsy) are hypothesized to be intrinsically more difficult to understand than the more concrete phenomena of broken bones or chicken pox. Holt (1967) mentioned the latter phenomena in her survey of 30 children's recall of a prior hospitalization following a five-year interval. Although no empirical data are available, few children in in her sample (age range of 8 to 10 years) had an understanding of their illness. Of those who did, visible surgical or orthopedic conditions were viewed more accurately than systematic diseases. Through exploring the relationships among Piagetian cognitive development, body concept, illness symptom cues, and children's conceptions of illness with hospitalized and healthy school children ranging in age from 5 to 16 years, our research seeks to redress this early neglect.

Preliminary data (Whitt, Dykstra, Johnson, & Taylor, 1980) support the hypothesis that childhood awareness of internal organs, measured by asking hospitalized children to "draw the inside organs of the body and label all the parts" (cf. Tait & Archer, 1955), increases as a function of the perceptual cues provided by each organ system. Acknowledgment of the skeletal system did not exceed children's knowledge of gastrointestinal and cardiovascular organs. However, recognition of these latter organ systems significantly exceeded awareness of the respiratory, nervous, and urinary/reproductive systems, which were in turn mentioned more than the endocrine system. For the developmental analysis, children were categorized into three age groups: 5 to 7 year-olds ($N = 23$), 8 to 11 year-olds ($N = 34$), and 12 to 16 year-olds ($N = 27$). Analysis of variance performed on the mean number of organs acknowledged indicated that awareness of internal organs increased with age for the gastrointestinal, cardiovascular, respiratory, urinary/reproductive, and endocrine systems. The nervous system was mentioned infrequently by any age group in the present sample, while even the youngest children acknowledged bones as a part of the body. Children demonstrated essentially parallel findings when the mean number of organs per system was analyzed by stage of cognitive development (preoperational, concrete operational, formal operational). These results suggest that children acknowledge the presence of internal organs of the skeletal, gastrointestinal, and cardiovascular system more than the respiratory, nervous, urinary/reproductive, and endocrine systems. Moreover, increasing awareness of most body systems occurs as a function of both age and cognitive stage of development, but not IQ, of these children. These findings, like the results of other investigations (Gellert, 1978; Nagy, 1953a; Smith, 1973; Tait & Archer, 1955), suggest that illness explanations may be influenced not only by the structure of the child's conceptual focus, but also by the capacity to imagine the inner workings of the body.

Congruence of specific illness cues with cognitive-developmental aspects of comprehension may also be a factor. For example, the lack of children's recognition of the nervous system in combination with the absence of concrete perceptual cues provided to the child with a seizure disorder would augur poorly for accurate comprehension of this disease at all ages. On the other hand, even young children may be expected to comprehend the treatment of a broken bone or skin irritation for which perceptual cues of both the illness and organ system in question are readily apparent.

## DISCUSSION

The studies reported have evolved relatively independently, creating an admixture of methodologies which makes direct comparison difficult and limits generalization. Future collaboration may focus the miscellany of interview questions and explanatory taxonomies surveyed in Table 1.

Disentangling the currently confounded developmental effects of age, Piagetian stage of cognitive development, stress of hospitalization or illness, and personality dimensions on children's illness conceptions will require further methodological refinement. For example, many investigators (e.g., Bibace & Walsh, 1979, 1980) presume that the cognitive stage of their sample children increases with age, and only analyze the effects of age on illness comprehension. Even those investigators who include direct assessment of children's Piagetian stage functioning in their protocols (e.g., Perrin & Gerrity, 1981; Simeonsson, Buckley, & Monson, 1979; Whitt, Dykstra, Johnson, & Taylor, 1980) fail to distinguish statistically the qualitative impact of these cognitive structures (e.g., concrete or formal operational thought) from the more general maturational effects of age on the structure and content of childhood illness explanations. (For further discussion of this challenging problem, see Neuhauser, Amsterdam, Hines, & Steward, 1978; Whitt & Prentice, 1977).

Illnesses vary dramatically in their perceptual presentation to the child. The number of concrete symptoms presented, the accuracy with which these perceptual cues reflect the dysfunctional organ system, the developmental salience of each organ system, physician's explanations, and the clarity of the treatment effects are but a few of the stimulus factors requiring investigatory attention. As yet, only the attempt to compare healing of a cut versus an illness has been published on this topic (Neuhauser, Amsterdam, Hines, & Steward, 1978) likely due to the length of time and tenacity of clinical research efforts required to assemble controlled developmental samples of children having target illnesses from a single medical center (cf. Whitt, Johnson, Dykstra, & Taylor, 1981).

The absence of well-controlled research with both hospitalized and well children has left moot the question of whether children who have more extensive contact with illness develop a more sophisticated understanding of health care phenomena or if, on the other hand, heightened affect regarding illness interferes with these cognitions (or both, depending upon individual variability in the developmental factors mentioned above). Our results (Whitt, Johnson, Dykstra, & Taylor, 1981) support the hypothesis of Carandang, Folkins, Hines, and Steward (1979) and the data of Myers-Vando, Steward, Folkins, and Hines (1979), which report unexpectedly low cognitive functioning in children with chronic illness. While some authors (e.g., Blos, 1978) have discussed stress-induced distortions of thought content and emotional regressions associated with long-term hospitalization and life-threatening childhood illness, testing an hypothesis of diminished Piagetian cognition as a function of chronic illness will require carefully planned methodology comparing children matched on environmental, cultural, and innate potentialities. Previous research exploring the cognition of ill and healthy children has compared intelligence, not attainment of Piagetian stages. However, one provocative study (Cayler, Lynn, and Stein, 1973) found that children *misdiagnosed* as having cardiac disease performed lower on intellectual measures than a matched control group. Misdiagnosed children who were restricted from social activities attain the lowest scores, suggesting that the impositions of chronic disease may have an effect on cognitive functioning even beyond the effects of the illness itself.

Despite the limitations of current developmental research on children's understanding of health care phenomena, these investigations suggest a coherent maturational progression in childhood conceptions of illness causality, health care, and medical treatment procedures. In parallel with the developmental characteristics of thought described by Piaget, the child's awareness of illness realities increases in qualitative, structural ways. Centered focus on isolated, concrete symptoms broadens to include first multiple symptom clusters and, later, abstract, internal process. As illness causality becomes less magically linked to contiguity in space and time with increasing age, children begin to grasp the necessity of contact with a contaminating organism, mechanisms for germ intrusion of the body, the role of bodily susceptibility, and, finally, the interlocking synergism of multiple organ systems in health and disease.

Below the age of three or four, the role of childhood cognition seems secondary to the protective presence of emotionally supportive parental figures. Given the egocentricity of children's thinking at this age, explanation and reason may provide little support against the perceived realities of fear, pain, and separation (Blos, 1978). Children's distress at this age is heightened by the unexpected departure of an anxious parent. Statements of fact such as "This will hurt a bit" or "I am going to leave you now until tomorrow" become important not as explicatory comments, but as reassurance based on their honesty, emotional tone, and invitation for subsequent elaboration.

Older preoperational children up to around seven years, despite rapid increases in vocabulary, are unlikely to understand internal processes, link associated illness symptoms, or grasp the mechanisms of therapeutic change. Rather, illness is perceived as a single perceptual experience, explained through transductive or magical connections to "causality." Explanations at this age must be simple and perceptually based, with an ear tuned to the reverberations of the inevitable distortions.

The onset of concrete operational thinking engenders the perception of relationships among multiple symptom events, although not the cognitive capacity to form hypothetical deductions about causality or understand internal physiological processes. The child can, however, comprehend the connection between one observable occurrence, for example, swallowing, and the onset of perceptual aspects of an illness (i.e., external sensory symptoms). Thus, illnesses are attributed to germs, but with little knowledge of action specificity of interaction between these external agents and bodily susceptibility or resistance to disease.

Only with the onset of formal operational thinking beginning around 11 or 12 does the child begin to think abstractly of illness in terms of internal physiological structure and systems whose dysfunction is manifest by a variety of changing external symptoms. The abstract complexity of thought at this stage, coupled with the ability to understand various contributory causes of illness and the interaction of illness agents and bodily resistance, allows preadolescents a fresh opportunity for participation in preventive health care.

# IMPLICATIONS FOR PEDIATRIC CLINICIANS

Recognition of the developmental factors which limit the child's capacity to apprehend illness and medical procedures has important implications for physicians, nurses, parents, and others who care for sick and hospitalized children. More than empathy regarding these cognitive limitations is required. Physician-child communication begins with the earliest encounters, a relationship of trust or mistrust based upon clinical sensitivity to the informational and security needs of the child and his or her family.

## The Parents' Roles in Health Care

Especially for the younger children to whom parents are omniscient protectors, the pediatric clinician's responsibility includes soliciting parental involvement and encouraging more than passive receipt of medical care (Stacy, 1979). Parents can play a major role in reducing the discontinuities between home and hospital, health and disease. In addition to maintaining the parent-child bond during stressful health care experiences, progressive hospital policies offer parents the opportunity to provide emotional support (e.g., Spinetta & Maloney, 1978), cognitive stimulation through play, and mediation with medical staff on behalf of the child (Webb, 1977).

Although no clear consensus exists in practice, several authors (e.g., Powers, 1980; Stacey, 1979) seek the development of a partnership role for parents in pediatric case management. Such a role precludes definitions of either parents or the nursing staff as babysitters. Rather, the responsibility for the care of the child is shared, a relationship facilitated by nursing awareness of normal parental discomfort with unfamiliar health care procedures, and educational efforts that address parents' mastery of limit-setting and leave-taking skills, infrequent visitation, and reluctance to interact with their "sick" child (e.g., the monitored infant). While parent partnership and advocacy at times appear to strain ward or clinic regime, who can doubt the value of the parents' sensitive insistence that their child's medical procedures occur in a treatment area separate from the hospital isolation room where he or she sleeps and plays.

### Preparation for and Mastery of Health Care Phenomena

It cannot be overemphasized that every child of suitable age requires proper and honest preparation for health care phenomena that provides pre- and post-procedure opportunities to talk, ask questions, and repeat what has been heard (Visintainer & Wolfer, 1975; Wolfer & Visintainer, 1979). Mastery is enhanced by hospital provisions for normal child-life and play activities (cf. Petrillo & Sanger, 1980) and accredited academic education. Playrooms stocked with books, crayons, games, and other activities are helpful in this regard. But most important is the interpersonal communication by both the physician in charge of the child's care and child-life persons trained in interpreting the meanings of childhood expressions in ways that allow both emotional catharsis and mastery. The hospital always has potential for benefit for children, not just healing of physical and psychosomatic disease. Opportunities for viewing X-rays, helping nurses, and feeling in control via praise which says not "you're a good boy" but rather "thank you for holding still," assist the child in obtaining this potential.

Health care practice requires a recognition that changes in routine are a threat to the child. Providing the child with choices often serves mastery and lessens feelings of helplessness regarding the reality of illness. Only at times can oral medication be adminstered instead of an injection, but the choice of which arm can almost always be left to the child. Dietary restrictions, physical restraints, and bed confinement are, of course, necessary at times. However, balancing these with normalizing play activities, however inactive they may be, often serves to compensate and allows expression of pent-up feelings (Johnson, 1979; Johnson, Martin, Whitt, & Weisz, 1980).

### Interpersonal Format of Physician-Child Interaction

The maturational passage from early childhood reliance on parental presence for security to individual understanding and participation with health care phenomena is a lengthy developmental process. By adolescence we can expect a person to relate autonomously to the physician, to recognize that a variety of symptoms represent a single illness or syndrome, to understand the course of illness through a progression of different phases, and to comprehend the logic of using oral medication to treat a rash on the skin (Perrin & Gerrity, 1981).

But what of a child of eight who not only has the ability to understand concretely provided explanations of illness, but also, according to Rashkis (1965), begins to view the physician as his or her primary health protector? At this stage, direct contact with the physician would appear to be indicated. Indeed, despite the utility of interdisciplinary health care teams, children and parents clearly view the physician as bearing primary responsibility for communicating medical information (Kupst, Blatterbauer, Westman, Schulman, & Paul, 1977). However, inspection of the format and content of this communicative process raises questions regarding current patterns of physician involvement.

Whitt and Dykstra (1981) surveyed 500 pediatricians providing subspecialty fellowship training at major medical centers in the care of children with epilepsy, asthma, diabetes, cystic fibrosis, scoliosis, leukemia, hemophilia, sickle cell anemia, and nephrotic syndrome. Requested was information by age of child on whether the illness is explained directly to the child, the format of the explanation process, identity of other helping professionals, perceived significance of disease concepts to chronically ill children, and verbatim descriptions of the phrases and metaphors used in physicians' illness descriptions. The illness explanations of responding physicians to children were characterized by considerable variability in recognition of developmental differences in childhood understanding. For example, the accounts given of epilepsy to nine-year-old youngsters included: "Too much electricity"; "Nothing to worry about; anyone can have one"; "Electrical short circuiting of the CNS"; "Like a short circuit in the wires that come out of the wall"; and "A small number of nerve cells are very excitable; this occurrence makes surrounding cells excitable, like a vacuum cleaner interfering with TV reception."

The variability of these responses cannot be attributed to inexperience. The mean number of years since residency for these physicians was 12.4 years. Nor was the explanation of illness perceived as unimportant to these professionals. Indeed, the proportion of physicians in this sample giving the highest rating on a four-point scale of importance to the impact of childhood understanding of illness on medical compliance, symptom management, personality development, peer interaction, family stability, and school performance was 73.9, 60.8, 51.1, 49.5, 49.8, and 29.0 percent, respectively. However, as a group the physicians surveyed evidenced a disinclination towards meeting alone with children of any age. Only 15.9 percent of the overall sample met alone with children between the ages of 8 and 11 years to explain their illness, a figure which increased only to 40.6 percent for children between the ages of 12 and 16 years of age.

## Content of Physician-Child Communication

Although the infrequency of direct explanations of illness to children alone may reflect the constraints of time in busy medical practices, the anecdotal comments of the physicians surveyed reflected considerable uncertainty regarding what to say. It is here that understanding of children's development of illness concepts provides awareness of what is "concrete" for each child, enabling the design of illness explanations targeted no more than one step above the child's level of cognitive ability (cf. Bibace & Walsh, 1980; Whitt, Dykstra, & Taylor, 1979). For example, the terminology used with children requires thoughtful selection. Consistent with Piagetian theory, developmental research on linguistic ambiguity indicates that with the attainment of concrete operational thought processes, the child decenters from single interpretations to recognize the multiple meanings of words (Shultz & Pilon, 1973). Likewise, peak enjoyment and comprehension of jokes based on homonymic structure, such as the children's riddle: "Q. Why is a packed baseball field always cool? A. It has fans on every seat!" is not attained until second and third grades (Whitt & Prentice, in press). Just as the preoperational child is unable to appreciate that "fans" can mean *both* "people who cheer for a team" and "cooling devices," when told the doctor will inject some "dye," this child may center his or her focus on "death" rather than the intended linguistic meaning. Likewise, in a description where epilepsy is likened to excess "electricity" in the brain, the preoperational child's association may be only to the wall socket of which Mom has severely admonished avoidance lest shocking and perhaps terminal consequences follow. Thus, "being concrete" means the avoidance of explanatory terminology that may have unintended second meanings from which young children may be cognitively unable to decenter their perceptions (Whitt, Dykstra, and Taylor, 1979).

The degree to which an illness provides concrete perceptual referents seems a significant variable for designing childhood illness explanations. In contrast to broken bones, lacerations, or a skin rash, many illnesses provide few cues to the child's awareness. Understanding of epilepsy, for example, requires a grasp of multiple concepts which are outside the child's perceptual field. "Being concrete" in the explanation of epilepsy to a preadolescent child requires the provision of concrete perceptual referents both to describe the underlying physiological process (brain activity) and the symptom events (seizures), as well as to account for the causalty of the disorder. For the young preoperational child, explanation may consist of reassurance associated with the perception of aura and the sleepiness which follows the episodes, in addition to focus on mastery of feelings of anxiety associated with separation and/or hospitalization. The ability to conceptualize fully an abstract internal process like epilepsy may come only with the attainment of formal operational thought during adolescence. However, the younger school-aged child and some preschool children can use a simplified explanation if appropriate concrete perceptual cues are provided by the physician.

In our efforts to explain illness to young children, we include the parents, both to aid their understanding and to reinforce their central role in clarifying their child's conceptions. We gather the child's and parents' perceptions for use as concrete anchor points, including the aura, seizure events, and postictal experience. Then, using these cues as referents, we explain brain functioning (using drawing as indicated) to the child, saying: "Your brain works like a telephone. With it you can send messages to all parts of the body. I can use my brain to tell my finger to move, my foot to kick, my mouth to talk," and so forth. (We have the child send "messages" to various parts of his or her body.) "Does your telephone at home ever get a wrong number?" (We discuss the occurrence of wrong numbers.) "Sometimes a part of your brain sends out accidental messages like a wrong number on your telephone at home. That's what a seizure is. When you don't want it to, your brain sends a message to your _____." (Here we use the aura and/or the child's other perceptual cues to illustrate the seizure event). "When it's over you may feel sleepy or tired, but then you feel better. Just like your telephone at home, after the wrong number, the phone works fine again. After you stop feeling sleepy, you can make your brain send messages to your body just like you want it to . . . ," and so on until the child's questions and concerns are clarified. Examples of similar explanations using this metaphoric format are described in Whitt, Dykstra, and Taylor (1979).

## Emotional Aspects of Communication with Children

The emotional aspects of communication with children are frequently difficult for pediatric practitioners. A physician contact is not psychotherapy. However, cognition and affect are inextricably intertwined. Identification of the child's feelings and recognition of their legitimacy often diminishes interpersonal confusion and avoids roadblocks in later communication. A hospital milieu that allows and accepts feelings, including sadness and anger, while conveying the message that "while your feelings are understandable, they can not affect medical decisions about what is best for you" provides security to children who are torn between the desire to express their feelings and a fear that their emotional omnipotence may in some way diminish the quality of their health care (Geist, 1979). Comments like, "You seem angry," or affective permission such as "I don't blame you for being angry because you have to stay in a hospital" or "It's O.K. to be afraid. Even grown-ups are afraid, but remember the doctors know how to help," often serve this purpose. There is no expectation that these feelings will of necessity go away. It is unnecessary for a physician to feel pressed to create an atmosphere of gaity and intractable agreeableness (Geist, 1979). These attempts, however well intended, may undermine the child's spontaneous expressions ("If she's so nice to me, how can I be angry?").

The affective communications of children sometimes assume the metaphoric form described above. In this regard I am reminded of John, a 10-year-old boy who initially voiced his feelings about the lengthy but futile treatment of his rhabdomyosarcoma in a tale about fishing in the pond behind his house. John's skill was taxed by the minnows which stole his bait at every turn. He tried worms, dough balls (with and without corn), cornbread, and meat as bait with no success. Although close, according to John, even a trap constructed of a tin can could not capture the little varmints. Sometimes, said John, "I just feel like tossing a cherrybomb (a firecracker) into the pond and blowing them up."

John's story was true, confirmed by experience. However, it was also a metaphor for the multiple chemotherapy protocols (baits) and single surgical procedure (trap) that failed to control his cancer (minnows)—a frustration that on occasion led John to consider self-injury (fire cracker). The only response necessary to John, as he metaphorically broached the topic of his death, was to acknowledge his anger and frustration at the fishing experience, while wondering if he sometimes felt the same about the treatment of his disease. This recognition of John's message, a simple statement of understanding to which he readily agreed, cemented a relationship of honesty and open communication regarding feelings, which continued until his subsequent, peaceful death.

## CONCLUSION

Adequate discussion of health care phenomena with children is not a single isolated procedure. Repeated physician-child interaction and parental support are frequently required for resolution of childhood misconceptions. Children's comprehension of illness, hospitalization, and health care reflect a complex interplay of cognitive-developmental and affective elements within the child and his or her family system. Continued investigation of these factors and their impact on children's adaptation to illness, hospitalization, and health care procedures will benefit pediatric clinicians and parents who seek to avoid the common behavioral and emotional reactions associated with childhood illness.

## ACKNOWLEDGMENTS

The author thanks Helen T. Brantley, Melissa R. Johnson, and Donald K. Routh for their constructive critiques of an earlier draft. The support of NIMH Psychiatry Education Branch, Grant Number MH 13471-05 and a research grant from the Spencer Foundation are also acknowledged.

## REFERENCES

Anderson, N. H., & Cuneo, D. O. The height + width rule in children's judgments of quantity. *Journal of Experimental Psychology: General*, 1978, *107*, 335-378.

Association for the Care of Children in Hospitals. *Child life activity study section position paper.* Washington, D.C.: ACCH, 1979.

Belmont, H. S. Hospitalization and its effects upon the total child. *Clinical Pediatrics*, 1970, *9*, 472-483.

Bergmann, T. *Children in the hospital.* New York: International Universities Press, 1965.

Bernstein, A. C., & Cowan, P. A. Children's concepts of how people get babies. *Child Development*, 1975, *46*, 77-91.

Beverly, B. I. The effect of illness upon emotional development. *Journal of Pediatrics*, 1936, *8*, 533-543.

Bibace, R., & Walsh, M. E. Developmental stages in children's conceptions of illness. In G. Stone, F. Cohen, & N. Adler (Eds.), *Health psychology: A handbook.* San Francisco, Ca.: Jossey-Bass, 1979.

Bibare, R., & Walsh, M. E. Development of children's concepts of illness. *Pediatrics*, 1980, *66*, 912-917.

Blom, G. E. The reactions of hospitalized children to illness. *Pediatrics*, 1958, *22*, 590-599.

Blos, P. *An investigation of the healthy child's understanding of the causes of illness*. Unpublished thesis, Yale University School of Medicine, 1956.

Blos, P. Children think about illness: Their concepts and beliefs. In E. Gellert (Ed.), *Psychosocial aspects of pediatric care*. New York: Grune & Stratton, 1978.

Bowlby, J. Some pathological processes set in train by early mother-child separation. *Journal of Mental Science*, 1953, *99*, 265-272.

Bowlby, J. Separation anxiety: A critical review of the literature. *Journal of Child Psychology and Psychiatry*, 1960, *1*, 251-269.

Brain, D. J., & Maclay, I. Controlled study of mothers and children in hospital. *British Medical Journal*, 1968, *1*, 278-280.

Breger, L. *From instinct to identity: The development of personality*. Engelwood Cliffs, N.J.: Prentice-Hall, 1974.

Bridge, E. M. Emotional disturbances in epileptic children. *Nervous Child*, 1947, *6*, 11-21.

Campbell, J. D. Illness is a point of view: The development of children's concepts of illness. *Child Development*, 1975, *46*, 92-100.

Carandang, M. L. A., Folkins, C. H., Hines, P. A., & Steward, M. S. The role of cognitive level and sibling illness in children's conceptualization of illness. *American Journal of Orthopsychiatry*, 1979, *49*, 474-481.

Cayler, G. G., Lynn, D.B., & Stein, E. M. Effect of cardiac "nondisease" on intellectual and perceptual motor development. *British Heart Journal*, 1973, *35*, 543-547.

Chapman, A. H., Loeb, D. G., & Gibbons, M. J. Psychiatric aspects of hospitalizing children. *Archives of Pediatrics*, 1956, *73*, 77-88.

Childers, P., & Wimmer, M. The concept of death in early childhood. *Child Development*, 1971, *42*, 1299-1301.

Cuneo, D. O. A general strategy for quantity judgments: The height + width rule. *Child Development*, 1980, *51*, 299-301.

Douglas, J. W. B. Early hospital admissions and later disturbances of behavior and learning. *Developmental Medicine and Child Neurology*, 1975, *17*, 456-480.

Elkind, D. The child's conception of his religious denomination. *Journal of Genetic Psychology*, 1962, *101*, 185-193.

Flavell, J. H. *Cognitive development*. Englewood Cliffs, N.J.: Prentice Hall, 1977.

Freud, A. The role of bodily illness in the mental life of the child. *Psychoanalytic Study of the Child*, 1952, *7*, 69-81.

Geist, R. A. Onset of chronic illness in children and adolescents: Psychotherapeutic and consultative intervention. *American Journal of Orthopsychiatry*, 1979, *49*, 4-23.

Gellert, E. Reducing the emotional stresses of hospitalization for children. *American Journal of Occupational Therapy*, 1958, *12*, 125-129.

Gellert, E. What do I have inside me? How children view their bodies. In E. Gellert (Ed.), *Psychosocial aspects of pediatric care*. New York: Grune & Stratton, 1978.

Ginsberg, H., & Opper, S. *Piaget's theory of intellectual development*. Engelwood Cliffs, N.J.: Prentice Hall, 1959.

Goslin, E. R. Hospitalization as a life crisis for the preschool child: A critical review. *Journal of Community Health*, 1978, *3*, 321-346.

Harter, S. A cognitive-developmental approach to children's expression of conflicting feelings and a technique to facilitate such expression in play therapy. *Journal of Consulting and Clinical Psychology*, 1977, *45*, 417-432.

Heinicke, C. M. Some effects of separating two-year-olds from their parents. *Human Relations*, 1956, *9*, 105-175.

Holt, J. L. *Children's recall of preschool age hospital experience after an interval of five years.* Unpublished dissertation, University of Pittsburgh, 1967.

Howe, J. Children's ideas about injury. *Proceedings of the ANA Regional Clinical Conferences, 1967.* New York: Appleton-Century-Crofts, 1968.

Johnson, M. R. Mental health interventions with medically ill children: A review of the literature 1970–1977. *Journal of Pediatric Psychology,* 1979, *4,* 147–164.

Johnson, M. R., Martin, B., Whitt, J. K., & Weisz, J. *Anxiety reduction through fantasy in chronically ill and normal children.* Paper presented at the meeting of the American Psychological Association, Montreal, September 1980.

Katz, E. R., Kellerman, J., & Siegel, S. E. Behavioral distress in children with cancer undergoing medical procedures: Developmental considerations. *Journal of Consulting and Clinical Psychology,* 1980, *48,* 356–365.

Kennedy, D. A. Planning a new children's hospital. In M. E. Shore (Ed.), *Red is the color of hurting: Planning for children in the hospital.* Rockville, Maryland: NIMH Clearinghouse for Mental Health Information, 1971.

Klaus, M. H., & Kennell, J. H. *Maternal-infant bonding.* St. Louis, Mo.: C. V. Mosby, 1976.

Koocher, G. P. Childhood, death, and cognitive development. *Developmental Psychology,* 1973, *9,* 369–375.

Korsch, B. M. The pediatrician's approach to his patient. *American Journal of Diseases of Children,* 1973, *126,* 146–148.

Kupst, M. J., Blatterbauer, S., Westman, J., Schulman, J. L., & Paul, M. H. Helping parents cope with the diagnosis of congenital heart defect: An experimental study. *Pediatrics,* 1977, *59,* 266–272.

Langford, W. S. Physical illness and convalescence: Their meaning to the child. *Journal of Pediatrics,* 1948, *33,* 242–250.

Langford, W. S. The child in the pediatric hospital: Adaptation to illness and hospitalization. *American Journal of Orthopsychiatry,* 1961, *31,* 667–684.

Levy, D. M. On the problem of movement restraint. *American Journal of Orthopsychiatry,* 1944, *14,* 644–671'

Lynn, D. B., Glaser, H. H., & Harrison, G. S. Comprehensive medical care for handicapped children. III. Concepts of illness in children with rheumatic fever. *American Journal of Diseases of Children,* 1962, *103,* 42–50.

MacCarthey, D. Communication between children and doctors. *Developmental Medicine and Child Neurology,* 1974, *16,* 279–285.

Mahler, M. S., Pine, F., & Bergman, A. *The psychological birth of the human infant: Symbiosis and individuation.* New York: Basic Books, 1975.

Mattsson, A. Long-term physical illness in childhood: A challenge to psychosocial adaptation. *Pediatrics,* 1972, *50,* 801–811.

McGhee, P. E. Cognitive mastery and children's humor. *Psychological Bulletin,* 1974, *81,* 721–730.

Melamed, B. G., Meyer, R., Gee, C., & Soule, L. The influence of time and type of preparation on children's adjustment to hospitalization. *Journal of Pediatric Psychology,* 1976, *1,* 31–37.

Melamed, B. G., & Siegel, L. J. Reduction of anxiety in children facing hospitalization and surgery by use of filmed modeling. *Journal of Consulting and Clinical Psychology,* 1975, *43,* 511–521.

Miller, M. The traumatic effect of surgical operations in childhood on the integrative functions of the ego. *Psychoanalytic Quarterly,* 1951, *20,* 77–92.

Ministry of Health and Central Health Services Council. *The welfare of children in hospital.* (The Platt Report) London: H.M.S.O., 1959.

Myers-Vando, R., Steward, M. S., Folkins, C. H., & Hines, P. The effects of congenital heart disease on cognitive development, illness causality concepts, and vulnerability. *American Journal of Orthopsychiatry,* 1979, *49,* 617–625.

Nagera, H. Children's reactions to hospitalization and illness. *Child Psychiatry and Human Development*, 1978, *9*, 3-19.

Nagy, M. H. Children's ideas of the origins of illness. *Health Education Journal*, 1951, *9*, 6-12.

Nagy, M. H. Children's concepts of some bodily functions. *Journal of General Psychology*, 1953, *83*, 199-216. (a)

Nagy, M. H. The representation of "germs" by children. *Journal of Genetic Psychology*, 1953, *83*, 227-240. (b)

Naylor, K. A., & Mattsson, A. "For the sake of the children:" Trials and tribulations of child psychiatry-liaison service. *Psychiatry in Medicine*, 1973, *4*, 389-402.

Neuhauser, C., Amsterdam, B., Hines, P., & Steward, M. Children's concepts of healing: Cognitive development and locus of control factors. *American Journal of Orthopsychiatry*, 1978, *48*, 335-241.

Paplia, D. E., & Olds, S. W. *A child's world: Infancy through adolescence.* New York: McGraw-Hill, 1975.

Paternaude, A. F., Szymanski, L., & Rappeport, J. Psychological costs of bone marrow transplantation in children. *American Journal of Orthopsychiatry*, 1979, *49*, 409-422.

Perrin, E. C., & Gerrity, P. S. There's a demon in your belly: Children's understanding of illness. *Pediatrics*, 1981, *67*, 841-849.

Peters, B. M. *Concepts of hospitalized children about causality of illness and intent of treatment.* Unpublished dissertation, University of Pittsburgh, 1975.

Petrillo, M., & Sanger, S. *Emotional care of hospitalized children: An environmental approach.* Philadelphia: J. B. Lippincott, 1980.

Piaget, J. *The origins of intelligence in children.* (M. Cook, trans.) New York: International Universities Press, 1952. (Originally published, 1936).

Piaget, J. *The psychology of intelligence.* (C. K. Ogden, Ed.). Patterson, N. J.: Littlefield, Adams, 1963. (Originally published, 1947).

Powazek, M., Goff, J. R., Schyving, J., & Paulson, M. A. Emotional reactions of children to isolation in a cancer hospital. *Journal of Pediatrics*, 1978, *92*, 834-837.

Powers, J. *Working with parents of the learning disabled child.* Panel presentation and personal communication at the meeting of the American Orthopsychiatric Association, Toronto, April 1980.

Prentice, N. M., Manosevitz, M., & Hubbs, L. Imaginary figures of early childhood: Santa Claus, Easter Bunny, and the Tooth Fairy. *American Journal of Orthopsychiatry*, 1978, *48*, 618-628.

Prentice, N. M., Schmechel, L. K., & Manosevitz, M. Children's belief in Santa Claus: A developmental study of fantasy and causality. *Journal of the American Academy of Child Psychiatry*, 1979, *18*, 658-667.

Prugh, D. G. Emotional aspects of the hospitalization of children. In M. F. Shore (Ed.), *Red is the color of hurting: Planning for children in the hospital.* Rockville, Maryland: NIMH National Clearinghouse for Mental Health Information, 1971.

Prugh, D. G., & Eckhardt, L. O. Children's reactions to illness, hospitalization, and surgery. In A. Freedman & H. Kaplan (Eds.), *Comprehensive textbook of psychiatry.* Baltimore: Williams & Wilkins, 1974.

Prugh, D. G., Eckhardt, L. O. Stages and phases in the response of children and adolescents to illness and injury. In B. W. Camp (Ed.), *Advances in behavioral pediatrics.* Vol. 1. Greenwich, Connecticut: JAI Press, 1980.

Prugh, D. G., Staub, E. M., Sands, H. H., Kirschbaum, R. M., & Lenihan, B. S. A study of the emotional reactions of children and families to hospitalization and illness. *American Journal of Orthopsychiatry*, 1953, *23*, 70-106.

Rashkis, S. Child's understanding of health. *Archives of General Psychiatry*, 1965, *12*, 10-17.

Reddihough, D. S., Landau, L., Jones, H. J., & Rickards, W. S. Family anxieties in childhood asthma. *Australian Pediatric Journal*, 1977, *13*, 295-298.

Robertson, J. *Young children in hospitals.* New York: Basic Books, 1958.

Robertson, J., & Bowlby, J. Responses of young children to separation from their mothers. II. Observations of the sequences of response of children aged 18 to 24 months during the course of separation. *Courrier,* 1952, *2,* 131–141.

Rutter, M. *Maternal deprivation reassessed.* Harmondsworth, Middlesex: Penguin Books, 1972.

Rutter, M. Maternal deprivation, 1972–1978: New findings, new concepts, new approaches. *Child Development,* 1979, *50,* 283–305.

Seagull, E. A. W. *Children's reactions to hospitalization: Policy implications for cross cultural research.* Paper presented at the Fifth International Congress of the International Association of Cross Cultural Psychology, Bhubaneswar, India, December 1980.

Shaklee, H. Bounded rationality and cognitive development: Upper limits on growth? *Cognitive Psychology,* 1979, *11,* 327–345.

Shore, M. F. (Ed.) *Red is the color of hurting: Planning for children in the hospital.* Rockville, Maryland: NIMH National Clearinghouse for Mental Health Information, 1971.

Shultz, T. R. Development of the appreciation of riddles. *Child Development,* 1974, *45,* 100–105.

Shultz, T. R., & Pilon, R. Development of the ability to detect linguistic ambiguity. *Child Development,* 1973, *44,* 728–733.

Simeonsson, R. J., Buckley, L., & Monson, L. Conceptions of illness causality in hospitalized children. *Journal of Pediatric Psychology,* 1979, *4,* 77–84.

Skipper, J., & Leonard, R. Children, stress, and hospitalization: A field experiment. *Journal of Health and Social Behavior,* 1968, *9,* 275–287.

Smith, E. C. *School-age children's concepts of body organs and illness.* Unpublished dissertation, University of Pittsburgh, 1973.

Spinetta, J., & Maloney, L. J. The child with cancer: Patterns of communication and denial. *Journal of Consulting and Clinical Psychology,* 1978, *46,* 1540–1541.

Spitz, R. A., & Wolf, K. M. Anaclitic depression: An inquiry into the genesis of psychiatric conditions in early childhood. *Psychoanalytic Study of the Child,* 1946, *2,* 313–342.

Stacey, M. Practical implications of our conclusions. In D. Hall & M. Stacey (Eds.), *Beyond separation: Further studies of children in hospital.* London: Rouledge & Kegan Paul, 1979.

Steward, M. S., & Steward, D. S. Children's concepts of medical procedures. In R. Bibace & M. Walsh (Eds.), *The development of children's conceptions of health and related phenomena.* San Francisco: Jossey-Bass, in press.

Stimson, G. The child's view of the general practitioner. *Journal of the Royal College of General Practitioners,* 1974, *24,* 37–41.

Strickland, R. Internal-external expectancies and health-related behaviors. *Journal of Consulting and Clinical Psychology,* 1978, *46,* 1192–1211.

Tait, C. D., & Archer, R. C. Inside-of-the-body test, a preliminary report. *Psychosomatic Medicine,* 1955, *17,* 139–148.

Tomlinson-Keasey, C., Eisert, D. C., Kahle, L. R., Hardy, K., & Keasey, B. The structure of concrete operational thought. *Child Development,* 1979, *50,* 1153–1163.

VanderVeer, A. H. The psychopathology of physical illness and hospital residence. *Quarterly Journal of Child Behavior,* 1949, *1,* 55–71.

Vernon, D. T. A., Foley, J. M., & Schulman, J. L. Effect of mother-child separation and birth order on young children's responses to two potentially stressful experiences. *Journal of Personality and Social Psychology,* 1967, *5,* 162–174.

Vernon, D. T. A., Foley, J. M., Sipowicz, R. R., & Schulman, J. L. *The psychological responses of children to hospitalization and illness.* Springfield, Illinois: Thomas, 1965.

Visintainer, M. A., & Wolfer, J. A. Psychological preparation for surgical pediatric patients: The effect on children's and parents' stress responses and adjustment. *Pediatrics,* 1975, *56,* 187–202.

Webb, B. Trauma and tedium: An account of living-in on a children's ward. In A. Davis & G. Horobin (Eds.), *Medical encounters.* London: Croom Helm, 1977.

Whitt, J. K., & Dykstra, W. *Patterns and content of physician's communication with physically ill children.* Unpublished manuscript, University of North Carolina, 1981.

Whitt, J. K., Dykstra, W., Johnson, M. R., & Taylor, C. A. *Cognitive-developmental and illness factors in children's conceptions of the human body.* Unpublished manuscript, University of North Carolina, 1980.

Whitt, J. K., Dykstra, W., & Taylor, C. A. Children's conceptions of illness and cognitive development: Implications for pediatric practitioners. *Clinical Pediatrics,* 1979, *18,* 327-339.

Whitt, J. K., Johnson, M. R., Dykstra, W., & Taylor, C. A. *Children's conceptions of illness: The effects of cognitive development and illness experience.* Unpublished manuscript, University of North Carolina, 1981.

Whitt, J. K., & Prentice, N. M. Cognitive processes in the development of children's enjoyment and comprehension of joking riddles. *Development Psychology,* 1977, *13,* 129-136.

Whitt, J. K., & Prentice, N. M. The development of children's enjoyment and comprehension of thematic riddles. *American Journal of Orthopsychiatry,* in press.

Wilkening, F. Combining of stimulus dimensions in children's and adults' judgment of area: An information integration analysis. *Developmental Psychology,* 1979, *15,* 25-33.

Wines, D. B. Architectural aspects of services for children. In M. F. Shore (Ed.), *Red is the color of hurting: Planning for children in the hospital.* Rockville, Maryland: NIMH National Clearinghouse for Mental Health Information, 1971.

Wolfer, J. A., & Visintainer, M. A. Prehospital psychological preparation for tonsillectomy patients: Effects on children's and parents' adjustments. *Pediatrics,* 1979, *64,* 646-655.

# RESEARCH ON PARENTING:
## IMPLICATIONS FOR PRIMARY HEALTH CARE PROVIDERS

Robert W. Chamberlin and

Barbara B. Keller

## INTRODUCTION

Because of his or her long-term contact with families having children, the pediatrician is in a strategic position to influence evolving parent-child relationships for better or for worse. The purpose of this chapter is to review what is known about how parents influence the developing child, what factors influence the parent's ability to parent, and how this knowledge can improve the delivery of primary health care by the pediatrician and other providers. This review will be largely limited to the infant and preschool periods because it is during this time that visits

Advances in Developmental and Behavioral Pediatrics, vol. 3, pages 203–231
Copyright © 1982 by JAI Press Inc.
All rights of reproduction in any form reserved.
ISBN: 0-89232-223-3

to the primary care provider are most frequent and thus potentially have the most impact.

# PARENTAL INFLUENCE ON CHILDREN'S DEVELOPMENT AND HEALTH STATUS

*The Concept of Competency*

Previous conceptions of desirable or undesirable child development outcomes which emphasized IQ and/or various behavioral traits such as being aggressive or dependent have given way to more multidimensional aspects of coping with the environment, often subsumed under the category of "competence" (White & Watts, 1973; Appleton, Clifton, & Goldberg, 1975). This concept is operationally defined differently at different ages. In the newborn period, the competent infant is one whose skills such as visual following and consolability facilitate early social interaction with adults (Brazelton, 1980). These skills are possessed by the majority of infants.

Between one and two years of age, one of the most widely used markers of "social competence" is the quality of the infant's attachment to the mother. Ainsworth et al. (1978) have described eight categories of mother-infant relationships which are based on the young child's response to separation from and then reunion with the mother. These categories can be summarized into three groups: A, B, and C. Infants in Group B are "securely attached" to their mother. They approach their mothers upon reunion with them and are relatively easily consoled at that time. The infants in the other two groups are "insecurely attached." Those infants in Group A avoid their mother upon reunion, while those in Group C show ambivalence (e.g., cling to mother and then resist consoling from her).

The validity of this conception of "competence" is supported by its cross-sectional and longitudinal association with other measures of functioning. Bell (1970) reported that securely attached infants as measured at age 11 months were more advanced than insecurely attached infants in the development of object permanence. At 18 months of age, securely attached infants have been found to socially interact more often and in a more sophisticated way with peers than more anxiously attached ones (Esterbrooks & Lamb, 1979).

In longitudinal studies, infants having a secure attachment at 12 months of age have been found to score one standard deviation higher on the mental scale of the Bayley Scales of Infant Development at 20 months of age than those classified as insecurely attached (Main, 1973). However, this difference may have reflected the young children's cooperativeness more than actual mental competence. Other comparisons of mental functioning as measured by Bayley Scales at 24 months and the Stanford-Binet Scale at 36 months (Bell, 1978; Ainsworth et al., 1978), or the Stanford-Binet Scale at 30 months (Connell, 1976; Ainsworth et al., 1978) did not reveal any significant differences between infants who were securely and insecurely attached at about 12 months of age.

More marked relationships have been found between quality of attachment and later socially oriented skills. In contrast to insecurely attached babies, infants who were previously evaluated as securely attached at 11 months of age showed more positive affective tone in behaviors toward their mother in a free play situation at 24, 30, and 36 months of age (Bell, 1978). Infants who were securely dent of developmental quotient and the child's temperament. In addition, infants less frustration and crying or whining at 48 months of age than insecurely attached infants (Matas, Arend, & Sroufe, 1978). This relationship was independent of developmental quotient and the child's temperament. In addition, infants classified as "securely attached" at 18 months were found to be more curious and better at interpersonal problem-solving skills at about five years of age (Arend, Gove, & Sroufe, 1979). Security of attachment in three-year-olds was positively related to assessments of peer competence such as reciprocal interaction and negatively related to negative behavior (such as violent play and threats) (Lieberman, 1977). These types of associations over time appear to link the concept of competence in infancy to that of the preschool child as described by White and Watts (1973).

In an extensive study of nursery school and kindergarten children, White and Watts (1973) identified 6 percent of the 3- to 6-year-old children in their original sample as "very high on overall competence, able to cope in superior fashion with anything they met, day in and day out" (p. 10). They observed these children weekly over an eight month period. These observations indicated that competent children had the following strengths in comparison to less competent children: They were able to get attention from adults in socially acceptable ways and to use them as resources; they were able to express both affection and hostility to adults and peers; they could lead, follow, and compete with their peers and show pride in their individual accomplishments; they had expressive language skills (grammar, vocabulary, and articulation), and intellectual competence (able to detect discrepancies, anticipate consequences, deal with abstractions, take another's perspective and make interesting associations). Executive abilities (carrying out multistep activities and using resources effectively) and the ability to attend to two things at once also reflected strengths of the competent young children.

This description of competence has limitations. First of all, it is post hoc in nature. A group of children was first identified as competent, and then described. This description has not actually been tested prospectively to validate that the skills described are both necessary and sufficient for successful coping with the environment. Secondly, as Appleton, Clifton, and Goldberg (1975) pointed out, the constellation of skills which the infant and young child need to acquire to become "competent" varies according to the child's milieu. A child appearing competent by middle-class standards may lack the necessary skills to get along in a ghetto environment, for example. Nevertheless, the concept of competence appears to be an advance in our thinking about what types of skills are necessary to successfuly cope with daily life.

*Parental Responsivity*

Just as conceptions of desirable child development outcomes have changed, so have conceptions of what types of parenting skills are necessary to produce them. Considerations of global styles (permissive vs. strict) have given way to detailed assessments of parental behaviors. From these observations comes the concept of "social responsivity" as an important determinant of child functioning. The precise operational definition of parental responsivity, however, varies with almost every study. Some researchers limit their assessment to one measure (Bradley & Caldwell, 1971), while others include many measures in a multiple regression approach (Cohen & Beckwith, 1979). Some general constructs can be identified however. For infants, "responsive parents" are generally considered to be available, interpret their baby's cries and other signals correctly, and promptly attend to the baby's needs. Attention given to the child is contingent on the child's behavior in a consistent way. For preschool children, White and Watts (1973) have identified parenting characteristics that are associated with competency for this age period. Parents of competent children structure the physical surroundings for their children in such a way as to motivate the child to learn more about the environment, and they encourage their children through verbal and social interaction appropriate for the child's level of understanding. In addition these parents are able to set reasonable limits, prohibiting particular activities (such as playing with sharp objects).

## RELATIONSHIPS BETWEEN PARENTAL RESPONSIVITY AND COMPETENCE

*Social Competence*

Ainsworth et al. (1978) have summarized studies of the development of the infant's attachment to his mother. They concluded that infants who were found to have a secure attachment to the mother at 12 months of age had mothers who were more responsive than those of insecurely attached babies during the first year of life. Specifically in the first three months of their baby's life, these mothers were more sensitive to their baby's signals during feeding (Ainsworth & Bell, 1969). In their face-to-face interaction they more often showed gentle, contingent pacing of their interventions, increasing their stimulation as the baby responded so as to encourage interaction (Blehar, Lieberman, & Ainsworth, 1977).

Situations or events that compromise the mother's ability to respond sensitively to her infant also appear to result in less adequate social development. An example is from a recent study on families of twins. Hock, Coady, and Cordero (1973) compared the attachment behavior of premature twins and singletons. The twins exhibited more avoidant behavior upon reunion with their mothers after a brief separation than the singletons did at 12 months of age. The authors speculate that this may be the result of the mother's limited capacity to respond promptly to both infants' signals.

Other investigators have looked at the influence of adults' modeling (setting an example) and verbal reasoning on preschool children's prosocial behaviors. These have been reviewed recently by Rushton (1976). Typically these studies have either been naturalistic observations of the concurrence of child and parent behaviors at one point in time or have been experiments in which the short-term effects of certain child-rearing approaches have been evaluated in a laboratory setting. The general findings are that children exposed to such models show more of this type of behavior than children not exposed to them. Taking a somewhat different approach, Zahn-Waxler et al. (1979) did a nine-month longitudinal study of 16 children who were 15 to 20 months of age at the start of the study. Mothers were trained to collect naturalistic data on their child's response to their child-rearing behaviors in situations in which the child was the cause of another's distress or in which the child was just a witness to another's distress. They found that mothers who had children showing altruism and reparation were most likely to explain to the child the consequences of his or her behavior for the victim. This explanation was usually rather emotional, not calm, in nature.

Although the vast majority of research on infant development focuses on the mother-infant relationship, most infants develop multiple attachments in the first year of life (Ainsworth, 1967; Schaffer & Emerson, 1964; Lamb, 1977). The nature of the father's early social interaction is increasingly being studied (Lamb, 1976), but as of yet there is little information on implications of the effects of the nature (not merely the absence) of this relationship on later social development. Some researchers have suggested that the father's influence on the young child may be indirect (through the marital relationship) as well as direct (Parke, 1979; Belsky, 1981).

## Cognitive Competence

Studies of the acquisition of mental skills also indicate the importance of the child's interaction with a responsive caregiver. Ainsworth and her colleagues evaluated this relationship in 26 white, middle-class families. Through home observations every three weeks throughout the first year of life, data was collected for ratings of the caregiver's behaviors and attitudes toward her baby. Maternal sensitivity was positively correlated (.46) to the General Quotient as measured by Griffiths Scale at around 11 months of age (Ainsworth & Bell, 1974).

In a longitudinal study of the development of preterm infants, Beckwith, et al.

(1976) found that infants who were more advanced on Piagetian cognitive tasks at 9 months had received more face-to-face gazing from the caregiver at 1 month of age, a higher percentage of prompt (within 45 seconds) responses to cries at three months and more contingent vocal responses to their noncrying vocalizations at eight months of age than less advanced infants. A subsequent follow-up of these children revealed that the mother's social behavior (contingent response to vocalization, mutual gazing, affectionate touching and social play) were positively related to scores of the Gesell and Bayley mental scales and Piagetian sensorimotor task performance at age 2 years (Cohen & Beckwith, 1979). A further follow-up of these children at five years of age with the Stanford-Binet intelligence test shows that these associations are still present (Beckwith 1981).

Additional evidence for the positive effect of maternal involvement on children's capabilities comes from research with the HOME measurement of Bradley, Caldwell, and Elardo (1979). This method, which has been recently reviewed in detail (Bradley & Caldwell, 1981), consists of a checklist of items describing the child's home environment. Typically, a researcher completes this form by observing the child in the home and interviewing the mother. The overall checklist can be subdivided for analysis of results, allowing assessment of separate aspects of the environment.

One such aspect, emotional and verbal responsivity of the mother, appears particularly important. This responsivity rating at 12 months was related to Binet IQ at 3 years (Bradley & Caldwell, 1980) and this rating at 24 months was predictive of Binet IQ at 54 months of age (Bradley & Caldwell, 1976). This relationship was especially strong for girls in comparison to boys (Bradley & Caldwell, 1980). Among their low-income families (one-half of which had preterm infants), Bakeman and Brown (1980) found that mothers who were more verbally and emotionally responsive during a home visit at 20 months of age had children who had higher Binet IQs at three years of age. In this sample, the mothers of preterm infants were not rated as different in responsivity from mothers of full-term infants. A related home variable, maternal involvement, at 18 months has been found to contribute substantially to the prediction of Binet IQ at 36 months of age in a sample of children at high risk for sociocultural retardation (Ramey, Farran, & Campbell, 1979). There is evidence however, that the early relationship between responsivity of the mother and the child's cognitive development at 12 months is less strong among upper middle-class, educated people. Using the HOME measure and the Bayley scales, Stevenson and Lamb (1979) found this relationship only for the first-born infants of this group of mothers.

Other aspects of the infant's environment which are controlled by the parent also appear to influence the young child's later cognitive development. In studies of families relatively low in SES (Bradley & Caldwell, 1976), in middle-class families (Ainsworth & Bell, 1974; Chazan, 1981), and among groups of families varying widely in SES (Beckwith, et al., 1976; White & Watts, 1973), the way the mother structures the physical environment and the amount of floor freedom given the infant were also found related to later IQ scores. In the Ainsworth and Bell study (1974) the variance explained by adding a measure of floor freedom to the measure of responsivity increased from 21 percent to 40 percent.

The father's influence on early cognitive development has also begun to be investigated. His mere presence in the home does not appear to favorably influence the child's Binet IQ at five years of age (Kohn & Rosman, 1973), but his involvement in parenting does seem to be positively related to advancement in his child's development (Clarke-Stewart, 1978). The relationships between parental child-rearing practices and intellectual functioning in 30 four-year-old boys were examined by Radin (1973). Lower- and middle-class fathers were observed at home interacting with their sons. Nurturance was measured through observations of father and son during a supposed "interview" of the father while the child was present. Assessments of intellectual functioning were made using the Stanford-Binet IQ test and the Peabody Picture Vocabulary Test within a few weeks of the home observation and one year later. For the sample as a whole and within the middle-class sample (n=17), the father's nurturance was significantly related to both sets of cognitive tests initially and at follow-up. The fathers in the lower-class sample were observed to be substantially less nurturant in their social interactions with their sons. Yet, despite the limited range of nurturance and small sample size (n=13) there was still a significant correlation with the initial IQ measures (r=.61 and r=.57) and a positive but not significant correlation with the IQ measures after one year (r=.38, r=.44).

Other evidence that it is these types of parenting skills that influence the child come from intervention projects such as those described by Gutelius, et al. (1972), Levenstein (1977), and Gordon (1969) in which home visitors teach the mother simple interactive games that she can play with her child. Children experiencing these types of stimulation score significantly higher on various developmental tests than control children, at least during the time the project is in progress. The outcomes of these interventions over time have been recently reviewed (Guinagh & Jester, 1981). Finally, studies by Ramey et al. (1979) and Heber and Garber (1975) with extremely deviant populations have shown that similar IQ gains can be produced with minimal involvement of either parent if the child receives similar types of stimulation from teachers or trained volunteers who work directly with the child in the home or center.

Longitudinal follow-up of early intervention studies have raised the question of whether these IQ gains really represent a significant change in cognitive structures or are just temporary phenomena, since most differences between experimental and control groups decrease or wash out with time after the program ceases. Kagan (1976) also raised this question after studying Guatemalan children in a rural village. He found that children raised in windowless huts with no conventional toys and limited verbal interaction with adults for their first 15 to 16 months of life were initially considerably behind on measures of cognitive development when compared to American children of the same age. However, once out of this early environment, the children appear to rapidly catch up, because older children in the village performed as well as American children on culture-free tests designed to assess cognitive competency. This suggests their basic cognitive competence is intact. However, these same children continue to be considerably behind American children on culture-specific skills such as reading, writing, and arithmetic. These skills would, of course, determine to a large degree how they would do in school. In fact it is "school competency" that appears to be the most lasting effect of early stimulation. In recent reports of the long-term follow-up of 12 early stimulation programs, children participating in the programs were less likely to fail in school or be placed in special classes than children not participating (Darlington et al., 1980). Further support for this comes from the Island of Kauai study (n=750) where the variables most strongly associated with doing well in school at age 10 were the amount of educational stimulation and emotional support received in the home as measured at age two years (Werner et al., 1971).

The Brookline Early Education Program is an attempt in part to test White and Watt's (1973) theory of what types of parenting skills are necessary and sufficient to produce "competent" children (Pierson, 1973). In this program home visitors skilled in early childhood education worked with mothers during the preschool years to help them become more responsive to their child's developmental needs. The children also participated in preschool classes led by responsive teachers. Recent reports of the school performance of these children indicate they are functioning closer to White and Watts' model of overall competence than children who did not receive those extra services (Pierson et al., 1981).

*Language Development*

Although the sequence of language acquisition has been thoroughly studied (e.g., see review by Bloom, 1975), knowledge of precisely how children develop language skill is still lacking. Lenneberg (1969) has described language development as occuring in a fixed maturational sequence in normal children with specific parental training presumably having little or no effect, as long as the environment provides some minimal level and variety of language as examples. The question of what the nature of this minimal level is may be best described by Nelson (1977). He states: "In order to fully acquire syntactically governed language the child must engage in active communication in meaningful contexts with partners who are fluent in the language and who display . . . a full range of grammatical structures." Observations that the passive watching of television is apparently not adequate for learning a language support this. Neither a hearing child of deaf parents (Bard & Sachs, 1977) nor Dutch children watching German-language television (Snow et al., 1976) acquired language from their television viewing.

Additional support for the facilitative role of active communication has been found. Early social communication behaviors of the mother (affectionate touching, social playing, contingent response to vocalization) measured at one month of age are positively related to the child's receptive language skill at two years of age (Cohen & Beckwith, 1979). Also, mothers who more often stimulated their babies at four months of age by encouraging their attention to people and objects have been found to have babies with larger expressive vocabularies at 12 months (Ruddy & Bornstein, 1981).

Specific training procedures have not proven useful, however. For example, it was once thought that the "expansion" of child's speech would facilitate language acquisition. (For example if the child said "Dog gate," the parent would reply "The dog is at the gate"). This does not seem to be the case. In fact, one group of children subjected to expansions for forty-minute periods daily for three months showed lesser gains in language than a group in which the children were spoken to in a less didactic manner (Cazen, 1968). Thus, it would seem that in order to be successful, attempts to facilitate language development should focus on enriching social interaction and not just on the correction or practice of isolated aspects of speech.

## Motor Development

The sequence of motor skill development in normal infants and preschoolers has been documented (ex. Bayley, 1969; Holt, 1977; Knobloch & Pasamanick, 1974). Since there is little recent work on parental influences on the acquisition of motor skills, the existing literature will be briefly reviewed.

The rate of achievement of motor milestones in the first year of life can be affected by child-rearing practices at least on a short-term basis. The acceleration of gross motor development often seen in black infants has been shown to be related to more permissive child-rearing approaches even within socioeconomic classes of an all-black sample (Williams & Scott, 1953). "Permissive caregivers" as defined do not restrict the child's movements to certain areas of the house, do not punish the child for "nonapproved habits" such as hair pulling and thumbsucking and encourage the child's reaching behaviors. This kind of permissiveness may be more often found in low rather than middle socioeconomic status families (Williams & Scott, 1953). If so, this may explain rather consistent social class differences (which are often confounded with race) found in the attainment of early motor skills in the United States.

In studies of other cultures, motor precocity has been found in many relatively undeveloped regions of India, Guatemala, and Africa (Phatak, 1970; Cravioto et al., 1967; Liddicoat, 1969; Super, 1976) where child care practices stimulate motor development. In contrast motor milestones are not as quickly obtained by Japanese infants (Caudill & Weinstein, 1969) who are raised in a much more restrictive fashion. Interpretation of these differences must be cautious due to the possibility that there is a lower mean birth weight of babies in the undeveloped regions and some kinds of motor behavior may be easier for smaller infants. Yet, it appears likely that early child-rearing practices substantially affected motor development in the first year of life.

Nevertheless, by one year of age, these kinds of motor precocities seem to fade. Studies of the attainment of walking (e.g., Dennis & Dennis, 1940) indicate that substantial restriction of early physical movement for the first year of life (e.g., Hopi Indian infants on cradle boards) does not significantly delay the onset of walking unless this restriction is extreme and is combined with social deprivation (Dennis & Najarian, 1957). Although the development of motor skills seems to proceed with no specific encouragement by caregivers, these findings should not be interpreted to mean that no child's motor development can be facilitated. Some children (such as those disabled with cerebral palsy) may well benefit from habilitative programs as described by Henderson (1981). Also the long-term effects of preschool physical fitness programs such as "fit by five" in this country need evaluation.

## Parenting and Child Health Outcomes

Studies relating parenting skills to health outcomes have generally not been as precise as those relating parenting skills to development. Variables that appear to influence the child's health status include the mother's health habits during pregnancy, her coping ability in general and her ability to care for a sick child in particular, her utilization of preventive services, her knowledge of nutrition and her feeding techniques, and her ability to protect the child from environmental hazards.

One of the first recognizable acts of parenting in the new family are the mother's health habits during pregnancy. The mother's use of prenatal care and the extent of undesirable health habits such as poor diet, cigarette smoking, alcohol ingestion and drug use are all significantly related to fetal growth and the child's weight at birth (Miller & Merritt, 1979).

After birth, whether or not the child is hospitalized during the first year of life is also related to the mother's parenting skills. Longitudinal studies indicate that 10–15 percent of infants are admitted to the hospital during the first year of life. Many of these admissions are related to lower respiratory infections, gastroenteritis, and feeding problems, which in turn have been related to the mother's coping ability (Miller et al., 1960; Drillen, 1964; Douglas & Bloomfield, 1965; Glass et al., 1971).

Household accidents are often associated with lapses of parental supervision. Of the 2,000 youngsters under age 15 who die in fires every year about one-third were left unattended at the time of the fire (Wheatley, 1973). Others have reported a higher incidence of lapses of supervision in children hospitalized or being seen in the emergency room for other types of accidents (Holter & Friedman, 1968; Meyer et al., 1963). A recent report by Larson (1980) indicates that better training of mothers in accident prevention may be beneficial at least during the infants' first year.

Other aspects of parenting related to child health are: use of proper automobile seat restraints; keeping the child up to date on immunizations; recognizing potential streptococcal sore throats and finishing out the prescribed duration of treatment to prevent rheumatic fever; recognition and follow-through on treatment for amblyopia and chronic supperative otitis media; and obtaining proper dental care and prophylaxis.

## SELECTED FACTORS INFLUENCING PARENTAL BEHAVIOR

From the previous section it is clear that how parents function in their child-rearing role is an important determinant of the child's health and developmental status. In this section we will look at selected factors that have been identified as having an influence on how parents carry out these tasks. These are: individual differences among children; maternal age; mother-child separations; and the ecologic context within which the parents are trying to function.

### Effects of Individual Differences In Infants and Children on Parenting

Although certain aspects of the parenting process appear to facilitate the development in young children of "competence" in several areas, this process is continually influenced by the young child. When counseling parents to increase (or decrease) certain of their behaviors toward their child, this limitation must be realized.

Children of all ages (including neonates) have been shown to vary considerably in behavioral characteristics which have an important effect on how their parents respond to them (Brazelton, 1980; Goldberg, 1977; Bell & Harper, 1977; Thomas & Chess, 1977; Korner, 1971). Evidence supporting infants' and children's effects on adults rather than vice versa can be deduced from a variety of research designs (Bell & Harper, 1977). Four basic types follow.

Cross-lagged correlations such as those done by Clarke-Stewart (1973) have been useful in weighing the influences of children vs. adults. For example, she found that the relationship between a child's positive emotional behavior at 11 months of age (Time A) was correlated to the mother's positive emotional behavior six months later (Time B). This relationship was stronger than that between the mother's emotional behavior at Time A and the infant's positive emotion at Time B, suggesting that the infant's effect may be more influential. Further analysis of autocorrelations and partial correlations helped clarify the relationship.

Another approach is to look within an observational session at which behaviors follow others. For instance, during a home visit, certain behaviors of three-month-old infants (fussing, gross movement) were found to be followed fairly predictably by the maternal responses of vocalization or touching (Lewis, 1972). Vietze et al (1978) studied other intrasession relationships between infant and maternal behaviors over a ten-month period in the first year of life. In the early months, infant vocalizations had a much greater effect on parent behavior than in later months.

A third major way of studying the effects of children on adults' child-rearing techniques is to vary the children's characteristics experimentally and study the results on adults. For example, Bates (1975) trained four 11-year-old boys to vary attentiveness and smiling to adults while being taught mathematics. When the boys were attentive and smiled, they received more positive nonverbal expressions from the adult. In Keller and Bell's (1979) laboratory situation, adults tried to persuade 9 year-old girls to perform altruistic tasks. The girls were trained to vary their behavior systematically, appearing responsive to only one-half the adults with whom they were paired. The results showed that the adults paired with girls who behaved responsively to them used a higher proportion of reasoning statements than those paired with girls who had little eye contact with them and were slow to respond to the adults' verbalizations.

A fourth strategy has been to identify infant characteristics early in life and see if these are more predictive of later parenting behaviors than other known influences such as socioeconomic status or early and extended contact at birth. For example, Field's (1977) study of pre-term, term and post-term infants suggested that early social interaction characteristics of neonates (measured on the Brazelton Neonatal Behavioral Assessment Scale) were more predictive of later mother-infant interaction than early opportunities for mother-infant contact. Other groups of newborns have been found to have lower than average social interaction skills: small for gestational age infants (Als et al., 1976; 1977); infants exposed to phototherapy; (Telzrow et al., 1980); and infants exposed to obstetric medication during labor (Aleksandrowicz & Aleksandrowicz, 1974). One would hypothesize that mothers of these babies would have more parenting difficulties than average, but well-controlled studies to confirm this are lacking.

Other evidence of the relationship between early infant characteristics and later parenting problems has been reported by Thomas, Chess, and Birch (1968). In their study of early "temperament" differences, they found that babies identified as "difficult" at around 3 months of age were at higher risk for later disturbances in parent-child relationships than babies identified as "easy."

*Maternal Age: Adolescents As Parents*

There has been much recent concern about the increasing number of adolescent pregnancies. This has raised the question about what effect, if any, age of the mother has on her child-rearing skills. Most of the investigators who have looked at this issue have not controlled for differences in socioeconomic status and ethnicity. Thus, reports that teenage mothers (in contrast to older mothers) have unrealistic expectations about when their infants will obtain various developmental milestones, play and verbalize less with their infants, use more physical punishment and do not respond as readily to infant cries because of fear of spoiling, are hard to interpret because similar patterns have been described for mothers of low socioeconomic status in general (Williams, 1974; Phipps-Yonas, 1980). When socioeconomic status, ethnicity, and birth order are controlled, differences related to maternal age are few and not very striking when compared to environmental effects (Broman, 1981; Field, 1980). However, even if the reported parenting problems are not related to age per se, they do indicate that this group of mothers could benefit from more emotional support, and information, and training in the area of child care and child development (Furstenberg & Crawford, 1978).

## Effects of Parent-Child Separations

Separations in unfamiliar surroundings appear to affect infant behavior. Fagin (1966) observed anxious attachment in 18 to 48 month-old children after their hospitalization of a week or less. All children had mothers who visited them daily but only one-half had mothers who spent the night with them. Reports of the mother at a week and at one month after returning home from the hospital indicated that the behavior of the children whose mothers did not stay overnight was noticeably disturbed in relation to their behavior prior to hospitalization. The children were reported to be much more dependent and more easily upset by a very brief separation from their mother. Those children whose mother spent the night with them in the hospital showed none of these unfavorable changes. An earlier study of hospitalization with children under a year of age revealed that disturbances similar to those reported by Fagin (1966) had faded by two months in most children; by 80 days no children showed any remaining symptoms (Schaffer & Callender, 1959).

The effects of repeated, daily separations of mother from infant on the development of the infant's attachment to the mother is not so clear a relationship. Although Blehar (1974) reported effects consistent with those of major separations (such as hospitalization) when children began attending full-time day care after about 25 months of age, other investigators have found no adverse effects on the infant's attachment to the mother when infants began attending group day care in the first one-half year of life (Kagan, Kearsley, & Zelazo, 1978) or at three years of age (Portnoy & Simmons, 1978). This literature has recently been reviewed by Rutter (1981) who concluded:

> We know that good quality day care does not disrupt children's emotional bonds with their parents, . . . children continue to prefer their parents over alternative caregivers. Furthermore, even day care for very young children does not *usually* result in serious emotional disturbance. On the other hand there are indications that day care influences to some extent the form

of children's social behavior. . . . The ways in which it does so may be determined by the specific characteristics of the day care . . . by the age and other characteristics of the child, and by the characteristics of the family.'' (pp. 20–21).

## Parenting As Seen From An Ecologic Context

There is an increasing consensus among students of human development that a focus broader than the parent-child relationship or even the home environment is necessary if one is to understand the forces shaping the development of the child (Brim, 1975; Bronfenbenner, 1979). Ecologic theorists see factors affecting the child in terms of nesting systems such as shown below. The implications of this are that the ability of parents to function effectively in their child-rearing role depends a great deal on how much support they as individuals get from each other, relatives and friends, community institutions, cultural values and government policies.

Evidence supporting this model has recently been reviewed by Bronfenbrenner (1979). Further evidence of particular interest to pediatricians comes from epidemiologic studies of the incidence and prevalence of such problems as child abuse and neglect, accidents, low birth weight babies, and children with behavioral and learning problems. Family settings in which these types of problems are most likely to occur are characterized by some combination of the following:

1. The parents have little knowledge and/or experience with childbirth and child care.
2. The parents are receiving little in the way of emotional support from each other, relatives, friends, and other community organizations and groups.
3. The family is disorganized and under stress from a variety of sources including poor living conditions, poor working conditions, health problems, child care problems, unwanted pregnancies and geographic mobility.

(Harvard Task Force, 1977; Silver, 1973; Birch & Gussow, 1970; Miller, 1975; Kane et al., 1976; Preventive Medicine U.S.A., 1976; Morse, et al., 1977; Miller et al., 1976; Richmond & Weinberger, 1970; Newberger, Newberger, & Richmond, 1976; Brent & Harris, 1976).

Perhaps the most dramatic example of the need for an ecologic approach to understanding parenting comes from the literature on child abuse and neglect (Belsky, 1980). Parenting defects noted in the studies of child-abusing families include: inconsistent and harsh physical punishment; lapses in supervision; unrealistic expectations about what children at different stages of development are capable of doing; and negative attitudes toward the pregnancy and later the child (Smith & Hanson, 1975). Early views held that these defects were almost entirely related to parent psychopathology and/or early experiences of the parents

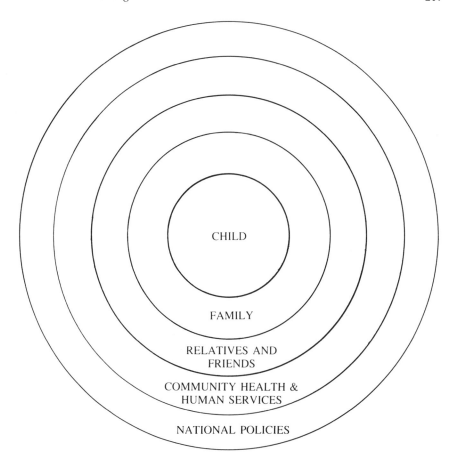

*Figure 1.* An ecologic model of development.

being abused in their own upbringing (Spinetta & Rigler, 1972). Further evidence has shown this to be a far too simplistic model. Studies have shown that abused children often differ from control children in birth weight and in exhibiting developmental delays and having personality traits of irritability, hyperactivity and impulsivity (Friedrich & Boriskin, 1976). This has resulted in the abuse of some of these children by foster care families after they have been removed from their original homes.

Stress and support data is still sketchy because of lack of uniform measures and adequate comparison groups, but almost all ecologically oriented investigators have found that abusive and neglectful families are under greater stress and more isolated from family and friends than families of similar socioeconomic circumstances (Smith, Hanson, & Noble, 1974; Justice & Duncan, 1976; Lauer et al., 1974; Newberger et al., 1977; Giovanni & Billingsley, 1970). Finally, Gil

(1970) has shown a connection between child abuse and cultural values relating to the use of physical punishment and institutional policies.

Approaching the problem on a community-wide basis, Garbarino (1976) found that high rates of reported abuse and neglect are associated with other correlates of low socioeconomic status such as lower use of prenatal care and higher rates of low birth weight babies and infant mortality. Similar findings of increased family stress and decreased support have been reported from studies of household accidents. Investigations have shown a higher incidence of family illness, recent moves, new pregnancies, unemployment or some other recent change requiring adaptation at the time of the accident (Meyer et al., 1963; Sibert, 1975; Sobel, 1970). In a prospective study Padilla et al. (1976) found that families with high "life change" scores had a significantly higher accident rate over a five-month follow-up period than families with lower "life change" scores. Measures of support are very sketchy, but several investigators have found a higher frequency of single parent and/or isolated families among children having accidents (Meyer et al., 1963; McCormick et al., 1980; Plionis, 1977; Holter & Friedman, 1968). Better measurement of both these variables should increase our understanding of the conditions that lead to accidents and what steps might be taken to prevent them. Overall, these studies indicate that programs designed to improve child health and development outcomes will have to pay attention to parent support systems as well as providing health care and education.

## INFLUENCE OF HEALTH CARE SYSTEMS ON PARENT AND CHILD FUNCTIONING

Increasing technical competence in the care of sick children is the most obvious way that the health care system can improve child development. Recent developments in the treatment of low birth weight infants are an impressive example of this. Once survival is insured, however, gains or losses in the neonatal period tend to be overshadowed by effects related to a child's socioeconomic environment (Werner et al., 1971; Sameroff & Chandler, 1975; Birch & Gussow, 1970).

Today, as compared to ten years ago, there are considerably more single parent families, families in which the mother is young and inexperienced in child care, families that are isolated from relatives and friends because of a recent move to a new area and/or a divorce, and families that are having increasing difficulty in meeting their basic needs for food, clothing, shelter, and medical care, because of un- or underemployment and the inroads on the dollar caused by inflation (Children's Defense Fund, 1979; U.S. Department of Health, Education and Welfare, 1978; America's Children, 1976; Allen Gutmacher Institute, 1976). In few other cultures is so much expected of parents with so little provided in the way of emotional and material support (Clark, 1981). Because of this there has been increasing interest in what the health care system can do to provide more help to parents in their child-rearing role. Following is a summary of the evaluation research related to attempts to provide such services.

## Hospital Birthing Procedures

Much recent attention has been focused on changes in birthing procedures so as to provide early and extended mother-infant contact. Some evidence has been presented to indicate that these procedures enhance the emotional bonding between parent and child which in turn leads to more effective parenting. However, recent research on this (see review by Morgan, 1981) has yielded equivocal results.

Investigators limiting their sample to low SES, primiparous women who plan to bottle feed their infants have found that early contact seems to enhance mother-infant interaction (Klaus & Kennell, 1976) and reduce the incidence of inadequate parenting (O'Connor et al., 1980). Findings are more equivocal in studies in which the samples have a preponderance of middle-class (Leiderman, 1978), multiparous (Siegel et al., 1980), or breast-feeding women (Svejda et al., 1980).

One explanation that has been proposed to explain these results is that previous findings of the effects of early contact procedures were actually due to the mother receiving extra attention from the hospital staff. Svejda et al. (1980) carefully controlled several dimensions of this variable in their study and found no substantial differences between the early and later contact group at 36 hours after delivery. This result is notable because investigators who have *found* parenting differences between traditional and extra contact groups have not controlled more than one aspect of special attention, such as the amount of time that nurses spend with the mothers (O'Connor et al., 1980).

It is possible that early contact between mothers and infants in the hospital (which is confounded in most studies with extra attention or hospital privileges) is actually one *means* to an *end* (namely confidence in mothering skills and interest in the infant). Svejda et al.'s (1980) results could be reinterpreted to support this hypothesis. They limited their sample to mothers planning to breast feed their infants. It is plausible that these mothers are already very interested in their infants and somewhat confident of their caregiving skills (especially with regard to feeding). Thus, a hospital-based intervention designed to enhance these characteristics would be limited in its effects because of a "ceiling" effect. The influence of intervention (through early contact procedures) would be more pronounced in women having less of these characteristics to start with.

This analysis of studies suggests that the encouragement by hospitals of early mother-infant contact is most effective in promoting positive contact between mothers and infants among certain subgroups of mothers: namely, primiparous women of low SES who plan to bottle feed their babies. Nevertheless, since modification of hospital practices to foster early contact is relatively inexpensive and our ability to predict who might benefit from such services is relatively poor, we would recommend such services be routinely available to all. However, it should be made clear to mothers that such an experience is by no means necessary or sufficient to insure adequate maternal infant bonding or to enhance parenting skill.

Preliminary data is being collected on the effects of early extended contacts between fathers and infants (Keller, Hildebrandt, & Richards 1981). Follow-up measures indicate that the fathers who were randomly assigned to the extended contact group played more with their infants and had taken on more caretaking responsibilities at six weeks postpartum than those assigned to the less intensive infant contact group.

## Other Methods of Support During Labor and Delivery

In most cultures other than our own, the mother is attended by a relative or friend during labor. Until recently, hospital procedures in this and some other developed countries either ignored this or actively tried to discourage it. Such attitudes and routines are often picked up in less developed countries striving to achieve a similar level of technology. In a recent report from Guatemala, a person to accompany the mother during labor was reintroduced into the care system (Sosa et al., 1980). Twenty mothers attended by such a person had shorter labors, were awake more after delivery and smiled and talked to their babies more than twenty control mothers who went through labor unattended. While the usual conditions of delivery in that hospital are somewhat different from those in many hospitals in this country, there are unattended mothers here who might benefit from such a person and it is a relatively simple procedure that could be easily evaluated.

## Anticipatory Guidance and Counseling in the Physician's Office

The American Academy of Pediatrics and others have long stressed the importance of the pediatrician providing education and support to parents during well child visits. However, over the past two decades a number of studies of well child care around the country suggest that this is not done very well by many physicians (Stine, 1962; Starfield & Borkart, 1969; Korsch et al., 1971; Mindlin & Denson, 1971; Foye et al., 1977). In the most recent of these (Reisinger & Bires, 1980) a random sample of pediatricians (n=33) in the metropolitan Pittsburgh area was studied. The total time spent with each family in a well child visit averaged 10.3 minutes and only about 90 seconds of this was focused on anticipatory guidance and counseling.

When the physician (or combination of physician and nurse practitioner) does spend considerably more time in this area, there are some beneficial effects (Chamberlin et al., 1979; Chamberlin & Szumowski, 1980). In this study, the amount of physician teaching effort was related to various measures of mother and child functioning over time. Mothers receiving care from high teaching physicians (and nurses) felt more supported in their child-rearing role and reported more use of positive contact with their child than mothers receiving care from low teaching physicians. However, there were no differences in the developmental status of the children. A content analysis of a small sample of visits showed that even the high teaching physicians did not focus directly on trying to enhance the mother's responsivity. One recent report indicated that if the physician does do this, the effect is greater and has some carry over on child functioning as well (Casey & Whitt, 1980). Improving the supportive and educative aspects of well child visits is certainly one approach to making pediatric care more effective in its influence on parenting.

However, improving the way well child visits are conducted will not, by itself, have much effect on the major problems of child health and development today because the families in which most of these problems occur are poor utilizers of preventive services (Miller, 1975; Harvard Child Health Care Task Force, 1977; Kane et al., 1976; Children's Defense Fund, 1976, 1977). Thus many studies have shown that pediatricians spend the bulk of their time delivering preventive care to the families that need them the least (Miller, 1975; Schonfield et al., 1962; Gallagher, 1967; Barsky, 1969; Staub et al., 1969; Cervantes, 1972; Hoekelman, 1978; Leopold, 1974). Because of this, additional methods of providing support and education to parents will have to be found.

## Other Approaches to Parent Support

There have been a number of demonstration projects in medical settings that have achieved some success in teaching parenting skills such as behavior modification and cognitive stimulation (Gutelius et al., 1972; Scarr-Salapatek & Williams, 1973; Jason & Kimbrough, 1974; Cornell & Gottfried, 1976; Morris, 1976; Masterpasqua et al., 1980). In spite of positive results, most of these programs are discontinued after the initial grant runs out because third party payers have not been willing to pay for them.

Efforts to set up parent-child centers and "home start" programs in selected communities have run into some of the same hurdles. These programs have been reasonably comprehensive and have had some documented positive effects on parenting but each has only served a small number (80 to 100) of families per year (Johnson et al., 1974; Keliher, 1969; Collins, 1980). The problems with these programs are that they are limited in availability by categorical funding and often require introducing a whole new system into communities, which makes them expensive, difficult to sustain, and often poorly coordinated with other ongoing programs. Working through already established institutions such as health departments that have a long history of providing maternal child health services could bypass many of these problems and make the services more cost-effective.

However, the effectiveness of health department programs are also frequently compromised by fragmentation related to categorical funding, poor coordination with private sector health care programs, lack of built-in evaluation techniques, bureaucratic rigidity, and inadequate funding (Harvard Task Force, 1977; Children's Defense Fund, 1976, 1977; Blum et al., 1968; Komaroff & Duffell, 1976; Kessner et al., 1974; Wallace & Goldstein, 1975; Schlesinger et al., 1976).

## Home Visitor Approaches

One approach to providing parent support that looks promising and could be run out of a public health department or other existing community agency is the use of home visitors. Silver (1973) describes a number of nurse home visitor programs in operation in other countries. Few evaluation studies are available, but infant mortality rates in most of these countries are less than those in the United States.

In this country, trained lay home visitors have been shown to be able to bridge cultural gaps and bring hard to reach families into the health care system for prenatal, postnatal and well child care, and for developmental screening (Adair & Deuschle, 1970; Conn, 1968; Westheimer et al., 1970; Fox et al., 1968; Colombo et al., 1979; Children's Defense Fund, 1977; Domke & Coffee, 1966; Kent & Smith, 1967). They can provide health education, increase immunization rates for target populations, and detect household health hazards (Wise et al., 1968; Cons & Leatherwood, 1970; Cauffman, 1970; Stewart & Hood, 1970). They can provide emotional support to families with a chronically ill child and to those at risk for child abuse and neglect, (Rice et al., 1976; Pless & Satterwhite, 1972; Gray et al., 1977), and they can teach parenting skills such as cognitive stimulation to new mothers (Levenstein, 1977; Gordon, 1969; Lourie et al., 1967). Lay persons have also been trained to serve as family advocates with landlords, social agencies, and government bureaucracies and can maintain the confidentiality of sensitive information (Wise et al., 1968; Torrey et al., 1973; Hoff, 1969; Gales, 1967). Finally, they have been able to work well along with physicians and nurses (Wise et al., 1968).

In most of these programs, however, the home visitor has been trained in only one or two tasks and the programs have not been organized on a community-wide basis. Recent attempts to do this have achieved mixed results (Larson, 1980; Siegel et al., 1980). At a recent conference on home visitors in Washington (1980)[1] it was clear that programs vary widely in scope and intensity and that some kind of collaborative study employing uniform program components and outcome measures will be necessary to achieve sample sizes large enough to demonstrate significant effects over the relatively long periods of time necessary for follow-up.

# SUMMARY

In the past decade considerable data has accumulated about how parenting skills affect the developing child. Of equal importance has been the knowledge gathered about what factors influence the ability of parents to parent. Overly simplistic notions have given way to the realization that parenting must be viewed in an ecologic context with multiple levels of influence and that child development programs must be geared to meet the needs of parents as well as their children if they are to have any long term success. The challenge for health care providers is how to incorporate this knowledge about human development into their care programs so that they provide the education and support that parents need to function effectively.

# ACKNOWLEDGMENTS

This work was supported in part by the Commonwealth Fund Grant 5-29829-210 to train pediatricians in the knowledge and research skills of Developmental Psychology. We also wish to thank Judy O'Hara for her help in preparing the manuscript.

# NOTE

1. Improving the Delivery of Preventive Services to Families with Young Children: The Home Visitor Approach; Sponsored by the American Academy of Pediatrics, June, 1980, Washington, D.C.

# REFERENCES

Adair, J., & Deuschle, K. *The Peoples Health: Medicine and Anthropology in the Navajo Community.* New York: Appleton Century Crofts, 1979.

Ainsworth, M. D. S. *Infantry in Uganda: Infant Care and the Growth of Love.* Baltimore, Md.: The Johns Hopkins University Press, 1967.

Ainsworth, M. D. S., & Bell, S. M. Some contemporary patterns of mother-infant interaction in the feeding situation. In A. Ambrose (Ed.), *Stimulation in Early Infancy.* New York: Academic Press, 1969.

Ainsworth, M. D. S., & Bell, S. M. Mother-infant interaction and the development of competence. In K. J. Connolly and J. Bruner (Eds.), *The Growth of Competence.* New York: Academic Press, 1974.

Ainsworth, M. D. S., Blehar, M. C., Waters, E., & Wall, S. *Patterns of Attachment: A Psychological Study of the Strange Situation.* Hillsdale, N.J.: Lawrence Erlbaum, 1978.

Aleksandrowicz, M. K., & Aleksandrowicz, D. R. Obstetrical pain-relieving drugs as predictors of infant behavior variability. *Child Development,* 1974, *45*, 935-945.

Allan Gutmacher Institute. *11 Million Teenagers: What Can Be Done About Epidemic of Adolescent Pregnancies in the United States?* Planned Parenthood Federation of America, Inc., 1976.

Als, H., Tronick, E., Adamson, L., & Brazelton, T. B. The behavior of the full-term yet underweight newborn infant. *Developmental Medicine and Child Neurology,* 1976, *18*, 590.

Als, H., Tronick, E., Lester, B. M., & Brazelton, T. B. The Brazelton Neonatal Behavioral Assessment Scale (BNBAS). *Journal of Abnormal Child Psychology,* 1977, *5*, 215-231.

America's Children 1976, Washington, D.C., National Council of Organizations for Children and Youth, 1976.

Appleton, T., Clifton, R., & Goldberg, S. The Development of behavioral competence in infancy. In F. D. Horowitz (Ed.), *Review of Child Development Research*, Vol. 4. Chicago, Ill.: University of Chicago Press, 1975.

Arend, R., Gove, F., & Sroufe, L. Continuity in early adaptation: From attachment theory in infancy to resiliency and curiosity at age five. *Child Development*, 1979, *50*, 950–959.

Bakeman, R., & Brown, J. V. Early interaction: Consequences for social and mental development at three years. *Child Development*, 1980, *51*, 437–447.

Bard, B., & Sachs, J. *Language Acquisition Patterns in Two Normal Children of Deaf Parents.* Paper presented at the Second Annual Boston University Conference on Language Acquisition, Boston, 1977, and Cited in P. A. de Villiers and J. G. de Villiers (Eds.), *Early Language.* Cambridge, Mass.: Harvard University Press, 1979.

Barsky, P. An evaluation of well child clinics in the Province of Manitoba. *Canadian Journal of Public Health*, 1969, *60*, 307–14.

Bates, J. E. Effects of a child's imitation vs. nonimitation on adult's verbal and nonverbal positivity. *Journal of Personality and Social Psychology*, 1975, *31*, 840–851.

Bayley, N. *Bayley Scales of Infant Development.* New York: The Psychological Corporation, 1969.

Beckwith, L., Cohen, S., Kopp, C., Parmelee, A., & Marci, T. Caregiver-infant interaction and early cognitive development in preterm infants. *Child Development*, 1976, *47*, 579–587.

Beckwith, L. *Preterm Children's Cognitive Competence at Five Years and Early Caregiver-Infant Interactions.* Paper presented at meeting of Society for Research in Child Development, Boston, Mass.: April, 1981.

Bell, S. M. The development of the concept of the object and its relationship to infant-mother attachment. *Child Development*, 1970, *41*, 291–312.

Bell, R. Q., & Harper, L. V. *Child Effects on Adults.* Hillsdale, N.J.: Lawrence Erlbaum, 1977.

Bell, S. M. Cognitive development and mother-child interaction in the first three years of life. Monograph in preparation, 1978. Cited in M. D. S. Ainsworth, M. C. Blehar, E. Waters, & S. Wall (Eds.), *Patterns of Attachment: A Psychological Study of the Strange Situation.* Hillsdale, N.J.: Lawrence Erlbaum Assoc., 1978.

Belsky, J. Child maltreatment: An ecological integration. *American Psychology*, 1980, *35*, 320–335.

Belsky, J. Early human experience: A family perspective. *Developmental Psychology*, 1981, *17*, 3–23.

Birch, H., & Gussow, J. *Disadvantaged Children: Health, Nutrition and School Failure.* New York: Harcourt-Brace, 1970.

Blehar, M. C. Anxious attachment and defensive reactions associated with day care. *Child Development*, 1974, *45*, 683–692.

Blehar, M. C., Lieberman, A. F., & Ainsworth, M. D. S. Early face-to-face interaction and its relation to later infant-mother attachment. *Child Development*, 1977, *48*, 182–194.

Bloom, L. Language development review. In F. D. Horowitz, (Ed.) *Review of Child Development Research*, Vol. 4 Chicago, Ill.: University of Chicago Press, 1975.

Blum, H. L., Wahl, F., Lemon, G. M., Jorlin, R., & Kent, G. W. The multi-purpose worker and the neighborhood multi-service center: Initial experiences and implications of the Rodea Community Service Center. *American Journal of Public Health*, 1968, *58*, 458–462.

Bradley, R. H., & Caldwell, B. M. The relation of infants' home environments to mental test performance at fifty-four months: A followup study. *Child Development*, 1976, *47*, 1172–1174.

Bradley, R. H., Caldwell, B. M., & Elardo, R. Home environment and cognitive development in the first 2 years: A cross-lagged panel analysis. *Developmental Psychology*, 1979, *15*, 246–250.

Bradley, R. H., & Caldwell, B. M. The relation of home environment, cognitive competence, and IQ among males and females. *Child Development*, 1980, *51*, 1140–1148.

Bradley, R. H., & Caldwell, B. M. Pediatric usefulness of home assessment. In B. W. Camp (Ed.), *Advances in Behavioral Pediatrics,* Vol 2. Greenwich, Conn.: JAI Press, 1981, 61-80.

Brazelton, T. B. Behavioral competence of the newborn infant. In P. M. Taylor (Ed.), *Parent-Infant Relationships.* New York: Grune and Stratton, 1980.

Brent, R. L., & Harris, M. (Eds.), *Prevention of Embryonic, Fetal and Prenatal Disease.* Bethesda: Fogarty International Center of Advanced Study in the Health Sciences, 1976.

Brim, O. Macro-structural influences on child development and the need for childhood social indicators. *American Journal of Orthopsychiatry,* 1975, *45,* 516-524.

Broman, S. Long-term development of children born to teenagers. In K. Scott, T. Field, & E. Robertson (Eds.), *Teenage Parents and Their Offspring.* New York: Grune and Stratton, 1981, 195-224.

Bronfenbrenner, U. *The Ecology of Human Development: Experiments by Nature and Design.* Cambridge, Mass.: Harvard University Press, 1979.

Caudill, W., & Weinstein, H. Maternal care and infant behavior in Japan and America. *Psychiatry,* 1969, *32,* 12-43.

Casey, P., & Whitt, K. Effect of the pediatrician on the mother-infant relationship. *Pediatrics,* 1980, *65,* 815-820.

Cauffman, J. Community health aides: How effective are they? *American Journal of Public Health,* 1970, *60,* 1904-1909.

Cazden, C. B. Some implications of research on language development for preschool education. In R. D. Hess, & R. M. Bear (Eds.), *Early Education: Current Theory, Research and Action.* Chicago: Aldine, 1968.

Cervantes, R. The failure of comprehensive health services to serve the urban Chicano. *Health Service Report,* 1972, *87,* 432-40.

Chamberlin, R., Szumowski, E., & Zastowny, T. An evaluation of efforts to educate mothers about child development in pediatric office practices. *American Journal of Public Health,* 1979, *69,* 875-885.

Chamberlin, R., & Szumowski, E. A follow-up study of parent education in pediatric office practices: Impact at age two and a half. *American Journal of Public Health,* 1980, *70,* 1180-1188.

Chazan, S. E. Development of object permanence as a correlate of dimensions of maternal care. *Developmental Psychology,* 1981, *17,* 79-81.

Children's Defense Fund: *Doctors and Dollars and Not Enough. How to Improve Health Services for Children and Their Families.* Washington, D.C.: Children's Defense Fund, 1976.

Children's Defense Fund: *EPSDT: Does it Spell Health Care for Poor Children.* Washington, D.C.: Children's Defense Fund, 1977.

Children's Defense Fund: *America's Children and Their Families: Basic Facts.* Washington, D.C.: Children's Defense Fund, 1979.

Clark, A. (Ed.), *Culture and Childbearing.* Philadelphia: F. A. Davis and Co., 1981.

Clarke-Stewart, K. A. Interactions between mothers and their young children: Characteristics and consequences. *Monographs of the Society for Research in Child Development,* 1973, *38,* No. 6-7, Serial No. 153.

Clarke-Stewart, K. A. *Child Care in the Family.* New York: Academic Press, 1977.

Clarke-Stewart, K. A. And daddy makes three: The father's impact on mother and young child. *Child Development,* 1978, *49,* 466-478.

Cohen, S. E., & Beckwith, L. Preterm infant interaction with the caregiver in the first year of life and competence at age two. *Child Development,* 1979, *50,* 767-776.

Collins, R. Home start and its implications for family policy. *Children Today,* 1980, *9,* 12-16.

Colombo, T. J., Freeborn, D. K., Mullooly, J. P., & Burnham, V. R. The effect of outreach workers educational efforts on disadvantaged preschool children's use of preventive services. *American Journal of Public Health,* 1979, *69,* 465-473.

Conn, R. Using health education aides in counseling pregnant women. *Public Health Report,* 1968, *83,* 79-82.

Connell, D. B. Individual differences in attachment: An investigation into stability, implications, and relationships to structure of early language development. Unpublished doctoral dissertation, Syracuse University, 1976. Cited in M. D. S. Ainsworth, M. C. Blehar, E. Waters, & S. Wall (Eds.), *Patterns of Attachment: A Psychological Study of the Strange Situation.* Hillsdale, N.J.: Lawrence Erlbaum Assoc., 1978.

Cons, N., & Leatherwood, F. Dental services in community child care programs. *American Journal of Public Health,* 1970, *60,* 1245-1249.

Cornell, E., & Gottfried, A. Intervention with premature human infants. *Child Development,* 1976, *47,* 32-39.

Cravioto, J., Licardie, E. R., Montiel, R., & Birch, H. G. Motor and adaptive development of premature infants from a preindustrial setting during the first year of life. *Biologia Neonatorum,* 1967, *11,* 151-158.

Darlington, R. B., Royce, J. M., Snipper, A. S., Murray, H. W., & Lazar, I. Preschool programs and later school competence of children from low-income families. *Science,* 1980, *208,* 202-208.

Dennis, W., & Najarian, P. Infant development under environmental handicap. *Psychological Monographs,* 1957, *71* (Whole No. 436).

Dennis, W., & Dennis, M. G. The effect of cradling practice upon the onset of walking in Hopi children. *Journal of Genetic Psychology,* 1940, *56,* 77-86.

Domke, H. R., & Coffey, G. The neighborhood based public health worker: Additional manpower for community health services. *American Journal of Public Health,* 1966, *56,* 603-608.

Douglas, J., & Bloomfield, J. *Children Under Five.* London: George Allen and Unwin Ltd., 1958.

Drillien, C. M. *The Growth and Development of the Prematurely Born Infant.* Baltimore: Williams and Wilkins Co., 1964.

Easterbrooks, M. A., & Lamb, M. E. The relationship between quality of infant-mother attachment and infant competence in initial encounters with peers. *Child Development,* 1979, *50,* 380-387.

Fagin, C. M. *The Effects of Maternal Attendance During Hospitalization on the Post-hospital Behavior of Young Children: A Comparative Study.* Philadelphia: F. A. Davis, 1966.

Field, T. M. Effects of early separation, interactive deficits, and experimental manipulations on infant-mother face-to-face interaction. *Child Development,* 1977, *48,* 763-771.

Field, T. Interactions of Preterm and Term Infants with Their Lower and Middle Class Teenage and Adult Mothers. In T. Field (Ed.), *High Risk Infants and Children-Adult-Peer Interaction.* New York: Academic Press, 1980.

Fox, R. I., Goldman, J. J., & Brumfield, W. A., Jr. Reaching the target population for prenatal and postnatal care. *Public Health Report,* 1968, *83,* 597-602.

Foye, H., Chamberlin, R., & Charney, E. Content and emphasis of well child visits: Experienced nurse practitioners vs. pediatricians. *American Journal of Diseases of Children,* 1977, *131,* 793-797.

Friedrich, W., & Boriskin, J. The role of the child in abuse: A review of the literature. *American Journal of Orthopsychiatry.,* 1976, *46,* 580-590.

Furstenberg, F., & Crawford, A. Family support: Helping teenage mothers to cope. *Family Plan Perspective,* 1978, *10,* 322-333.

Gales, H. The community health education project: "Bridging the Gap." *American Journal of Public Health,* 1970, *60,* 322-327.

Gallagher, E. Prenatal and infant health care in a medium sized community. *American Journal of Public Health,* 1967, *47,* 127-137.

Garbarino, J. A preliminary study of some ecological correlates of child abuse: The impact of socioeconomic status on mothers. *Child Development,* 1976, *7,* 178-185.

Gil, D. *Violence Against Children: Physical Child Abuse In The United States.* Cambridge, Mass.: Harvard University Press, 1970.

Giovanni, J., & Billingsley, A. Child neglect among the poor: A study of parental adequacy in families of three ethnic groups. *Child Welfare,* 1970, *49,* 196.

Glass, L., Kolko, N., & Evans, H. Factors influencing predisposition to serious illness in low birth weight infants. *Pediatrics,* 1971, *48,* 368-371.

Goldberg, S. Social competence in infancy: A model of parent-infant interaction. *Merrill-Palmer Quarterly,* 1977, *23,* 163-177.

Gordon, I. Stimulation via parent education. *Children,* 1969, *16* 56-58.

Gray, J. D., Cutler, C. A., Dean, J. G., & Kempe, C. H. Prediction and prevention of child abuse and neglect. *Child Abuse and Neglect: The International Journal,* 1977, *1,* 45-58.

Guinagh, B. J., & Jester, R. E. Long-term effects of infant stimulation programs. In B. W. Camp (Ed.), *Advances in Behavioral Pediatrics.* Greenwich, Conn.: JAI Press, 1981, 81-110.

Gutelius, M., Kirsch, A., MacDonald, S., Brooks, M., McErlean, B., & Newcomb, C. Promising results from a cognitive stimulation program in infancy. *Clinical Pediatrics,* 1972, *11,* 585-593.

Harvard Child Health Project Task Force, *Toward a Primary Medical Care System Responsive to Children's Needs.* Cambridge, Mass.: Ballinger Publishing Company, 1977.

Heber, R., & Garber, H. The Milwaukee Project: A study of the use of family intervention to prevent cultural-familial mental retardation. In B. Z. Friedlander, G. M. Sterritt, & G. E. Kirk (Eds.), *Exceptional Infant Vol. 3: Assessment and Intervention.* New York: Brunner/Mazel, 1975.

Henderson, A. Research in occupational therapy and physical therapy with children. In B. W. Camp, (Ed.), *Advances in Behavioral Pediatrics,* Vol. 2. Greenwich, Conn.: JAI Press, 33-59, 1981.

Hock, E., Coady, S., & Cordero, L. *Patterns of attachment to mother of one-year-old infants; comparative study of full-term infants and prematurely born infants who were hospitalized throughout the neonatal period.* Paper presented at the biennial meeting of the Society for Research in Child Development, Philadelphia, 1973.

Hoekelman, R. Child Health Supervision. In R. Hoekelman, S. Blatman, P. A. Brunell, S. B. Friedman, & H. M. Seidel (Eds.), *Principles of Pediatrics: Health Care of the Young.* New York: McGraw-Hill, 1978.

Hoff, W. Training the disadvantaged as home health aides. *Public Health Report,* 1969, *84,* 617-623.

Holt, K. S. *Developmental Paediatrics: Perspective and Practice.* Boston: Butterworths, 1977.

Holter, J. C., & Friedman, S. B. Child abuse early case finding in the emergency department. *Pediatrics,* 1968, *42,* 128.

Jason, L., & Kimbrough, C. A preventive program for young economically disadvantaged children. *Journal of Community Psychology,* 1974, *2,* 134-139.

Johnson, D. L., Leler, H., Rios, L., Brandt, L., Kahn, A. J., Mazeike, E., Frebe, M., & Biset, B. The Houston Parent-Child Development Center: A parent education program for Mexican-American families. *American Journal of Orthopsychiatry,* 1974, *44,* 121-128.

Justice, B., & Duncan, D. F. Life crises as a precursor to child abuse. *Public Health Reports,* 1976, *91,* 110-115.

Kagan, J. Resilience and continuity in psychological development. In A. Clark & A. Clark (Eds.), *Early Experience: Myth and Evidence.* London: Open Books, 1976.

Kagan, J., Kearsley, R., & Zelazo, P. *Infancy: Its Place in Human Development.* Cambridge, Mass.: Harvard University Press, 1978.

Kane, R., Kasteler, J., & Gray, R. (Eds.), *The Health Gap: Medical Services to the Poor.* New York: Springer Pub. Co., 1976.

Keliher, A. V. Parent and child centers. *Children,* 1969, *16,* 63-66.

Keller, B. B., & Bell, R. Q. Child effects on adult's method of eliciting altruistic behavior. *Child Development,* 1979, *50,* 1004-1009.

Keller, W. D., Hildebrandt, K. A., & Richards, M. *Effects of extended father-infant contact.* Paper presented at meeting of Society for Research in Child Development, Boston, April, 1981.

Kent, J. A., & Smith, C. H. Involving the urban poor in health services through accommodation: The employment of neighborhood representatives. *American Journal of Public Health,* 1967, *57,* 997-1003.

Kessner, D., Snow, C., & Singer, J. *Assessment of Medical Care for Child In Contrasts in Health States,* Vol. 3. Washington, D.C.: National Academy of Sciences, 1974.

Klaus, M. H., & Kennell, J. H. *Maternal-Infant Bonding.* St. Louis: Mosby, 1976.

Knobloch, H., & Pasamamick, B. (Eds.), *Gesell and Amatruda's Developmental Diagnosis,* 3rd Ed. New York: Harper & Row, 1974.

Kohn, M., & Rosman, B. L. Cognitive functioning in five year old boys as related to social-emotional and background demographic variables. *Developmental Psychology,* 1973, *8,* 277–294.

Komaroff, A., & Duffell, A. An evaluation of selected federal categorical health programs for the poor. *American Journal of Public Health,* 1976, *66,* 255–261.

Korner, A. F. Individual differences at birth: Implications for early experiences and later development. *American Journal of Orthopsychiatry,* 1971, *41,* 608–619.

Korsch, B. M., Negrete, V. F., Mercer, A. S. & Freemon, B. How comprehensive are well-child visits. *American Journal of Diseases Children,* 1971, *122,* 483–488.

Lamb, M. E. The role of the father: An overview. In M. E. Lamb (Ed.), *The Role of the Father in Child Development.* New York: John Wiley, 1976.

Lamb, M. E. Father-infant and mother-infant interaction in the first year of life. *Child Development,* 1977, *48,* 167–181.

Larson, C. Efficacy of Prenatal and Postpartum Home Visits on Child Health and Development. *Pediatrics,* 1980, *66,* 191–197.

Lauer, R., Brocch, E., & Grossman, M. Battered child syndrome: Review of 130 patients with control. *Pediatrics,* 1974, *54,* 67.

Leiderman, P. H. The critical period hypothesis revisited: Mother to infant social bonding in the neonatal period. In F. D. Horowitz (Ed.), *Early Developmental Hazards: Prediction and Precautions,* AAAS Selected Symposium, Vol. 19. Boulder, Col.: Westview Press, 43–77, 1978.

Leifer, A. D., Leiderman, P. H., Barnett, C. R., & Williams, J. A. Effects of mother-infant separation on maternal attachment behavior. *Child Development,* 1972, *43,* 1203–1218.

Lenneberg, E. H. On explaining language. *Science,* 1969, *164,* 635–643.

Leopold, E. Whom do we reach? A study of health care utilization. *Pediatrics,* 1974, *53,* 341–348.

Levenstein, D. The mother-child home program. In M. C. Day, & R. K. Parker (Eds.), *The Preschool in Action: Explaining Early Childhood Programs,* 2nd Ed. Boston: Allyn & Bacon, 1977.

Lewis, M. State as an infant-environment interaction: An analysis of mother-infant interaction as a function of sex. *Merrill-Palmer Quarterly,* 1972, *18,* 95–121.

Liddicoat, R. Development of Bantu children. *Developmental Medicine and Child Neurology,* 1969, *11,* 821–822.

Lieberman, A. F. Preschooler's competence with a peer: Relations with attachment and peer experience. *Child Development,* 1977, *48,* 1277–1287.

Lourie, R. S., Rioch, M. J., & Schwartz, S. The concept of a training program for child development counselors. *American Journal of Public Health,* 1967, *57,* 1754–1758.

Main, M. Exploration, play, and cognitive functioning as related to child-mother attachment. Unpublished doctoral dissertation, Johns Hopkins University, 1973.

Masterpasqua, F., Shuman, B., Gonzalez, R., & O'Shea, L. Integrating early parent-infant psychosocial support into neighborhood health clinics: An ecological intervention. *Infant Mental Health,* 1980, *1,* 108–115.

Matas, L., Arend, R., & Sroufe, L. Continuity in adaptation in the second year: The relationships between quality of attachment and later competence. *Child Development,* 1978, *49,* 547–556.

Meyer, R., Roclofs, H., Bluestone, J. & Redmond, S. Accidental injury to the preschool child. *Journal of Pediatrics,* 1963, *63,* 95.

McCormick, M. C., Shapiro, S., & Starfield, B. Injury and its correlates among one-year-old children. *American Journal Diseases of Children,* 1981, *135,* 159–163.

Miller, C. A. Health care of children and youth in America. *American Journal of Public Health,* 1975, *65,* 353.

Miller, F., Court, S., Walton, W., & Knox, E. *Growing up in NewCastle upon Tyne.* London: Oxford University Press, 1960.

Miller, H. C., Hassanein, K., Chin, T. D., & Hensleigh, P. Socioeconomic facts in relation to fetal growth in white infants. *Journal of Pediatrics,* 1976, *89,* 638-643.

Miller, H., & Merritt, A. *Fetal Growth in Humans.* Chicago: Year Book Publishers, 1979.

Mindlin, R. L., & Densen, P. M. Medical care of urban infants: Health supervision. *American Journal of Public Health,* 1971, *61,* 687-697.

Morgan, L. J. Methodological review of research on mother-infant bonding. In B. W. Camp (Ed.), *Advances in Behavioral Pediatrics,* Vol. 2. Greenwich, Conn.: JAI Press, 1981.

Morris, A. The use of the well baby clinic to promote early intellectual development via parent education. *American Journal of Public Health,* 1976, *66,* 73-74.

Morse, A., Hyde, J., Newberger, E., & Reed, R. Environmental correlates of pediatrics social illness: Preventive implications of an advocacy approach. *American Journal of Public Health,* 1977, *67,* 612-615.

Nelson, K. E. Aspects of language acquisition and use from age 2 to age 20. *Journal of the American Academy of Child Psychiatry,* 1977, *16,* 584-607.

Newberger, E., Newberger, C., & Richmond, J. Child Health in America: Toward a Rational Public Policy. *Millbank Memorial Fund Quarterly: Health and the Society,* 1976, *54,* 249.

Newberger, E., Reed, R., Daniel, S., Hyde, J., & Rotochuch, M. Pediatric social illness: Toward an etiologic classification. *Pediatrics,* 1977, *60,* 178.

O'Connor, S., Vietze, P. M., Sherron, K. B., Sandler, H. M., & Altemeier, W. A. Reduced incidence of parenting inadequacy following rooming in. *Pediatrics,* 1980, *66,* 176-182.

Padilla, E., Rohsenow, B., & Bergman, A. Predicting accident frequency in children. *Pediatrics,* 1976, *58,* 223-226.

Parke, R. D. Perspectives on father-infant interaction. In J. D. Osofsky (Ed.), *Handbook of Infant Development.* New York: John Wiley, 1979, 549-590.

Phatak, P. Motor growth patterns in Indian babies and some related factors. *Indian Pediatrics,* 1970, *7,* 619-624.

Plionis, E. Family functioning and childhood accident occurrence. *American Journal of Ortho-psychiatry,* 1977, *47,* 250-263.

Phipps-Yonas, S. Teenage pregnancy and motherhood. A review of the literature. *American Journal of Orthopsychiatry,* 1980, *50,* 403-431.

Pierson, D. *The Brookline Program For Infants and Their Families: The First Operational Year.* Brookline, Mass.: Brookline Early Education Project, 1973.

Pierson, D. *The Integration of Multiple Perspectives in the Assessment of Children's Educational Problems.* Presented at the Society for Research in Child Development Meetings, April 4, 1981.

Pless, I. B., & Satterwhite, B. Chronic illness in childhood selection, activities, and evaluation of non-professional family counselors. *Clinical Pediatrics,* 1972, *11,* 403.

Portnoy, F. C., & Simmons, C. H. Day care and attachment. *Child Development,* 1978, *49,* 239-242.

Preventive Medicine U.S.A. *Social Determinants of Human Health.* New York: Prodist, 1976.

Radin, N. Observed paternal behaviors as antecedents of intellectual functioning in young boys. *Developmental Psychology,* 1973, *8,* 369-376.

Ramey, C. T., Farran, D. C., & Campbell, F. A. Predicting IQ from mother-infant interactions. *Child Development,* 1979, *50,* 804-814.

Reisinger, K. S., & Bires, J. A. Anticipatory guidance in pediatric practice. *Pediatrics,* 1980, *66,* 889-892.

Rice, N., Satterwhite, B., & Pless, I. Family counselors in a pediatric specialty clinic setting. *Social Work in Health Care,* 1976-77, *3,* 193-203.

Richmond, J., & Weinberger, H. S. Program implications of knowledge regarding the physical, intellectual, and emotional growth and development and the unmet needs of children and youths. *American Journal of Public Health*, 1970, (Supp) 60, 23.

Ruddy, M. G., & Bornstein, M. H. *Cognitive Correlates of Infant Attention and Maternal Stimulation Over the First Year of Life*. Paper presented at meeting of Society for Research in Child Development, Boston, April, 1981.

Rushton, J. P. Socialization and the altruistic behavior of children. *Psychological Bulletin*, 1976, *83*, 898-913.

Rutter, M. Social-emotional consequences of day care for preschool children. *American Journal of Orthopsychiatry*, 1981, *5*, 4-28.

Sameroff, A., & Chandler, M. Reproductive risk and the continuum of care-taking casualty. In F. D. Horowitz, Hetherington, S. Scarr-Salapatek & Siegel, (Eds.) *Review of Child Development Research*, Vol. 4. Chicago: University of Chicago Press, 1975.

Scarr-Salapatek, S., & Williams, M. The effects of early stimulation on low-birth weight infants. *Child Development*, 1973, *44*, 94-101.

Schaffer, H. R., & Callender, W. M. Psychologic effects of hospitalization in infancy. *Pediatrics*, 1959, *24*, 528-529.

Schaffer, H. R., & Emerson, P. E. The development of social attachments in infancy. *Monographs of the Society for Research in Child Development*, 1964, *29*, (Serial No. 94).

Schlessinger, E., Skoner, M., Trooskim, E., Markel, J. & Nath, F. The effects of anticipated funding changes on maternal and child health projects: A case study of uncertainty. *American Journal of Public Health*, 1976, *66*, 385-388.

Schonfield, J., Schmidt, W. M., & Sternfeld, L. Variations in prenatal care and well-child supervision in a New England city. *Journal of Pediatrics*, 1962, *61*, 430-437.

Sibert, R. Stress in families of children who have ingested poisons. *British Medical Journal*, 1975, *3*, 87.

Siegel, E., Bauman, K. E., Schaefer, E. S., Saunders, M. M., & Ingram, D. D. Hospital and home support during infancy: Impact on maternal attachment, child abuse and neglect, and health care utilization. *Pediatrics*, 1980, *66*, 183-190.

Silver, G. *Child Health: America's Future*. Germantown, Maryland: Aspen Systems Corporation, 1973.

Smith, S., Hanson, R., & Noble, S. Social aspects of the battered baby syndrome. *British Journal of Psychiatry*, 1974, *125*, 568-582.

Smith, S., & Hanson, R. Interpersonal relationships and child rearing practices in 214 parents of battered children. *British Journal of Psychiatry*, 1975, *127*, 513-525.

Snow, C. E., Arlman-Rupp, A., Hassing, Y., Jobse, J., Joosken, J., & Vorster, J. Mother's speech in three social classes. *Journal of Psycholinguistic Research*, 1976, *5*, 1-20.

Sobel, R. The psychiatric implications of accidental poisoning in childhood. *Pediatric Clinics of North America*, 1970, *17*, 653-686.

Sosa, R., Kennell, J., Klaus, M., Robertson, S., & Urrutia, J. The effect of a supportive companion on parental problems, length of labor, and mother-infant interaction. *New England Journal of Medicine*, 1980, *303*, 597-600.

Spinetta, J., & Rigler, D. The child abusing parent: A psychological review. *Psychological Bulletin*, 1972, *77*, 296-304.

Starfield, B., & Borkart, F. Physicians' recognition of complaints made by parents about their children's health. *Pediatrics*, 1969, *43*, 168-172.

Staub, H., Hoekelman, R. A., Bien, S. J., & Drazek, B. A. Health supervision of infants on the Cattaraugus Indian Reservation, New York. *Clinical Pediatrics*, 1976, *15*, 44-52.

Stevenson, M. B., & Lamb, M. E. Effects of infant sociability and the caretaking environment of infant cognitive performance. *Child Development*, 1979, *50*, 340-349.

Stewart, J. C., & Hood, W. R. Using workers from "hard-core" areas to increase immunization levels. *Public Health Reports,* 1970, *85,* 177-185.

Stine, O. Content and method of health supervision by physicians and child conferences in Baltimore. *American Journal Public Health,* 1962, *52,* 1858-1865.

Super, C. Environmental effects on motor development: The case of "African infant precocity". *Developmental Medicine Child Neurology,* 1976, *18,* 561-567.

Svejda, M. J., Campos, J. J., & Emde, R. N. Mother-infant "bonding": Failure to generalize. *Child Development,* 1980, *51,* 775-779.

Telzrow, R., Snyder, D., Tronick, E., Als, H. & Brazelton, T. B. The effects of phototherapy on neonatal behavior. *Developmental Medicine and Child Neurology,* 1980, *22,* 317-326.

Thomas, A., Chess, S., & Birch, H. G. *Temperament and Behavior Disorders in Children.* New York: New York University Press, 1968.

Thomas, A., & Chess, S. *Temperament and Development.* New York: Brunner/Mazel, 1977.

Torrey, E., Smith, D., & Wise, H. The family health worker revisited: A five-year followup. *American Journal of Public Health,* 1973, *63,* 71-74.

U.S. Department of Health, Education and Welfare. *Health: United States, 1978.* DHEW Publication No. (PHS) 78-1232, 1978.

Vietze, P. M., Abernathy, S. R., Ashe, M. L., & Faulstich, G. Contingent interaction between mothers and their developmentally delayed infants, in G. P. Sackett (Eds.), *Observing Behavior, Vol. 1: Theory and Application in Mental Retardation.* Baltimore: University Park Press, 1978.

Wallace, H. M., & Goldstein, H. Child health care in the United States: Expenditures and extent of coverage with selected comprehensive services. *Pediatrics,* 1975, *55,* 176-180.

Werner, E. K., Bierman, J. M., & French, F. *The Children of Kauai: A Longitudinal Study from the Prenatal Period to Age Ten.* Honolulu: University of Hawaii Press, 1971.

Westheimer, R. K., Cattell, S. H., Connell, E., Kaufman, S. A., & Swartz, D. P. Use of paraprofessionals to motivate women to return for post-partum check-ups. *Public Health Report,* 1970, *85,* 625-635.

Wheatley, G. Childhood accidents, 1952-72, an overview. *Pediatric Annals,* 1973, *2,* 10-28.

White, B. L., & Watts, J. C. *Experience and Environment: Major Influences on the Development of the Young Child.* Englewood Cliffs, N.J.: Prentice-Hall, 1973.

Williams, J. R., & Scott, R. B. Growth and development of Negro infants: IV. Motor development and its relationship to child rearing practices in two groups of Negro infants. *Child Development,* 1953, *24,* 103-121.

Williams, T. Childrearing practices of young mothers: What we know, how it matters, why it is so little. *American Journal of Orthopsychiatry,*

Wise, H. B., Torrey, E. F., McDade, A., Perry, G., & Bogard, H. The family health worker. *American Journal of Public Health,* 1968, *58,* 1828-1838.

Zahn-Waxler, C., Radke-Yarrow, M., & King, R. A. Child rearing and children's prosocial initiations toward victims of distress. *Child Development,* 1979, *50,* 319-330.

# THE NEONATAL BEHAVIORAL ASSESSMENT SCALE:
## ASSESSING THE BEHAVIORAL REPERTOIRE
## OF THE NEWBORN INFANT

Frances Degen Horowitz and

Patricia L. Linn

The newborn period is defined as the first 28 to 30 days of postnatal life. Self and Horowitz (1979) have reviewed ten instruments available for assessing the status of the infant during this period. Some of them, like the Gesell Development Scale, (Knobloch & Pasamanick, 1974) are useful only toward the end of the neonatal period as the infant reaches one month of age; others, like the Apgar (1953) and the Dubowitz (Dubowitz, Dubowitz, & Goldberg, 1970), are intended for use immediately after birth and have largely clinical applications. Still

**Advances in Developmental and Behavioral Pediatrics, vol. 3, pages 233–255**
**Copyright © 1982 by JAI Press Inc.**
**All rights of reproduction in any form reserved.**
**ISBN: 0-89232-223-3**

others, like Prechtl's evaluation (Prechtl & Beintema, 1964), are limited with respect to the fuctional domain being evaluated (e.g. reflexes) though it is an intensive investigation of this domain. There are two assessments designed to provide a more general review of the infant's behavioral repertoire—the Graham/Rosenblith Scale (Rosenblith, 1979) and the Brazelton Scale (Brazelton, 1973) which is officially titled the Neonatal Behavioral Assessment Scale (NBAS). Of these two, the NBAS is now the most widely used.

The NBAS grew out of T. Berry Brazelton's own observations during his examinations of normal newborn infants. He became aware of the range of behavioral interaction that was possible with a newborn infant if one carefully brought the infant through a variety of states. Using some systematic procedures that had been developed by other investigators (namely some from the early Graham scales) Brazelton began to develop a technique for eliciting different kinds of behavior from the newborn infant. What eventually became the Brazelton Scale or the NBAS was the result of a collaborative effort between Brazelton and several pediatricians and psychologists which was designed to provide an assessment procedure that could be reliably administered and scored, and which permitted the examiner to tap into the normal infant's states, state control, and behavioral abilities.

At the same time as the NBAS was being developed there was a growing body of evidence from experimental laboratories that the normal newborn infant comes into the world far more competent than had once been thought. Not only was it demonstrated that the infant could respond to visual, auditory, tactile, and olfactory stimuli but that the infant was capable of recognizing repeated stimulation and of making associative connections. If the normal newborn infant's capabilities are so extensively developed then speculations about the nature and import of early environmental experience affecting early development and/or behavior become more tenable. While a lively debate continues regarding the ultimate importance or impact of early intervention programs (Horowitz, 1980) there is no doubt that the newborn infant's behavioral repertoire and the individual differences that exist within the infant population are functional factors affecting mother-infant or infant-caregiver interactions. Much of the interest in the NBAS is stimulated by the possibility that the examination will enable us to better understand the genesis of some early mother-infant interaction difficulties and eventually, in some form, provide us with a clinical tool for pediatric practice.

In this chapter we will briefly describe the nature of the NBAS examination, its scoring and how the scores from the exam may be evaluated. We will then review the database that currently exists on normal infants, present the developments with regard to special populations, and evaluate the relationships between NBAS performance and other variables. Finally, we will attempt to discuss the present practical uses of the NBAS and crystal-gaze concerning its future utility.

# A DESCRIPTION OF THE NEONATAL BEHAVIORAL ASSESSMENT SCALE

The NBAS, in its originally published from (Brazelton, 1973) provided for the scoring of the infant's behavior on a nine point scale for 27 items. The list of items is shown in Table 1. In addition to these behavioral ratings the score sheet provides for a three point evaluation of the strength and symmetry of 16 reflexes and for recording a descriptive paragraph about the infant. The basic manual for the examination (Brazelton, 1973) provides a description of the exam, an explanation of the scoring and advice on administration of the assessment. Unlike traditional psychometric evaluations, the NBAS is administered in a fixed order only through the first four items. Following the first four items the examiner is trained to follow the baby's state changes and to administer items when the infant's state for the item is optimal. The NBAS also differs from standard psychometric procedures in that the original form of the exam provides for the

*Table 1.* NBAS Items

|  |  |
|---|---|
| 1. Response decrement to light | (2,3)* |
| 2. Response decrement to rattle | (2,3) |
| 3. Response decrement to bell | (2,3) |
| 4. Response decrement to pinprick | (1,2,3) |
| 5. Orientation inanimate visual | (4 only) |
| 6. Orientation inanimate auditory | (4,5) |
| 7. Orientation animate visual | (4 only) |
| 8. Orientation animate auditory | (4,5) |
| 9. Orientation animate visual & auditory | (4 only) |
| 10. Alertness | (4 only) |
| 11. General tonus | (4,5) |
| 12. Motor Maturity | (4,5) |
| 13. Pull-to-sit | (3,5) |
| 14. Cuddliness | (4,5) |
| 15. Defensive movements | (4) |
| 16. Consolability | (6 to 5,4,3,2) |
| 17. Peak of excitement | (6) |
| 18. Rapidity of buildup | (from 1,2 to 6) |
| 19. Irritability | (3,4,5) |
| 20. Activity | (alert states) |
| 21. Tremulousness | (all states) |
| 22. Startle | (3,4,5,6) |
| 23. Lability of skin color | (from 1 to 6) |
| 24. Lability of states | (all states) |
| 25. Self-quieting activity | (6,5 to 4,3,2,1) |
| 26. Hand-mouth facility | (all states) |
| 27. Smiles | (all states) |

*Note:*

*Numbers in parentheses indicate state in which item is to be scored.

examiner, on a number of the items, to score the infant's *best* behavior observed during the exam. Finally, each of the items is to be scored only in terms of performance on the item during a specified state. Thus, the orientation items are to be administered and scored only when the infant is in an awake, alert state.

Being trained to give the exam requires a significant investment of time. An individual interested in acquiring the skill to administer and score the NBAS must first read the manual, and is then advised to observe a training film or to observe a trained examiner administer the exam. Following this, one must practice administering and scoring the exam on a minimum of 20 infants. At this point it is advisable to work with a trained tester and finally one must go to Boston, Kansas, or Washington to check the reliability in scoring and technique of administration. All three reliability testing centers stress the importance of appropriate technique for administering the exam because part of the assessment involves the examiner's skill in bringing the infant through a series of state changes, creating the conditions in which optimal states for behavioral assessment are likely to occur, and for taking advantage of the presence of these states for the skillful evaluation of the infant's behavioral performance. While the results of the examination are not likely to be seriously distorted by small differences in examiner technique, it is quite clear that basic departures from the recommended techniques will produce quite different results.

Examiner reliability then requires the use of comparable scoring criteria as well as acquiring the proper skills in administering the exam. At Kansas, individuals coming to test their reliability must achieve a 0.90 or above reliability with three different trained testers and must, as well, be passed in the administration of the exam. Because of the necessary artfulness in the proper use of the NBAS, it is not possible to acquire competence in the administration of the exam without receiving direct training at one of the training centers.

One major variation in the NBAS has been developed by the Kansas group and is referred to as the NBAS-K (Horowitz, Sullivan, & Linn, 1978; Lancioni, Horowitz, & Sullivan, 1980a) or the Neonatal Behavioral Assessment Scale with Kansas Supplements. The supplements are of three kinds. The first is the development of scoring criteria that makes it possible to score the modal or characteristic behavior of the infant on the orientation items, on consolability, and on defensive response as well as the best behavior; the second is the addition of an orientation item that provides for assessing attention to an inanimate visual and auditory stimulus (which was left out of the original scale) and the changing of the scoring criteria for the 7, 8, and 9 score points on the orientation items so that both modal and best scores could be assigned. The third modification in the NBAS-K is the addition of several new scales which can be thought of as "qualifiers" or new items. Table 2 provides the new items in the NBAS-K as well as some of the additional scores that can be derived. Other investigators and centers have also been adding qualifying items in different research projects and ultimately one can expect to see a revision of the scale based upon the experience

*Table 2.*   New Items and Scores Added to the NBAS-K

---

Orientation Inanimate Visual and Auditory
Quality of Infant's Alert Responsivity*
Examiner's Persistence
General Irritability
Reinforcement Value of Infant's Behavior

Modal Scores for all Orientation Items, for Defensiveness and for Consolability
Sum of Orientation Items—Best
Sum of Orientation Items—Modal
Difference between Sum of Orientations Items Best and Modal

---

*Note*:
*This was taken from the Als et al., (1980a; 1980b) exam for use with premature infants.

with the qualifiers and modifications. However, when the NBAS is used at the present time it is most likely to be the original version as published in 1973 or the NBAS-K version.

Administering the NBAS or the NBAS-K takes about 30 minutes. It is recommended that the exam be carried out about midway between feedings and is probably optimally used at three days of age for normal infants or at two weeks of age (Lancioni, Horowitz, & Sullivan, 1980a). It can, however, be administered as early as 12 hours after birth and through one month of age. Because of the convenience of doing the examination during the hospital stay, and due to the changing patterns of hospital release for new mothers and infants, the exam is increasingly being given on the second day of life. This may not be the optimal day but the overall pattern of results in a given population is not likely to be greatly distorted by second compared to third day results. For a number of reasons, some of which are reviewed below, multiple assessments may provide a more informative picture of an infant than a single assessment.

Scoring the examination requires about ten to fifteen minutes. The immediate results consist of anywhere from 27 to 32 separate item scores plus possible modal and orientation summary scores. From a clinical standpoint, to be discussed in a later section, the raw score results of an individual examination may be used as a profile picture of the strengths and differences for a particular infant. Medical and psychological personnel often find this profile useful as an aid in talking with parents about the individual characteristics of an infant. However, for purposes of research, the results of the NBAS are most often looked at in terms of population characteristics related to means and variability of scores and in terms of clusters or factors that may provide for comparisons between populations.

Across a number of samples it has now become clear that the NBAS contains two to three major factors or clusters around which the exam items group. Orientation, state control, and motor maturity appear repeatedly in various factor analytic studies of the structure of the NBAS (Sameroff, 1978); in a study of the factor structure of the NBAS-K over repeated tests two major factors emerged: Orientation-Alertness and Irritability-State Control (Lacioni, Horowitz, & Sullivan, 1980a). Some investigators use the factor structure of the examination against which to evaluate the role of other variables in differentiating newborn populations. The more popular data reduction technique in the published literature, however, has been the use the "*a priori* clusters" described by Als (1978).

The *a priori* cluster technique reduces the 28 scores of the NBAS to four cluster scores: (1) Interactive Processes; (2) Motoric Processes; (3) Organization Processes, State Control; and (4) Organization Processes, Physiological Response to Stress. Within each cluster the infant is assigned a score of 1, 2, or 3. Some investigators have felt that the reduction of the 28-item scale to four clusters involving a 3-point discrimination simplified the results more than necessary. A more recent and more promising cluster technique has been devised by Lester (1981). It retains seven clusters and uses a summary score for each cluster based upon the items within the cluster. Undoubtedly, the NBAS has provided investigators with a tool for evaluating and quantifying the behavioral repertoire of the newborn infant. In the section that follows we review the recent research using the NBAS and the NBAS-K.

# CURRENT RESEARCH

## Normative Data

Several investigators have published items, means, and standard deviations against which different populations of infants may be compared. In the original publication of the NBAS the means and standard deviations as well as test-retest reliabilities gathered by Self (1971) were reported by Horowitz and Brazelton (1973) on a population of 60 normal infants, largely Caucasian, born in Kansas. Subsequently, Osofsky and Danzger (1974) published some normative information concerning a black, lower SES sample of infants tested in Philadelphia. Horowitz, et al. (1977) provided mean and standard deviation and some test-retest reliability on samples of Kansas, Israeli, and Uruguayan infants. Normative data for the NBAS-K have been published by Lancioni, Horowitz, and Sullivan (1980a, 1980b) on a sample of 200 Kansas infants.

The means and standard deviaitons do not appear to vary for relatively heterogeneous American samples, though, as discussed below, there do appear to be some differences in different cultural groups. (Evidence of cross-cultural differences in neonatal behavior was reported as early as 1969 by Freedman and Freedman (1969) using an early version of the NBAS).

The largest normative database has been collected by the Kansas group and is currently under analysis. Test results from the NBAS-K are available for over

1,300 infants and a major report of the normative characteristics of this sample will be forthcoming (Horowitz, Sullivan, & Byrne, in preparation).

In an interesting side analysis, Lancioni, Horowitz, and Sullivan (1980b) analyzed the components that contributed to one of the new scales of the NBAS-K: Reinforcement Value of Infant Behavior. This scale is a judgmental scale that attempts to measure how much the examiner liked the infant. Lancioni, Horowitz, and Sullivan have reported that in the first three days of life the higher the quality of the infant's responsiveness, the lower the irritability, the less need for examiner persistence and the higher the modal orientation scores the more likely it was that the examiner would judge the infant as reinforcing and likable. At two weeks high quality of responsiveness, low general irritability, and high modal and best orientation scores accounted for over one-half the variance on reinforcement value of the infant. By one month of age the low general irritability, high modal orientation, and less examiner persistence accounted for over 58% of the variance on reinforcement value scores. But, what was interesting was that at one month of age general irritability was the dominant factor accounting, by itself, for over one-half the variance. On the first day of life general irritability was absent from the predictor variables and on days 2 and 3 and at 2 weeks of age it was second or third. By one month of age it was the first and most powerful predictor variable.

## Stability of Performance

One of the major questions of interest is whether an infant's performance on the NBAS on one day resembles the infant's performance on another day. The answer to this question in part depends upon the method for deriving an estimate of test-retest reliability. In several reports it has now been demonstrated that test-retest reliability estimates on the NBAS and on the NBAS-K using the Pearson correlation technique are low to moderate (Horowitz, Sullivan, & Linn, 1978; Lancioni, Horowitz, & Sullivan, 1980a; Lancioni, Horowitz, & Sullivan, 1980b). However, in these same reports the degree to which the group correlation approach is the appropriate estimate of reliability is questioned. A group reliability estimate such as the Pearson basically tells you whether or not an individual infant's performance on one day is in relatively the same position within the group as on a second day. This, however, does not necessarily address the issue of the degree to which the infant's performance on one day is the same as that infant's performance on a second day. Such an individually estimated criterion of stability requires a comparison of the degree to which the scores on a given time on two test administrations are the same or different. Using a technique to evaluate stability across days to test the results show that within a sample of infants, day-to-day stability is generally higher than reliability estimates using group correlation analyses.

In the traditional psychometric literature, high test-retest reliabilities are the sine-qua-non for acceptance of a test instrument. As noted by Horowitz, Sullivan and Linn (1978) and more recently by Horowitz et al. (in press), such a criterion may be much less useful in evaluating neonatal behavior and may even be misleading. Linn (1979) and Buddin (1981) have both found that infants who show relatively high stability over two performances on the NBAS-K exhibit quite different patterns of mother interaction when compared with infants who show relatively lower stability on two examinations. Further, it is the infants whose behavior on the two tests is more variable who are involved in more active interactions as compared to the infants whose performance is more stable. Implications of these findings will be discussed below. However, Brazelton's advice that repeated evaluations may prove more useful than a single evaluation may be particularly true for investigating relationships of neonatal behavior to other variables.

Lester (1981) is working with a sample of infants looking at repeated performance and the possibility of deriving behavioral recovery curves using the repeated examination results. Both he and Lancioni (1978) have found that there are a large number of individual patterns across repeated tests, and that it is not easy to cluster these patterns into any useful groups at the present time. Some combination of stability measures and patterns may ultimately prove to be more useful than just stability or pattern information by themselves.

As more and more investigators are applying the NBAS and the NBAS-K to infant populations we can expect an increased understanding of the range and variation of normal infant behavior as measured by these instruments. This, in turn, should aid us in evaluating the kinds of results obtained from special groups or in relation to selected background and contemporaneous variables. Even without an extensive normative reference group, however, interesting patterns of relationships among different infant groups and relative to specific variables are beginning to emerge.

## Prenatal and Perinatal Factors in Relation to NBAS Performance

The effects of various prenatal conditions and perinatal procedures on the behavioral organization and smooth CNS functioning of the newborn have been assessed using the NBAS. While the placenta was once thought to buffer the fetus against harmful effects of maternal indulgences and illnesses, medical and developmental research has now laid this notion to rest. Biophysical and behavioral sequelae to maternal drug and alcohol ingestion, poor nutritional status, chronic illness, as well as treatments and procedures associated with modern obstetrical care have been known to relate to NBAS performance. Looked at from another perspective, it is possible to say that the NBAS permits us to detect behavioral differences associated with certain conditions.

Though specific behavioral effects of prenatal and perinatal challenges to the infant may disappear after the first postnatal days or weeks, current theoretical perspectives suggest that newborn behaviors influence interactions with the caregiver in a dynamic way (Lewis & Rosenblum, 1977; Sameroff & Chandler, 1975). Thus, while the infant may not continue to display a particular behavior, that behavior may have had a significant influence on the ongoing system of the caregiver-infant communication. For this reason, a behavioral effect of prenatal or perinatal condition may disappear quickly, but still have developmental significance.

The variables associated with pregnancy and delivery that have been studied with the NBAS range from maternal narcotics addiction to the choice of obstetrical medications. For narcotics-addicted infants, obvious clinical symptoms of irritability and poor motor control are apparent. More subtle effects in the alertness/orientation domain have been shown in studies using the NBAS (Kron et al., 1975; Strauss et al., 1975; Strauss et al., 1976). In addition to the obvious hyperarousal and irritability displayed in infants withdrawing from narcotics, these studies have also shown that there is decreased alerting and orienting to objects and faces, when these infants are compared to control infants. An infant who is both irritable and unlikely to alert or orient to faces may be a difficult infant for caregivers to get to know. Although such infants may be given barbituates for purposes of calming them, in two studies (Soule et al., 1974; Strauss et al., 1975) the authors noted that the consoling techniques used in the NBAS exam were quite successful in quieting the infants, thus suggesting a way to reduce the need to administer pharmaceutical agents to control symptoms of withdrawal.

Maternal malnutrition, evident from the mother's history or implied in the case of a low-weight-for-length newborn, has been associated with both poor NBAS performance and irregularities in the acoustical features of the infant's cry. In a study done in Greece, infants in an orphanage whose mothers had poor nutrition until intervention was instituted in the seventh month of pregnancy were compared with two well-nourished control groups (Brazelton, Tryphonopoulou, & Lester, 1979). In all four of Als' *a priori* cluster dimensions, the malnourished infants showed the poorest performance, when compared with the control groups, although with repeated testing the malnourished infants did show good recovery over the first ten postnatal days. Later (1979) studied the cry features of undernourished newborns, in addition to their NBAS performance. This study replicated the Brazelton, Tryphonopoulou, and Lester (1979) finding of poor NBAS performance in underweight newborns. It was also found that the cries of undernourished newborns in response to a pain stimulus differed from full-weight controls in several acoustical features. Perhaps most salient to a caregiver was the higher fundamental frequency found in these small infants' cries when compared to control infants' cries. Zeskind (1981) replicated these findings and demonstrated that these acoustical irregularities were to be found in infants on either end of the size distribution as overweight infants also exhibited unusual cry features. Both Lester (1979) and Zeskind (1981) suggested that CNS stress associated with inadequate weight gain may lead to both the poor NBAS performances and unusual cry features.

In one study infants were presumed to have experienced an atypical prenatal environment due to the fact that their mothers were diabetic. These infants of diabetic mothers (Yogman, Cole, & Als, 1978) were tested with NBAS three times. Their scores on the four *a priori* clusters were compared to scores from a control group. The infants of diabetic mothers had significantly lower scores on the "interactive processes" and "physiological stability" dimensions. More specifically, the study group showed less visual alertness and orienting, less cuddling, and more tremulousness and color changes than did the control group. It should be noted that infants of diabetic mothers were, themselves, a basically healthy group of infants, with normal blood glucose and calcium levels. However, the behavioral differences were still present on the infants' seventh day. The authors concluded that infants of diabetic mothers may be another group whose behavioral characteristics make early interactions more difficult for the caregiver.

Given a specific prenatal history, which may or may not have been complicated by the risk factors discussed above, decisions made by the parents and the physician about the delivery itself have also been shown to relate to newborn behavior. The effects of obstetrical medication on the newborn have been widely studied. Both depressive effects (Brackbill et al., 1974) and a lack of significant effects (Horowitz et al., 1977) on the newborn infant have been reported. Two recent studies have, however, provided a fresh approach in understanding medication effects by determining statistically the unique contribution of a variety of maternal, obstetrical, and infant variables that covary with obstetrical medication. Lester and his colleagues (Lester, Als, & Brazelton, 1980) reanalyzed data from a previous report by Tronick et al. (1976). In that study newborns were tested repeatedly with the NBAS. No significant effects of obstetrical medication were found. The reanalysis involved predicting NBAS performance based upon two types of drug scores, length of labor, parity, and the infants' ponderal index. The ponderal index is a weight-to-length ratio (weight/length$^3$ x 100) and provides an assessment of the relative thinness of the infant (Miller & Hassanein, 1971). Depending on the test day and the specific NBAS cluster Lester, Als, and Brazelton (1980) found that various combinations of variables did predict NBAS test performance best. The obstetrical medication scores and the ponderal index (PI) were found to be the most powerful predictors of NBAS performance, with low medication scores and a higher PI ratio invariably associated with more optimal NBAS scores.

Woodson and Da Costa-Woodson (1980) provided a similar perspective on the covariation of demographic, parturitional, and infant variables with obstetrical medication. Rather than try to control for these variables in their sample, they used statistical techniques to determine which variables lessened or increased the effects of medication on newborn behavior. Knowledge of the length of labor and maternal blood pressure during labor increased the power of the medication variable in predicting an NBAS irritability factor. Also, use of medication was not distributed randomly throughout the sample. Rather, mothers of a certain ethnic group, age, and parity tended to receive obstetrical medication. Based upon these two studies, it seems that some of the conflicting findings in the obstetrical medication literature may be related to the medication covariates that have not been controlled statistically or by the study design in the earlier studies. Variables such as the infant's PI or the mother's blood pressure may influence the degree to which a drug is stored by or transmitted to the infant. This, in turn, may affect the infant's behavior as measured by the NBAS. Thus such variables should be entered into future analyses of the effects of obstetrical medication on newborn behavior (Lester, Als, & Brazelton, 1980; Woodson & Da Costa-Woodson, 1980).

Another perinatal variable that has been studied recently is the effect of Caesarian section, versus vaginal delivery, on the behavior of the infant. Caesarian section may be either a planned, elective procedure (usually due to a previous Caesarian delivery by that mother) or an unplanned, emergency procedure (due to conditions such as cephalo-pelvic disporportion or preeclampsia). These procedures are very likely perceived as different kinds of experiences by the mother. It now seems, from two recent reports, that they may also differentially affect the newborn. In one study, infants delivered by emergency Caesarian section (CS) and vaginal deliveries were compared using the NBAS. No significant behavioral differences were found (Field & Widmayer, 1980). In another study, in which the potentially important covariate of obstetrical medication was controlled, infants delivered by elective CS scored significantly better on the NBAS "autonomic regulations" cluster than a vaginally delivered group with similar medication (Als et al., 1980). On the "range of state" cluster, the vaginally delivered group scored significantly better than the CS group. In general, the vaginally delivered group appeared more reactive and irritable than the CS group. A comparison group who had been delivered by CS, but with general anesthesia, were drowsy and difficult to interact with on the NBAS test.

Whether labor itself, experienced by the emergency-sectioned but not the elective-sectioned infants, may explain the different findings in these two studies is a question to be answered by further research. However, it now appears that both delivery route *and* the reason for the delivery procedure should be controlled in studies of newborn behavior.

It is clear that the NBAS has been useful in quantifying and describing the effects of prenatal and perinatal variables on the behavior of the newborn infant. The question remains, however, whether and how the differences in newborn behaviors, assessed in the relatively structured testing situation of the NBAS exam, relate to newborn behaviors in interaction with caregivers. Answering this question requires testing of the infant and an independent observation of the infant in interaction with a caregiver. Some research, discussed below, has been addressed to this topic.

A more difficult issue for the researcher employing newborn behavioral measures involves the complex interactions between maternal, obstetrical, and infant variables shown in these research reports. In designing a study and performing statistical analyses, it now appears that a variable may not only contribute an independent effect on newborn behavior, but it may also indirectly affect another variable, and its relationship to newborn behavior. For this reason very careful control of the variables shown to relate to NBAS performance is needed.

### Cross-Cultural Studies of the Newborn Using the NBAS

As newborn researchers attempt to unravel the complex interactions between infant and environment, one useful approach has been to study newborns from a variety of cultural backgrounds. Historically many newborn cross-cultural studies may have been designed to investigate genetic contributions to early behavioral diversity. Gradually we have come to understand that genetic and environmental effects on development exist in interaction and that environmental factors are already in operation during the prenatal period. Trying to specify the unique contributions of genetic and environmental factors using the newborn infant, who already has a nine-month history of environmental and genetic factors interacting is no longer a meaningful goal. Yet much remains to be learned from cross-cultural assessments of newborn behavior. (See Lester & Brazelton, in press; Super, in press, for further discussions of these issues and relevant reviews.)

The research reviewed in the previous section clearly describes newborn behavior as function of intrauterine environmental and perinatal factors. By studying infants from diverse cultural groups, our understanding of these variables may be aided in several ways. First, levels of variables which are not found (or are rarely found) in one culture may be prevalent in another. For example, Horowitz and her colleagues traveled to Israel and Uruguay to find larger samples of infants delivered without obstetrical medication (Horowitz et al., 1977).

Second, a cross-cultural perspective may clarify the variety of variable relationships for which we must account. Variables considered to be risk factors in one culture, based upon their correlations with poor newborn behavioral functioning, may not be risk factors in another culture. In one recent report, Coll, Sepkowski, and Lester (1978) studied a number of risk factors, including maternal age, in predicting newborn NBAS performance in Puerto Rico and the United States. While most of the risk factors (gestational age, Apgar scores, ponderal index) were equally powerful in both cultures in predicting NBAS performance, maternal age was a useful predictor only in the U.S. sample. At least two recent studies have shown that infants of teenage mothers in the United States are at risk for optimal NBAS performance in both preterm (Widmayer & Field, 1980) and term samples (Thompson, Cappleman, & Zeitschel, 1979). However, in the Puerto Rican sample described in the Coll et al. (1978) report, teenage childbearing was not a risk factor. The authors noted that most of the teenage mothers in the Puerto Rican sample were married, and their pregnancies were well accepted in their culture. Perhaps social acceptance of their pregnancy reduced maternal stress and increased the likelihood of early prenatal care.

In another report of the interrelationships of various biomedical factors in a Puerto Rican sample and two U.S. samples (Coll, Sepkowski, & Lester, in press) risk factors such as gestational age, Apgar scores and ponderal index were used to predict NBAS clusters. While for Black and White U.S. samples there were no or one significant predictors respectively, in the Puerto Rican sample, 6 of 7 NBAS clusters were significantly related to a combination of risk factors. Thus, again, it appears that the relationships between prenatal, perinatal, and newborn variables described in the previous section are themselves dependent upon another factor—the sociocultural environment.

There are difficulties associated with cross-cultural comparisons, however. The physical conditions of the testing situation, unfamiliar newborn care practices and rituals, parental attitudes concerning newborn robustness and frailty, and distrust of the foreign testers' contact with the infant have all been shown to influence NBAS test results in studies done in other cultures (DeVries & Super, 1978). Therefore, comparisons across cultures, where these factors may vary widely, need to include some estimate of variance due to such contextual factors. Keeping the importance of cultural context in mind may provide useful insights for researchers working within the United States. Significant variations in contextual factors may be present in different ethnic and racial groups in the United States but they have not been widely studied. They may, however, influence NBAS performance and should be considered in studies comparing groups of infants within a culture.

## The NBAS and Prediction of Infant Behavior

In the research discussed to this point newborn behavior has been used as an "outcome" variable. As such, it provides a type of yardstick against which one measures the effects of maternal, obstetrical, cultural, and other variables. The NBAS, however, has also been of interest as a predictor of other newborn behavior as well as later infant behavior.

In a sense, prediction from newborn test scores to later indices of infant functioning (such as Bayley or Stanford-Binet scores), without considering the infant's environment in between the two test points, denies a role to the infant's social, physical, and cultural milieu as an active contributor to developmental outcome. While NBAS scores have not shown significant test-to-test stability over the first month of life, some interesting relationships with NBAS test stability and variability have emerged. There have also been several recent reports describing significant longitudinal relationships between NBAS scores and later social, temperament, or cognitive measures. Let us review the longitudinal findings first.

Sostek and Anders (1977) investigated the relationships between day 8 NBAS scores, a modified version of the Carey Infant Temperament Questionnaire given at two weeks, and Bayley Mental and Motor Scales administered at ten weeks for a small sample of infants. The "distractability" Carey temperament cluster was significantly correlated with the NBAS "motoric processes" dimension and a total NBAS score. Both the NBAS "state control" dimension and the total NBAS score were significantly related to the Bayley Mental Scale at ten weeks. In comparing their results with other studies which found poor prediction from the NBAS test, Sostek and Anders suggested that delaying the NBAS assessment until the eighth postpartum day may have provided a description of newborn behavior less affected by the transition to extrauterine life. An eighth day evaluation coupled with the relatively short interval between the NBAS and Bayley tests may have enhanced the prediction that was found.

Egeland and his colleagues reported data gathered on a large sample of economically disadvantaged mothers and their infants in Minneapolis, Minnesota in which the NBAS was administered in the home at seven and ten days. The NBAS scores have been studied in relation to later interactive, attachment, and cognitive measures. In one report it was ntoed that more relationships with the NBAS were found as the infants grew older (Vaughn et al., 1980). At three months of age, factor scores derived from day 7 NBAS scores were not related to factor scores based on an observed mother-infant feeding interaction. At six months, however, several significant relationships were found between NBAS factor scores and the feeding factors. Factors derived from an observed mother-infant play interaction at six months related to NBAS factors as well. Analyses of variance revealed that infants classified as "worrisome" on the NBAS were less responsive to their caregivers in both a feeding and a play situation. At nine months, three of five NBAS factor scores were significantly correlated with Bayley Mental scores, but the amount of Bayley score variance explained by the NBAS scores was low. In this case, when infants were followed through their first year, NBAS scores, especially the derived "worrisome," "average," and "optimal" clusters, did predict interactive and Bayley measures significantly (Vaughn et al., 1980).

From this same study Vaughn, Crichton, and Egeland have reported that adding the performance on the NBAS to ratings of maternal behavior in the hospital significantly increased the prediction of the quality of maternal caregiving at three and six months. Interestingly, they found that the behavioral organization of the newborn as measured by the NBAS provided better added prediction for males compared to females. In a third report from this large study (Waters et al., 1980), 100 infants who had been tested with the NBAS at seven and ten days were observed in the Ainsworth (Ainsworth & Wittig, 1969) strange situation when the infants were one year of age. In this paradigm, the infant was observed in an unfamiliar room when alone, with the mother, or with an experimenter. Coders scored behaviors such as proximity seeking, proximity resisting, and crying before, during, and after the mother and infant were separated. The infant was then classified as belonging to one of three main attachment groups: secure attached, anxious avoidant, or anxious resistant.

Attachment groups were differentiated by their NBAS scores, with the anxious resistant group having least optimal NBAS scores on the orientation, motor maturity, and physiological regulation item clusters. These data suggest that infant behaviors, as described by the NBAS assessment may contribute to interaction patterns that lead to various attachment styles (Waters et al., 1980).

A report by Bakeman and Brown (1980) described an elaborate longitudinal design, in which infants were followed through their third year. Beginning with NBAS assessments upon discharge from the hospital and at one month, these infants were observed in early feeding interactions, were assessed in their home environments, were given developmental tests at one, two, and three years, and were observed for social participation and social competence in a summer camp situation at three years. The authors found that a summary score based on the mean of the NBAS orientation items across the two tests were significantly correlated with both the social participation and social competence measures at three years of age.

These reports provide some degree of predictive validity for the NBAS. However, it must be noted that although significant correlations have been found with later measures of social or cognitive functioning in these studies, the amount of variance explained by the newborn assessments is generally quite small (5%–25%). It may be that if newborn behavioral dimensions were weighted by some measure of that infant's environment, prediction to later measures of infant functioning would be enhanced.

Some indication that such a more complex picture is operating to link newborn behavior with later functioning is to be found in a program of research at Kansas. Linn (1979) studied 28 lower-class infants using the NBAS-K on the second and third days of life and had an independent observation of the infants in a feeding interaction with their mothers on the second day of life. She found that about half the infants in her sample could be classified as stable and half variable on the two NBAS-K examinations. Stable infants were those whose performance on half or more of the items on the NBAS-K was the same or only one scale score point different while the variable infants were those whose performance on half or more of the NBAS-K items differed by at least two scale score points. When the variable and stable infants were compared with respect to their interactions with their mothers it was found that the variable infants were more likely to be involved in an interaction with a mother who was classified as responsive to her infant while the stable infants were more likely to be involved in an interaction with a mother who was classified as unresponsive. The NBAS-K was administered again at two and four weeks of age. Using the variable-stable classification for the two- and four-week test Buddin (1981) found that an independent observation of the mother and the infant at home at four weeks revealed the same relationship. That is, infants classified as variable on the two- and four-week NBAS-K assessments were more likely to be involved in an interaction with a mother classified as responsive while those infants classified as stable were more likely to be involved in an interaction with a mother classified as unresponsive to her infant (Horowitz et al., in press).

In an analysis of maternal behavior in relation to individual NBAS-K item performance it was also found that infants whose modal orientation performance was lower tended to be involved in maternal behavior that was of closer proximity and more enveloping, but no stable patterns of infant behavior and maternal behavior were found for infants whose orientation performance was strong on the NBAS-K. This tended to be true of the infants and their mothers in the first few days of life when observed by Linn, as well as at one month of age when observed by Buddin (Horowitz et al., in press).

Smith has followed six of the infants seen by Linn and Buddin when the infants reached one year of age. He tested them with the Bayley Scale and found an almost perfect correlation between the degree to which the mother was responsive to her infant during the first few days of life and at one month and Bayley Mental Scale score performance. The more responsive the mother was, the higher the Bayley Mental scores (Horowitz et al., in press; Horowitz et al., 1981).

From the research just reviewed it is possible to hypothesize that neonatal behavior, as measured by the NBAS-K, affects the degree to which the mother's behavior is or is not responsive to the infant; in turn, maternal responsivity contributes to later developmental outcome. The ability to predict developmental outcome, accounting for more than a minimal amount of the variance, may thus require, as indicated above, documentation of the interrelationship between neonatal behavior, initial maternal responsivity, and the manner in which these combinations affect the nature of subsequent mother-infant interactions. It is interesting to note that the modal scores of the NBAS-K as well as the variability-stability dimension of performance on repeated NBAS-Ks may provide significant keys to a complex set of interacting variables that affect the developmental course of the infant.

## Evaluation of Special Populations

While the NBAS was originally developed for use with healthy, full-term infants, several investigators have attempted to describe the newborn behavioral characteristics of infants who fall outside of the healthy, full-term classifications. Studies using infants of diabetic mothers, malnourished infants, and infants withdrawing from narcotics have already been described. Additional studies of

NBAS performance on other groups of special infants have appeared in the literature. Prominent among these are studies of premature infants.

Due to recent clinical and technological advances in the field of neonatology, infants who are born prematurely are surviving in greater numbers than ever before. Infants born at 1,000 or 1,500 grams receiving optimal intensive care have a good chance to survive the neonatal period. The quality of their survival, in terms of physical, cognitive, social, and emotional development has been studied recently by health care providers and developmental psychologists. The NBAS scale, both in its standard form and in several revisions and alternate forms designed to suit the preterm behavioral repertoire, has been used to compare preterm and full-term behavior in the newborn period, and to understand how preterm infant characteristics contribute to early infant-caregiver interactions.

There have been several recent reports in which the NBAS has been used to characterize preterm and full-term functioning in a comparative design. The degree of prematurity of the infants described in these studies varies widely, so comparisons between studies are difficult. One study found gestational age to be the best single predictor of NBAS factor scores (Werner, Bartlett, & Siqueland, 1979). When preterm infants were compared with full-term infants in another study, the preterm group's NBAS scores were significantly lower than the full-term group on three or four *a priori* clusters (Field et al., 1980).

Sostek and her colleagues tested a large number of preterms at time of discharge from the hospital, and compared the factor structure of their test scores to a full-term factor analysis (Sostek et al., 1980). They reported that while the first factor was similar in both samples (an alertness-orientation factor), quieting and not the usual irritability formed the second factor for the preterms. From these data we can conclude that it is possible to distinguish preterm from full-term behavior with the standard NBAS. However, a question remains as to whether the standard NBAS is fully describing the behavioral characteristics displayed by preterm infants. It is quite possible that the NBAS is appropriate to the evaluation of the premature infant as he or she approaches what was the expected date of birth, but that a better description of premature infant behavior requires an instrument more especially designed to relate to the premature.

Als and her colleagues have chosen to develop the Assessment of Premature Infant Behavior (APIB) which involves the basic testing procedures of the NBAS, but provides for a more elaborate scoring of the premature infant's behavior. (See Als & Brazelton, 1979; Als et al., 1980a; 1980b). The APIB also includes additional scales that capture the particular motoric, interactive, regulatory, and physiological responses typically seen in young premature infants.

The NBAS-K has been used in one study to investigate the behavior of the premature infant. Daily (1981) tested 30 premature infants when they reached 1,800 grams and could tolerate a feeding outside of the isolette, and half the sample was tested again at the time of discharge. She found that orientation behavior on the NBAS-K, particularly the modal scores, predicted the weight of the infants at discharge. She also found that the infants generally tolerated the exam well at 1,800 grams.

The NBAS-K has also been used to study the behavior of infants subjected to phototherapy due to neonatal hyperbilirubinemia (Nelson & Horowitz, 1980). Infants with hyperbilirubinemia were tested just before being placed under the bili-lights, just after emerging from the treatment and then again when they were two weeks of age at home. A matched-control sample of normal infants was tested at comparable points. Few significant differences on the NBAS-K were found between the two groups though the treatment group tended to perform more poorly, particularly on the orientation items, than the control group. The magnitude of differences, however, was never large.

Further research with the NBAS, the NBAS-K, and the APIB may help to answer questions about how the behavioral repertoire of the preterm and at risk infant may contribute to early interaction patterns such as those described in Bakeman and Brown (1980), Als and Brazelton (1979) and Horowitz, et al. (in press).

# THE CLINICAL AND EDUCATIONAL USES OF THE NBAS

While neonatal behavioral assessment is of major interest to investigators concerned with trying to understand the variables involved in early development, physicians and psychologists have been interested in determining to what extent the new knowledge of the newborn infant's behavioral competence might be used to help parents and caregivers. Though the efficacy of the NBAS as a clinical aid has not been studied extensively, the NBAS is being used increasingly by medical and psychological personnel to demonstrate to parents what their infants can do. It is not uncommon for portions of the NBAS, particularly the orientation items, to be done in the presence of the mother and father by hospital personnel as part of a program to teach parents about their infants. In one of the few attempts to evaluate the impact of such demonstrations Widmayer and Field (1980) reported that one-month NBAS performance was optimized in a group of infants where the mothers had received an NBAS demonstration and had also been asked to respond to an instrument called the Maternal Assessment of the Behavior of her Infant (MABI).

It is not possible to document what effect the existence of the NBAS has had on medical and pediatric practice in sensitizing physicians to the capabilities of the newborn infant and thus changing how physicians talk to parents about their infants. Anedoctal evidence, however, would suggest that knowledge of the NBAS has affected the way in which physicians interact with parents of newborn infants. Nurses, physical therapists and occupational therapists have all shown an increasing interest in the NBAS. Many of these professionals have sought training in the administration of the scale. Some of this has been influenced by the fact that these individuals are involved in research programs where measuring the behavior of newborn infants is important. The NBAS provides the most complete assessment of the newborn infant's behavioral repertoire. However, the interest has gone beyond the needs of research. Because many of the items on the NBAS are scored using relatively small incremental steps within the 9-point scale, clinicians involved in working with at risk infant populations have found the scale useful in educating themselves as to the nature and direction of behavioral changes that might be expected from therapeutic and intervention programs.

Another clinical use of the NBAS is found when physicians ask for a behavioral assessment to add information to a medical workup of an infant about whom there is concern or question. The NBAS performance thus complements the picture on the physical side and is probably being increasingly used by physicians to influence their prognoses. Daily's (1981) findings that the more behaviorally organized prematures had higher discharge weight may be some indication that being "put together well" on the behavioral side is a factor that influences the physical side. To the extent that behavioral organization provides useful information in the evaluation of the newborn infant it can be exptected to become an increasingly standard source of the assessment of the status of newborn infants.

At the present time, however, the NBAS remains largely a research instrument. Though some of the items on the exam (e.g., the orientation items) may be used informally by physicians and allied health personnel, the exam, in its entirety, has not become a standard clinical tool. To some extent this is because of the time it takes to be trained on the NBAS and the length of the exam if it were to be used on a routine basis. Undoubtedly, further demonstrations of the clinical relevance of the NBAS would change this situation. In the meantime, physicians are generally receptive and interested in NBAS exam results if they are available, because others are testing the infants in their care as part of other ongoing research programs.

## SUMMARY AND CONCLUSIONS

In less than ten years the NBAS and its variations have become the most singularly used standard tool for investigating the behavioral repertoire of the newborn infant and for relating the behavioral repertoire to previous, contemporaneous and future variables. If one accepts the fact that no single assessment is likely to provide a meaningful prediction of later developmental outcome, and if one considers the possibility that there are many interacting variables contributing to the determination of the developmental course, then the NBAS provides us with an important investigatory tool for understanding development. It does this by offering a general assessment of the newborn infant's behavioral repertoire and by supplying, in its scores, a baseline level of behavioral performance from which one may proceed. It is quite possible that behavioral variability on the NBAS instead of, or in addition to, absolute scores or profiles, will prove to be particularly useful in explaining the factors responsible for early development. It is clear that there is important work to be done in determining how best to summarize or cluster the information received from a neonatal assessment. The modal scores available from the NBAS-K as well as some of the new scales for qualifiers in the NBAS-K and those being used by Brazelton and his colleagues may prove to be particularly helpful in the study of the newborn infant. The contribution of the APIB in detailing the special characteristics of the premature infant may provide us with some clues as to the specific factors associated with premature infant behavior that contribute to developmental risk. Further study of the normal population using the NBAS and the NBAS-K should aid us in describing the components of neonatal behavior that contribute to infant-environment interactions which, in turn, influence developmental outcome. All of the evidence to date can be seen as the basis for contributing to a sense of confidence that the NBAS is a useful tool in the study of early infant development. It is likely that information being gathered in ongoing research not reported here and in research of the near future will demonstrate the further utility of the NBAS.

## ACKNOWLEDGMENT

The writing of this chapter and some of the research reported in this chapter was supported in part by the National Institute of Child Health and Human Development in a grant to the senior author (HD 10608) and in part by the Bureau of the Education of the Handicapped through the Institute for Early Childhood Research at the University of Kansas (300–77–0308). The authors wish to acknowledge the help of Ellen Ganon in the preparation of this manuscript.

## REFERENCES

Ainsworth, M., & Wittig, B. Attachment and exploratory behavior of one-year olds in a strange situation. In B. M. Foss (Ed.), *Determinants of Infant Behavior*, (Vol. 4). New York: Barnes & Noble, 1969.

Als, H. Assessing an assessment: Conceptual considerations, methodological issues and a perspective on the future of the Neonatal Behavioral Assessment Scale. In A. J. Sameroff (Ed.), Organization & stability of new born behavior: A commentary on the Brazelton Neonatal Behavioral Assessment Scale. *Monographs of the Society for Research in Child Development*, 1978, *43*, 14–28.

Als, H., & Brazelton, T. B. Assessment of behavioral organization in a preterm and fullterm infant. Paper presented at the Meeting of the American Academy of Child Psychiatry, Atlanta, Ga.: 1979.

Als, H., Landers, C., Tronick, E., & Brazelton, T. B. Caesarian section: Differential impact on newborn behavior. Paper presented at the International Conference on Infant Studies, New Haven, Ct., April, 1980.

Als, H., Lester, B. M., Tronick, E., & Brazelton, T. B. Toward a research instrument for the assessment of preterm infants' behavior (APIB). In H. E. Fitzgerald, B. M. Lester, & M. W.

Yogman (Eds.), *Theory and Research in Behavioral Pediatrics* (Vol. 1). New York: Plenum Press, 1980a.

Als, H., Lester, B. M., Tronick, E., & Brazelton, T. B. Manual for the assessment of preterm infant behavior (APIB). In H. E. Fitzgerald, B. M. Lester, & M. W. Yogman (Eds.), *Theory and Research in Behavioral Pediatrics* (Vol. 1). New York: Plenum Press, 1980b.

Apgar, V. A proposal for a new method of evaluation of the newborn infant. *Current Researches in Anesthesia and Analgesia,* 1953, *32,* 260-267.

Bakemann, R., & Brown, J. V. Early interaction: Consequences for social & mental development at three years. *Child Development,* 1980, *51,* 437-447.

Brackbill, Y., Kanes, J., Manniello, R. L., & Abrahamson, D. Obstetric meperidine usage and assessment of neonatal status. *Anesthesiology,* 1974, *40,* 116-120.

Brazelton, T. B. *Neonatal Behavioral Assessment Scale.* London: William Heinemann Medical Books, 1973.

Brazelton, T. B., Tryphonopoulou, Y., & Lester, B. M. A comparative study of the behavior of Greek neonates. *Pediatrics,* 1979, *63,* 279-285.

Buddin, B. J. Mother-infant interaction & individual differences at one month. M. A. thesis in preparation, University of Kansas, 1981.

Coll, C. G., Sepkoski, C., & Lester, B. M. Cross-cultural study of teenage childbearing. Paper presented at American Psychological Association Meeting, 1978, Toronto, Canada.

Coll, C. G., Sepkowski, S., & Lester, B. M. Cultural correlates of neonatal behavior. *Developmental Psychobiology,* In Press.

Daily, D. Performance of premature infants on the NBAS-K. University of Kansas Master's Thesis, In Preparation, 1981.

Devries, M., & Super, C. M. Contextual influences on the Neonatal Behavioral Assessment Scale and implications for its cross-cultural use. In A. J. Sameroff (Ed.), Organization and stability in newborn behavior: A Commentary on the Neonatal Behavioral Assessment Scale. *Monographs of the Society for Research in Development,* 1978, *43,* 92-101.

Dubowitz, L. M. S., Dubowitz, B., & Goldberg, C. Clinical assessment of gestational age in the newborn infant. *Journal of Pediatrics,* 1970, *77,* 1.

Field, T. M., Widmayer, S. M., Stringer, S., & Ignatoff, E. Teenage, lowerclass, black mothers and their preterm infants: An intervention and development followup. *Child Development,* 1980, *51,* 426-436.

Field, T. M., & Widmayer, S. Developmental following in infants delivered by Ceasarian Section & general anaesthesia. *Infant Behavior and Development,* 1980, *3,* 253-264.

Freedman, D. G., & Freedman, N. C. Behavioral differences between Chinese—American & European-American newborns. *Nature,* 1969, *224,* 1227.

Horowitz, F. D. Intervention and its effects on early development: What model is appropriate? In R. Turner, & W. H. Reese (Eds.), *Life Span Developmental Psychology: Intervention.* New York: Academic Press, 1980, 235-248.

Horowitz, F. D., Ashton, J., Culp, R. E., Gaddis, E., Levin, S., & Reichmann, R. The effects of obstetrical medication on the behavior of Israeli newborns and some comparisons with American and Uruguayan infants. *Child Development,* 1977, *48,* 607-623.

Horowitz, F. D., & Brazelton, T. B. Research with the Brazelton Neonatal Scale. In T. B. Brazelton (Ed.), *Neonatal Behavioral Assessment Scale.* London: William Heinemann Books, Ltd., 1973, 48-54.

Horowitz, F. D., Linn, P. L., Buddin, B. J., & Smith, C. Neonatal assessment: Evaluating the potential for plasticity. In T. B. Brazelton (Ed.) *New Approaches to Developmental Screening of Infants* (In Press).

Horowitz, F. D., Linn, P. L., Smith, C., & Buddin, B. J. (Maternal responsivity in relation to developmental outcome. Paper presented at Biennial Meeting of the Society for Research in Child Development, Boston, 1981.

Horowitz, F. D., Sullivan, J. W., & Byrne, J. M. *An Atlas of the Behavior of the Normal Newborn Infant*, In Preparation.

Horowitz, F. D., Sullivan, J. W., & Linn, P. L. Stability & instability in newborn behavior: The quest for elusive threads. In A. Sameroff (Ed.), The Brazelton Neonatal Behavioral Assessment Scale: A Commentary. *Monographs of the Society for Research in Child Development*, 1978, *43*, 29–45.

Knobloch, H., & Pasamanick, B. *Gesell & Amatruda's Development of Normal & Abnormal Neuropsychologic Development in Infancy & Early Childhood*. New York: Harper & Row, 1974.

Kron, R. E., Finnegan, L. P., Kaplan, S. L., Litt, M., & Phoenix, M. D. The assesment of behavioral change in infants undergoing narcotic withdrawal: Comparative data from clinical & objective methods. *Addictive Diseases*, 1975, *2*, 257–275.

Lancioni, G. A study of the stability & structure of the NBAS-K over the first month of life. Unpublished Ph.D. dissertation, the University of Kansas, 1978.

Lancioni, G., Horowitz, F. D., & Sullivan, J. NBAS-K: I. A study of its stability & structure over the first month of life. *Infant Behavior and Development*, 1980a, *3*, 341–359.

Lancioni, G., Horowitz, F. D., & Sullivan, J. NBAS-K: II. Reinforcement value of the infant's behavior. *Infant Behavior and Development*, 1980b, *3*, 361–366.

Lester, B. M. The continuity of change in infant development. Paper presented at Biennial Meeting of the Society for Research in Child Development, Boston, Mass.: 1981.

Lester, B. M. A synergistic process approach to the study of prenatal malnutrition. *International Journal of Behavioral Development*, 1979, *2*, 377–393.

Lester, B. M., & Brazelton, T. B. Cross-cultural assessment of neonatal behavior. In D. Wagner & H. Stevenson (Eds.), *Cultural Perspectives on Child Development*. San Francisco, CA.: W. H. Freeman & Co., in press.

Lester, B. M., Als, H., & Brazelton, T. B. Regional obstetric anesthesia and newborn behavior. A Reanalysis Towards Synergistic Effects. Unpublished manuscript, 1980.

Lewis, M., & Rosenblum, L. A. (Eds.) *Interaction, Conversation, & the Development of Language*. New York: John Wiley & Sons, 1977.

Linn, P. L. Newborn Environments and Mother-Infant Interactions. Unpublished dissertation, University of Kansas, 1979.

Miller, H. C., & Hassanein, K. Diagnosis of impaired fetal growth in newborn infants. *Pediatrics*, 1971, *48*, 511–522.

Nelson, C., & Horowitz, F. D. The short-term behavioral sequelae of neonatal jaundice (Hyperbilirubinemia) & phototherapy. Submitted for publication, 1980.

Osofsky, J. D., & Danzger, B. Relationships between neonatal characteristics and mother-infant interaction. *Developmental Psychology*, 1974, *10*, 124–130.

Prechtl, H., & Beintema, D. *The Neurological Examination of the Full Term Newborn Infant*. London: Wm. Heinemann Books, 1964.

Rosenblith, J. F. The Graham/Rosenblith behavioral examination for newborns: Prognostic value & procedural issues. In J. D. Osofsky (Ed.), *Handbook of Infant Development*. New York: John Wiley, 1979, 216–249.

Sameroff, A. J. Organization and stability of newborn behavior: A commentary on the Brazelton Neonatal Behavior Assessment Scale. *Monographs of the Society in Research in Child Development*, 1978, *43*, (Serial No. 177).

Sameroff, A., & Chandler, M. Reproductive risk & the continuum of caretaking casualty. In F. D. Horowitz (Ed.), *Review of Child Development Research* (Vol. 4). Chicago, University of Chicago Press, 1975, 187–244.

Self, P. A. Individual differences in auditory & visual responsiveness in infants from three days to six weeks of age. Unpublished doctoral dissertation, University of Kansas, 1971.

Self, P. A., & Horowitz, F. D. Neonatal Assessment: An overview. In J. D. Osofsky (Eds.), *Handbook of Infant Development*. New York: Wiley, 1979, 126-164.

Soule, A. B., Standley, K., Copano, S. A., & Davis, M. Clinical uses of the Brazelton Neonatal Scale. *Pediatrics,* 1974, *54,* 583-586.

Sostek, A. M., & Anders, T. F. Relationships among the Brazeltons Neonatal Scale, Bayley Infant Scales, and early temperament. *Child Development,* 1977, *18,* 320-323.

Sostek, A. M., Davitt, M. K., Renzi, J., Born, W. S., & Kiely, S. C. Behavioral organization in preterm newborns. Unpublished paper, 1980.

Strauss, M. E., Lessen-Firestone, J. K., Starr, R. H., Jr., & Ostrea, E. M., Jr. Behavior of narcotics-addicted newborns. *Child Development,* 1975, *46,* 887-893.

Strauss, M. E., Starr, R. H., Ostrea, E. M., Chavez, C. J., & Stryker, J. C. Behavioral concomitants of prenatal addiction to narcotics. *Journal of Pediatrics,* 1976, *89,* 842-846.

Super, C. M. Behavioral development in infancy. In R. L. Munroe, R. H. Munroe, & B. B. Whiting (Eds.), *Handbook of Cross-Cultural Human Development.* New York: Garland Press, in press.

Thompson, R. J., Cappleman, M. W., & Zeitschel, K. A. Neonatal behavior of infants of adolescent mothers. *Developmental Medicine and Child Neurology,* 1979, *21,* 474-482.

Tronick, E., Wise, S., Als, H., Adamson, L., Scanlon, J., & Brazelton, T. B. Regional obstetric anesthesia and newborn behavior: Effect over the first ten days of life. *Pediatrics,* 1976, *58,* 94-100.

Vaughn, B. E., Crichton, L., & Egeland, B. Individual differences in qualities of caregiving during the first six months of life: Antecedents in maternal and infant behavior during the newborn period. Unpublished manuscript, University of Minnesota, 1981.

Vaughn, B., Taraldson, B., Crichton, L., & Egeland, B. Relationships between neonatal behavior organization and infant behavior during the first year of life. *Infant Behavior and Development,* 1980, *3,* 47-66.

Waters, E., Vaughn, B. E., & Egeland, B. R. Individual differences in infant-mother attachment relationships at age one: Antecedents in neonatal behavior in an urban, economically disadvantaged sample. *Child Development,* 1980, *51,* 208-216.

Widmayer, S., & Field, T. M. Effects of Brazelton demonstrations on early interactions of preterm infants and their teenage mothers. *Infant Behavior and Development,* 1980, *3,* 78-89.

Werner, J. S., Bartlett, A. W., & Siqueland, E. R. Assessment of preterm and fullterm infant behavior. Unpublished manuscript, Brown University, 1979.

Woodson, R. H., & Da Costa-Woodson, E. M. Covariates of analgesia in a clinical sample and their effect on the relationship between analgesia and infant behavior. *Infant Behavior and Development,* 1980, *3,* 205-213.

Yogman, M. W., Cole, P., & Als, H. The behavior of newborns of diabetic mothers. Paper presented to American Pediatrics Society—Society for Pediatric Research, New York, 1978.

Zeskind, P. S. Behavioral demensions and cry sounds of infants of differential fetal growth. *Infant Behavior and Development,* 1981, *4,* In Press.

# SPECIFIC LANGUAGE IMPAIRMENT IN CHILDREN

Rachel E. Stark and Paula Tallal

## CLASSIFICATION OF LANGUAGE DISORDERS IN CHILDREN

Specific language impairment in children, sometimes referred to as developmental dysphasia, is defined by exclusion, that is, as a language disorder occurring in the absence of hearing impairment, mental retardation or severe behavioral or emotional disorder (Benton, 1964). Thus, the definition is based upon a traditional view of the classification of language disorders in children and, ultimately, upon a medical model. It has been assumed that children with language disorders may be assigned to treatment groups on the basis of this model, that is, according to presumed etiology.

Advances in Developmental and Behavioral Pediatrics, vol. 3, pages 257–271
Copyright © 1982 by JAI Press Inc.
All rights of reproduction in any form reserved.
ISBN: 0-89232-223-3

In practice, the traditional classification of language disorders in children has not been a useful one. While the classification system has a certain face validity, it does not segregate children with respect to variables that are related in any useful way to treatment options. This failure may be related to the presence of multiple problems in language impaired children and to the current lack of understanding of the etiologies of language impairments in children. The classification may not have a valid basis.

## STATISTICAL TEST OF DIAGNOSTIC CATEGORIES OF CHILDHOOD LANGUAGE DISORDERS

Rosenthal, Eisenson, and Luckau (1972) employed a statistical analysis approach in addressing this problem. They selected 82 children with significant language impairment from their case load who could be assigned *a priori* to the following diagnostic categories:

1.   mentally retarded
2.   severe hearing impairment
3.   neurologically handicapped/aphasic
4.   oral apraxic
5.   dysarthric
6.   maturational lag (organic)
7.   autistic

They then performed a cluster analysis, employing 32 variables that were routinely included in the evaluation of these children. Some of these were medical history or medical assessment variables, for example, history of pre- and perinatal CNS insult and EEG abnormalities; other variables related to the psychological and social functioning of the child and to speech motor abilities.

It was expected that the cluster analysis would group the children according to the *a priori* classification scheme, that is, the scheme employed in their initial selection. The results of the procedure, however, were quite different. Only two clusters were formed; one including mentally retarded and autistic children, the other including children with severe hearing impairment, aphasia and maturational lag. These results were supported by additional chi square analyses of the distributions according to the above categories.

In addition, a discriminant function analysis was carried out in order to determine which of the 32 evaluation variables best differentiated the two groups identified by the cluster analysis. It was found that the major basis on which the two clusters of children differed was that of general performance on intelligence tests as well as performance on intelligence scale subtests. Other variables such as presence of hearing impairment, auditory discrimination measures, and medical history variables did not differentiate the two groups.

# DEFINING SPECIFIC LANGUAGE IMPAIRMENT IN CHILDREN

## Specific Language Deficit vs. Hearing Impairment

The results of the Rosenthal et al. (1972) study, although they do not support the utility of the original classification scheme, suggest that specific language deficit in children may be differentiated from language disorders associated with mental retardation and autistic-like behaviors on the basis of standard language and intelligence test results. Specific language deficit (dysphasia) was not differentiated, on the basis of the 32 variables employed, from language delay (maturational lag) or hearing impairment.

Hearing impairment was defined on the basis of hearing threshold for the pure tones in the frequency range important for speech (500 Hz to 2KHs). The average threshold for the frequencies 500, 1K, and 2KHz in the better ear, and *also* the average of the two best (lowest) thresholds in the better ear, was required to be 50 dB or greater in children classed as hearing impaired. Thus, a considerable range of hearing impairment must have been subsumed under this category as well as different types of hearing impairment. It is probable that the children so classified would form a heterogeneous group. Children who present with language impairment in the absence of hearing loss or mental retardation are also likely to form a heterogeneous group. In the Rosenthal et al. (1972) study, for example, children with neurologic deficits and children with maturational lags were both included. Thus, it would not be surprising if such variables as laterality, delayed motor development, and auditory discrimination failed to discriminate between hearing impaired and dysphasic children whose selection was based on such broadly defined categories.

Other investigators have pointed out that hearing impaired and dysphasic children may resemble one another quite closely in auditory processing abilities, language comprehension and language production. These similarities, if substantiated, would offer support for the hypothesis that specific language impairment or dysphasia (SLI) in children is a manifestation of auditory processing deficit. It has been stated repeatedly in the literature that children with specific language deficits present auditory processing disorders (Eisenson, 1966; Hardy, 1965; Myklebust, 1954; Benton, 1966; Tallal & Piercy, 1974; and others). The affected children may give inconsistent responses to both speech and nonspeech sounds. They may show a lack of interest in or a selective inattention to speech, in spite of normal peripheral hearing sensitivity. The nature of the relationship between language impairment and auditory disorders, however, is not clear. It could be approached by considering different types of dysphasia that have been identified in children.

## Congenital vs. Developmental Dysphasia

The term dysphasic suggests that language impairment in the children so classified is related to neurologic deficit or lesion. Clearly, this is the case of children with acquired aphasia. Benton (1964) suggests that in children with developmental dysphasia, neurologic lesions are also frequently present. It is presumed that these lesions are congenital in nature and, because of the inconsistent and aberrant manner in which auditory input, particularly speech, is dealt with by dysphasic children (Benton, 1966; Gordon & Taylor, 1964; Ewing, 1967; Myklebust, 1954), it is believed that extensive bilateral damage to the central auditory system must be present. Bilateral lesions are implicated because otherwise, the intact auditory cortex and subcortical structures, given their plasticity in the very young child, should be able to take over the functions proper to the damaged structures on the affected side. A number of the conditions associated with neurologic damage to the fetus and the newborn infant are known to be capable of inflicting bilateral auditory system lesions. These conditions include asphyxia neonatorum, kernicterus, and maternal viral infections.

Only one case of congenital aphasia has come to post mortem examination thus far but, in that case, atrophy of both white and gray matter over large areas of both cerebral hemispheres was present. The auditory radiations to the temporal lobes on both sides were affected and there was retrograde degeneration of the medial geniculate nuclei bilaterally (Landau, Goldstein, & Kleffner, 1960).

Children with less severe dysphasia or specific language impairment may be less likely to present a history of congenital neurologic insult. It has been suggested that the language impairment in these children may be familial in nature and that genetic factors may have a prominent etiologic role (Ingram, 1960). It is assumed that, in these children, the development of different groups of nuclei in the central auditory system or of different portions of the auditory or auditory association cortex may be affected (Eisenson, 1972). Geschwind (1978) and Galaburda, et al. (1978) have suggested that inferior language abilities may be associated with anatomical differences in the size and structure of certain portions of the left hemisphere. Specifically language impaired (SLI) children may be at one extreme of a continuum representing the normal variation in language abilities rather than members of a population that is quite different from normal.

Thus, it has been suggested that specific language impairments in children that are present from the earliest stages of language development may be related to neurologic lesions sustained before or immediately after birth, or they may be related to differences in central nervous system structure or functioning which are possibly familial in nature. The term ''congenital'' has been applied to the former type and the term "developmental" to the latter type (Chase, 1972), although these terms are not, by definition, mutually exclusive.

The "congenital" type has generally been described as more severe than the "developmental" type. The distinction is reminiscent of the classification of mental retardation as exogenous or endogenous. The central nervous system insult, anomaly, or difference that is presumed to be present in children with specific language impairment is thought to be localized in the language areas of the left hemisphere and to be characterized by auditory processing disorders. A possible definition, then, of specific language impairment might be a "language impairment secondary to an auditory processing deficit."

## PERCEPTUAL FUNCTIONING IN CHILDREN WITH SPECIFIC LANGUAGE IMPAIRMENT

### Studies of Auditory Processing

In a number of investigations conducted over the past 15 years, auditory processing deficits in children with language and learning disabilities have been described in greater detail. These include auditory temporal integration, sequencing of speech-like and non-speech sounds, and serial memory for speech-like and non-speech sounds (Aten & Davis, 1968; Rosenthal et al., 1972; Swisher & Hirsh, 1972; Lowe & Campbell, 1965; Tallal & Piercy, 1973; Tallal & Piercy, 1974; Golick, 1977).

Tallal and Piercy (1973, 1974) showed that a group of children with developmental dysphasia age 7½ to 9 years, were significantly impaired in discrimination of auditory stimuli that (1) were presented rapidly; that is, separated by very brief intervals or with no interval separating them; and (2) were characterized by rapid changes: for example, changes in energy concentrations taking place over a very short period of time. Their dysphasic subjects demonstrated these impairments in their responses to both speech-like and non-speech stimuli. Discrimination of speech-like signals improved when transitions within them were extended, that is, made to take place over a longer period of time. On the basis of this work, Tallal and Piercy (1974) believed that auditory sequencing and serial memory deficits in dysphasic children might be secondary to their auditory discrimination deficits. They found that their subjects had no difficulty in discriminating or sequencing rapidly presented visual stimuli. Tallal and Piercy believed that the auditory deficits they demonstrated in their subjects were primary deficits and that the relationship of these deficits to language impairment was a causal one.

There is, however, a general lack of agreement with respect to the relationship of auditory processing deficits with language impairment. Rees (1974, 1981) has suggested that children with delayed language may show speech-processing disorders as a result of their language deficits, rather than as their primary or more basic deficit. She has also suggested that the primary deficit in children with specific language impairment may be a subtle cognitive or representational deficit, not an auditory deficit. (See also Morehead and Ingram, 1973.) It has further been shown that auditory processing deficits, in particular those related to attentional deficits and failure on vigilance tasks, may be present in hyperactive children who do not have a language disorder (Ludlow, 1981).

## Study of Perceptual and Motor Functioning

A comprehensive study of both perceptual and motor disorders in children receiving treatment for specific language impairment (SLI) was recently conducted by Stark and Tallal (1980). The objectives of this study were to determine:

1.  whether or not the SLI children were significantly inferior to the normal children in auditory or visual perceptual functioning;
2.  whether or not the SLI children were significantly inferior to the normal children in gross or fine motor skills;
3.  whether perceptual deficits, if present in the SLI children, were confined to the auditory modality or involved both the auditory and the visual modality, and whether or not they included deficits in cross modal integration; and
4.  whether or not there was a relationship between patterns of perceptual and motor deficits, if present, and patterns of language impairment in SLI children.

*Subjects.* Thirty-five children with SLI were compared with thirty-eight normally developing children. The children in these two groups were 5 to 8½ years in age and were matched with respect to age, performance IQ on the WPPSI (Wechsler, 1963) or WISC-R (Wechsler, 1974), race, and socioeconomic status as measured by the Hollingshead Scale (1957). The children in both groups had normal hearing sensitivity, normal oral motor functioning as determined by a speech/language pathologist, and a performance IQ between 85 and 130. Children with a history of neurologic impairment or indications in neurologic assessment of CNS lesion and children with a history of severe emotional or behavioral disorder were excluded from the study. Additional criteria emloyed in subject selection were as follows.

Normal control subjects were required to:

a.  have a level of language development commensurate with their performance mental age (MAP) and chronological age (CA); that is, their language skills had to be at a level no more than six months behind their MAP and their CA;

b.  have a level of reading skill on standardized reading tests commensurate with their CA and full scale mental age (MAF) that is, their reading skills had to be at a level no more than six months behind their MAF and CA; and
c.  be without speech errors other than those developmental misarticulations which might be expected on the basis of their chronological age.

Children with language impairment were required to:

a.  have a "language age" at least one year below their MAP. The "language age" was derived from a composite score representing both expressive and receptive language skills. In addition these subjects had to have a receptive language age at least six months behind performance mental age (MAP) and an expressive language age at least one year behind MAP;
b.  have a level of reading skill no more than six months below their "language age"; and
c.  have a level of speech articulation skill no more than six months below their "expressive language age."

Further detail with respect to subject selection is given in Stark and Tallal (1981). Demographic and standard test data for the two groups of subjects are shown in Table 1. This table shows that the two groups of subjects were significantly different from one another in verbal IQ (and hence in full-scale IQ also) and on all speech and language measures.

*Methods.*  A battery of experimental tests were given to the children in the two subject groups. This battery included experimental auditory and visual perceptual

*Table 1.* Description of Demographic Variables for the Normal and Language Impaired Children Included in the Present Study.

| Variables | Normal | Language Delayed |
|---|---|---|
| Number of Subjects | 47 | 39 |
| Mean CA (months) | 75 (SD ± 14.2) | 78 (SD ± 15.6) |
| Verbal IQ | 110 (SD ± 13.15) | 82 (SD ± 11.4) |
| Performance IQ | 105 (SD ± 11.10) | 100 (SD ± 8.8) |
| Full Scale IQ | 108 (SD ± 12.43) | 90 (SD ± 9.0) |
| Sex | 23 M, 24 F | 28 M, 11 F |
| Race | 40 white, 7 black | 30 white, 9 black |
| SES (Hollingshead Scale) | 3.3 (SD ± 1.6) | 3.4 (SD ± 1.8) |
| Lang. Dev. History | 44 normal, 3 delayed | 29 normal, 10 delayed |
| Maternal Education | 35 high school + | 28 high school + |
|  | 12 high school − | 11 high school − |

tests, tests of oral motor and oral stereognostic functioning and an experimental neurodevelopmental test battery. These are described below.

*Experimental Perceptual Tests—Auditory and Visual Modality.*    In this battery a series of test items was constructed and applied in both the auditory and the visual modality. These tests were referred to as the Repetition Test Procedure. In each test item a stimulus pair was presented which might be auditory, visual, or both auditory and visual (cross-modal) in nature. These pairs were presented in binary sequences or series. The child was required to press one of two panels on a response box in response to each of the elements of the stimulus pairs. Each test item included a number of subtests that were always given in the same order. First the child was taught to respond appropriately by pushing one button or the other in a Detection Subtest. An Association Subtest, in which the child was required to respond to the elements of the stimulus pair presented in a random series one at a time was administered. These subtests were followed by a Sequencing Subtest, in which the elements were presented in random order two at a time, and a Serial Memory Subtest, in which they were presented in random order three to seven at a time. Special sequencing subtests in which the rate of transition from a consonant (C) to a vowel (V) within a computer-generated CV syllable pair or the interval between the two stimuli presented was varied were included in some test items as well as the standard Sequencing Subtest. Those subtests that included brief interstimulus intervals were referred to as Rate Processing Subtests. If the children failed the standard Sequencing Subtest they were, in some test items, given a Same/Different Discrimination Subtest as a means of exploring the reasons for failure at the sequencing level.

Some of the test items were known from previous work (Tallal, 1976; Tallal & Piercy, 1973, 1974) to vary in level of difficulty. Difficulty of a task was thought to be related to (1) number of elements presented within a binary series, (2) the duration of the stimulus elements and/or the interstimulus interval within a subtest, and (3) the rate of change of important parameters within the stimulus elements.

The stimulus pairs presented included complex tones, vowels, computer-generated consonant-vowel (CV) and consonant-vowel-consonant (CVC) syllables, words, lights of different hues, letters (graphemes) and nonletter two-dimensional shapes, and tone and light combinations. The test items were presented in random order except that a training test item (with either long-duration complex tones or light flashes as the stimulus pair) was always presented first.

*Oral Motor and Perceptual Tests.*    In this battery a test of Isolated and Sequenced Volitional Oral Movements (Yoss & Darley, 1974), a test of rapid word production and a test of rapid syllable production (Fletcher, 1972) were included. A test of tactile extinction involving unilateral or bilateral stimulation of the margins of the tongue and two tests of oral stereognostic perception employing three-dimensional forms prepared by the National Institute for Dental Research were also included.

*Neurodevelopmental Test Battery.* The neurodevelopmental battery included tests of motor control and coordination, balance and station, tactile perception, and laterality relationships. These tests were in some cases modified versions of tests from published batteries. They are described in detail in Johnston et al. (1981). The test groups were presented in random order and were administered and scored systematically.

*Results.* In the subject-selection phase of the project, 132 children were referred as potential language-impaired subjects. Of these, three were found to be hearing impaired and 50 were found to be borderline or below normal in their nonverbal cognitive abilities. It was thought that some of these 50 children were neurologically impaired. Only one of those children referred to the project who had a nonverbal IQ of more than 85 was found to have a neurologic lesion or to present hard neurologic signs. This finding suggests that the majority of children presently receiving intervention in classes or programs for SLI in public school systems may show developmental lags in language functioning rather than dysphasias secondary to neurologic insult. Demographic and IQ test data are presented in Table 1 (see p. 154).

*Medical and Family History Variables.* More detailed medical, family, and social history information is presented in Tables 2 through 5. These data indicate that the normal and SLI children did not differ from one another significantly in physical growth measurements (height, weight, or head circumference); birth and medical history variables; or family history variables, with the exception of the history of achievement of language milestones in the children themselves. The data showed that the SLI children were significantly delayed in comparison with the normal children.

It is hardly surprising that the two groups of children did not differ with respect

*Table 2.* Mean Percentile Rank for Height, Weight, and Head Circumference for the Two Groups of Children.

| Physical Measurements | Normal | | Language Impaired | |
|---|---|---|---|---|
| | Mean | SD | Mean | SD |
| Percentile rank for | | | | |
| Height | 57.70 | 23.06 | 67.33 | 29.73 |
| Weight | 59.13 | 29.32 | 64.20 | 31.08 |
| Head Circumference | 62.11 | 22.06 | 62.88 | 23.96 |

*Table 3.*   Birth History Variables Reported for the Normal and Language
Impaired Children.

|  | Normal | | Language Impaired | |
|---|---|---|---|---|
|  | Mean | SD | Mean | SD |
| Maternal age in years | 26.53 | 5.11 | 25.35 | 6.79 |
| Gestational age in weeks | 39.84 | 1.98 | 39.80 | 1.53 |
| Birth weight in pounds | 7.00 | 1.49 | 6.97 | 1.22 |
| Gravid | 2.56 | 1.65 | 2.11 | 1.86 |
| Para | 1.75 | 1.50 | 1.55 | 2.01 |
| Abortions | .34 | .64 | .23 | .62 |
| Birth order | 2.32 | 1.60 | 1.97 | 1.58 |
| Siblings (incl. subjects) | 2.57 | 1.35 | 2.43 | 1.52 |

to incidence of perinatal CNS insult, seizures in infancy, or significant illness, since children suspected of having neurologic impairment were excluded from the study. It *is,* however, surprising that the two groups did not differ with respect to a family history of late development of language. It is true that over 50 percent of the SLI children had family members who were reported as delayed in language, but the families of one-third of the normal children gave this history also. It might also have been expected, on the basis of reports in the literature (for example, Ferry, 1981), that the SLI children would have presented a history of left handedness or ambidexterity more significantly often than the normal children. It may be that such a finding is more characteristic of SLI children whose language impairment is clearly related to CNS insult.

*Experimental Perceptual Tests—Temporal Processing.*   The results of the experimental tests of auditory processing confirmed those of previous studies. The SLI children had more difficulty than the normal children on all tests in which rapid changes occurred within an element, two elements followed one another in rapid succession, or longer series (three to seven elements) were presented. They did not have difficulty when single steady-state elements were presented, even if these elements were, themselves, very brief. They *did* have difficulty if rapid changes were present within singly presented elements. In the auditory modality, the effects of rapid changes within an element, of brief duration intervals between successive elements, and of the length of series of elements were more important in relation to impaired performance than was the effect of the verbal vs. nonverbal (syllables vs. tones) nature of the stimuli presented. The results suggested that a basic impairment in auditory temporal processing was present, affecting the ability of the SLI children to discriminate rapidly changing cues. Such cues are highly characteristic of the speech signal. The results also

*Table 4.* Frequency of Occurrence of Medical History Variables for the Normal and Language Impaired Children.

|  | *Normal Group N=38* | *Language Impaired Group N=35* |
|---|---|---|
| Prenatal insult | 9 | 7 |
| Perinatal insult | 10 | 10 |
| Postnatal insult | 2 | 3 |
| Delay in motor dev. | 0 | 2 |
| Poor general health | 0 | 1 |
| Significant illness | 6 | 6 |
| Febrile seizures infancy | 3 | 2 |
| Presently on medication | 3 | 7 |
| Stigmata (including short digits, epicanthal folds, etc.) | 15* | 15* |

*Missing data points

suggested that their ability to discriminate real words incorporating these cues might be impaired (Tallal et al., 1980).

These results appeared to substantiate the earlier findings of Tallal and Piercy (1974). They also provided additional support for the hypothesis that there is a relationship between auditory temporal processing and language disorders in children.

*Table 5.* Frequency of Occurrence of Social and Family History Variables for the Normal and Language Impaired Children.

|  | *Normal Group N=38* | *Language Impaired Group N=35* |
|---|---|---|
| Poor social adjustment |  |  |
| Home | 1 | 2 |
| School | 1 | 2 |
| Poor progress in school | 1 | 3 |
| Repeated absences from school | 2 | 1 |
| Delayed development |  |  |
| Words | 0 | 22 |
| Phrases | 4 | 21 |
| Sentences | 2 | 28 |
| Family history of speech or language problems | 11 | 17 |
| Left handedness or ambidexterity | 7 | 11 |
| Change in handedness | 6 | 3 |
| Family history of left handedness or ambidexterity | 11 | 13 |

It was also found, however, that the SLI children were inferior to the normal children in their processing of visual and cross-modal stimuli. The effects of rapid presentation (brief duration of the intervals between stimuli) and of series length were again found to be significant. There were no changing parameters within the elements of visual and cross-modal stimulus pairs; therefore the effects of rapid transitions in visual stimuli cannot be assessed from these data. Responses to visual verbal stimuli were not significantly different from responses to nonverbal visual or nonverbal cross-modal stimuli.

The findings with respect to the visual modality differ from those reported by Tallal and Piercy (1974) who found the SLI children did not show impairment in the processing of rapidly presented visual stimuli. This difference in the results of the earlier and of the later study may be related to the age of the subjects included. The subjects of the earlier study were older (7 to 9 years) than those of the later study, and there is some evidence from both studies that temporal perceptual processing in the visual and the auditory modality, as measured by the Repetition Test Procedure, improves with age. This improvement could be taking place at different rates in the two sensory modalities in SLI children.

These results have been reported in greater detail in Stark and Tallal (1980) and Tallal et al. (1980). In summary, the findings indicated that temporal processing deficits were characteristic of SLI children but were not confined to the auditory modality. A more general immaturity or developmental lag, not confined to the central auditory system, might be implicated.

*Oral Motor and Perceptual Tests.*    Performance on the test of Isolated Volitional Oral Movement was not significantly different for the normal and the SLI children. There were no significant differences between groups in performance on an oral tactile (tactile extinction) or the oral stereognostic tests. There were significant differences, however, on all tests of sequenced oral movements, that is, on the Sequenced Volitional Oral Movement Test (a nonspeech test), and on the tests of rapid production of series of monosyllablic and multisyllablic words and the tests of rapid production of series of nonsense syllables.

*Neurodevelopmental Test Battery.*    The results of the neurodevelopmental examination indicated that the normal and the SLI children were not significantly different in their performance on tests of balance and station, touching finger-to-nose, postures assumed in running, associated or overflow movements observed on tongue protrusion, visual tracking, finger opposition, or diadochokinetic rate of hand movement. The SLI children were not less accurate or precise in their movements on these tasks. In addition, the two groups did not differ on measures of lateral dominance. They did differ however, in *rate* of movement. The SLI children hopped, touched fingers-to-thumb, performed on a diadochokinetic rate of hand movement task, and placed coins in a box, all at a significantly slower rate than normal children. They also performed on a simple visual cancellation (paper-and-pencil marking) task at a slower than normal rate. This rate of movement difference was observed whether the movements were carried out on the right or left side of the body, on the preferred or the nonpreferred side, and for both gross and fine movements. The SLI children also showed significantly more choreiform/athetotiform movements on the left side than did the normal children, when they were asked to hold their arms outstretched, their hands pronated. No differences between groups in onset and duration on these movements were observed on this task on the right side.

In addition, the SLI children made significantly more errors than the normal children on a number of tests of tactile perception in the neurodevelopmental battery. They had difficulty on a test of double simultaneous stimulation, in which widely separated surfaces were touched by the examiner (face and hand) on either side of the body; on a task in which the child had to identify two fingers on the same hand that were touched by the examiner; and on tests of graphesthesia in which figures were drawn on the child's palm. These findings suggested that for the SLI children, difficulty on a simultaneous tactile stimulation task might represent a special case of temporal processing deficit.

Finally the SLI children had significantly greater difficulty than the normals on verbal right-left discrimination tasks (for example, "Show me your right ear; touch your left ear with your right hand.") It was thought that this difficulty might be a linguistic one, reflecting their language impairment, rather than a true right-left discrimination problem. These results are reported in greater detail in Johnston et al. (1981).

## SUMMARY AND CONCLUSIONS

The results of this study indicate that a group of children with SLI may be identified from among larger groups of children demonstrating below normal language abilities. SLI children may be differentiated from children who are hearing impaired by audiological testing, and from children presenting overall retardation by means of standard speech, language, and intelligence tests. SLI children do not, however, form a homogeneous group with respect to speech articulation and receptive and expressive language abilities.

The results also suggest that SLI children do not frequently present with a frank history of neurologic impairment or with hard neurologic signs. Instead, they show a specific pattern of developmental delay on neurodevelopmental examination and perceptual testing. This pattern is characterized by delayed development of temporal processing in auditory and visual perception, difficulty in perceiving simultaneous stimulation in the tactile modality, and delay in the development of ability to sequence motor movements rapidly. The children are not, as a group, poorly coordinated in gross or fine movement. Their balance and station are unaffected except that minor athetotiform and choreiform movements appear when they are asked to maintain a fixed posture of the arms and hands.

These findings are consistent with Geschwind's (1978) view of language and learning disabilities in children as the expression of normal variation in genetic endowment within the population. The children concerned may have superior skills in other areas on which less value is placed in school programs, for example, musical abilities. Children with specific language impairments that are clearly based upon neurological insult sustained prenatally or very early in life may present different patterns of speech and language impairment from those who are developmentally delayed in language development. These considerations are important both for the development of a more satisfactory model for language disorders in children and for the management of specific language impairment in children.

# REFERENCES

Aten, J., & Davis, J. Disturbances in the perception of auditory sequence in children with minimal cerebral dysfunction. *Journal of Speech and Hearing Research,* 1968, *11,* 236-245.

Benton, A. L. Developmental aphasia and brain damage. *Cortex,* 1964, *1,* 40-42.

Benton, A. L. Language disorders in children. *Canadian Psychologist,* 1966, *1,* 298-312.

Chase, R. A. Neurological aspects of language disorders in children. In J. V. Irwin and M. Marge (Eds.), *Principles of Childhood Language Disabilities.* New York: Appleton Century Crofts, 1972.

Eisenson, J. Perceptual disturbances in children with central nervous dysfunction and implications for language development. *British Journal of Disorders of Communication,* 1966, *1,* 21-33.

Ewing, A. W. G. *Aphasia in Children,* New York, Hafner (1967).

Ferry, P. C. Neurological considerations in children with learning disabilities. In R. W. Keith (Ed.), *Central Auditory and Language Disorders in Children.* Houston: College Hill Press, 1981.

Fletcher, S. G. Time-by-count measurement of diadochokinetic syllable rate. *Journal of Speech and Hearing Research,* 1971, *15,* 763-770.

Galaburda, A. M., Kemper, T. L., & LeMay, M., & Geschwind, N. Right-left asymmetries in the brain. *Science*

Geschwind, N. *Anatomical Foundation of Language and Dominance.* Paper presented at NINCDS symposium entitled "The Neurological Bases of Language Disorders in Children". Bethesda, MD., 1978.

Golick, M. Language disorders in children: A linguistic investigation. Unpublished doctoral dissertation. McGill University, Montreal, 1977.

Gordon, N., & Taylor, I. G. The assessment of children with difficulties of communication. *Brain,* 1964, *87,* 121-140.

Hardy, W. G. On language disorders in young children: A reorganization of thinking. *Journal of Speech and Hearing Disorders,* 1965, *30,* 3-16.

Hollingshead, A. B. Two-factor Index of Social Position. New Haven, Connecticut, 1957.

Ingram, T. T. S. Pediatric aspects of specific developmental dysphasia, dyslexia, and dysgraphia. *Cerebral Palsy Bulletin,* 1960, *2,* 254-277.

Johnston, R. B., Stark, R. E., Mellitis, E. D., & Tallal, P. Neurological status of language impaired and normal children. *Annals of Neurology,* In Press.

Landau, W. M., Goldstein, R., & Kleffner, F. R. Congenital aphasia: A clinicopathological study. *Neurology,* 1960, *10,* 915-921.

Lowe, A. D., & Campbell, R. A. Temporal discrimination in aphasoid and normal children. *Journal of Speech and Hearing Research,* 1965, *8,* 313–314.

Ludlow, C. The differential effect of stimulant drugs on perception, language and communication. Paper presented at a conference on The Spectrum of Developmental Disabilities: The Learning Disabled Child from Birth to Adolescence. John F. Kennedy Institute and Johns Hopkins University. March 1981.

Morehead, D. M., & Ingram, D. The development of base syntax in normal and linguistically deviant children. *Journal of Speech and Hearing Research,* 1973, *16,* 331–352.

Myklebust, H. R. *Auditory Disorders in Children.* New York: Grune and Stratton, 1954.

Rees, N. S. Auditory processing factors in language disorders: The view from Procrustes' bed. *Journal of Speech and Hearing Disorders,* 1974, *38,* 304–315.

Rees, N. S. Saying more than we know: Is auditory processing a meaningful concept? In R. W. Keith (Ed.), *Central Auditory and Language Disorders in Children.* Houston, Tx.: College Hill Press, 1981.

Rosenthal, W., Eisenson, J., & Luckau, J. A statistical test of the validity of diagnostic categories used in childhood language disorders: Implications for assessment procedures. *Papers and Reports in Child Language Development.* Pala Alto, CA.: Stanford University Press, 1972.

Stark, R. E., & Tallal, P. Perceptual and motor deficits in language impaired children. In R. W. Keith (Ed.), *Central Auditory and Language Disorders in Children.* Houston, Tx.: College Hill Press, 1980.

Stark, R. E., & Tallal, P. Selection of children with specific language impairment. *Journal of Speech and Hearing Disorders,* 1981, *46,* 114–122.

Swicher, L., & Hirsh, I. J. Brain damage and the ordering of two temporally successive stimuli. *Neuropsychology,* 1972, *10,* 137–151.

Tallal, P. Rapid auditory processing in normal and disordered language development. *Journal of Speech and Hearing Research,* 1976, *19,* 561–571.

Tallal, P., & Piercy, M. Developmental aphasia: Impaired rate of nonverbal processing as a function of sensory modality. *Neuropsychologia,* 1973, *11,* 389–398.

Tallal, P., & Piercy, M. Developmental aphasia: Rate of auditory processing and selective impairment of consonant perception. *Neuropsychologia,* 1974, *12,* 83–94.

Tallal, P., Stark, R. E., Mellits, E. D., & Kallman, C. Perceptual constancy for phonemic categories: A developmental study with normal and language impaired children. *Applied Psycholinguistics,* 1980, *1,* 49–64.

Wechsler, D. Wechsler Preschool and Primary Scale of Intelligence. New York: The Psychological Corporation, 1963.

Wechsler, D. Wechsler Intelligence Scale for Children—Revised. New York: The Psychological Corporation, 1974.

# Advances in
# Human Psychopharmacology

Edited by **Graham D. Burrows**
*Department of Psychiatry, University of Melbourne*
and **John S. Werry**
*Department of Psychiatry, School of Medicine, University of Auckland*

Psychopharmacology, or the study of drugs given to change psychosocial rather than physical disease, has been one of the most significant growth areas in medicine in the last twenty years. It has given psychiatry a strong foothold in medicine and made it one of the major contributions to the neurosciences. Much of the literature on psychopharmacology is animal psychopharmacology and there is need for a series which will concern itself with human psychopharmacology, both adult and child, and its clinical applications to provide on a regular basis authoritative reviews and perspectives on new developments in what is an intellectually effervescent and exponentially developing branch of medicine. In general, the emphasis in this series will be on topicality (publication within twelve months), clinical relevance, critical, authoritative research and reviews so that the series will stand as an up to date informant readily available reference resource for psychiatrists, other mental health professionals, physicians, who use psychotropic drugs, work with patients who receive them or who are studying to do so.

**REVIEW:** "Psychopharmacology in recent years has been a considerable medical growth area, matched by only a few others, *e.g.* publishing. Both have now joined forces and this is the first volume of a series, and of an increasing number of books devoted to the study of drugs used to change psychosocial disease. It consists of 11 chapters on generally unrelated subjects which are strong on topicality. The writers are leading research and clinical workers in their repective fields, and their contributions are authoritative and critical. The reviews are well written and suprisingly balanced, and are followed by exhaustive lists of helpful and up-to-date references."
— *Developmental Medicine and Child Neurology*

**Volume 1,** 1980, 365 pp.
ISBN 0-89232-142-3

**CONTENTS: Introduction,** *Graham D. Burrows and John S. Werry.* **Preface. Cholinergic Mechanism in Mental and Nervous Disorders,** *Leo E. Hollister, Kenneth L. Davis and Philip A. Berger, Veterans Administration Hospital School of Medicine-Palo Alto.* **Anticholinergic Sedatives,** *John S. Werry, University of Auckland.* **Enkephalin and Endorphin,** *Geoffrey W. Tregear and John P. Coghlan, University of Melbourne.* **Plasma Levels of Psychotropic Drugs and Clinical Response,** *Trevor R. Norman and Graham D. Burrows, University of Melbourne.* **Lithium and the Kidney: Research and Clinical Implications,** *Priscilla Kincaid-Smith, Royal Melbourne Hospital and Brian Davies, University of Melbourne.* **ECT: Its Place and Value in Present Day Psychiatry,** *Leslie C. Kiloh, University of New South Wales, Prince Henry Hospital.* **Long-Acting Neuroleptics (Antipsychotics),** *A.O. Odejide, University College Hospital, Ibadan, Nigeria and Thomas A. Ban, Vanderbilt University-Nashville.* **Cortical Evoked Potentials and Psychopharmacology,** *Jeannette Friedman and Russell Meares, Austin Hospital, Heidelberg-Australia.* **Tissue Studies in Dementia,** *A.I.M. Glen and L. J. Whalley, University Department of Pharmacology, Edinburgh-Scotland.* **A Validation of Conners TQ and a Cross-Cultural Comparison of Prevalence of Hyperactivity in Children,** *Roslyn A. Glow, University of Adelaide.* **The Feingold Hypothesis: Review and Current Status,** *Florence Levy, Prince of Wales Children's Hospital, Randwick-Australia.* **Author/Subject Index.**

**Volume 2,** 1981, 342 pp.
ISBN 0-89232-193-8

**Volume 3,** In preparation,   Ca. 350 pp.
ISBN 0-89232-284-5

---

*University libraries depend upon their faculty for recommendations before purchasing. Please encourage your library to subscribe to this series.*

*INSTITUTIONAL STANDING ORDERS will be granted a 10% discount and be filled automatically upon publication. Please indicate initial volume of standing order.*

*INDIVIDUAL ORDERS must be prepaid by personal check or credit card. Please include $2.00 per volume for postage and handling on all domestic orders; $3.00 for foreign.*

---

**JAI PRESS INC., 36 Sherwood Place, P.O. Box 1678**
**Greenwich, Connecticut 06836**
**Telephone: 203-661-7602          Cable Address: JAIPUBL**

# Advances in
# Substance Abuse
# Behavioral and Biological Research

Edited by **Nancy K. Mello**

*Alcohol and Drug Abuse Center, Harvard Medical School — McLean Hospital*

**Advances in Substance Abuse** reviews and critically evaluates current research on alcohol and drug abuse problems. Behavioral and biological research on commonly abused drugs, alcohol, opiates, tobacco, depressants, stimulants, alcohol, and hallucinogens as well as other abused substances, such as food, are included. Each review provides a comprehensive assessment of recent developments in the area, within the context of an historical perspective, and discusses promising directions for future research. Substance abuse patterns are compared and the question of possible behavioral and biological similarities among addictive behaviors is critically examined.

**REVIEWS:** "This new series is a welcome addition in the field of substance abuse and will help to make sense of the growing literature on the subject. The first volume provides a most auspicious start for the series." — *Journal of Medicinal Chemistry*

"This first volume in a projected annual series edited by Nancy Mello is excellent and fills an important niche in the field." — *Amercian Journal of Psychiatry*

**Volume 1,** 1980, 384 pp.
ISBN 0-89232-128-8

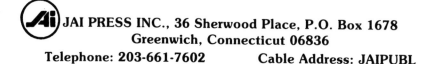

**JAI PRESS INC., 36 Sherwood Place, P.O. Box 1678**
**Greenwich, Connecticut 06836**
**Telephone: 203-661-7602**     **Cable Address: JAIPUBL**

# Advances in
# Learning and Behavioral Disabilities

Edited by **Kenneth D. Gadow**
*Office of Special Education and Developmental Studies*
*State University of New York — Stony Brook*
and **Irv Bialer**
*Division of Child Mental Health, Long Island Research Institute*
*State University of New York — Stony Brook*

**Volume 1,** 425 pp.
ISBN 0-89232-209-8

**CONTENTS: Part I: Learning Disabilities. Coding and Planning Processes in Children with Reading Disability,** J.P. Das, University of Alberta and James Cummins, Ontario Institute for Studies in Education. **Neurometrics in the Analysis of the Learning Handicapped Child,** Herbert Kaye, State University of New York University Medical Center. **Learning and Behavioral Difference: Theoretical Issues and Practical Considerations,** Darryl A. Newberger, West Virginia Wesleyan College. **Decoding Skill Development of Reading-Disabled and Nondisabled Children,** Ellis Richardson, Barbara DiBenedetto, Long Island Research Institute and Arlene G. Adler, Downstate Medical Center, State University of New York, Brooklyn. **Achievement Motivation: Construct, Research and Application in Learning Disability,** David A. Sabatino, Southern Illinois University. **Memory in Learning Disabled Children: Some Issues and Answers,** Joseph K. Torgesen, Florida State University. **Proactive Inhibition in Retarded Persons: Factors Influencing Accumulation and Release,** John J. Winters, Jr., Edward R. Johnstone Training and Research Center, Bordentown, New Jersey. **Part II: Behavior Disorders. Childhood Depression,** Ronald J. Friedman, Lenora Butler, Barbara R. Moyal and Solveiga Meizitis, Ontario Institute for Studies in Education. **Curricular Considerations in Treating Behavior Problems of Severely Handicapped Students,** Robert Gaylord-Ross, San Francisco State University. **Socialization and Peer Relations in Hyperactive Children,** Richard Milich and Steven Landu, University of Iowa. **Peer Interactions in Hyperactive Children: Assessment and Treatment,** William E. Pelham and Mary E. Bender, Florida State University. **Office Diagnosis of Hyperactivity by the Physician,** Esther K. Sleator, University of Illinois. **Follow-up Studies of Hyperactive Children: A Review,** Esther K. Sleator, University of Illinois. **Author/Subject Index.**

**Volume 2,** Ca. 350 pp.
ISBN 0-89232-285-3

**CONTENTS: Specific Reading Retardation: Traditional Concepts of Etiology,** Michael G. Aman, and Nirbhay Singh, University of Auckland. **Communicative Competence in Learning Disabled Children,** Tanis Bryan, Mavis Donahue, and Ruth Pearl, University of Illinois at Chicago Circle. **Stimulus Control in Developmentally Disabled Children: Analysis of Individual Differences,** Michael H. Dixon, Lois S. Dixon, and Joseph E. Spradlin, University of Kansas. **Measuring Response to Instruction as an Assessment Paradigm,** James L. Hamilton, U.S. Department of Education. **Relationship of Phonemic Analysis to Reading Disability in Children,** Donald K. Routh, and Barbara Fox, University of Iowa. **Interaction of Pharmacological and Behavioral Management in Children with Learning or Behavior Disorders,** Stephen R. Schroeder, Mark H. Lewis, and Morris A. Lipton, University of North Carolina. **Social Integration of Learning Disabled Children in Regular Classroom,** Gary N. Siperstein, and Melinda J. Goding, University of Massachusetts, Boston. **Learned Helplessness and Learned Confidence in Learning Disabled Children,** Jon D. Swartz, Jesse E. Purdy, and Billie Garrett Fullingim, Southwestern University. **Obesity in Developmentally Disabled Children: Etiology and Management,** Anthony F. Rotatori, Harvey N. Switzky, Northern Illinois University and Robert Fox, Ohio State University.

*University libraries depend upon their faculty for recommendations before purchasing. Please encourage your library to subscribe to this series.*

*INSTITUTIONAL STANDING ORDERS will be granted a 10% discount and be filled automatically upon publication. Please indicate initial volume of standing order.*

*INDIVIDUAL ORDERS must be prepaid by personal check or credit card. Please include $2.00 per volume for postage and handling on all domestic orders; $3.00 for foreign.*

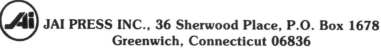

**JAI PRESS INC., 36 Sherwood Place, P.O. Box 1678**
**Greenwich, Connecticut 06836**
Telephone: 203-661-7602        Cable Address: JAIPUBL

# Advances in
# Developmental and
# Behavioral Pediatrics

Edited by **Mark Wolraich**
*Department of Pediatrics, College of Medicine University of Iowa*
and **Donald K. Routh**
*Department of Psychology, University of Iowa*

**Volume 1,** 1980, 266 pp.
ISBN 0-89232-076-1

**Volume 2,** 1981, 232 pp.
ISBN 0-89232-185-7

**Volumes 1 and 2** were published under the editorship of **Bonnie W. Camp,** *University of Colorado.*

---

 **JAI PRESS INC., 36 Sherwood Place, P.O. Box 1678
Greenwich, Connecticut 06836**
Telephone: 203-661-7602          Cable Address: JAIPUBL

# Research Annuals in the
# *BEHAVIORAL SCIENCES*

**Advances in Behavioral Measurement of Children**
Series Editor: Roslyn A. Glow, *University of Adelaide*

**Advances in Behavioral Pediatrics**
Series Editors: Mark Wolraich and Donald K. Routh, *University of Iowa*

**Advances in Descriptive Psychology**
Series Editor: Keith Davis, *University of South Carolina*

**Advances in Early Education and Day Care**
Series Editor: Sally Kilmer, *Bowling Green State University*

**Advances in Energy Use and Conservation: Behavioral and Social Factors**
Series Editor: Edwin P. Willems, *University of Houston*

**Advances in Family Intervention, Assessment and Theory**
Series Editor: John P. Vincent, *University of Houston*

**Advances in Human Psychopharmacology**
Series Editors: Graham D. Burrows, *University of Melbourne* and John S. Werry, *University of Auckland*

**Advances in Law and Child Development**
Series Editor: Robert L. Sprague, *University of Illinois*

**Advances in Learning and Behavioral Disabilities**
Series Editors: Kenneth Gadow and Irv Bialer, *State University of New York—Stony Brook*

**Advances in Motivation and Achievement**
Series Editor: Martin L. Maehr, *University of Illinois—Champaign*

**Advances in Nutritional Behavior**
Series Editor: J. Preston Harley, *Braintree Hospital*

**Advances in Reading and Language Research**
Series Editor: Barbara Hutson, *Virginia Polytechnic Institute and State University—Washington, D.C.*

**Advances in Special Education**
Series Editor: Barbara K. Keogh, *University of California—Los Angeles*

**Advances in Substance Abuse: Behavioral and Biological Research**
Series Editor: Nancy K. Mello, *Harvard Medical School—McLean Hospital*

*Please inquire for detailed brochure on each series.*

 **JAI PRESS INC.**